THE
# DORY BOOK

# THE
# DORY
# BOOK

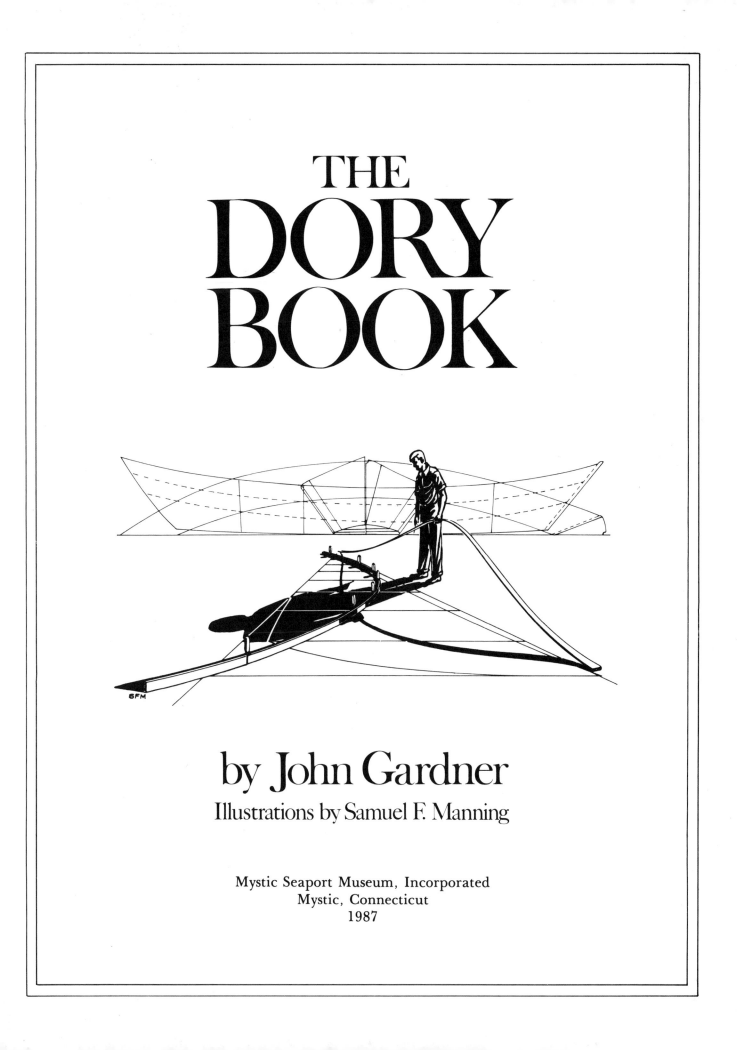

## by John Gardner

### Illustrations by Samuel F. Manning

Mystic Seaport Museum, Incorporated
Mystic, Connecticut
1987

# CONTENTS

# PREFACE

The *Maine Coast Fisherman*'s affair with the dory started back in June, 1951, when it printed a modest little article I had written about the Hammond dory. The piece was short, a beginner's effort, but it did provide some useful building information including a set of lines carefully drawn to scale. This was the first time, I believe, that lines for a small, round-sided, pulling dory of the Swampscott type had appeared in print. Perhaps it was these lines, freely offered, or the builder's approach to the subject that appealed to the readers. In any case, this maiden effort struck a spark of interest. Readers wrote in, and they have been writing ever since. Not just about that first Hammond dory, of course, but about all the dories since. During the last twenty-five years, a long line of my articles on how to build dories of various sorts and sizes has passed across the pages of the *Fisherman* (now known as the *National Fisherman*).

It is nice to get letters. We love to hear from our readers at home and abroad, to share in their enthusiasms, and to assist them in their boatbuilding efforts, if possible. We like to help. Yet questions from prospective builders, especially from the inexperienced, are not always easy to deal with. Lengthy answers are often required. Sometimes such inquiries can be handled by reference back to *Fisherman* articles, but many of these are now difficult to obtain. Photostats are not the answer, particu-

larly when cross references to a number of different articles are involved.

The fact is that a book is needed, a book that amplifies and gathers together in one package the scattered material on dories that has appeared in the *Fisherman*. It is desirable that the construction data and related information be systematically arranged, expanded in places, brought up to date, and illustrated for better comprehension.

There must be something about the dory that intrigues people. How else explain the persistent vigor of the type and its continuing popularity? There is no easy means for knowing just how many dories have been built from *Fisherman* plans and details. I believe an estimate of several hundred could be formed from the number of letters from dory enthusiasts, builders, or prospective builders that have accumulated in my files. Often those who display the greatest enthusiasm never get to the building stage for one reason or another. And some who do build never write, so that when one learns of their accomplishment, if at all, it is by accident.

The two boats which have proved most popular are the 27-foot St. Pierre fisherman's dory, and the 19-foot Marblehead gunning dory. In the wake of plans published for the St. Pierre dory more than ten years ago, scores of these big dories were completed, mostly as powerboats, but a few rigged for sail.

The big St. Pierre has ranged widely: from the Caribbean to the Gulf of Maine, and in the Pacific, from British Columbia to Okinawa and New Zealand. The gunning dory has covered almost as much territory. Over 160 sets of building plans and directions for the gunning dory have gone out to amateur builders in all parts of North America, with several to Europe. Dories from our published plans have been built in Australia. Two of our double-ended surf dories have given outstanding performance in the Pacific surf on the west coast of Nicaragua. One of our 19-foot outboard semi-dories, built in the Canadian northwest, was an enlarged version of our 16-foot model, drawn up for an engineer in Venezuela who wanted it for off-shore fishing. Dory plans and building instructions have been sent upon request to Spain and to Sweden, to Ireland and to Germany. Dories taken from the pages of the *Fisherman* now cleave the waves of the seven seas.

My own affair with dories dates from the late Thirties, when I came to Essex County, Massachusetts, to work as a boatbuilder. Hailing from Down East—as far east as it is possible to go in coastal Maine—I had known a good many dories. Among these was a small Bank dory that I had built for my own use, as a boy, on the St. Croix River.

But the dories I had rowed and sailed on the upper reaches of Maine's Passamaquoddy Bay were not the dories I found on the Lynn and Swampscott beaches, along the shores of Marblehead, Salem, and Beverly, and at the Cape Ann towns of Gloucester and Rockport. These round-sided dories, the double-enders in particular, were a choicer breed than the straight-sided Bank dories used by fishermen elsewhere on the New England coast. The sweet lines of some of them all but took my breath when I saw them for the first time, out of the water in all their naked elegance. I revelled in their good looks and desired them as much for their beauty as for their use.

Next best to possessing a boat is to possess her lines, carefully laid out on paper, neatly and painstakingly faired. There is recurrent satisfaction in thinking that one might someday build the boat, having drafted her lines in preparation for the event. Readers who tell me that they clip drawings of hull lines

and carefully save them in folders apparently do so from this sort of motivation. The lines serve as surrogate for the boat.

Thus my recording of dories began as an intensely personal experience in which the aesthetic element bulked large. Far from intending to publish the data resulting from my first measuring of dories and recording the lines and the details of representative specimens, I wanted those shapely, svelte, round-sided boats for myself.

An early object of my attentions was the lovely 19-foot double-ender I noticed one day drawn up on the beach at Barnegat* in a cove frequented by Marblehead lobstermen. I was told that this was Will Chamberlain's personal gunning dory that had lain for a number of years drying out under a veranda after Will's eyesight had grown too dim to see beyond the gunsights. Following his death, the dory had lain there until his widow was finally persuaded to sell her to a part-time lobsterman who now used her to tend his strings of pots. In spite of her long retirement the boat had tightened up again after some swelling, and although she was a lightweight craft, built for duck hunting on the islands of the outer harbor, she proved strong enough to carry heavy loads of lobster pots with only one light brace affixed across the gunwales amidships to keep the sides from working.

I looked up the owner. He readily granted me permission to take off the lines. The next pleasant Saturday morning found me on the beach bright and early with notebook, tape, rule, chalk line, thin pine template stock, and all the other tools and equipment I could think of as possibly needed for the job.

I had built boats and passed for a boatbuilder at the time, yet never before had I essayed to take off a set of lines from a completed hull. But as an avid reader of the many superb historical articles on representative American small craft written by H. I. Chapelle in *Yachting* during the Thirties, I had a pretty good idea of how it was done. I had also practiced redrawing the hull lines that accompanied Chapelle's articles.

That practice stood me in good stead. Of

---

*Local name for a section of Marblehead in the vicinity of Beacon Street.

course my boatbuilding experience also helped. I must admit that I approached my task with some trepidation, but once I had made the plunge, the water was fine. The day flew by. I am not sure I even stopped to eat. There was so much to get on paper, so much not to be overlooked, so many measurements to be checked and doublechecked against error, always lurking close at hand. But at the end of the day, pretty well worn out by the excitement and the unaccustomed concentration, I had a notebook full of sketches and figures and an armful of pine templates.

The boat, that is to say, the boat's essential shape, was mine. And it is now yours or anyone's, whoever might want to build her, study her, or merely contemplate her beauty.

The lines were taken off none too soon. The handsome gunning dory, too lightly built for a rough workboat, and old to begin with, was overloaded and abused, and soon started going to pieces. She did not last long thereafter. Broken up and destroyed, she has been departed for a good many years.

While so far no exact reproduction of this 19-foot Chamberlain gunning dory has been built, her lines, with slight changes, are those upon which James S. Rockefeller's 18-foot gunning dory are molded, and a derivative boat, but somewhat huskier, is the Texaco surf dory built for use as a workboat on the west coast of Nicaragua.

Not long after recording the lines and details of the Chamberlain double-ender, I became involved with another similar dory, the last decrepit survivor of a number of surf dories acquired by the Metropolitan District Commission early in this century for use as lifesaving craft on the public beaches of Greater Boston. One of these still used to lie in readiness during the summer season on a high wagon in a turn-out just off the sidewalk at the entrance to King's Beach in Lynn, not far from the Swampscott line. Every time I passed by I would stop to admire this boat. She must have been in service for a long time, for when I first saw her, she was an old boat, weak in her fastenings, rent in her garboard planks, and heavily encrusted inside and out with layers of white paint, an additional coat of which she apparently had received at the beginning of each beach season for many, many years.

After some letter writing back and forth, I secured permission from the MDC to measure the boat and lost no time in taking off her lines. During this operation, in attempting to set an awl on which to hook a chalk line, I discovered a small brass builder's name plate buried under thick paint. The plate proved the boat to have been built by Will Chamberlain, although at first I had surmised she might have been an early George Chaisson boat, because of the location of her berth close to the Swampscott line. Most of the dories at nearby Fisherman's Beach in Swampscott were of Chaisson build.

As in the case of the gunning dory, I took off the lines none too soon. The next season the boat was retired. I made inquiries as to her whereabouts some time after, but by then no one had heard of the boat and she could not be located. Fortunately, before this surf boat was removed, I got Colonel Smith* of the Peabody Museum of Salem to photograph her for the record. Some years later in *Yachting* (March, 1954) I showed for purposes of comparison a series of lines of representative dory types drawn to the same scale. The Chamberlain surf dory was included in this series.

The newer boats procured by the Boston MDC to replace the old Chamberlain dories are pathetically inferior both in design and ability to the old boats, although I suppose they are adequate for what they have to do. Surf dories of the original Chamberlain model would, I expect, be prohibitively expensive today, if, indeed, any boatshop could be found that would undertake to build them.

The building of dories and other lapstrake types, in Essex County as nearly everywhere else in this country, is a forgotten trade. The old-time Essex County dory builders are an extinct species. In barely fifty years the social and economic conditions that molded and nourished them are gone beyond recall, and to some extent, beyond recollection. The boats they built with such care and pride, the round-sided Swampscott dories that reached their apogee during the onset of the present century, have nearly slipped into oblivion.

---

*Col. Smith, now passed on, was an honorary curator of, I believe, ethnology at the Peabody Museum in Salem.

The dory of the turn of the century in Marblehead and Swampscott must be considered in the context of the culture that then existed. It was a simpler time. People worked longer hours for less wages, but probably had more of the essentials. Fishermen rowed their dories to their fish traps and lobster pots. The young village bloods who raced in Beachcombers and X-dories on Sunday mornings, on the Fourth of July, and on Labor Day had little means of escaping workaday routine and neighborhood surveillance except in their dories. There were the trolley cars and various horse-drawn vehicles, it is true, but they did not offer much real freedom. The spatial liberation brought about by the auto, and by the motorboat to a lesser degree, was yet to come for those with moderate incomes. Around 1910, the waters of northern Massachusetts Bay were white with dory sails. By 1930, most of them were gone. The change came with the gasoline engine.

The gas engine in the automobile on land, and to a lesser extent in the motorboat on the water, opened up a dimension of mobility to the American people that exploded the confines of the village. The population took to cars and powerboats in a big way, and overnight the quality of American life was altered. Small craft of the older types, including dories on saltwater and canoes on lakes and streams, slipped into decline.

Now the tide has turned. Seeking respite from gas fumes, the mechanized madness of deadly superhighways, and the confinement of crowds, increasing numbers of people in their leisure hours are turning back to the small craft of an earlier day, back to sail and oar. The dory revival is part of this larger general revival of small craft. The increase in canoes is spectacular, even to the return of canoe liveries as profitable enterprises after a lapse of more than a quarter of a century. Of course there are lots of outboards, and more to come, which is another reason for the increase in dories. Some of the modified dory types, suitably fitted out, make the best of outboard boats.

This expanding small-craft revival is to a large extent an amateur undertaking. Amateur boatbuilding is certainly nothing new in this country, but the "backyard builder," to adopt the late Sam Rabl's phrase, is on the increase.

Many more people with a great deal more leisure are turning to handwork. Not since pioneer times have there been so many busy home workshops. For those who love the out-of-doors, and the sea, and desire a real challenge of skill, what better project than building a boat?

Dories as a type possess several characteristics that make them especially suitable for amateur construction and commend them to wide general acceptance. To begin with, dories are fine sea boats, especially the perfected, round-sided models developed along Essex County's North Shore. Second, they are low-cost boats, economical to build and to maintain. Finally, they are easy to construct, and adaptable to the use of easily obtainable modern materials without alteration in basic design.

Dory building costs are relatively low because expensive materials are not required, and because the simplified construction of dory-type boats makes the costs of labor lower than for most other small craft. Of course this saving in labor is not too much of a consideration to the recreational builder, whose own labor costs him nothing more than his spare time. In the matter of maintenance, dories are inexpensive because of their rugged construction, which will take abuse that would wreck more fragile boats.

The relative simplicity of dory construction makes the type particularly attractive to the first-time builder. Furthermore, the ordinarily more difficult round-sided dories become much easier to build when traditional construction is modified in order to utilize modern, easily obtainable materials, in particular plywood, elastic sealants, synthetic reinforcements, and thermoplastic adhesives.

It has been established to my satisfaction that almost anyone can put together a passable dory if he has normal faculties, a few hand tools, a corner to work in, and a fair amount of patience and drive. It is also necessary, in the case of a tenderfoot builder, to have reliable construction plans and comprehensible directions. The directions should be laid out in a series of progressive steps or stages. If a boat-building project is to turn out correctly, it is necessary to do the right thing, in the right sequence.

The dory-building directions in the chapters

that follow have been thoroughly tested and proven. The plans are for boats that have been successfully built and used, either by myself or others. As for the historical chapters, this material was originally published in the *National Fisherman* in 1964 and has recently been revised to include additional facts which have since come to light.

John Gardner
Mystic, Connecticut

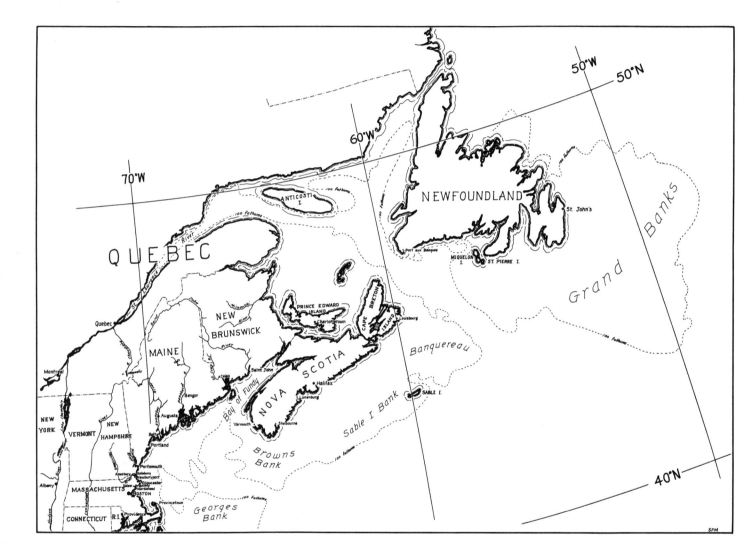

# PART ONE

# HISTORY OF THE DORY

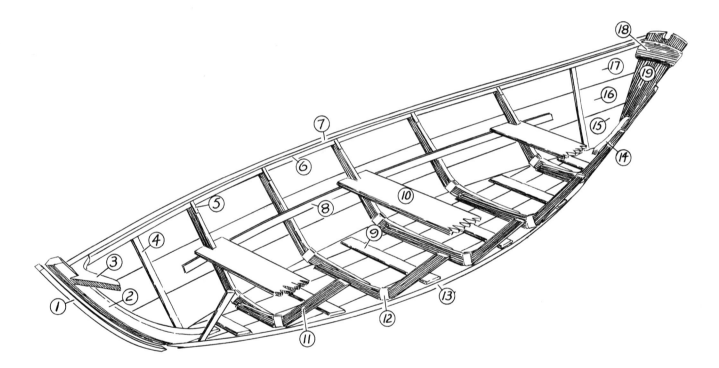

*Dory nomenclature.*

1. False stem
2. Stem
3. Breast hook
4. Side cleat
5. Frame head iron
6. Gunwale log
7. Cap rail
8. Riser
9. Bottom cleat
10. Thwart
11. Frame
12. Frame gusset plate
13. Bottom plank
14. Stern knee
15. Garboard plank
16. Broad plank
17. Sheer plank
18. Stern cleat
19. Transom or "tombstone"

# 1  A SEARCH FOR BEGINNINGS

In August, 1719, Captain Nathaniel Uring, in an English vessel bound from Madeira to Jamaica, was cast away on a reef. The captain noted in his report to the owners that his crew got ashore in the longboat, and with their dory they were able to pass back and forth over the reef, when the seas abated, to take off part of the cargo. This dory appears to have been smaller than the longboat and of less draft. Whether they waited for the seas to calm because of the dory's characteristics is not clear.

This is the earliest reference to a dory so far found. Because of the familiar, matter-of-fact way in which Captain Uring tells about the dory and its use, it may be assumed that neither the name nor the type were new at the time.[1]

E.P. Morris notes the mention of a "doree" in the Boston *Gazette* in 1726, and it seems that this "doree" was large enough to carry five men. Apparently the boat was in use at the Isles of Shoals.[2]

Toward the end of the century, reference to the dory becomes more common. Starting in 1789, dories are frequently mentioned in the account books of James Topham, Marblehead boatbuilder.[3] William Bentley, Salem diarist, records a dory in local waters in 1795.[4]

A report in 1819 relates that Marblehead fishing vessels, or "jiggers," had recently adopted the practice of taking out several dories to fish from instead of fishing from the vessels themselves. Apparently in Swampscott, prior to the arrival in 1795 of the *Dove,* Swampscott's first fishing schooner, all fishing was done in dories off the beach.[5]

In no instance to date has any detailed description of eighteenth century dories been found.

In 1790, Topham at Marblehead sold two new dories for three pounds each, while a 13-foot boat, presumably round-bottomed, went for nine pounds, indicating an easier and cheaper construction for the dories of that day, just as the Bank dory a century later cost less than other fishing types.

With boatbuilders' wages at approximately five shillings per day, according to Topham's accounts, and making allowance for the cost of materials, an estimate of one week's building time for a dory that cost three pounds seems not too far from the mark. A week to build a dory would have been about right 100 years later, when we know what a dory was.

Compare this with the "week's labor" it cost two amateurs in 1839, the brothers Thoreau, to build the craft for their famous boating trip on the Concord and Merrimac rivers. Henry David Thoreau describes their boat as being "in form like a fisherman's dory, fifteen feet long by three and a half in breadth at the widest part." This does not tell us much, considering that we have no description of what a fisherman's dory of that time, or before, was like. The length is normal for a small dory but the beam is scant. Even on quiet inland waters, a dory this narrow must have been tender.[6]

Until about 1870, there are to be found no recorded dory lines, details, nor any list of particulars that would enable us to say with certainty what the earlier dories were really like. It is reasonable to assume, however, that the type has not changed too radically over the years. There must have been evolution to some extent, but with continuity of inheritance also.

It appears that the classic Bank dory shape, which is the image that generally first comes to mind when the word "dory" is mentioned, was established before 1870. In 1880, the U.S. National Museum issued a bulletin containing rather complete specifications for a number of standard sizes of Bank dories as employed at that time in the various American fisheries.[7]

The old practice was to measure dories on the bottom, and included were dories with bottom lengths of 13, 14, 14½, 15, and 15½ feet. The 15½-footer, of extra width and depth like the winter haddock dory, measured 19 feet 8 inches on top with a beam of 5 feet 5 inches and a bottom width of 2 feet 11 inches. The depth amidships was 1 foot 10 inches, and the depth at the ends, 2 feet 7 inches. Built extra strong, with six and sometimes seven pairs of frames, and with a wide band on top outside to bind and protect the sheer, such big dories were little used by American fishermen, but were shipped in large numbers each year to the French at St. Pierre and Miquelon Islands off Newfoundland. In addition to these Bank models, the National Museum bulletin noted the occurrence of other less common kinds of dories, including round-bilged Cape Ann sailing dories and a Nantucket dory.

Four years after this catalog was issued by the U.S. National Museum, Henry Hall's Tenth Census *Report On The Ship-Building Industry of the United States* was published. Here, for the first time, appeared a printed representation of the general lines of the Bank dory, but without a dimensioned layout. According to Hall, building these dories for Bank fishing schooners, which seldom set sail without buying from one to five or six new dories, was a brisk business centered at Salisbury, Massachusetts. Seven shops, each producing from 200 to 650 Bank dories annually, operated on piece-work production. In addition, Hall reported, dories in lesser quantity were built all along the coast from Maine to New York. He found five principal sizes in use with bottom lengths ranging from 12 to 16 feet, the largest being for the halibut fishery.

"Dories," according to Hall (and he means the Bank dory), "are swift, easily handled, capacious and safe, and, if properly handled,

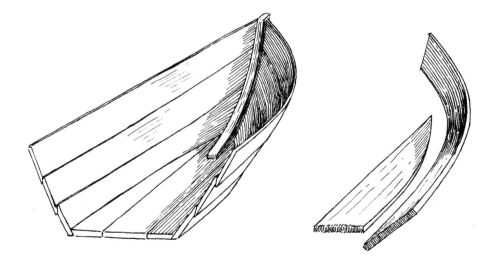

*What is a dory? A dory is a flat-bottomed boat, with sides and bottom planked lengthwise and with no keel structure other than the bottom planking.*

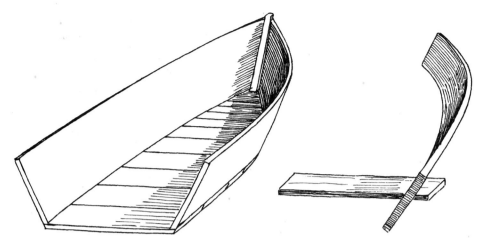

*A cross-planked, flat-bottomed boat is not a dory. Cross planking is a more recent innovation in flat-bottomed craft. It requires an abundance of nails or other plank fastenings not readily available to the classic builders of dories.*

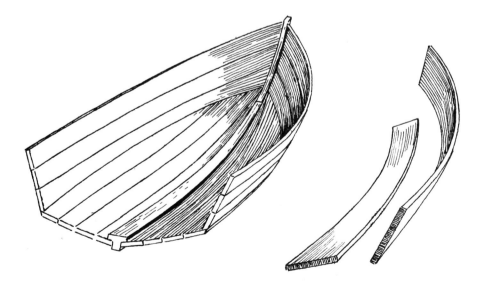

*A vee-bottom, or deadrise hull. Although planked lengthwise with wide lumber, this type is built on a keel. This is a box reproduction of a round-bottomed hull. Not a dory.*

hard to capsize." He also noted their comparatively light weight. The dory, says Hall, is a "Yankee invention" that came into widespread use in the fisheries since the changeover in fishing, which he explains had formerly been done with handlines over the sides of the vessels, but in "late years" was being carried on from small boats, that is to say dories, sent out from the mother ship. Hall is referring to the advent of trawl fishing, which appears to have been first introduced in the Grand Banks cod fishery in about 1832 by fishermen from Dieppe, France.

Precisely what kind of small craft were used originally by the French fishermen who devised the trawl is not known, although it is possible that they were of the dory type in spite of Hall's patriotic claim for the Yankees. Although it is true that before the trawl was introduced, cod fishing on the Grand Banks had been done over the side of the vessel without intervention of small boats, it is not to be understood from this that small boats had not

seen large-scale use in the north Atlantic fisheries prior to the trawl.

The extensive shore fisheries at Newfoundland and along the Gulf of St. Lawrence in early times employed small boats manned by two to four men. Putting out from the coast each morning, these boats returned at night with their catch of cod. It appears that the French may have started using small craft in the Newfoundland fishery some 300 years before their compatriots from Dieppe devised the trawl.[8]

Certain it is that both the English and the French made extensive use of small craft at Newfoundland in the sixteenth and seventeenth centuries. In large part they used round-bottom shallops or, in French, *chaloupes*. But quite definitely some were flat-bottomed row-boats of the dory type.

A pictorial representation of the Newfoundland shore fishery, drawn about 1700 by Herman Moll, a Dutch cartographer then resid-

*Unloading fish from a dory flat alongside a wharf. Dory flats were introduced to North America by transient fishermen working the cod grounds of Newfoundland. This illumination, from Herman Moll's map, c. 1710, is the earliest known representation of a dory flat in North America.*

*Enlargement of a dory flat in Moll's illumination, as redrawn line by line under magnification. The map was printed from a wood engraving.*

ing in London, shows a boat about 16 or 18 feet long, laden with codfish and lying alongside a wharf. Two men are unloading it with pitchforks. The boat has a broad, moderately raking transom, a pointed, well-sheered bow, and from the way its straight, slightly flaring, clinker sides rise from the water, it has to be flat-bottomed. This is a deep, capacious rowboat, for all the world like a large, heavily built dory skiff of the first decades of this century, and in fact not dissimilar to a modern semi-dory for outboard power.[9]

It might be objected that Herman Moll never visited Newfoundland. Be that as it may, it is certain he didn't invent the craft that he drew

in all its accurate and authentic detail. If Moll had not observed such a dory type in use in Newfoundland, it is more than likely that he had seen such boats in his youth in Holland.

By 1792, or forty years before the trawl is said to have come into use, the French were already employing great numbers of two-man "flats" in Newfoundland. At St. Pierre and Miquelon alone, some 600 to 700 of these flat rowboats were in use.[10]

In localities where the French based shore-fishing operations in the summertime but were not permitted to remain over the winter, they brought out a fresh stock of small fishing boats each spring in a knocked-down condition in

*Handlining for cod prior to the expansion of the fishery by use of dories. Enlarged detail from Moll's illumination.*

the holds of their vessels, along with the season's supply of salt. These cheap, expendable rowboats, which were easily and quickly assembled on the beach prior to the start of fishing operations, seem to have been dory-type flats. The flat bottoms, completely constructed ahead of time, could be easily and compactly stored, and frames and planking could be cut to shape and beveled ahead of

time, ready to be nailed together. This could not have been done, or at least not so easily, for round-bilged boats.[11]

There seems to be no doubt that both the English and the French made use of small, flat rowboats of the dory type in the North American fisheries during the eighteenth century. We do know precisely what the fishermen called such boats. In New England waters at this time

*Sixteenth-century French fishermen assembling knocked-down dory flats on the beach in Newfoundland. The drawing is pure conjecture, but the boat and details are derived from Moll's map illumination.*

such craft seem sometimes to have been called wherries, sometimes dories, and then sometimes skiffs. At Halibut Point on Cape Ann, William Bentley in 1799 observed numerous "small flat-bottom row boats" called "wherries" by him, "which in good weather make two fares a day & sometimes take as many as five hundred Cod & Haddock. They are rowed cross-handed by one man & even by boys of 10 & 12 years."

On the Merrimack at this time, at Salisbury Point, later to become Amesbury and toward the end of the nineteenth century the manufacturing center for the Bank dory, Simeon Lowell was building an improved flat-bottomed rowboat, which he called a wherry. Some of these were hauled by oxcart to Swampscott, then a part of Lynn, where the fishermen had not yet taken to building their own boats.[12] The Swampscott fishermen called these Salisbury Point wherries "dories." Incidentally, Simeon Lowell is reputed by local tradition to have invented the Bank dory.

Earlier than this, that is during the French and Indian War at the mid-point of the eighteenth century, a citizen of Albany, New York, and an officer in a Provincial company stationed at Lake George, wrote in a letter to England: "Our Battoes are small kind of wherries . . ."[13] The nineteenth-century lumberman's batteau, a direct descendant of the colonial "battoe," markedly resembled the Bank dory.*

The nineteenth century river-driving batteau, as perfected for the rapids of the West Branch of the Penobscot River in Maine, might well be called the dory of the inland waterways, if its predecessor, the double-ended cargo boat of the St. Lawrence fur trade, did not have prior claim. The Colonial "battoe" may well be the direct ancestor of the Bank dory, as we shall see.

At St. Pierre and Miquelon, almost to this day, one kind of wide, dory-type boat was to be found called *le wary*. This apparently is a corruption of the English "wherry." A *Dictionnaire de Marine*, published in France in 1846, states that at the time some 200 or 300 *warys* were employed in cod fishing in Newfoundland waters, especially around St. Pierre and Miquelon. Such *warys* could have been the very boats used by fishermen out of Dieppe for tending the first trawls before cheaper New England dories arrived on the scene.

Wherry may be translated in French as *bachot* or *petit bac*, signifying a small ferry. *Bac*, derived from the Latin, *baccarium*, a vase, is the name of a very ancient and widely distributed European type, a wide, flat boat for crossing rivers and narrow straits and for constructing pontoon bridges in military operations since Roman times.

On the strength of this it appears that we should view with skepticism Henry Hall's claim for "Yankee invention." Our search for beginnings leads farther back to an Old World origin.

Until a few years ago it was not generally known that several examples of small flat-bottom, dory-like boats were native to the British Isles, and that they could have existed relatively unchanged for centuries in isolated fishing communities in the west of England adjacent to Bristol. One of these is the Bridgwater flatner, native to the River Parret, which discharges into the Severn estuary. The likeness of this flatner to the Bank dory is striking, and, in fact, according to Allan Shaw, this flatner is called a "dory" on its native beaches.[14]

Another of these North Somerset flatners takes its name from Weston-Super-Mare Bay, which opens into the Bristol Channel. The Weston-Super-Mare-flatner[15] with its knuckled, or rounded, clinker sides closely resembles some of the old New England wherries as well as Staten Island skiffs and Saint John River salmon boats. These flatners are also like the cots formerly employed by County Wexford herring fishermen, and described by Dixon Kemp.[16] The occurrence of similar flat-bottom fishing craft on both sides of St. George's Channel is no strange coincidence, as Somerset fishermen are known to have been working the Irish Coast as early as 1427, and even before. By this time, had other North Somerset fishermen in Bristol vessels reached as far west as Newfoundland? Some evidence has recently come to light that they had, and that they were bringing back dried cod (stockfish) before the voyages of John Cabot.[17] If this is what happened, it could be that West Country fishermen took their flatners with them to fish off the Newfoundland beaches. Conceivably, these boats could have been the first European dories in the Western World, but it is not likely we shall ever know for sure.

Turning to the continent of Europe and to the shores of the Mediterranean, in particular to Italy and Spain, and around and up to Portugal, we find to this day numbers of flat-bottomed craft still in use resembling in form or in construction the three closely related American flats—the dory, the wherry, and the river batteau.

It is not generally known that the Venetian gondola has a flat bottom, and, out of the water it might pass for a type of batteau. The

---

*Bateau* (plural, *bateaux*) is French for any small boat.

*Batteau* (plural, *batteaux*) seems generally to have been adopted in English as the name of one particular boat, or rather class of boats, the double-ended river boats whose origin in America I have attempted to sketch here. This is the form I will use in a general discussion of the type.

*Batteau* (plural, *batteaus*) is the proper spelling for the American river-driving and lumberman's boat, according to Fannie Hardy Eckstrom (*The Penobscot Man*), an authority whose dictums deserve respect.

*Batoe* (plural, *batoes*) is the spelling generally employed in the British colonies during the French and Indian Wars.

double-ended *betes* of Provence have flat bottoms, raking batteau ends, and Bank dory sides. These fishing boats, with their lateen sails, like that of the 19-foot Gloucester dory *Nautilus* in which the Andrews brothers of Beverly, Massachusetts, sailed to England and France in 1878, are widely known from Vincent Van Gogh's painting of boats on the beach at Les Saintes-Maries de la Mer.

In Portugal, a large high-sided, double-ended flat with towering stem and enormous sheer is probably a survival from very ancient times, going back to the Egyptians and beyond to wide, flat dugouts of Neolithic build, such as those still to be found in the Lake Chad area of Africa.[18] Some authorities think that double-ended, flat-bottom boats at one time had a range from Egypt to Denmark. The fact is that the flat-bottom is indigenous throughout Asia, and, indeed, seems to be worldwide in occurrence. Alan Villiers, who favors a Portuguese origin for the Bank dory, suggests that judging from their appearance, the ancestry of these dories might go back to the sewn surf-boats of southern Arabia, and to craft still used by Arab fishermen.[19] Looking still farther to the East, we find such flat-bottom types as the patalias of the Upper Ganges and the Chittagong sampans of south-eastern Pakistan.[20] A numerous assortment of Chinese riverboats of the Yangtze and the Yellow Rivers are built with flat bottoms, as well as Japanese sampans and yamato boats. In no instance has the origin of any of these been traced back to their primal beginnings, although some authorities believe that the Chinese flats are more likely to have been derived from rafts than from dugouts.[21] Whatever its derivation, flat-bottom construction unquestionably is extremely ancient as well as widespread.

Stone Age man seems early to have become a proficient boatbuilder experimenting with craft of many sorts—rafts, dugouts, and bark- and skin-covered craft, the latter supported internally with basketwork of other arrangements of wooden strips of small saplings, similar to the Welch curragh or the Eskimo umiak.

As time passed, the Stone Age artisan learned to split logs lengthwise, and to dress the radial sections to proper thickness and shape with a flint adz in order to form the strakes for a planked hull. Stone saws, while workable for some things, are not suitable for splitting logs lengthwise into planks and boards, and even the first clumsy, thick, bronze saws of Egypt and Crete, lacking down-raked teeth and files to sharpen them,[22] would have taken an eternity to go through a long log from end to end.

Centuries later, by Roman times, a fairly efficient two-man frame saw for splitting timber had come into use, with a narrower, thinner blade of iron, and with uniform, file-sharpened teeth. But even with such improvements, it is doubtful that two sawyers could keep up with a single boatbuilder riving out boat strakes in the old manner with axe and wedges, and dressing them to thickness and shape with iron cutting tools, including the adz, drawknife, and plane, all of which the Romans had.[23]

In either case, plank so produced either by riving or by manual sawing would tend to be of comparatively narrow width for reasons of economy of labor. Narrow planks saw much easier and faster than wide ones when sawn by hand. And because narrow strakes bend and twist easier than wide ones, they are better adapted for planking the round-bilged, full-bowed craft that made an early appearance in southern Europe. Probably the first round-bilged hulls took the shape they did to a large extent because of the narrow planking at first most easily and economically available.

It seems to follow that the development of wide-board types like the dory would tend to be delayed until wide boards became plentiful and relatively cheap. This did not occur until after the introduction of the power sawmill toward the end of the medieval period. According to Professor Beckman, sawmills were first introduced in Germany. One is known to have been set up at Augsburg in 1322.[24] This great technological advance quickly spread throughout Europe. Soon water-powered gang-saws were producing cheaper lumber in quantity throughout the continent. In North America, a power sawmill was in operation on the Piscataqua River before 1635. In England, however, due in part to the opposition of rioting pit-sawyers, and in part to local lumbering practices, the changeover to power sawmills lagged until late in the nineteenth century. This could well have had some bearing on the fact that wide-board, flat-bottom types were never widely distributed in the British Isles.

When do dory-type boats enter history? Not, apparently, during the centuries when boat plank was split or riven from logs for the lack of better tools. Split radially from the log as shown, riven plank is tough and flexible due to its clear, straight, unbroken grain. Long lengths of plank may be obtained this way, but the width is necessarily narrow. Riven plank having unbroken grain is highly contortable.

Below: Riven lumber in its best application produces a canoe-like boat—long, rather than wide, with sharply rounded bilge sections and upswept complex planking curves at the ends. The use of riven plank may have dictated the design of Mediterranean craft starting in Neolithic times and the hull forms identified with the Vikings in Scandinavia. The practice of riving, or splitting, plank from logs is said to have flourished in Norway until the middle of the sixteenth century.

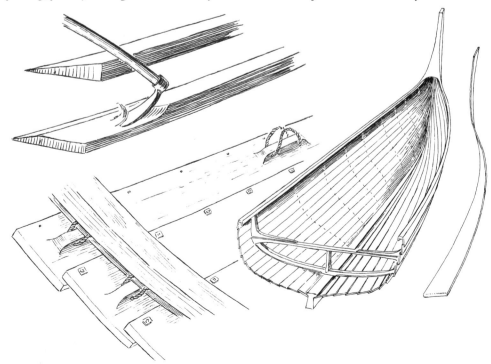

Practical ripping of boards from logs waited until Iron Age technology had developed long, thin saw blades, raked teeth, and files for sharpening. Pit sawing of plank is done today in remote parts of the world. In the upper left of the drawing is a classic frame saw in use; in the lower right is a modern pit saw.

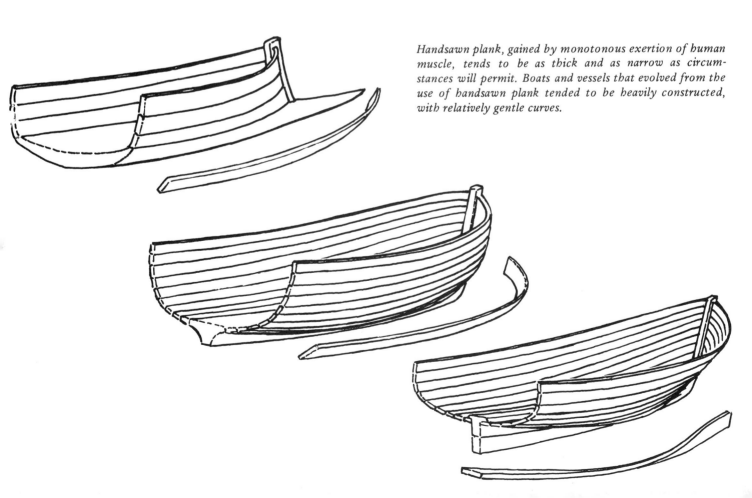

Handsawn plank, gained by monotonous exertion of human muscle, tends to be as thick and as narrow as circumstances will permit. Boats and vessels that evolved from the use of handsawn plank tended to be heavily constructed, with relatively gentle curves.

An up-and-down sawmill, water powered, operating a gang of four blades in reciprocating motion. Such a machine produced volume amounts of wide, thin lumber.

The dory, it should be emphasized, is a wide-board type. And if it is not the only wide-board type, it is among the foremost, for dory construction is one of the easiest, quickest, and cheapest methods yet devised for utilizing wide-board lumber in building boats for a wide variety of uses. It should be well understood. that it is the dory's special mode of construction, not hull shape, that sets it and its related sub-types apart from other boats.

It is true that considerable variations in hull shape can be achieved by dory construction. It is also true that certain hard-bilged round types with "flat floors," so called, have broad bottoms that for all useful purposes may be considered flat, and in effect make them flatter on the bottom than some slack-bilged Swampscott dories.

The advent of the dory type, or, more properly, of dory construction, did not bring any radically new and different hull shapes. What happened was an adaptation to new materials of old and tested shapes and proportions that had been passed down through an immemorial evolution of use. The old shapes remained basically and hydrodynamically the same, although their fabrication from wide boards gave a new look.

Dory construction starts with a flat bottom of wide boards cleated together and cut to shape on the outside edges. The shape of the bottom determines to a considerable extent the shape of the finished hull. Bend and fasten wide-board sides around the bottom, and the Bank dory is essentially built.

Such simplicity makes for an inexpensive boat, which is one reason why the Bank dory had no rivals. Such simplicity also makes it possible for dory types to be put together quickly and easily under adverse building conditins, as were the thousands of military batteaux constructed in backwoods outposts during the French and Indian Wars. And it is because of this simplicity that dory construction remains, as always, a favorite of the amateur builder.

As suggested, we might expect to discover dory construction making an appearance shortly after the new power sawmills had begun to produce abundant supplies of wide boards—and so we do.

At that early time workers in the manual trades were illiterate, and trade matters, such as small-craft design and construction, were not subjects of literate consideration and written record. Also, the boats of that remote day have long since utterly disappeared. We might never know what small craft of the late Middle Ages and early Renaissance were like except that a few of them found their way into the pictures of the great realistic artists of that time.

Sometime between 1495 and 1497 the German painter and engraver Albrecht Durer did a charming chromatic idyll in watercolor of a rustic cottage on an island in a fish pond near Nurnberg.[25] Drawn up on the beach in

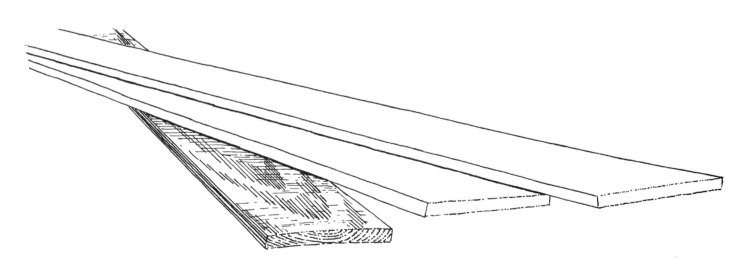

*Wide lumber, sawn by machines, may be what produced dory-type boats in Renaissance Europe as well as in maritime North America. Apparently cheap, quickly built, these were the "plywood skiffs" of yesteryear.*

*The earliest known representation of a dory flat in Europe. This is an enlarged detail from Albrecht Durer's watercolor* Little House on a Fish Pond, *c. 1497-8.*

*Durer's dory flat straightened up by mechanical perspective. If this is the boat viewed by the painter, and if this reconstruction is plausible, then it indicates a dramatic change in the science of boatbuilding afforded by the new, wide boards.*

the foreground and exhibited in full detail is a small double-ended boat, not unlike a lumberman's batteau in miniature, or a small Bank dory, notwithstanding that it antedates such craft by nearly 400 years. Its long raking ends are obviously contrived to slide up on the high banks so passengers may step ashore without wetting their feet.

Durer's boat has a flat bottom, boarded lengthwise, and flaring dory sides apparently made from a single wide board each. Natural crook frames are indicated. It is a wide-board boat of the dory type, in all particulars precisely like what we might build today for a similar purpose. Besides, this little double-ender does not bear the slightest constructional resemblance to older, round-bilged types planked continuously from keel to sheer with numerous narrow, sprung and twisted strakes.

Peter Breughel (the Elder), sixteenth century Flemish artist and a master of realistic detail, noticed the common, lowly things and drew them with honesty and precision. He sometimes put boats into his pictures, both round and dory types in the same scene, and this practice permits illuminating comparison.

In one of his whimsical fantasies done in 1556 called "Big Fish Eat Little Ones," Breughel shows us a dory skiff which looks much like one of our Amesbury rowing skiffs of a few years back, that is except for a more pointed, peaked-out bow section. But this bow, which looks slightly odd to American eyes, is nearly identical with the bow of a small contemporary French skiff featured on the cover of the October 1963 issue of *Toute la Peche*. It would seem that some small European dory skiffs have not changed much in the last 300 years.

This skiff of Breughel's would be about 12 or 13 feet long, judging from the size and position of its two occupants. The bottom cannot be seen, but definitely it must be flat. The two wide boards to a side on natural crook frames typify dory construction. The sheer is rather flat aft, not unlike a modern semi-dory, and the transom, set at about a normal rake, is ample to support an outboard motor.

All in all, this Flemish skiff is substantially a smaller version of the heavy working skiff, already mentioned, that Herman Moll showed in use in the Newfoundland fishery some 150 years later. While it has not yet been established for a certainty, it is most likely that wide-board boats of the dory type were employed in the Newfoundland cod fishery from its inception at the beginning of the sixteenth century, and thus were in use in the New World over a century before the Pilgrims landed at Plymouth.

NOTES

1. Uring, Capt. Nathaniel, *A History Of The Voyages And Travels*, London, 1726.
2. Morris, E.P., *The Fore-and-Aft Rig In America*, New Haven: Yale University Press, 1927.
3. Topham, James, Marblehead, Day book, Jan'y, 1784. Collection, Essex Institute, Salem Massachusetts.
4. Bentley, William, D.D., *Diary*, Essex Institute, Salem, Mass. 1907.
5. Albree, John, "The Swampscott Beaches", *Register*. Lynn Historical Society, Lynn, Mass., 1905.
6. Thoreau, Henry David, *A Week on the Concord and Merrimack Rivers*.
7. Goode, G. Brown, Bulletin 21, U.S. National Museum. No. 18, *The Exhibit of the Fisheries and Fish Culture of the United States of America, Berlin, 1880*. Washington, D.C., U.S. Government Printing Office.
8. Innis, Harold A., *The Codfisheries—The History of an International Economy*. New Haven: Yale University Press, 1940.
   Lounsbury, R.G., *The British Fishery at Newfoundland, 1634-1763*, New Haven, 1934.
   Judah, C.B., *The North American Fisheries and British Policy to 1713*. Urbana, 1933.
9. Prowse, D.W., *A History of Newfoundland*, London, 1896.
10. Légasse, Ferdinand L., *Evolution Economique des Iles Saint-Pierre et Miquelon*, Paris, 1935
11. Innis, op. cit. page 216-Note 7.
12. Albree, op. cit.
13. Pargellis, Stanley, *Military Affairs in North America, 1748-1765*. New York, American History Association, 1936 (Peter Wraxall to Henry Fox, p. 142).
14. Shaw, Alan, "The Bridgwater Flatner", *Mariners' Mirror*, Vol. 55, pp. 411-416.
15. McKee, Eric, "The Weston-Super-Mare Flatner," *Mariners' Mirror*, Vol. 57, pp. 25-39.
16. Kemp, Dixon, *Manual of Yacht and Boat Sailing and Yacht Architecture*, London, 1913.
17. Sauer, Carl O. *Northern Mists*, University of California Press, 1968
18. Lethbridge, T.C., *Boats and Boatmen*, Thames and Hudson, London: New York, 1952
19. Villiers, Alan, *Mariners' Mirror*, Vol. 37, p. 185.
20. Greenhill, Basil, *Boats and Boatmen of Pakistan*, David & Charles, Newton Abbot, England, 1971.
21. Worcester, G.R.G., *The Junks & Sampans of the Yangtze*, Naval Institute Press, Annapolis, Maryland, 1971.
22. Jones, P. d'A., and Simons, E.N., *Story of the Saw*, Newman Neame for Spear & Jackson, Ltd., Sheffield, England, 1961.
23. Mercer, Henry C., *Ancient Carpenters' Tools*, The Bucks County Historical Society, Doylestown, Pa., 1929.
24. Beckman, *Concise History of Ancient Institutions, Inventions, and Discoveries In Science And The Mechanic Arts*, London, 1823.
25. Waetzoldt, Wilhelm, *Dürer And His Times*, Phaedon Publishers, Oxford, 1950.

# 2 THE BATTEAU ANCESTOR

The first flat-bottomed boat, or "flat," built in the New World of which positive record has so far been found was a "flat batteau" outfitted at Montreal in the spring of 1671 at the order of M. de Courcelles, Governor of New France, who had conceived the idea of taking a flat batteau up the St. Lawrence River through the rapids to Lake Ontario.[1]

The Governor had two object in view. He foresaw the possibility of future trouble with the Iroquois, and he wished to demonstrate to the Five Nations that he could move effectively against them in a fleet of substantial planked boats if necessary. But more than that, it was becoming urgent to open up the interior wilderness to a volume of commerce not possible to be transported in bark canoes alone.

Neither the French nor the friendly Algonquins believed a planked boat could be taken up through the rapids. Undeterred, the Governor had one readied and provisioned and placed in charge of a sergeant with a crew of eight soldiers. On June 3, the batteau left Montreal in company with thirteen bark canoes carrying fifty-six persons. On June 12, the canoes and the batteau, after much travail in the rapids, reached Lake Ontario. The little fleet started back the same day.

The return downstream was made without mishap, taking only five days to retrace the 175 miles to Montreal, half the time required for the trip going out. The "promenade" had been a success, the Governor had proved his point, a great natural barrier to westward penetration of the continent had been overcome, and a new era in trade and warfare was initiated.

M. de Courcelles was failing in health; soon he returned to France, and a new Royal Governor, the able and illustrious Frontenac, took his place. One of Frontenac's first and most important measures was to erect a fort on Lake Ontario near the outlet of the St. Lawrence. To accomplish this purpose, he left Montreal on June 28, 1673, with 400 men, 120 canoes, and two flat batteaux. The batteaux were brightly painted and carried six small cast-iron cannon that he had found in the fort at Quebec. The Indians on the upper river were astonished at the size of this flotilla—and impressed, no doubt, by the cannon in the two batteaux.[2]

Frontenac and his task force arrived at their destination on July 12 in good order. A suitable site was selected and fortification immediately started. Here, shortly, rose the fort that later bore Frontenac's name. Fort Frontenac remained in French hands until it finally

*A River dory, or batteau, as developed by the French for conquest and commerce on the St. Lawrence River and its tributaries. Batteaux were the white man's canoe on the river systems of New England and French Canada throughout the colonial days. Experience with this type of boat in the Indian wars may have prompted New England fishermen to develop a cheaply produced seagoing dory for the offshore cod fishery. The ultimate American development of the batteau design was to be found in the log-driving batteaux of nineteenth-century Maine and in the Adirondack guideboats of the late nineteenth and early twentieth centuries.*

19

fell in 1758 to Colonel John Bradstreet's batteau-borne troops and the men of Bradstreet's special Battoe Service.

But the eventual eviction of the French from this spot, in which batteaux were destined to take a principal part, was still far in the future. In the meantime, an interim of eighty-five years, the French prospered on the upper reaches of the St. Lawrence and penetrated far into the interior by natural waterways. The fur trade flourished, and it was a trade based primarily upon batteau transportation.

Perhaps more than any other single factor, it was the batteau that not only built the power and wealth of New France, but also contributed to her downfall at the end. For when New France finally became too powerful and too close an economic threat for the British colonists to tolerate, they moved against her in "batoes." The logistics that defeated the French was a logistics based upon batteaux.

Was M. de Courcelles's first "flat batteau" borrowed from the Newfoundland cod fishery, or was it derived by some other route from an Old World small craft heritage? It would be naive to suppose that M. de Courcelles's "flat batteau" was invented on the spot. We are told it was a craft of from two to three tons, which may be assumed to be its total *loaded* displacement. Otherwise it could never have been portaged around rapids by nine men—or twice that number. Probably this first batteau did not differ too greatly from the batteaux later employed on the St. Lawrence, for its successful passage up the river and back through shoals and rapids, and the good time made, indicate the same special characteristics later familiar in the classic river batteau.

But perhaps Courcelles's batteau was not the first one on the river. Perhaps there was a prior local model. In the early spring of 1658, fifty refugees from the Jesuit mission at Onondaga,[3] in what is now upstate New York, fleeing from Iroquois treachery, had come down the St. Lawrence to Montreal in eight canoes and two boats. In two weeks, the little party of escapees had come down the Oswego River, crossed the eastern end of Lake Ontario, at times chopping their way through ice, and thence descended the St. Lawrence. In the Great Sault, one of their canoes capsized, drowning three men, but the two boats came through safely.

These two boats, each capable of carrying fourteen or fifteen men and some 1,600 pounds of additional weight, seem to have been flat. Built in secret and in haste—for the Indians delayed the massacre of the French garrison only because they believed the latter did not have the means for escape—these boats must have been crude in construction, but they could not have been too heavy to have been portaged around the falls on the Oswego.

From an account of one who was there, we learn that these boats were "contrived" from "deale boords" and had "large bottoms."[4] Father Simon le Moyne, also present, mentions that the two "batteaux" drew but little water yet carried much freight and were of a novel and excellent shape to pass through the rapids.[5] For this they would have required high ends, especially if the freeboard amidships was only half a foot, as the account states.

Given some prior knowledge of flat craft such as might be remembered from France, perhaps; some pine ("deale") boards and little else; being under desperate need to produce without delay a craft at once burdensome yet light, and of minimum draft; and working under the eyes of watchful but unsophisticated savages who believed the "Black Robes" were making additions to the interior of their house—taking all this into consideration—it might have been just possible that they could have improvised a batteau. What would have made it possible, in the final analysis, is the natural, inherent inclination of wide boards to peak up at the ends when bent as flaring sides around a pointed, flat bottom.

It is quite possible that the American river batteau dates from the Onondaga escape. The arrival of these boats at Montreal, then a small backwoods outpost, could not have passed unnoticed. Boats that had previously come safely through the perilous rapids of the upper St. Lawrence under such adverse circumstances might well have been remembered and offered as models to Courcelles thirteen years later.

In any case, after the middle of the seventeenth century and for more than 100 years subsequently, the batteau dominated transportation in that important region extending up the valley of the St. Lawrence to the Great Lakes, southward to the New York lakes, the upper Hudson, the Mohawk, and westward to the Allegheny. It was in this theater that the contest for the continent between Britain and France mainly took place, coming to a climax in the middle years of the eighteenth century. It was to a considerable extent a contest waged with, and in, batteaux. Each side employed many thousands of the flat-bottomed craft.

Whether the English originally derived their "batoes" from the French is unclear. Indications are that they did. But they might have obtained their model from the New York Dutch, who certainly would have been long familiar with flat craft, in use for centuries on the rivers of Germany and the Low countries. In any case, the English were using batteaux in military operations on the New York lakes and rivers as early as Queen Anne's War at the beginning of the eighteenth century.

Batteaux were built in many different sizes and with considerable minor variation. It appears that the model generally favored by the English colonials was appropriate for lake use, but not as well suited for violent rapids as the French model.

General Jeffrey Amherst, proceeding down the St. Lawrence in September, 1760, with 10,000 men in 800 batteaux and whaleboats, lost in the Cedars Rapids 84 batteaux and upwards of 300 men by French estimate, but only 66 batteaux and 84 men, according to the British. Whether these accidents were due to unfamiliarity with the river or to a model of boat unsuited to violent rapids is still an open question.[6]

The final struggle of Britain and France for North America, joined at the mid-point of the century, developed slowly, and at first the British had the worst of it. The year 1755 has been called "a year of disaster" for the British. Braddock's rout at Fort Duquesne, Johnson's failure at Crown Point, and Shirley's and Pepperill's equally abortive attempt against Fort Niagara sum it up for the interior.

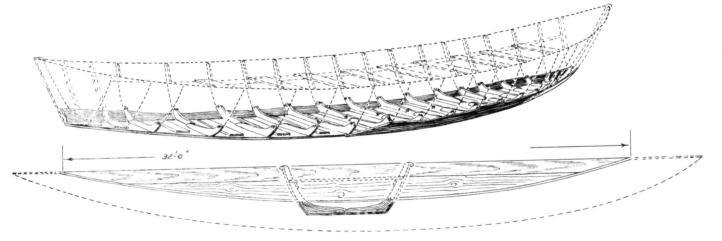

*An ancient batteau bottom raised from Lake George in 1960. The boat's overall length was possibly 36 feet. The reconstruction (dotted lines) is based on the draft of the 1776 colonial batteau shown in Howard I. Chapelle's* American Small Sailing Craft.

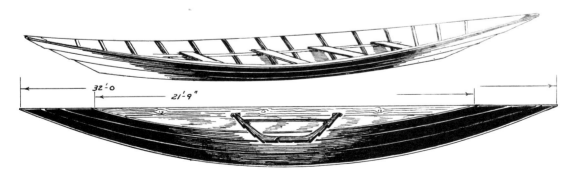

*A nineteenth-century Maine log-driving batteau.*

William Shirley, Esq., Governor of Massachusetts, was at this juncture the commanding general of the British forces in North America. His expedition against Niagara had proceeded in batteaux up the Mohawk from the great batteau depot at Schenectady to the Oneida carrying place, and then down the Oswego to Lake Ontario, over the regular batteau route.

Having learned first-hand of batteau transportation and its military urgency, General Shirley lost little time in proclaiming, in January, 1756, the formation of a Battoe Service for recruiting 2,000 experienced men along the coast as battoemen to report at Albany no later than March.[7] The new service was placed under the command of Lieutenant Colonel John Bradstreet, already in charge of building and repairing batteaux and whaleboats. Special inducements were offered for enlistment.

Items in the newspapers in the spring of 1756 frequently mention the Battoe Service. For example, when sixteen whaleboats from Cape Cod, with six men in each, arrived in New York City on the way to Albany to join the Battoe Service, one of the whaleboats rowed a race against a New York pettiauger for the then substantial wager of twenty dollars, and it won "with greatest ease."[8]

There seem never to have been enough boatbuilders and carpenters. In 1755, Bradstreet wrote to General Shirley of his need for carpenters. In 1758, he wrote General James Abercrombie that carpenters sent from New England included many boys, that he would like 200 more carpenters from New Jersey and Pennsylvania, and that he would not have 1,200 boats ready by May 15. In March of 1760 Bradstreet wrote to Joshua Loring that he required fifty good ship carpenters over and above the fifty already promised, "to build batteaux at Albany."

A turning point for British fortunes was the capture and razing of the French Royal Fort Frontenac on Lake Ontario in the summer of 1758 by a daring foray of a force of 2,737 men in batteaux led by Colonel Bradstreet over the Mohawk route from Schenectady and back.[9]

The great batteau factories were at Schenectady. For the thousands of batteaux that went up the Mohawk, as many more thousands went up the Hudson to Lake George, including thousands more carried across to Lake Champlain. The total of all these batteaux has never been reckoned, but it would be a staggering figure.[10]

Colonel John Bradstreet's Battoe Service and

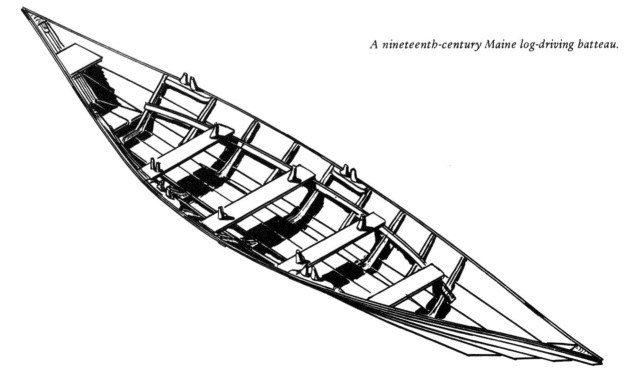

*A nineteenth-century Maine log-driving batteau.*

*A Maine log-driving batteau at work.*

the attached corps of carpenters and boatbuilders, aside from their specific military function, served as a practical school in small craft design and construction for a generation of American boatbuilders at a time when watercraft were still the chief means of transportation. In recruiting and gathering artisans and watermen from Maine to the Chesapeake, the Battoe Service became a melting pot of boatbuilding know-how and experience, as well as experimentation. While the batteau, whaleboat, and scow, in that order, were the principal types, many other kinds of small craft were tried and used to a minor extent. Besides, all kinds of larger vessels saw service on the lakes. Military necessity as well as the hard conditions of the backwoods frontier forced all manner of expedients.

With the successful conclusion of the French and Indian Wars, there began for the colonies a period of rapid economic growth and territorial expansion. Without railroads, and lacking anything like an adequate system of wagon and coach roads, especially in the interior behind the fast-advancing frontier, the colonials depended on waterborne transportation, with its requirements for all manner of small and medium craft as well as for larger vessels, to an extent that cannot be overestimated.

Veterans of the Battoe Service took home experience and knowledge they never would have acquired in the local boatshop. Above all, they took back familiarity with dory construction acquired in building, repairing, and operating batteaux.

Some of the grandsons and great grandsons of the veterans of the Battoe Service built the Massachusetts Bank dories that went to Newfoundland and were carried back to Europe by fishermen from Brittany and Portugal.

So, in the course of several centuries, the dory had traveled in a great spiral, as it were, from the Old World west to Newfoundland, up the St. Lawrence and across to the New York lakes, eastward to New England, and north and eastward still, until finally arriving back at its European site of origin. A minor eddy in the evolution of dory types turned the river-driving batteaux of the Penobscot lumbermen westward again, as lumbering moved west in the nineteenth century, first to the Adirondacks, then to Michigan, to Wisconsin, and to Oregon.

The wide diffusion of the batteau-building experience acquired by the veterans of Col. John Bradstreet's Battoe Service unquestionably influenced the future course of boatbuilding along our North Atlantic Coast, but to precisely what extent can only be guessed. This is because so little that is definite is known about the design and construction of small craft other than the batteau in Colonial America. For all we definitely know, there could have been several different flat-bottom contemporaries or precursors of the eighteenth-century military batteaux in use in various localities along the coast. But lacking such definite knowledge or any reliable indication of the existence of such craft, it is tempting to assume that a number of distinctive flat-bottom working small craft that came into view in the nineteenth century, were, in fact, directly derived from the earlier military batteaux. These are the Saint John River salmon boat, various New England wherries, including the Maine salmon wherries and the Piscataqua River wherry, Bank and Swampscott dories, the Staten Island skiff, known in the Chesapeake as the Yankee skiff, and the Jersey sea skiff, originally called a dory.

## NOTES

1. Preston and Lamontagne, *Royal Fort Frontenac*, Champlain Society. Toronto, 1958.
2. Ibid.
3. Thwaits, Ruben Gold, Ed., *Jesuit Relations*. Vol. 44, p. 175.
4. *Voyages of Peter Radisson: Experience Among the North American Indians, 1652 to 1684*. Introduction, Gidion D. Scull, Prince Society, Boston, 1885.
5. *Documentary History of New York*, Vol. 1, pp. 52-54.
6. Knox, Capt. John, *An Historical Journal of the Campaigns in North America for the Years 1757, 1758, 1759, and 1760*. The Champlaign Society, Toronto, 1914.
7. *Boston Weekly News Letter*. Feb. 5, 1756.
8. Ibid. May 6, 1756.
9. *An Impartial Account of Lieut. Col. Bradstreet's Expedition to Fort Frontenac*, London, 1759. Reprinted, Rous & Mann, Ltd., Toronto, 1940.
10. J.W. Bradstreet to His Ex. Gen. Amherst, Albany, Dec. 31, 1756. Amherst Papers, Library of Congress and Amherst College, WO34/57, folio 16.

# 3   THE BANK DORY EMERGES

After a century and a half of colonial preparation, the American Revolution opened the gateway to an era of material expansion and progress that accelerated unchecked until World War I. During that fabulous period of economic growth, American small craft shared in the general prosperity, multiplied in number, proliferated in design, and, at the onset, participated directly in the mainstream of economic activity as essential transportation. As time passed, and the standard of living rose for increasing segments of the population, bringing cultural change, small craft were turned increasingly to employment for sport and pleasure. By the end of the 1800s their original function had, to a considerable extent, been superseded. The workboat had become a pleasure boat. This, in briefest outline, recounts the final evolution of New England dories.

It is easy to see how a reporter for the U.S. Tenth Census picked up the notion that the dory was a "Yankee Invention."[1] The American fishing industry, then a prime contributor to the national wealth, was dominated by New England, and the bulk of its fishing was done from New England dories. It was only natural to accept the claim of local patriots that the dory had been originally devised in Massachusetts.

Gloucester, then the largest fishing port in the world, is situated in Massachusetts's Essex County, which at that time was also the center of dory building, both for local use and for export. Salisbury Point, north of Gloucester on the Merrimack River, had seven dory shops in the 1870s that utilized piece-work methods to assemble annually from pre-cut parts many thousands of Bank dories, nearly all of which were built in five standard sizes. Not since Colonel John Bradstreet's great batteau factory at Schenectady more than a century before had boats of standardized model been mass-produced in such quantity.

The place where the dory was supposed to have been born was the boatshop at Salisbury Point (now Amesbury) founded in 1793 by Simeon Lowell and operated until a few years ago by his direct descendants. The lines of old Simeon's boat, which, strangely enough, he apparently called a "wherry," are lost. How much or how closely these lines resembled the classic form of the Bank dory is a matter of surmise. Certainly Simeon did not get up his "wherry" with the needs of the Bank fishery in view, because trawl fishing, which brought the Bank dory to the fore, was not introduced on the Newfoundland Banks until after 1830, the date of Simeon's death at the age of eighty-five.[2]

That Simeon's "wherry" was called a "dory" by the Swampscott shore fishermen, who imported these boats from Salisbury Point, sug-

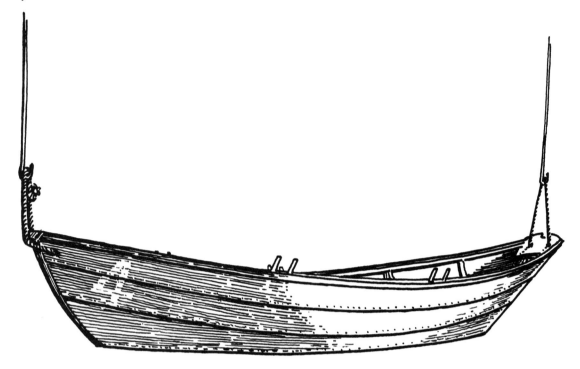

*The Bank dory, probably developed from the colonial batteau. It appeared in the New England fishery in the mid-1830s, when trawl fishing was introduced on the offshore banks.*

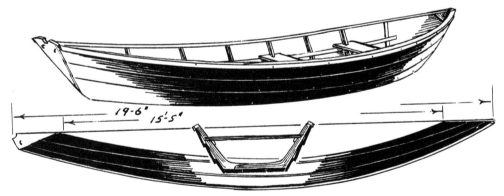

*A two-man, or double, Bank dory.*

*The flared, straight sides of the Bank dory permit these boats to be stacked one inside another. This schooner carried 16 dories in two stacks, or banks, port and starboard. Sometimes the dories were stacked upside down.*

*In a fishing schooner, the dories were hoisted in and out by tackles made up to the crosstrees of the schooner's masts. A hooked rod, or dory hook, at the end of the dory tackle permitted over-the-rail fishing for the rope beckets of a dory alongside.*

gests that in late colonial times both names might have been applied in and around the waters of Massachusetts Bay to the same general type of small, flat, rowing workboat. According to lines shown by Chapman in his *Architectura Navalis Mercatoria*, the English wherry of the eighteenth century was a round-bottomed boat with a keel instead of a flat bottom craft with a moderately slack bilge.

But there is evidence that the American wherry of the same period did have a flat bottom. The Reverend William Bentley, voluminous Salem diarist of the post-Revolutionary period who frequently recorded his observations of Essex County small craft, definitely described one-man rowing "wherries" used in the Cape Ann shore fishery as being "flat."[3]

There also were wherries on the Merrimack at this early date. The account book of Richard Hackett, a Salisbury oar maker who exported large numbers of whaleboat oars to Nantucket, shows an entry dated 1753 for oars for a "whary."[4] Some of Hackett's fellow townsmen, including an older brother of Simeon Lowell and several of Simeon's cousins, served on the New York lakes during the French and Indian War, repairing whaleboats and building batteaux as well as a sloop. Newburyport, a few miles below Salisbury Point at the mouth of the Merrimack, was a principal center of colonial shipbuilding, and the neighborhood supplied many artisans for the campaign against the French.

Boatbuilders and shipwrights by the scores, if not the hundreds, were recruited from the shore towns of Massachusetts and New Hampshire for Bradstreet's Battoe Service and they mingled with carpenters from New York, New Jersey, Pennsylvania, and even as far south as the Chesapeake, in the greatest boatbuilding operation America had then seen. When these mechanics returned to the Merrimack tidewater, they must have brought back new ideas if not new models. Thus Ben Glaiser, young boatbuilder from nearby Ipswich, who tells in his war diary[5] of "Building Botems for Batoes," may well have picked up notions of mass production such as later materialized in the Salisbury Point dory factories. Undoubtedly the youthful Simeon Lowell must have heard his relatives and other local veterans recount on numerous occasions their war experiences of building batteaux and whaleboats.

Tradition usually is not completely wrong. The likely kernel of truth in this instance is that some modifications in the form and construction of flat-bottomed colonial wherries probably did take place at the mouth of the Merrimack at the onset of the nineteenth century. And it is wholly natural that Simeon Lowell, as proprietor of the leading boatshop and a successful businessman, should have been accorded the credit by local annalists.

It is probable that the knuckles were taken out of the sides of the flat-bottomed but semi-roundsided wherry to produce a straight, uniform side flare running back to the stern. To replace the wherry's smallish, high-tucked transom of wineglass curve, a narrow, straight-sided, V-shaped plank was substituted, which when raked steeply aft on the approximate profile angle of the stem, produced in effect a double-ended boat.

Such a boat would not have rowed or handled quite as easily as the wherry, and unless it were loaded and expertly managed, it would have proved somewhat cranky in rough water. Yet, such a boat would have been much easier and cheaper to build than the round-sided wherry; in addition it would be admirably suited to mass production out of the native white pine and oak lumber then abundant in the Merrimack valley.

Until more precise information is uncovered, we may assume that this, in substance, was the breakthrough that yielded the Bank dory, making due allowance for some minor changes and improvements before the classic mold of the type was set some time about midway in the nineteenth century.

At the Peabody Museum in Salem there is a model originally from the old Boston Museum that purports to represent a dory of 1830. This flat-bottomed rowboat has straight, flaring sides like a Bank dory. But its transom is wider, like the familiar dory skiff of which so many variations were once popular as rowboats along the New England shore before the outboard motor. One of the best of these, and perhaps the best known, was the Amesbury skiff, once widely used in children's summer camps requiring a safe, easy-rowing boat. It took its name, obviously, from the dory-building town of Amesbury.

It may be that the Bank dory owes as much to the skiff as it does to the wherry. Today

*Dorymen tending trawl on the Grand Banks.*

*A jumbo-size modern power dory seen today in the French fishery at St. Pierre et Miquelon. This is probably the ultimate development of the Bank fishing dory.*

the name skiff means in general a light rowboat, but not a flat-bottomed boat exclusively. Just what colonial skiffs were like we do not know, nor how precisely the name was then applied—whether to a single type or to several. But it is clear that small, flat rowboats, uncommonly like the nineteenth century dory skiffs of Massachusetts's Essex County, were in use in Europe from 200 to 300 years earlier, witness the pictures by Breughel and Herman Moll referred to earlier.

In his diary in 1791, Reverend Bentley twice mentions skiffs as being in use off Marblehead, once when he and others engaged a "Marblehead skiff" to take them through the surf for a landing on the beach. Perchance might Bentley's "Marblehead skiff" have been one of the "dories" listed in the account book of the contempory Marblehead boatbuilder James Topham?

Two years later, Bentley watched fishermen on the Merrimack, above tidewater, seining for salmon, alewives, pickerel, shad, and suckers. "Their method was a flat boat of about fourteen feet in length, and three in breadth with a stern upon which is a table for the seine, which is furnished with scuppers to void the water." This "flat boat" sounds like a skiff, although Bentley's estimated beam of three feet would seem to have been too narrow.

Simeon Lowell was not the only Essex County Lowell in the boatbuilding business in the post-Revolutionary War years. The account book of his nephew David,[6] started in 1781, lists numerous craft constructed: whaleboats, a "12 feet Moses boat," wherries, gundelos, a "Raftsman's wherry," and a shad boat. The Moses boat went for 72 shillings, while the shad boat brought exactly half that sum, indicating, it would seem, a simpler, lower-cost construction.

Perhaps the Merrimack shad boat of that period, when the river teemed with the succulent shad, was a flat-bottomed skiff of the sort observed by Bentley. If so, it would be unlike the nineteenth century Hudson River shad boat, a more elaborate and expensive craft closely related to the Whitehall in its build.

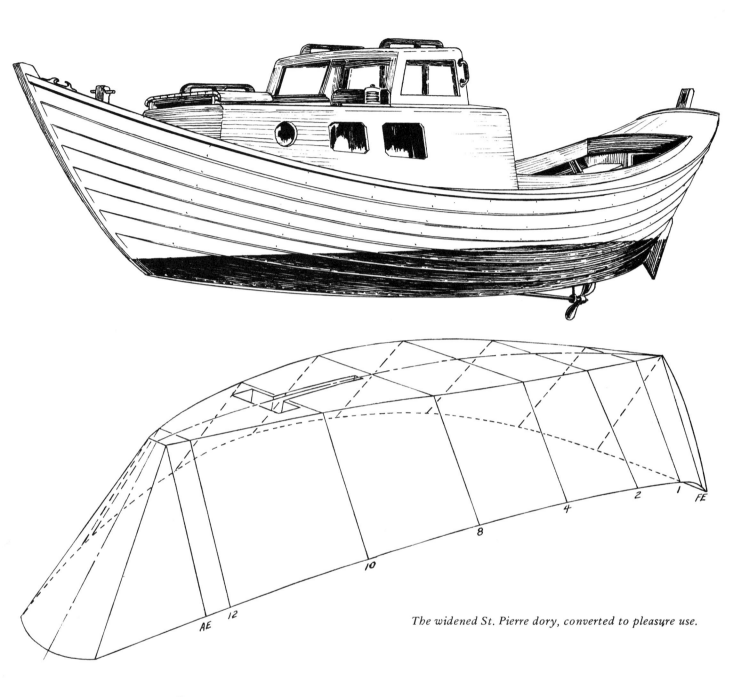

*The widened St. Pierre dory, converted to pleasure use.*

*The round-sided Swampscott dory.*

It has frequently been supposed that the round-sided Swampscott dory, which became so widely popular toward the end of the century for pleasure sailing and power boating as we shall see, constitutes a refinement of the fisherman's straight-sided Bank dory, erroneously taken to have been the prior and original dory type. This is definitely not the fact. The knuckle-sided Swampscott dory is too close in resemblance and historical connection to the round-sided colonial wherry, whatever the Swampscott type may have borrowed of the rationalized construction of the mass-produced Bank fishing dories.

As the century progressed, a new spirit burgeoned, and scientific interest turned to the workaday world of the common man. The equipment and methods of the fisheries were intensively examined and cataloged in the 1880s in preparing exhibits for the several international fisheries expositions held during that decade in Berlin, London, and New Orleans. A one-time master of Gloucester fish-

ing schooners, working for the U.S. Fish Commission, started the Watercraft Collection of the U.S. National Museum, the early bulletins of which contain the first complete descriptions of dories used in the Bank fisheries.[7]

At about this time the Bank dory began to receive attention from a different quarter. A new breed of boating amateurs, home builders, and devotees of boats as recreation, emerging in this era of expanding prosperity, turned to the dory along with other small craft. The pioneer sporting and amateur boating publication, *Forest & Stream*, in 1887 printed lines and partial details for a 14-foot Bank dory as built by Higgins & Gifford of Gloucester. And what appears to be much the same dory is to be found in the 1889 edition of W.P. Stephens's famous amateur manual of *Canoe and Boat Building*, also issued by Forest and Stream Publishing Company. Since then, lines and details for Bank dories have appeared over and over again in many diverse publications.

The Bank dory, due to its enormous repu-

*The round-sided Swampscott dory, the shore fisherman's boat, individually built and refined toward better rowing and sailing qualities.*

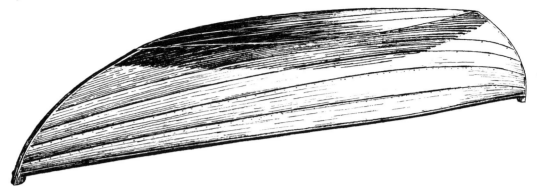

*A surf dory of the Chamberlain model.*

*A lightly built, double-ended gunning dory for the sport hunting of ducks.*

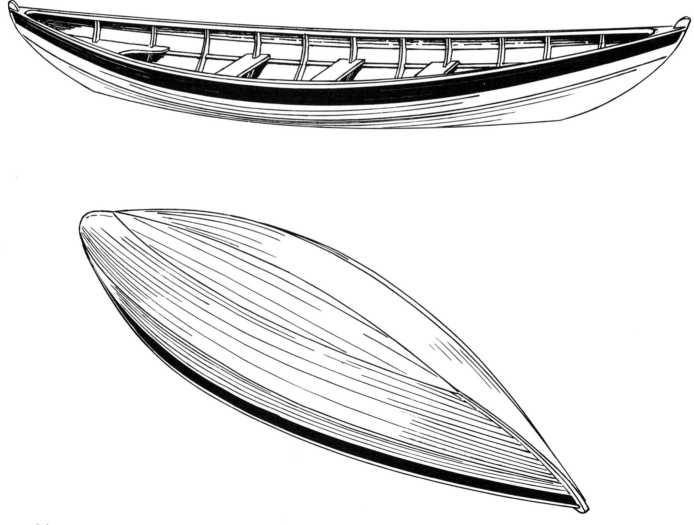

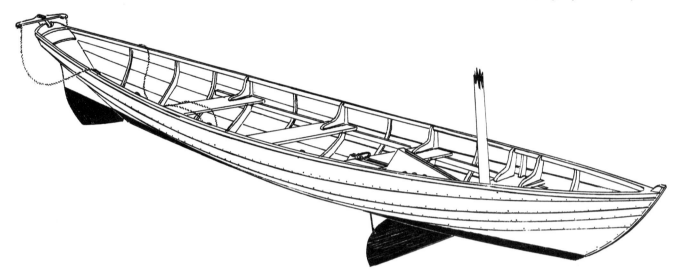

*The Beachcomber dory, an extreme model of the Swampscott type. The Beachcombers, Alphas, and X-dories, similar types, were groomed into racing machines during the opening decades of the twentieth century.*

*The sailing Swampscott dory.*

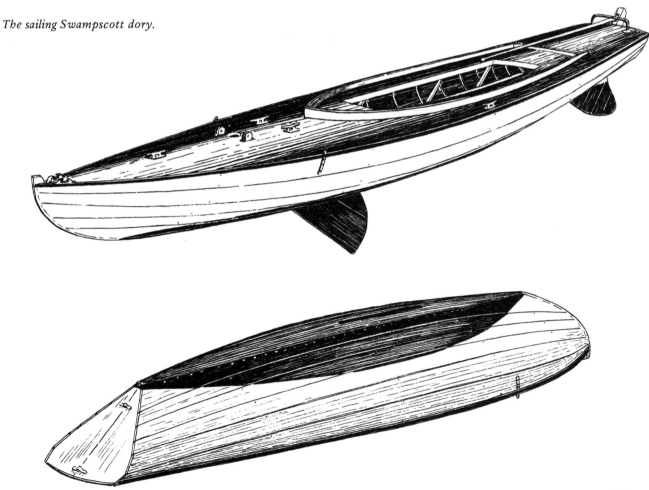

*The decked, sailing Swampscott at the final degree of dory development.*

tation as a fishing craft, is the best known of all the dories, yet it is not as well suited to the requirements of recreational boating as the round-sided types. Its single great virtue is ease and simplicity of construction. That it is an excellent sea boat, if properly handled, goes without saying. But it does not sail as well as a round-sided Swampscott dory. And it does not make as good a general-purpose rowboat as a well-designed dory skiff. As an economical, low-cost power launch, where high speed is not required, a large Bank dory offers distinctive advantages when fitted with a properly engineered well for an outboard motor. The big St. Pierre dory is in actuality an over-size Bank dory, and in this boat the Bank type attains its peak potential for adaptation to pleasure use.

The modern St. Pierre dory with its high crescent sheer, its deeply rounded bottom rocker, and its widely flaring sides, closely recapitulates the basic lines of the original Bank model contrived for deep water and the open sea. Dories for the shore fisheries generally carried less sheer and were made straighter on the bottom, giving a shallower draft, which enabled them to ground out higher on the beach. Often the side flare was lessened in these shore dories. The wider bottoms increased initial stability but made a boat less reliable in rough water.

Originally, the different sizes of Bank dories were designated according to bottom length, which is sometimes confusing to those not acquainted with this convention. The practice undoubtedly arose in nineteenth-century dory factories where all except the very largest and the very smallest dories were assembled from identical, standardized, pre-cut parts, excepting the bottoms and planking. In building, the bottom first had to be put together and cut to shape. For each size of dory built, a separate bottom half-pattern of the required length was kept on hand, marked with the location and spacing of the frames for that particular size. At first, dories would probably have been specified by mentioning the length of bottom, for instance, a dory with "a 14-foot bottom." Later this was naturally shortened to "a 14-foot dory." In actuality, however, a 14-foot dory is several inches over 18 feet in total length.

Bulletin 21 of the U.S. National Museum, published in 1880, describes five sizes of straight-sided fishing dories, in connection with which it states that the size built on the 15-foot bottom was most used and was called the "Bank dory." The smallest in this series listed by the Bulletin is a 13-footer, and the larger bottom lengths run 14, 14½, 15, and 15½ feet.[8]

We know, however, that dories both larger and smaller than these sizes were built at this time for the fisheries. Henry Hall in his *Ship-Building Industry Report* of 1884 lists bottoms of 12, 13, 14, 15, and 16 feet, the last and largest being used for halibut.

The 1880 Bulletin of the U.S. National Museum, however, states that the 15-foot bottom, or the "Bankdory" was the halibut dory. Its 15½-foot dory, which was 19' 8" on top, was described as an out-size model little used by American fishermen, being exported mainly to the French fishermen at St. Pierre and Miquelon. It was built extra heavy with six and sometimes seven pairs of frames, instead of the usual four pairs.

Almost everyone knows the fisherman's dory, that is to say the Bank dory. This distinctive boat-type is easily recognized, with its crescent sheer, straight, flaring sides, narrow "tombstone" stern, and comparatively narrow, flat bottom. But few look closely enough at individual specimens to see in just what dimensions and proportions these components are blended. Unless one uses dories, builds them, or has studied them, the considerable variations among the numerous examples of this general type are not obvious and go unnoticed, however important such differences may be under certain conditions or for some particular purpose.

Quite often the Bank dory is referred to as the Gloucester dory. This is because of association. In the heyday of the Gloucester fisheries, thousands of these dories were standard equipment on Gloucester fishing schooners. But the dory did not originate in Gloucester, and the general characteristics of the type seem to have been established before Gloucester assumed dominance in the Bank fisheries.

The Gloucester boatbuilding firm of Higgins & Gifford, world-famous for its batten-seam mackerel seine boats, built fishing dories for a period after setting up its boatshop in 1873, but by that time the fishing dory had attained classic form. It was a Higgins & Gifford dory

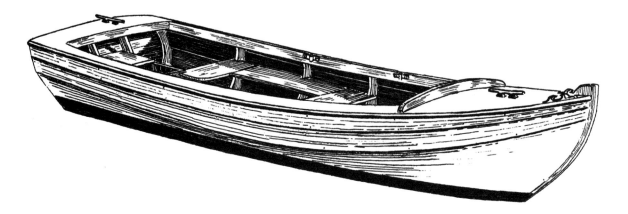

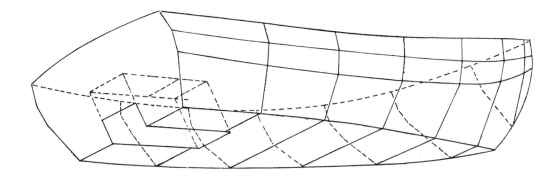

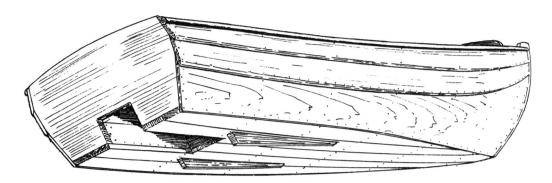

*An outboard-powered semi-dory.*

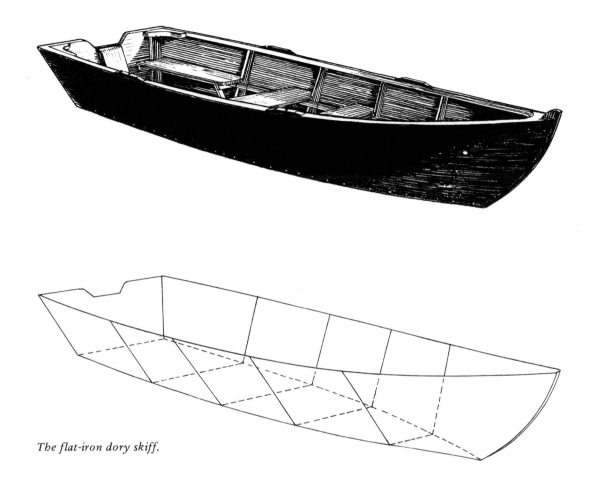

*The flat-iron dory skiff.*

that Captain Alfred "Centennial" Johnson in 1876 sailed single-handed to England in ninety-six days. The 19-foot dory in which the Andrews brothers of Beverly crossed the Atlantic two years later in only forty-five days was also built in Gloucester by Higgins & Gifford. The same firm patented an "improved" fishing dory construction, employing batten seams as on their seine boats, and also a special gunwale reinforcement, but these improvements did not catch on. In the 1890s, they gave up building dories, and in their catalog they referred those interested in dories to Hiram Lowell & Son of Amesbury.

If the classic, straight-sided, fishing dory, or Bank dory, first assumed its characteristic form in Essex County, Massachusetts, during the first part of the nineteenth century, it must very soon have spread widely up and down the coast. Hall in 1880 reports that these dories

were built from New York to Maine, but with the principal center at Salisbury. The U.S. National Museum acquired a model of a Nantucket dory of this general shape in 1876, so that it may be assumed that dories of this sort were known in the area of Cape Cod even earlier. The fisherman's dory is sometimes called the Cape Cod dory.

In considering small craft beginnings in this country, boatbuilding should not be confused with shipbuilding, which became a specialized trade (or more precisely, complex of trades) earlier and to a more exclusive extent. Boatbuilding, on the contrary, until well along in the nineteenth century, remained an occasional, part-time occupation diversified with spells of farming, fishing, lumbering, house carpentry, mason work, and much else.

Fishermen often built their own boats, just as they still do in some parts of Maine and the

Canadian Maritimes. Boats varied greatly from builder to builder and from town to town. One indication of this is the diversity of names applied with little attempt at uniformity or precision of meaning. Much of this rich diversity has long since passed beyond recall, although some interesting names remain. A good example is the "Joppa Shay," apparently a flat skiff once indigenous to Joppa Flats near Newburyport and the mouth of the Merrimack.

Contemporary writing relating to the New England shore in the first half of this century not infrequently mentions boats that must have been dories of one sort of another, or closely related types, as in the case of the flat-bottomed "skiffs" noted by a summer visitor to Swampscott in 1858, who estimated them as being about 13 feet long. There were no systematic descriptions, however, no precise and reliable dimensions, no detailed plans. Observers did not carry rules, apparently, or kept them in their pockets. But there was more to it than that. The literate classes then, as formerly, were rarely concerned with mechanical matters and artifacts of common utility.

## NOTES

1. Hall, Henry, *Report On The Ship-Building Industry of the United States.* Tenth Census. Washington, 1884.
2. Innis, Harold A., *The Cod Fisheries — The History Of An International Economy.* New Haven: Yale University Press, 1940, p. 219.
3. Bentley, William, D.D., *Diary.* Essex Institute, Salem, Mass., 1907, Vol. 2. p. 304.
4. Hackett, Richard, Account Book. Essex Institute, Salem, Mass.
5. Glasier, Benjamin, *Diary* (unpublished). Essex Institute, Salem, Mass.
6. Lowell, David, Account Book 1781. Amesbury, Mass. Essex Institute, Salem, Mass.
7. Collins, Capt. J. W., *Catalogue of the Collection Illustrating the Fishing Vessels and Boats, and Their Equipment; the Economic Condition of Fishermen; Anglers' Outfits, etc. of the United States of America.* Great International Fisheries Exhibition, London, 1883, Washington, Government Printing Office, 1884.
8. Goode, George Brown. Bulletin 21 of the U.S. National Museum. No. 18. *Exhibit of the Fisheries and Fish Culture of the United States of America, Made in Berlin in 1880.* Washington, Government Printing Office, 1880.

# PART TWO
# HOW TO BUILD A DORY

# 4  DORY LAYDOWN

The straight-sided dories, including the Banks dories and ordinary skiffs, have such simple lines that sometimes these need not be laid down full size for building. But for a good job, the lines of the larger, round-sided, Swampscott dories do require a full-sized laydown and careful fairing. Of course the basic reason for laying down the dory's lines full size is so the builder can later pick up the exact sizes and shapes of the boat's parts (all but the planks) from the laydown surface, and have some assurance that these parts, when assembled, will form a fair hull.

Perhaps you have never laid down the lines of a boat. If so, the dory is a good type to start on, for its lines are relatively easy. The operation should become clear with a little study. It may even prove enjoyable as a prelude to the actual building, for pencil lines are more tractable than wood and there is something satisfying in seeing the form of the boat-to-be unfold itself upon the floor.

The dory in all the shapes and stages of its evolution, going back some 400 years at the least, was developed and brought to perfection without benefit of lines. Lines were for large vessels, and are, at that, a comparatively late innovation in the ancient art of shipbuilding. Until yesterday, boats were built by eye and by rule of thumb.

## Patterns

Famous dory builders of the nineteenth century built from patterns taken from proven boats. In addition to preserving form and assuring uniformity, such patterns facilitated building by making it easy to mark out the shapes of the various parts on the building stock. As dories evolved and models were improved, patterns were altered or pieced out in conformity with the changes.

Patterns formed an important stock in trade. They were guarded from competitors, handed down from father to son, and stolen by ambitious hired help. In long-established boatshops, old patterns accumulated overhead on the rafters, under benches, in corners, or were tacked to the walls. They wore out, got lost, and were even burned sometimes to heat the shop during cold weather, as happened in the case of the frame molds for old Simeon Lowell's 1793 "wherry," erroneously credited by local patriots to have been the first and original dory of them all.

## Hull Lines

It is unfortunate that boatbuilders in the past did not work from lines, for, without this

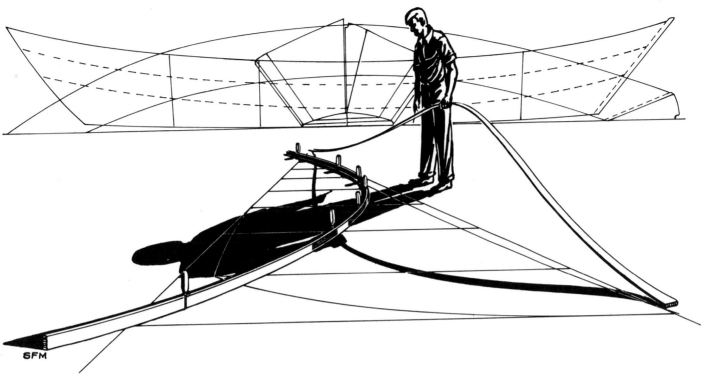

**1. Lines and the laydown.**

means of permanently recording design, much of our rich heritage of native small craft has been irretrievably lost. The old builders died. Their boats rotted away. Their patterns disappeared.

Lines are a real boon to the amateur builder once he gets the hang of using them. They are a great equalizer in the trade, for with lines the amateur leaps over years and years of arduous apprentice and journeyman training, and stands quite soon on a nearly equal footing with the masters of the trade in coping with form and design. Not wholly equal, it is true, for it still takes experience to perfect a boatbuilder's eye.

It should be understood at the outset that the basic dory form is very largely and directly derived from the *natural bend* taken by wide boards of uniform thickness. The precise form that this bend takes is controlled to some extent by such factors as bottom width, side flare, and end rake, but it is the easy, natural, curving sweep of the side plank that really shapes the dory. In some hull forms, the wood must be twisted, steamed, and tormented into place. Not so with the dory. The builder follows the natural inclination of the boards and

is guided by it. Incidentally, this is a large reason why dories are so strong and durable.

Because its shape is not forced, but already grown in the boards to some extent before they reach the builder, the dory requires only the simplest of lines. All that is needed are the curves of the bottom and sheer, the rake of the ends, a few heights and widths from which the shape of the frames is derived, and the lining of the plank on the frames. No buttocks, no diagonals, and no waterlines are required, although the half-breadths of the bottom and sheer and plank knuckles are treated somewhat as if they were waterlines. Lines for the straight-sided Bank type are utterly simple. For the round-sided Swampscott, the lines are not more difficult, but there are more of them.

I have no intention at this point of attempting to produce an extensive treatise on boat lines. That has already been adequately done in a number of excellent standard works on boatbuilding, which the prospective builder will do well to consult. Nevertheless, it will be helpful to recapitulate briefly from the standpoint of the dory builder's needs what the hull lines are and what they do.

### Profile, Halfbreadths, Sections

The lines show three views of the hull corresponding to the three dimensions of a solid (see Figure 3). First, the *profile* is the sidewise view of the boat plumbed upright on its bottom or keel. Second, in looking up at the boat from directly below one gets a breadth view, or rather a *half-breadth* view, because for convenience and simplicity only one of the halves of the symmetrical hull is usually drawn. Third, *section* views of the hull are obtained by considering the boat cut into a number of athwartship sections at the location of the frames and by looking at these from the ends of the boat, that is, in the hull's fore-and-aft direction.

The profile shows the sheer curve and the rocker curve of the bottom. The half-breadth view shows the side curves of the bottom and sheer, and of the knuckles in a Swampscott dory. The sections show the shapes of the frames and the appearance of the transom, foreshortened in its raked position. Dory lines are always drawn to the inside of the plank, rather than to the outside.

To obtain and locate points for laying out these three fundamental views of hull shape, two separate sets of measurements are employed: *heights* and *half-breadths*. Heights are plumbed up from an assumed base plane usually made parallel to the flotation plane of the boat. It is as if the boat were floating or suspended on an even keel in a large rectangular box. Heights are the distances plumbed up from the bottom of the box. Widths, that is to say, half-breadths, are distances measured "square" across the box (see Figure 4).

As previously stated, the half-breadth plan shows only half of the symmetrical hull, which is assumed to be divided by the vertical plane generated by the boat's fore-and-aft centerline. It is as if this half hull, enclosed in our imaginary rectangular box, were attached lengthwise to one of the box's vertical sides. Thus half-breadths are horizontal distances squared out from the vertical, lengthwise side of the box.

Now assume we cut up our long imaginary box and the half-hull it encloses into several short sections where frames are needed in the dory. The surfaces forming the ends of these sections will be plumb with the bottom of our box and square with its long sides. On these surfaces, or section faces, pairing heights and half-breadths are measured off, and the points where the heights and half-breadths intersect establish the shape and position of the frames at each respective station. Thus, at each station, a point in the sheer curve will be located by the intersection of a horizontal half-breadth measurement of width and a vertical measurement of height (see Figure 4). Likewise will be determined a point in the curve of the inside edge of the bottom. In the same manner, points are obtained in the plank lines that will be the knuckle lines in a Swampscott dory.

To establish a line, several points are required, generally connected, in the case of dory lines, by a fair sweep or curve. That is, the sheer, bottom, and planking longitudinals

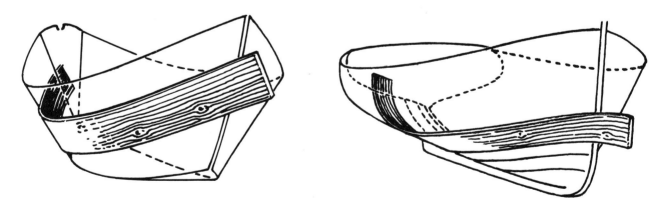

**2. Plank shapes.** (Left) *The shape of a dory is largely governed by the natural bend taken by wide boards of uniform thickness. (Right) In some hull forms, the wood must be twisted, steamed, and tormented into place.*

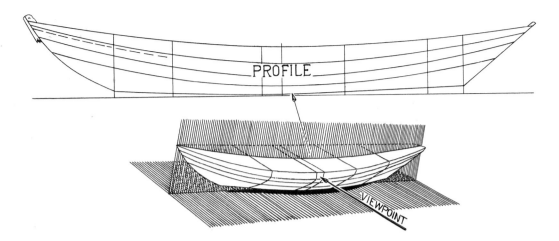

*3.(a). The profile is the elevation, or broadside view.*

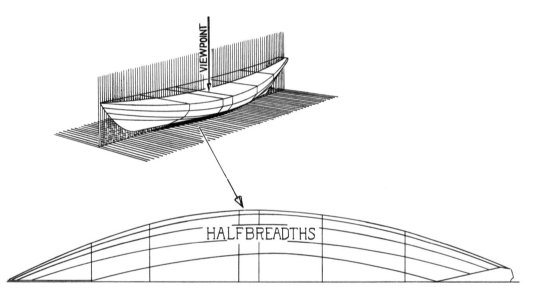

*3(b). The halfbreadths show the hull as seen from directly above (or directly below) in "plan" view.*

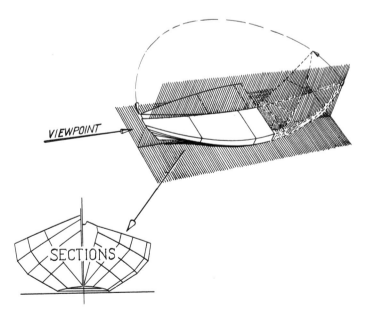

*3(c.). The sections or body plan give the cross-sectional views of the hull lines.* Bow and stern, seen head-on, represent the same side of the boat. Note that the stem and transom are foreshortened in length in this view.

are curves. But the shape of the frames is straight across the bottom, and straight from bottom to sheer in the Bank-type dory, and straight from knuckle to knuckle in the Swampscott.

To locate each point, three dimensions are required. The fore-and-aft location of the point is determined by the section in which it lies. Its height is measured above the horizontal plane generated by the base line. The point also has a width position, that is, its distance out from the vertical dividing plane of the hull, generated by the fore-and-aft centerline.

### Offsets

By using three interrelated sets of lines corresponding to the dimensions of a solid, by working back and forth from one to another,

and by correcting each in turn from the others, it is possible to lay out accurately the surface of the solid hull, or the shape of the dory, from a table of measurements. This is called a *Table of Offsets*, because to make a measurement is to *set off* a distance. By convention, heights and breadths are shown in the table for each section drawn in the lines. The distance between stations, and their fore-and-aft situation, will be found on the lines plan.

Measurements can be wrong, and too often are. Error can creep in at any time when measurements are first made, or when the figures are set down, read off, or laid out. Besides, offsets most frequently are scaled from drawings of reduced size—a sometimes practical necessity, which multiplies inaccuracies many times. Finally, single measurements have little absolute validity of their own, but are significant to the extent that they fair into the hull shape as a whole.

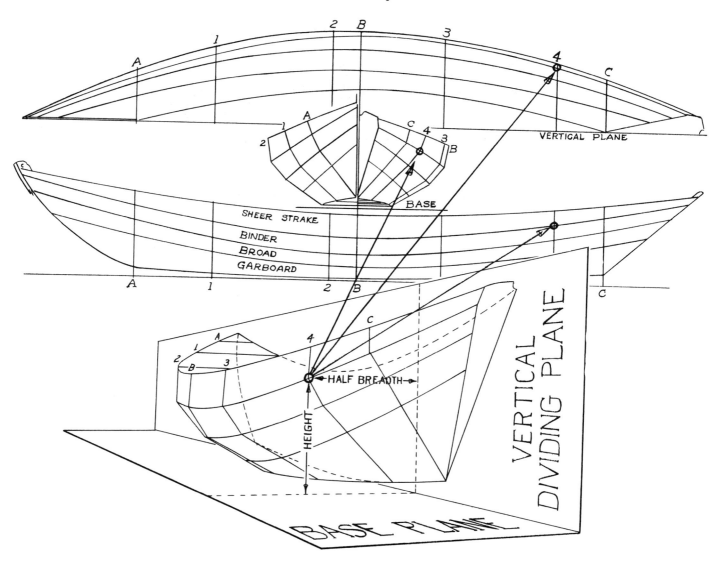

**4. The lines of Fred Dion's round-sided dory.** The top half of the drawing shows the lines as they appear on paper; the bottom half shows a 3-D diagram of the entire situation. The circled control points correspond to the circled offsets in the offset table (see Figure 5).

Height = 1-4-7 = 1'+4"+ ⅞"
Half Breadth = 1-6-6 = 1'+6"+ ⅝"

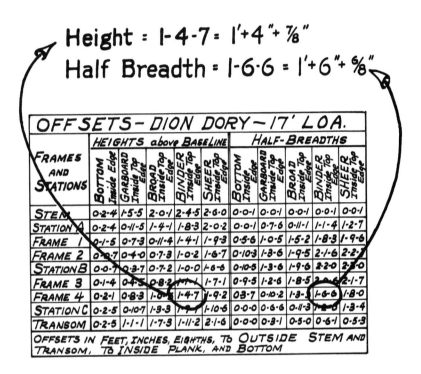

| FRAMES AND STATIONS | HEIGHTS above BASELINE | | | | | HALF-BREADTHS | | | | |
|---|---|---|---|---|---|---|---|---|---|---|
| | BOTTOM Inside Edge | GARBOARD Inside Top Edge | BROAD Inside Top Edge | BINDER Inside Top Edge | SHEER Inside Top Edge | BOTTOM Inside | GARBOARD Inside Top Edge | BROAD Inside Top Edge | BINDER Inside Top Edge | SHEER Inside Top Edge |
| STEM | 0-2-4 | 1-5-5 | 2-0-1 | 2-4-5 | 2-6-0 | 0-0-1 | 0-0-1 | 0-0-1 | 0-0-1 | 0-0-1 |
| STATION A | 0-2-4 | 0-11-5 | 1-4-1 | 1-8-3 | 2-0-2 | 0-0-1 | 0-7-6 | 0-11-1 | 1-1-4 | 1-2-7 |
| FRAME 1 | 0-1-5 | 0-7-3 | 0-11-4 | 1-4-1 | 1-9-3 | 0-5-6 | 1-0-5 | 1-5-2 | 1-8-3 | 1-9-6 |
| FRAME 2 | 0-0-7 | 0-4-0 | 0-7-3 | 1-0-2 | 1-6-7 | 0-10-3 | 1-3-6 | 1-9-5 | 2-1-6 | 2-2-1 |
| STATION B | 0-0-7 | 0-3-7 | 0-7-2 | 1-0-0 | 1-6-6 | 0-10-5 | 1-3-6 | 1-9-6 | 2-2-0 | 2-3-0 |
| FRAME 3 | 0-1-4 | 0-4-5 | 0-8-2 | 1-1-1 | 1-7-1 | 0-9-5 | 1-2-6 | 1-8-5 | 2-1-2 | 2-1-7 |
| FRAME 4 | 0-2-1 | 0-8-3 | 1-0-1 | 1-4-7 | 1-9-2 | 0-3-7 | 0-10-2 | 1-3-1 | 1-6-6 | 1-8-0 |
| STATION C | 0-2-5 | 0-10-7 | 1-3-3 | 1-7-2 | 1-10-6 | 0-0-0 | 0-6-6 | 0-11-3 | 1-2-0 | 1-3-4 |
| TRANSOM | 0-2-5 | 1-1-1 | 1-7-3 | 1-11-2 | 2-1-6 | 0-0-0 | 0-3-1 | 0-5-0 | 0-6-1 | 0-5-3 |

OFFSETS — DION DORY — 17' LOA.

OFFSETS IN FEET, INCHES, EIGHTHS, TO OUTSIDE STEM AND TRANSOM, TO INSIDE PLANK, AND BOTTOM

**5.** *The offsets table: the tabulation of measurements that determine a boat's shape. The experienced boatbuilder needs nothing else in the way of plans. The offsets locate control points on the surface of the hull.*

- *"Stations" (numbered A,1,2,B,3,4,C in the diagram) locate measurements forward and aft, and represent cross-sectional slices of the hull.*
- *Heights above the baseline (or base plane) locate vertical measurements.*
- *Halfbreadths measure half the breadth of the hull at that particular station point, giving the distance outward from the centerline (or plane) of the hull.*

*Offsets, in a dory, are measured to the frame knuckles behind the laps of the side planking. Thus "garboard," "broad," "binder," and "sheer" strakes are cited within the offset table instead of in reference to waterlines as in round-bottomed craft.*

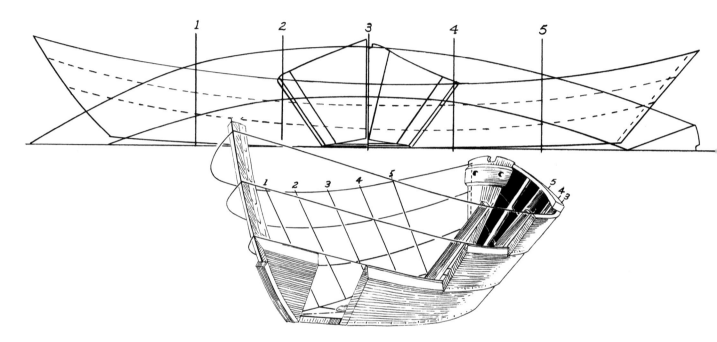

**6. Lines of the Bank dory adapted to wartime Coast Guard use.** *The lower part of the diagram shows where the lines are in the finished hull. In this boat (as denoted by its full plan) the lines are drawn to the outside of the frame members and inside of the planking. The stations occur at the after edge of the forward frames, and at the forward edge of the after frames. Offsets are taken where the station lines cross the inside upper edge of the side planking, and where the inside edge of the bottom meets the garboard plank.*

*On this plan the lines are drawn to the inside of the false stem and to the outside face of the transom. The offset table usually explains where the lines are drawn to.*

## Fairing the Lines

The process of correcting and adjusting a given set of hull measurements so that they correspond and harmonize throughout is called *fairing*. Fairing can best be done when the lines are laid down full-size and is a principal reason for this operation. Sometimes a great deal of minor dimensional adjustment is required. Lines must be shifted slightly back and forth to obtain a smooth locus; a curve will need softening here, filling-out there, with the changes carried over to the corresponding lines in the other views. Fairing is decidedly an art and, like most arts, is learned only through practice. Those who stay on the bank never learn to swim.

In dory building, total precision in reproducing an established set of dimensions is neither possible under ordinary conditions nor especially desirable. It is normal for offset figures, and especially those scaled from drawings, to vary by as much as an eighth of an inch, plus or minus. Sometimes even bigger discrepancies can be smoothed out without difficulty. So long as the hull turns out fair and symmetrical throughout, slight dimensional variation can be ignored. *But the lines of the hull must be fair.*

The best builders in the best boatshops of the past, even those who built carefully from patterns, never produced two dories exactly alike nor were they expected to. But Chamberlain of Marblehead, a builder with the highest of standards, is reported once to have smashed a newly finished dory by pushing it out of the loft of his shop to the rocks below when he detected unfairness.

Builders like Chamberlain, I have been told, frequently would make slight adjustments to suit their planking stock. So one dory might be an inch longer, another an inch shorter. Plank widths and knuckles would vary slightly, too, to suit the boards. And until a dory was in the water, no one could tell whether it was better or worse than its predecessors, nor did anyone really know then what was the cause of what, so long as dimensional variation was only slight.

Within narrow dimensional limits then, the fine, round-sided dories of the first decades of this century were each individual works of art rather than exact, mechanically formed and in-terchangeable replicas of one master model. In a perfectly proportioned Chamberlain dory, for example, every curve was sweet and true, and the whole expressed in unmistakable fashion the personality of the builder. This was done as much by eye as by measurement. After careful measurement had laid the groundwork, the trained eye took over.

What is *fairness*? What constitutes a *fair* curve? This is something simple and evident once you have seen it but very hard to put into words. It might be described as a continuous flow of curve without bunches, flats, holes, twists, or any other disharmonious interruption or deformity. There is no doubt that the standards of fairness originally derived from the natural bends of straight-grained boards of uniform thickness sprung to the gradual curves of seakindly shapes.

Fairness has its utilitarian functions, of course. Boards sprung to uniform, fair curves fit snugly together, making a tight boat. Fair shapes offer less resistance and slip easily through the water. But somewhere in the past the characteristic of fairness acquired aesthetic quality. The building of small craft became an art form. The look of a boat became a thing prized for itself. Thus, Essex County fishermen of fifty years ago took delight in their graceful, round-sided dories as objects of beauty as well as the means of their livelihood. Boats are not only to be rowed and sailed. They are also to be looked at.

## Fairing Battens

Fortunately for the inexperienced builder, there is a relatively simple and easy method for ensuring fairness, first in the laydown, and later in planking the hull. What is required are a few long, uniform strips of straight-grained wood, known in the trade as "battens." For dory work, I like battens of clear white pine, approximately ⅜-inch thick by 1½-inches wide, or slightly wider. If pine boards of sufficient length cannot be obtained easily, good battens of any desired length may be made up by splicing together shorter pieces, provided no kinks or unfair places result in the finished batten. Scarphed surfaces for gluing should be planed to a long, gradual taper on the flat of the batten. Scarphs should be in the proportion of at least 12 inches of length for ⅜-inch thickness of batten. After glue has been applied to both surfaces of the scarphed splice, and these have been joined, carefully aligned, and tacked with a few fine brads (later to be removed) to prevent slipping, the glued splice assembly is clamped between two stout blocks of wood with several 6-inch C-clamps or the equivalent, and set up tightly with plenty of pressure. A layer of waxed paper may be used to prevent the glue from sticking to the pressure blocks (see Figure 7).

After the well-made splice, as just described, has been cleaned and planed to size, it will be hard to find, and will bend exactly like any other part of the batten. One excellent method of making a spliced batten is to glue up a long strip considerably thicker and wider than the final desired dimensions, and then size and true it by running it several times, on alternate sides, through a sharp circular saw, preferably with a planer-tooth blade.

Northern white pine is far and away the best wood that I know of for battens. The selected pine should be soft, clear, perfectly straight-grained, and well-seasoned. To get long battens to meet such exacting specifications, it may be necessary to splice them up from several short lengths. White pine works easily, bends well, does not warp, twist, splinter, or check to any extent, and it takes nails well. This last is important, for it is generally convenient to hold battens in place on the laydown floor by nailing, that is to say, tacking through the center of the batten, laid on the flat, with 2d nails. Nails are better than brads, because their larger heads are easier to pull with a claw hammer.

The standard 1½-inch by ⅜-inch pine batten is generally bent on the flat. It is bent, or "run," to the desired curve on the floor, or on the planking stock, through a series of pre-marked points or "spots," and then tacked down in place (see Figure 7). It is usually best to commence nailing at the middle of the batten, working toward the ends, and to bend to the spots as one goes. After nailing, the batten is carefully sighted from different positions and directions to detect any unfairness of curve. Some builders stand backward to the curve, head low, and sight through spread legs. Flat spots are corrected by pulling a nail here or there to allow the batten to fill out slightly. A light sidewise tap with the hammer may give

the desired adjustment, to be held with an extra nail.

The fairing batten is one of the most important boatbuilding tools and is altogether indispensable. Just as the draftsman depends upon his straightedge for true lines, so the boatbuilder must depend upon his battens for fair curves. One way to define a fair curve is to say that it is the way a good batten naturally bends.

Different classes of curves in boat work are best obtained by a variety of battens of different sectional dimensions. Wider battens are stiffer, for instance, and better for achieving fairness in long gradual runs. For sharp curves, narrow battens of square or nearly square section are used; and sometimes flat battens are bent on edge (see Figure 7). Naturally, nails cannot be driven through them in this position, so they are bent around nails driven into the floor with other nails driven against the bends to keep them from springing back. Professional loftsmen find it convenient to use numbers of sharp awls or ice picks for holding their battens to curves. For dory work, with its simple, gradual bends and curves, battens of flat section, as described, bent on the flat and nailed through the center, will serve in nearly all cases. A variety of battens or battens of tapered section are not needed.

I have gone into the subject of battens somewhat extensively, not only because of their fundamental importance, but also because this basic tool of the trade is slighted or overlooked entirely in some boatbuilding manuals. It takes an experienced mechanic to value the fairing batten at its true worth.

By paying attention to his battens, the beginner can develop a good eye. In the meantime, by depending on his battens, he can manage to get by. Only by providing himself with true battens, and by accepting their guidance, can the novice hope to build a decent-looking dory. Exact dimensions from here to Doomsday are not enough. Fair shape is ultimately an affair of the boatbuilder's eye assisted by his battens.

We are not concerned here with designing a dory, or altering a design, or taking off, or reproducing the lines of a dory already built. We have been provided with a complete set of lines and a table of offsets. Our job is laydown, that is, merely to enlarge these lines full size so we can obtain the shape—"pick it up," as the loftsman would say—of the stem, transom, bottom, and frames, as well as the bevels and plank lines. While it is essential to lay out our measurements from the table of offsets as accurately as possible, it should now be clear that by no amount of exact measurement *alone* can we get the shape we want. A process

of adjustment—give and take—called fairing, which utilizes judgment, a good eye, and good battens, must come into play. When this is understood, and we are prepared to make the lines laydown, we must still find a suitable surface to work on and on which to transcribe our lines.

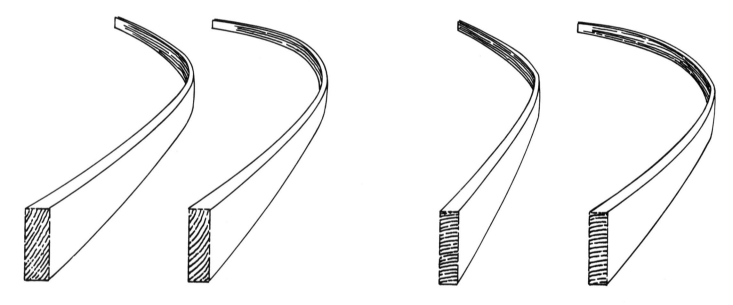

*7(a). Fair and unfair curves as seen when selecting battens for laying down the lines in full size prior to setting up the hull. The two battens at the right should be discarded.*

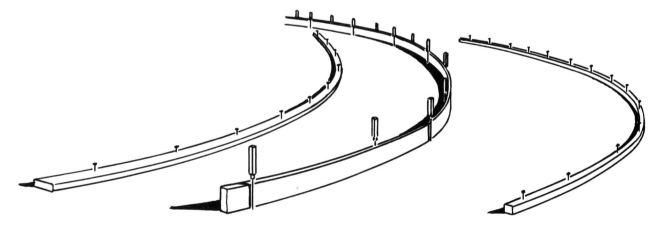

*7(b). Fairing battens sprung to curves on the floor.*

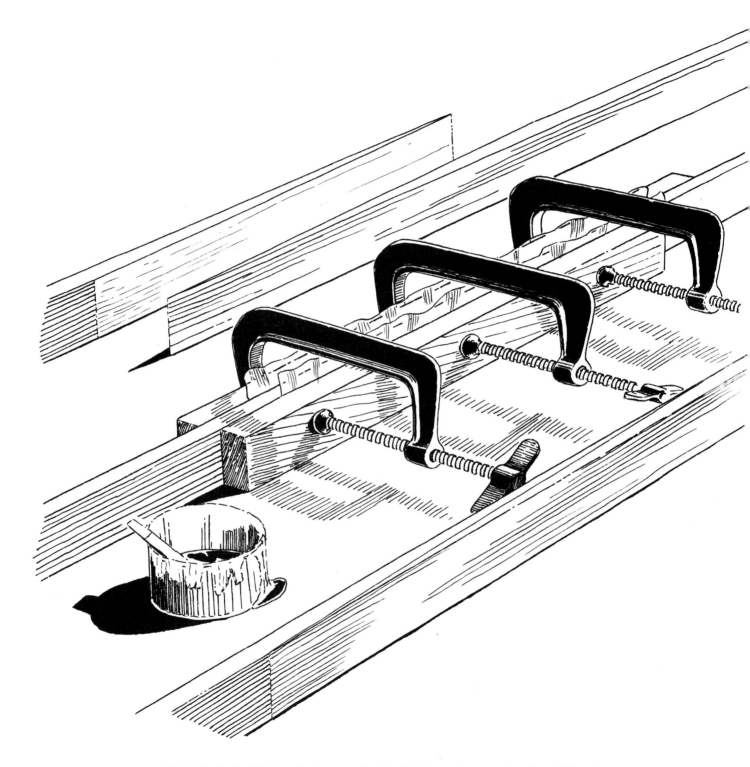

*7(c). Method of gluing a feather-scarph when joining strips to make a long fairing batten.*

## The Laydown Surface

Professional loftsmen use a clean, level, wood floor, sanded and painted a color that shows lines to advantage. The wood will take the loftsmen's sharp awls or batten nails. Lacking a suitable floor of this sort, the prospective dory builder can work on building paper spread out on any smooth surface of suitable expanse. If nails may not be driven into the surface, the battens can be held in place by weights. However, this is an awkward makeshift at best. Plywood makes a good surface for a laydown, and two or three ordinary 8-foot panels laid end to end will be adequate for most dories. If the dory is to be planked with plywood, as frequently is the case today, the planking stock can first be utilized for the laydown.

Dory lines are so simple and few, comparatively, that profile and half-breadth lines can be laid one over the other without confusion. A single straight line near one edge of the plywood will do for both centerline and baseline, and the width of one panel will be more than sufficient for the job. Bank dory lines are so rudimentary that the professional might not trouble to lay them down at all, but the home-workshop builder should. For Swampscott dories, on the other hand, there must always be a careful laydown.

One lofting operation that will be explained later is "expanding the transom," or drawing a plan of the transom by itself to set its true shape. This can't be taken directly from the lines, which show the transom only at an angle, and thus distorted. How to expand the transom will be detailed in Part III in the section on the widened St. Pierre dory, which has a more complicated transom than do most dories.

Taking bevels and other operations connected with lofting lines and establishing and fairing the full-size shape for building may be studied in detail in any standard boatbuilding manual, and it would be well for the prospective home dory builder to consult several of these works to see how different writers deal with these preliminaries to the actual construction. Here, we have only touched upon aspects of particular note to dory builders, and upon things not commonly taken up elsewhere.

# 5 DORY CONSTRUCTION

What makes a dory a dory? More than any-thing, the way it is constructed. As we have seen, dories are wide-board boats, and the boards have a lot to say about what is done with them and the form they take. The material possesses a will and character of its own, a natural bend, in literal fact, that goes a long way in shaping the boat.

We have assumed that when powered saws were introduced into the vast coniferous forests of central and northern Europe centu-ries ago, people were not long in devising new ways of building boats from the then-obtain-able wide lumber of pine and fir. Eventually, they found the easy way of joining wide boards to form a seakindly shape. Given half a chance, the boards cooperated. The boards showed the builders how to do it. The sides of a wide-board boat are separate and distinct from the flat bottom. Not so in the more ancient, rounded hulls, such as the Norse boats, in which the riven strakes of the bottom twisted imperceptibly into the topsides at the ends of the structure.

Whether round-bottomed or flat, boats con-structed for similar purposes may be so de-signed that there is no significant functional difference between them. These two basic hull forms can be very closely the same in capacity and performance. Their behavior in the sea, as well as their general form, may be so identical as to make any attempt to distinguish between them on this basis trivial and meaningless. In appearance, especially in the water, the two types may look much the same, as do the Marblehead gunning dory and some round-bottomed Maine peapods.

In construction, however, the flat and the round are radically different. Given suitable materials, the flat type is by far the easier to build. That is a principal reason why the dory drove the round types out of the New England fisheries.

All dories start with a flat bottom and grow out of it, as it were. Regardless of whether the dory is put together right-side up or up-side down, the bottom comes first. Put sides on the bottom, and the boat is built. It is almost as simple as that.

The wide-board strakes that form the sides of the dory are lapped together. Fastened thus to each other, they are vastly strong and rigid in themselves. But to spread, brace, and unite them even more securely, as well as to tie them to the bottom, a number of internal cross frames are required. At the bow, a stem pulls in and holds the ends of the strakes. At the stern, the strakes are gathered for nailing to some variety of transom or stern post, de-pending on whether the dory is a skiff, semi-dory, Banker, or sharp Marblehead double-ender. When the sides are on the bottom, the main structure is complete. The boat is made.

The rule that dory construction starts with

the bottom excludes an important class of flat boats, namely those with cross-planked bottoms. In such craft, the bottom is comprised of numerous athwartship pieces nailed on after the sides have been sprung to shape. Punts, flatirons, New Haven sharpies, and a number of special craft indigenous to the Chesapeake come to mind as examples.

The cross-planked bottom may be quite old. The sixteenth-century Flemish painter Jan Breughel shows crude box-like punts that appear to be cross-planked. Yet it seems likely that cross-planking, which requires much nailing, did not become common in this country until inexpensive, machine-made, iron nails came on the market at the beginning of the nineteenth century.

Some cross-planked flats are sharp, shapely, and good sea boats. They vie in looks and performance with the better dories. But a line must be drawn. Their construction is so distinctly different that we cannot include them with the dories. They are a specialized type by themselves, and, for that reason, none of the boats in this book have cross-planked bottoms.

What makes a dory a dory? History, a characteristic shape, performance in the sea—these all enter into it. But fundamentally and finally it is the unique construction that sets the dory apart and gives it exclusive right to its name.

## Construction Procedure

Dory construction, after laydown, normally follows a standard procedure that progresses through four distinct stages. These four stages, to be thoroughly explained later, may be listed as follows:

1. Getting out the pieces and making up the sub-assemblies.
2. Setting up the boat and fairing it for planking.
3. Planking.
4. Finishing the interior, painting, and miscellaneous.

It should be understood that what we are considering here is dory construction as a special process distinct from boatbuilding in general. We shall limit our attention at this point to the fabrication of the dory hull, that is, to the part that is most specifically dory. Whether the boat is destined to become a sailing dory, a power dory, or a pulling dory, or any combination of the three, does not concern us now. Eventually, a sailing dory must have a mast, rigging, sails, and usually a centerboard and rudder. A power dory may require engine beds or a motor well. But these, from our present standpoint, are extras to be added to the basic dory hull to adapt it to a specialized purpose. In analyzing dory construction, *per se,* and in learning to build the basic dory hull, such extras do not enter the picture at all.

### STAGE 1: *Getting out the parts and making up the sub-assemblies*

In the shop that specializes in dories, there will usually be a complete set of patterns for every part in the boat, including the strakes of planking. Every member can be gotten out ahead of time and beveled and otherwise prepared at the bench. A dory builds fast this way, and lumber can be marked and cut to best advantage.

Here, however, we shall assume that the boat is being built for the first time, and that we are proceeding from a laydown of the lines. We can pick up the shapes of all the parts from the floor, except the plank. Planking shapes cannot be determined from the laydown, but must be lined out on the boat after it has been set up and faired. Most of the bevels needed can also be taken from the floor without much difficulty. Pre-beveling of parts at the bench before assembly helps to expedite building, but is not necessary. The cautious beginner may prefer to wait to do most of his beveling during assembly. Perhaps the safest way is to cut only approximate bevels beforehand, leaving a margin of wood to be trimmed after the boat has been set up and when it is given its overall fairing before starting to plank. As the old-timer says, it's easier to take wood off than to put it back on.

The various parts of the dory naturally arrange themselves in a number of groups or sub-assemblies. First is the bottom, followed by the frames, transom, and stem. The plank comprise a special and later group. And last of all come miscellaneous parts including risers, thwarts, gunwales, breast hook, rub strips, gratings, and others.

*Bottom*

As we have already observed, the primary and most distinctive part of the dory is its bottom. The several sizes of standard Bank fishing dories were measured and named according to the length on the bottom. Shops that mass-produced fishing dories in the heyday of trawl fishing kept on hand half-breadth molds or patterns of the bottoms of each of the various sizes in demand, although stems, transoms, and frames for all were marked out from the same set of patterns, proportionally extended for the larger sizes.

The standard dory bottom is assembled from several full-length boards held together by flat cross-cleats located midway between the frame stations. The cross-cleats do not extend quite to the outside edges in order to permit the drainage of bilge water around their ends when the sides of the boat are on.

Northern white pine is the proper wood for dory bottoms; it should be not less than ⅞-inch in thickness. Knots in the bottom are no defect provided they are sound and solid. In fact, knotty bottom boards are tougher and wear better on rough beaches. Wide boards are stiffer, but open more at the seams when they dry out. Eight or nine inches wide is about minimum for bottom boards. Frequently the smaller Swampscott dories will have only two boards in their bottoms. Big semi-dories for outboard power with a 4-foot width of bottom, or more, will require five or six boards. Better fastening for the stem and the stern knee is obtained if the bottom is laid out so that no seam comes within several inches of the centerline.

After several boards have been chosen of sufficient aggregate width to give the required overall size when fitted, they are cut roughly to length, and their edges are jointed straight for a tight fit throughout. Caulking seam bevels are planed on the outside. The frame stations are measured off on the inside and squared out from the centerline. It is well to mark them on the outside also. Midway between the frame stations, the locations of the cross-cleats are marked.

*Cross Cleats*

The cross-cleats are oak of the same stock as the frames, which in dories of medium size will run about ⅞-inch thick. These strips, approximately 2 inches wide, are laid on the flat. The fastenings that hold them are put through from the outside, for fastenings take a firmer grip in oak than in pine. Formerly, the standard fastenings for these cleats were chisel-point, galvanized-iron boat nails, 1¾ to 2 inches long. Chisel-point nails are now virtually unobtainable. Screws are an acceptable modern substitute. When the bottom and the cross-cleats are both ⅞ inch in thickness, 1½-inch #12 or #14 screws are suitable, to be bunged with a half-inch bit.

While the cross-cleats are being fastened, the bottom may be held together by door clamps or it may be wedged tightly and nailed to temporary cross pieces (see Figure 8). The cross-cleats may be temporarily tacked in place on the inside to hold them while they are being fastened from the outside.

*Trimming and Beveling*

After the cross-cleats are on and the bottom is one solid piece, the bottom is marked and cut to final shape. Perhaps it was cut approximately to shape before it was fastened together. Now it must be trimmed exactly. With a half-breadth bottom mold to lay first on one side of the centerline and then on the other, it is simple to get both sides of the bottom alike. For the builder of a single boat, an easier method would be to transfer the half-breadth widths at each station from the laydown to the assembled bottom. A continuous line is faired through these spots with a batten. With care, both sides will be the same.

All that now remains to be done to the bottom at this stage is to bevel its edges. Great care must attend this operation (see Figure 8). If these bevels are wrong and the sides do not join the bottom later on with a touching fit throughout the inner edge of this seam, the boat will leak. The angle of bevel at each frame station is easily obtained from the section view in the laydown. The amount of wood to be taken off can be marked on the outside of the bottom at each frame station, and a fair batten can be run through the spots to give a continuous bevel line throughout, just as the edge of the bottom was previously marked. However, the prudent first-timer will not take off all of the wood directly down to this line, but will leave a little, as a margin of safety, not to be removed until the final fairing prior to planking.

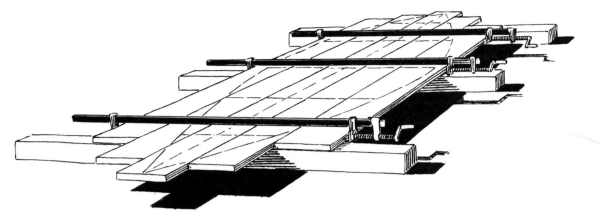

*8(a). **Lay out the bottom plank "inside"-up on horses or sleepers.** Clamp the planks together and mark the centerline, frame stations, and inside perimeter of the dory's bottom. Tack cleats temporarily on locations between the frames. Extend the cleat-location lines to the edges of the panel so they can be picked up on the opposite side.*

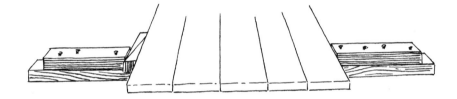

*8(b). **This wedge set-up may be used in lieu of cabinet clamps.***

*8(c). **Turn the bottom panel over so that screws may be driven through the pine bottom plank and into the oak cleats, not the other way around.***

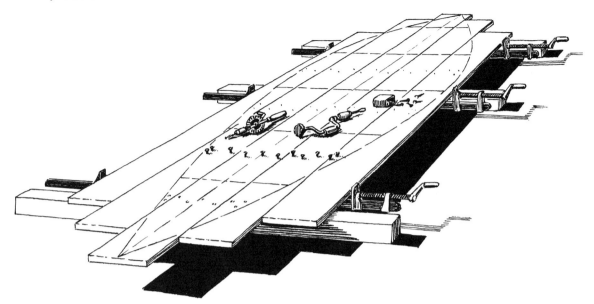

*8(d). Counterbore screw holes from the "pine" side.* Set the screws to fasten the cleats. For best control, drive the screws with a brace screwdriver.

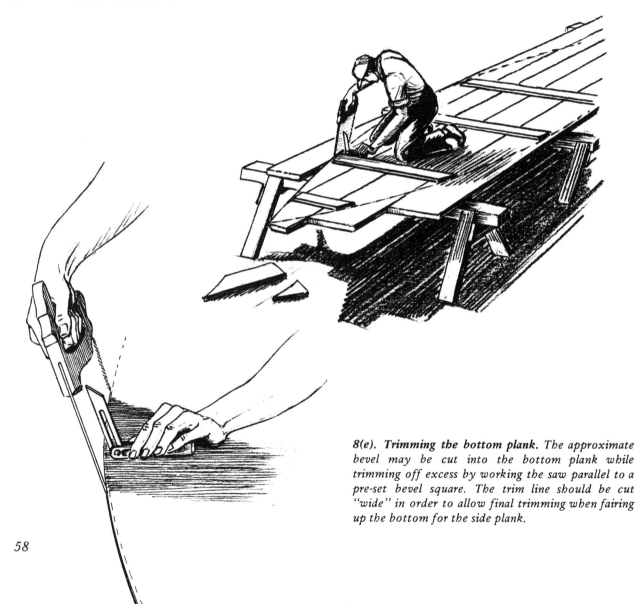

*8(e). Trimming the bottom plank.* The approximate bevel may be cut into the bottom plank while trimming off excess by working the saw parallel to a pre-set bevel square. The trim line should be cut "wide" in order to allow final trimming when fairing up the bottom for the side plank.

*Stem*

Usually the stem is cut out in a single piece from oak plank stock after its shape has been picked up from the laydown. Where there is considerable curve, as in the stems for some of the Swampscott dories, the stem may be spliced up from two pieces. This allows the use of narrower lumber, and gives a straighter, stronger grain. The splice should be made with a glued scarph at least a foot long and should be reinforced on either side with strips of ⅜-inch plywood also glued. Fastening through the plywood scabs with copper wire nails riveted over burrs will add strength to the splice.

The stem may also be laminated, as I show for the epoxy-glued spruce stem specified for the ultra-light gunning dory. In some of the very largest dories, it may be desirable to fasten the stem to the bottom with a bolted knee similar to the stern knee holding the bottom of the transom. This is what I have indicated for the big St. Pierre dory in order to avoid cross grain, and to get the stem out of a moderately wide plank. (Figure 9 shows these various stem construction methods, and Figures 12 and 13 give tips on making knees.)

Bevels for the stem are obtained by drawing a few special sections in the lines (see Figure 12). Such sections are laid out square with the stem curve in profile. Or put in another way, the bevel section is drawn in the same direction as a carpenter's bevel square is normally applied to the side of the stem in trying the bevel (see Figure 10). Here again the apprentice builder will do well to leave a little wood for later adjustment in the final fairing. Lastly, the location of the sheer line and the plank ends as obtained from the laydown should be plainly marked on the stem prior to set-up.

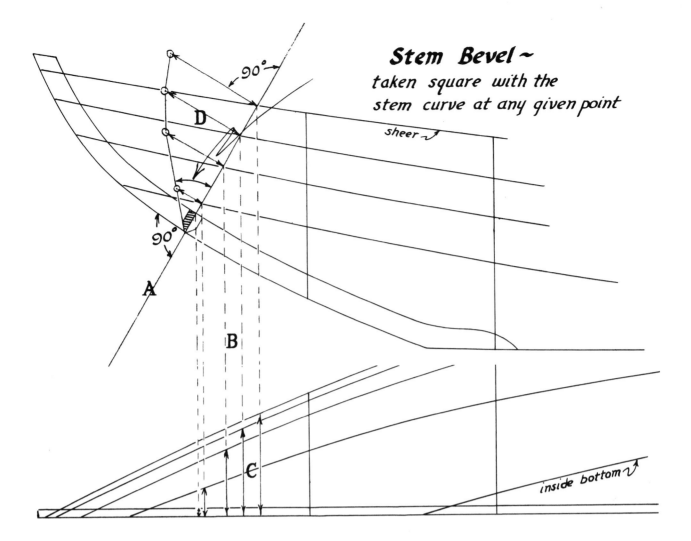

## Stem Bevel ~

taken square with the
stem curve at any given point

90°

D

sheer

90°

A

B

C

inside bottom

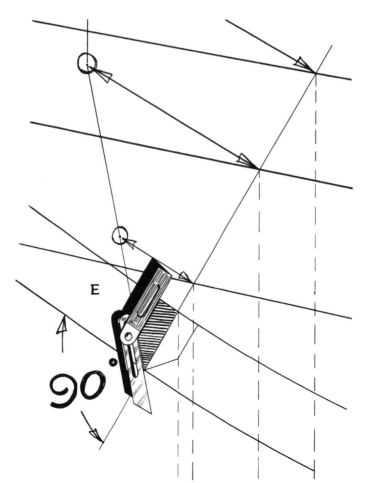

E

90°

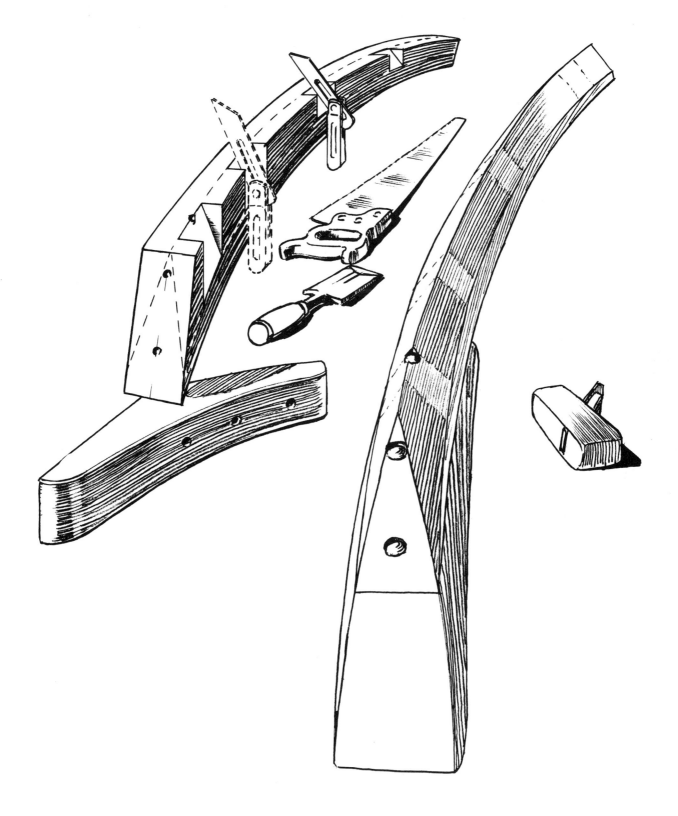

**9. Determining the stem bevels and cutting them into the stem timber.** *To obtain the bevel on the stem at any particular point, construct a special section of the boat at that spot on the loft drawing. The following steps apply:*

   *(A) On the loft profile, draw a line perpendicular to the stem at the spot where the bevel is to be taken.*

   *(B) Project to the halfbreadth plan all the intersections of this line with the stem and plank lines on the profile.*

   *(C) Where the projection lines cross corresponding elements on the halfbreadth plan, locate these intersections with measurements from the centerline.*

   *(D) Construct the special section with the measurements obtained from the halfbreadth plan.*

   *(E) Take the bevel from the special section.*

   *(F) Make cuts into the prepared stem timber to establish the bevels at the locations you have taken from the loft plan. Fair these spot cuts together when rough-beveling the entire timber. Leave enough wood for adjustments later. The knee, if used, should be joined to the stem and beveled with it.*

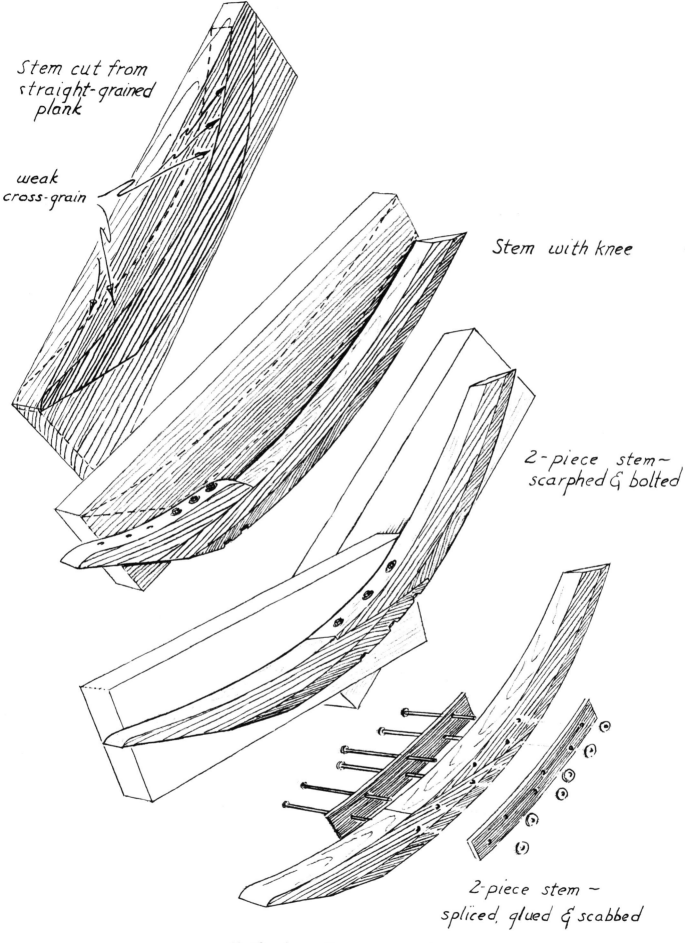

Stem cut from straight-grained plank

weak cross-grain

Stem with knee

2-piece stem ~ scarphed & bolted

2-piece stem ~ spliced, glued & scabbed

10. There is more than one way to make a stem.

*Transom or "Tombstone"*

The transom for a wide-sterned semi-dory may require a considerable number of parts. For the Bank dory, the "tombstone," so called, is often cut from a single width of oak plank. With this simple transom, there are only two additional parts, the inside cross-cleat at the sheer line, and the stern knee at the lower end that joins the transom to the bottom.

All dory transoms rake outward to greater or lesser extent. This means that in actuality they are longer than they appear to be in the lines. Before the transom can be made up, its true length and shape must be developed by a process called *expansion*. For most of the dories included in this book, the expanded shape of the transom is given with the lines.

When beveling the transom, the same rules apply as in beveling the stem. Bevels picked up from the laydown must be taken in the same direction that the carpenter's bevel square will be applied to the wood at any particular location. Bevels are always taken and applied square across the edge of the work, never slashwise or obliquely. The apprentice had best proceed with caution. Once again, discretion should be exercised and a little extra wood left on until the final fairing.

There is one other point to be understood prior to beveling the transom. While in this book dory lines are always drawn to the *inside* of the bottom, and because the bottom is beveled outward, no allownace of extra wood for beveling is required. The reverse holds for the transom. *The profile lines of our dories always show the outer face of the transom. The inside face will be wider.* (See Figure 11).

Thus in cutting out the transom, enough extra wood must be allowed to permit the bevel to "gain" wood. Of course the professional or exact way is to develop the shape of the inside of the transom in the laydown, using that as the cutout pattern. Most will not bother, for it is easy to guess the amount of extra wood required, allowing enough to be on the safe side. A sharp plane will take off the extra quickly enough when the boat is faired.

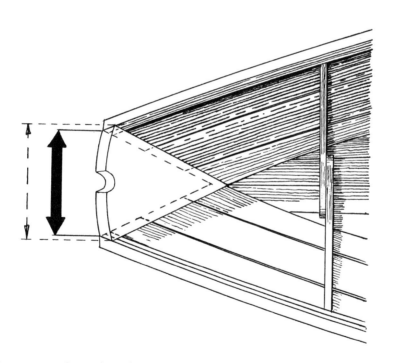

**11(a).** *To lay out the transom, determine whether the lines show the interior or the exterior face of the transom. Note that considerable extra width has to be retained to accommodate the bevel if the exterior face is laid out. If exactness is desired, either compute the amount of bevel or expand the interior face of the transom.*

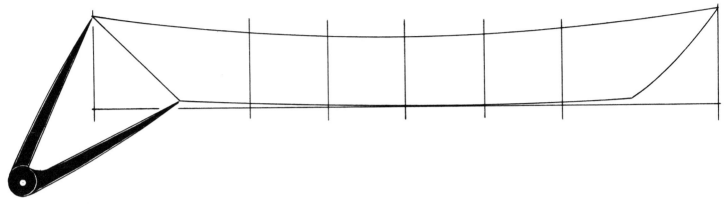

*11(b).  Take the length of the transom from the profile drawing. The transom is foreshortened in the other two views.*

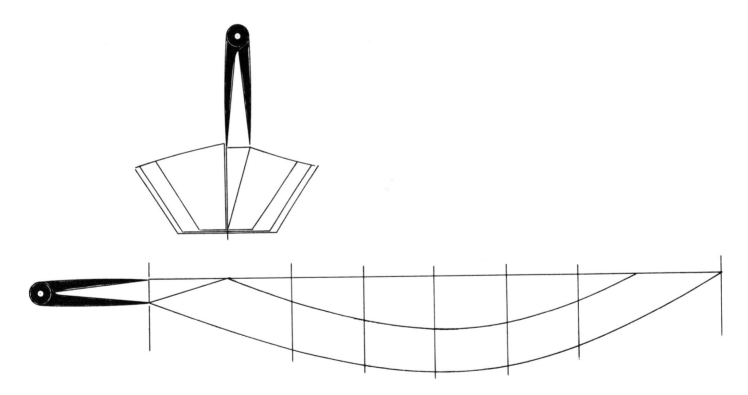

*11(c).  The width of the transom can be taken from either the halfbreadth or the section plan. Remember that only half the width of the transom is shown. It must be doubled.*

*11(d). Lay out these dimensions on your plank stock. If the exterior face is used and the angle of bevel is unknown, add at least an inch and a half to each side of the transom to accommodate the bevel. The top of the transom is a simple arc with a notch to hold a steering oar.*

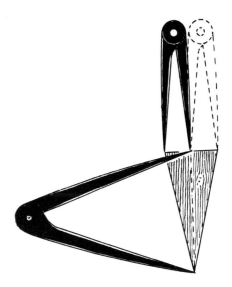

*11(e). A cross cleat, also cut to an arc, and transom knee should be added to the dressed-out transom.*

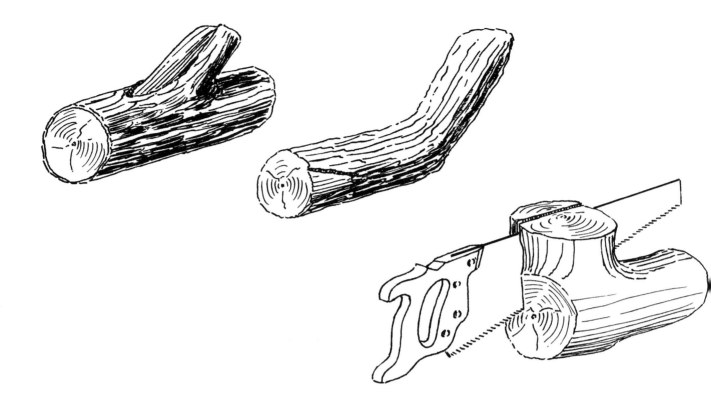

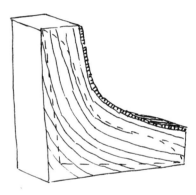

**12. Stem and transom knees.** *Crooked wood is the best stock for knees as well as the gussets and the breast hook used in a dory. Oak, elm, and apple woods are commonly used for these parts of a boat. Best source: your firewood pile or the dump used by the power company for depositing tree cuttings. Beware of accidents while machining crooked wood. Most sawmills today won't touch it.*

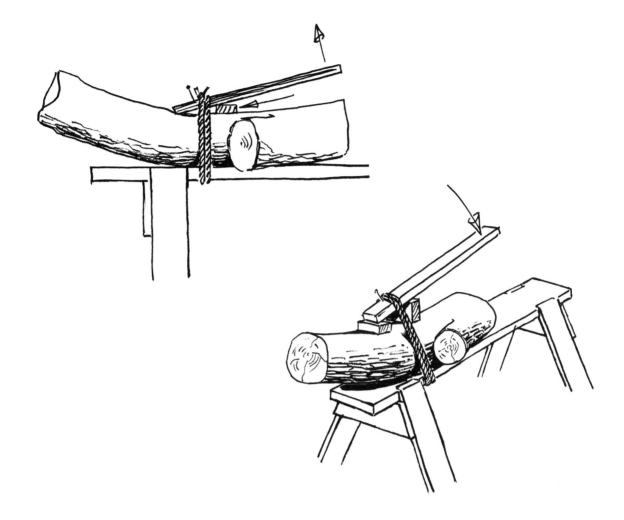

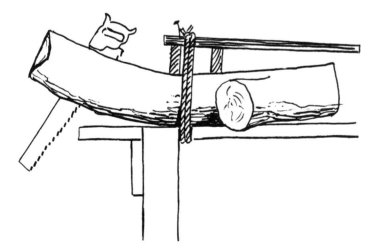

*13. A "crusher" for clamping round or crooked wood. This works by levering up a fixed lashing of rope or chain while alternately increasing the size of the two fulcrums. This device exerts tremendous force, is stable under pressure, and can be quickly released.*

*Frames and Frame Gussets*

The shape of the frames is obtained directly from section lines in the body plan. No allowance for plank thickness is required, for dory lines are purposely drawn to the *inside* of the planking. Originally, dory frames were cut out of root knees or limb crooks. They were made up in matched pairs for the two sides of the boat and, when set in place, extended by each other across the bottom. This was an exceptionally strong arrangement. Knees of white oak or hackmatack were commonly used for this purpose, or, more rarely, limb crooks of apple wood. But such natural-grown framing is limited in supply and comparatively costly.

When the expansion of trawl fishing caused dories to be mass produced, a cheaper, quicker way of making up dory frames had to be devised. This was to make the side frame separate from the bottom part, butting the two pieces at the chine knuckle where the bottom joins the side. To hold these two parts of the frame securely together, metal clips or plates drawn tight by several through-rivets were placed on either side of the joint.

While not as strong as one-piece, natural-grown timbers, this arrangement is adequate, and it eventually all but completely replaced the older method of timbering. Today, the metal clips are frequently replaced by gussets of glued plywood reinforced by screws or copper rivets. If this is properly done with marine plywood and an approved epoxy adhesive reinforced with glass fabric, the resulting joint will be closely equivalent to natural-grown frames. (Figure 14 shows these framing methods.)

In making up frames for Bank dories and the straight-sided skiffs, the run of the grain is no problem. In some of the round-sided Swampscott dories, the side frame pieces are bound to show some cross grain if cut out of ordinary straight boards. Crooked boards will help, but they cannot always be obtained. Besides, quite wide boards will be required, and there will be considerable waste of lumber in cutting out the curved frame pieces.

If cross grain in side frames cannot be avoided, it is best to have it come in the upper portion of the frame. One way of reinforcing cross grain here is to glue on a thin lamination with glass fabric between the layers, as I show for the lightly constructed gunning dory. Another method (successfully used in the deeply rounded surf dory, which had to be exceptionally strong) is to splice the frames halfway up the side under the thwarts rather than at the usual place at the bottom knuckle (see Figure 14). The joint is butted square, with reinforcing plywood gussets on both sides glued with epoxy adhesive and glass fabric further strengthened by copper rivets. Such frames are made in matched pairs for each station. When installed in the boat, they extend by one another across the bottom like natural-crook frames, with their ends fastened together, making a very strong job. The joint is hidden under the end of the thwart, which rests on the ends of the plywood scabs. The additional wood gives better fastening for the seat riser and altogether makes a very solid arrangement. Frames made this way are only slightly heavier then those made by the conventional method.

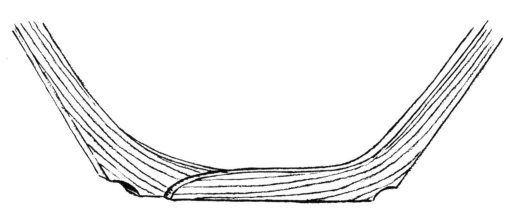

*14(a). Old-style frame of matched knees.*

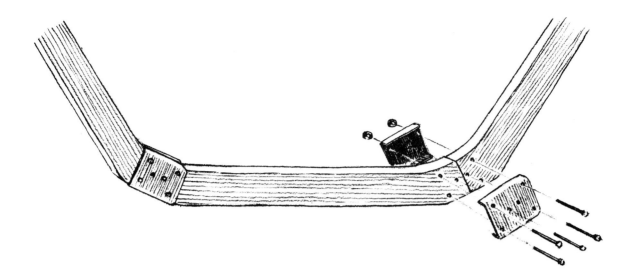

*14(b). **Production frame in a Bank dory.** Straight futtocks are joined with steel clips.*

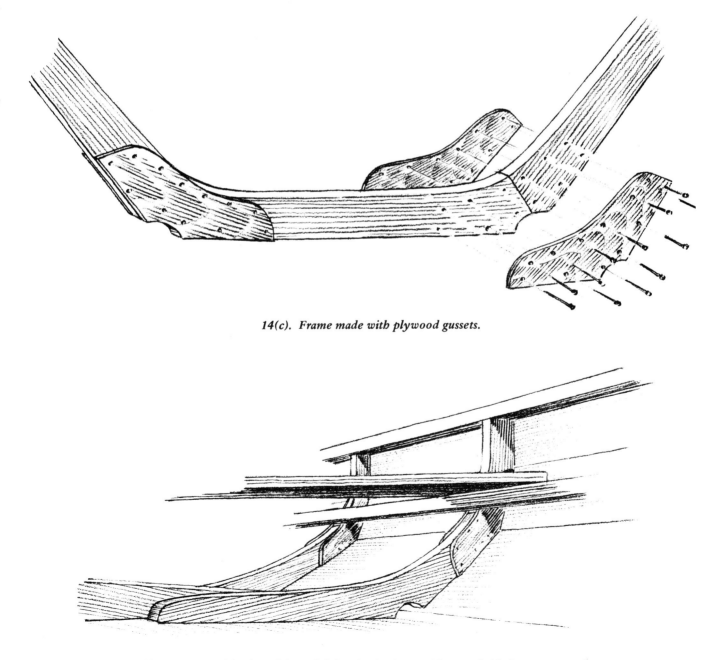

*14(c).  **Frame made with plywood gussets.***

*14(d).  **Proper positioning of futtock joints in the frames of a round-sided Swampscott dory.***

### Frame Bevels

The middle frames require little beveling. Frame bevels increase toward the ends of the boat. Bevels are taken from the laydown. *If there is any doubt about them, they may be left to be finished during the final fairing.*

In attaching the frames to the bottom planking, it is important to place frames that go forward of the center of the boat on the forward side of their respective station lines, and the frames that go aft of the boat's center on the after side of their station lines. This allows them to be beveled. Otherwise there would not be wood enough for beveling, or frames would have to be gotten out larger than their finished size to allow for beveling.

### Frames as Building Molds

In dories, the frames also serve as building molds. When the complete frame for each station is assembled, it is tied together at the top with a temporary brace called a *cross spall* (see Figure 15). The cross spall is put on with its top edge level with the sheer, and is held in place by two 1½-inch #12 or #14 screws in either end. Pine strips 2 to 3 inches wide will make adequate cross spalls, and may be gotten out of the same lumber as the dory bottom or the thwarts.

On each frame assembly, the centerline of the boat should be accurately squared up from the bottom and plainly marked on the bottom of the frame and the cross spall. This centerline is required in setting up. The sheer line is also needed and is previously marked in locating the cross spall.

### Framing Table

Frames must be assembled as accurately as possible, otherwise there will be trouble in setting up. This is particularly true for the more difficult Swampscott dories. A good system for putting together frames is to mark out the full outline of each frame in turn, as needed, either on the laydown, on a special piece of plywood, or on a framing table (see Figure 16). The pieces for the frame are laid over this outline, cut and fitted together to correspond precisely with it, and temporarily tacked or clamped or weighted down in position until permanently fastened together. Not until the cross spall is screwed on and the sheer and centerline are marked should the frame be removed from the framing table or floor. Bevels, it might be mentioned, are generally put on the various frame pieces before they are assembled, for the smaller pieces are most easily managed at the bench. However, there is no reason why beveling should not be left until after assembly.

When the side frame pieces are gotten out, they should be cut several inches longer than required for the finished boat. This extra length of frame head extending above the sheer is convenient for nailing braces and stay lathes to when the boat is set up and secured for planking. The extra length may also be needed for final adjustments to the sheer line. Later the frames will be cut off below the sheer in fitting the gunwales. Likewise, it is desirable to allow some extra on the stem head to be trimmed later.

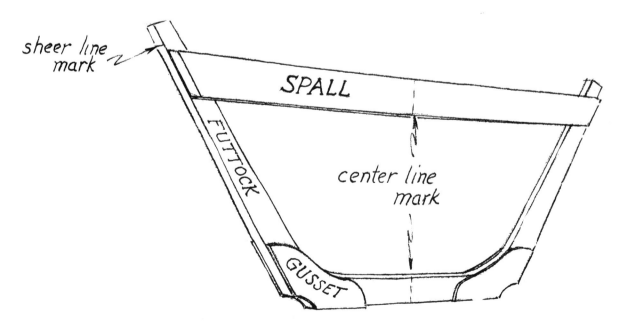

*15. A Bank dory frame with its cross spall in place.*

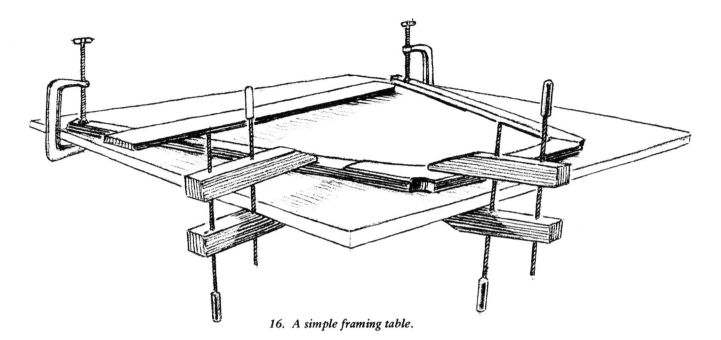

*16.  A simple framing table.*

*STAGE 2: Setting Up and Fairing*

When the sub-assemblies of the bottom, the transom, the frames, and the stem are complete, the boat is ready to be set up and faired for plank. During this stage, the shape of the boat is established. If the job is botched here, no amount of skill and effort later on can make a fair boat of it.

Prior to setting up, the stem, transom, and frames are fastened to the bottom panel (see Figure 17). They are fastened from the outside, with nothing less than 2-inch #14 screws, or equivalent boat nails, for a medium-sized dory.

The dory may be set up either right-side-up or bottom-up. For the Bank dory and the straight-sided skiffs, right-side-up is usual and the most convenient. Bottom-up is the procedure generally adopted for Swampscott dories, because in that position it is easier to get at their rounded, knuckled sides and under-cut bottoms. Their fussy planking bevels are easier if the builder does not have to lie down on the floor to work on them.

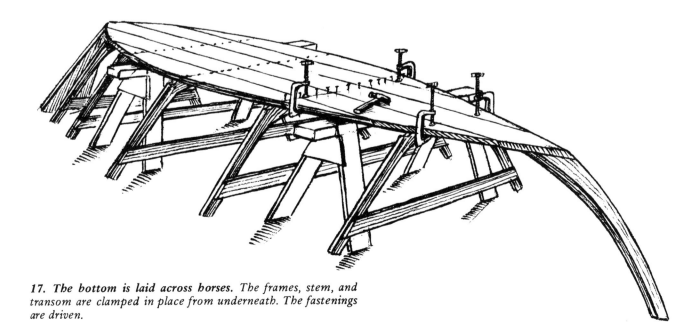

**17. The bottom is laid across horses.** *The frames, stem, and transom are clamped in place from underneath. The fastenings are driven.*

*Upside Down*

In setting a dory bottom-up, its bottom panel with stem, frames, and transom attached, is bent over a longitudinal strongback made from a plank sawn to the curve of the designed bottom rocker and notched to take the frames and bottom cleats (see Figure 18). With the plank strongback on legs that support it a little above waist height for convenience in working, the stem head will reach nearly to the floor on which the centerline for the boat is marked. The stem is centered on this line and secured at the correct fore-and-aft position by braces and by a short extension piece, or leg, which runs the stem to the floor for fastening. Likewise, the transom is centered over this line at the correct distance and is fastened by a couple of temporary legs nailed to the floor.

Legs are dropped from the frame timberheads to their respective station lines on the floor, as squared out from the center. The correct widths out from the center are also marked on these station lines for the location of the timberhead extensions. In a word, the boat is leveled, plumbed, and secured over a breadth plan grid drawn out on the floor.

Two-by-four shores from the ceiling or rafters are set up with a top maul and wedges to force the bottom assembly down on its strongback support. Everything should be firm and rigid. As a final check, the stem should sight plumb when viewed in the fore-and-aft direction, and the transom centerline likewise. The bubble of a spirit level set athwartships anywhere on the bottom should read exactly dead center. The assembly is now set up and ready for fairing.

**18. Set-up for a round-sided Swampscott dory, bottom up.** *(Top) The bottom, with attached frame members, is laid over a longitudinal strongback sawn to the curve of the designed bottom rocker and notched to receive the frames and bottom cleats. (Middle) The bottom assembly is bent down over the strongback by means of shores set against the ceiling. (Bottom) The frames, transom, and stem are plumbed and secured to their respective stations as marked on the floor.*

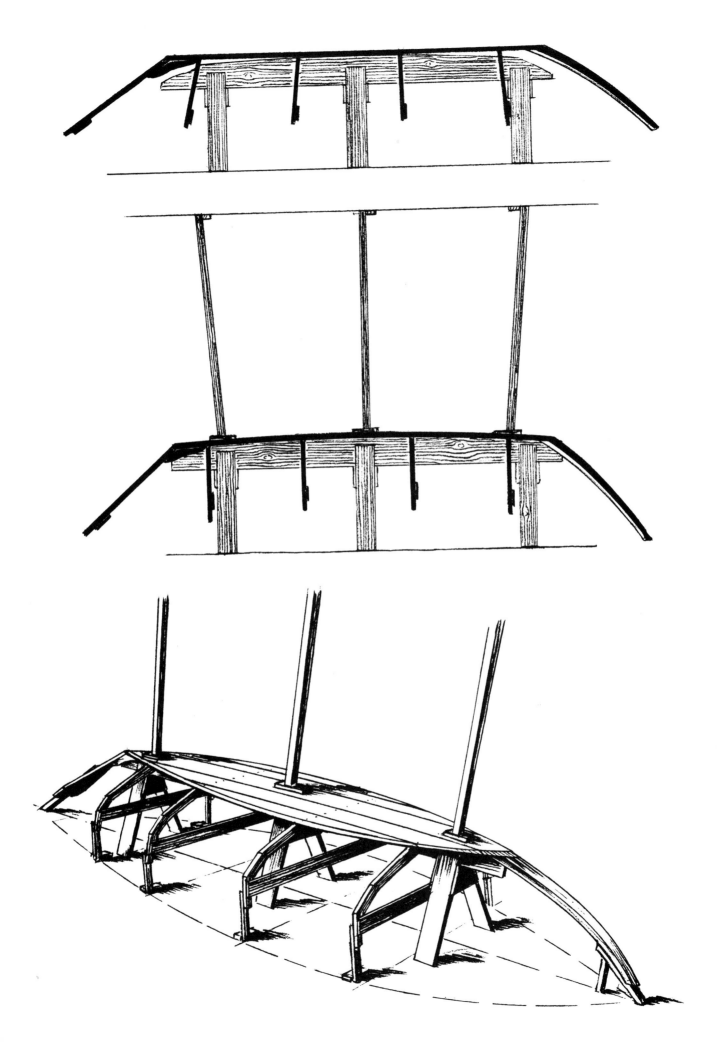

*Right-Side Up*

If it is a Bank dory or a straight-sided skiff that is to be set right-side-up, a couple of strong, low horses will do to rest the bottom on. The bottom, with stem, transom, and frames attached, is placed upright on the two horses far enough apart so that pressure or weight on the unsupported span of the bottom between will spring it down to the desired curvature or rocker. Shores to the ceiling may accomplish this, or heavy weights of cement blocks or lead ballast may substitute for shores. In any case, the horses will have to be nailed in place, and the dory bottom should be temporarily nailed to the horses. Stem and transom are plumbed athwartships and secured by braces or stay laths run to the walls and ceiling. (See Figure 19).

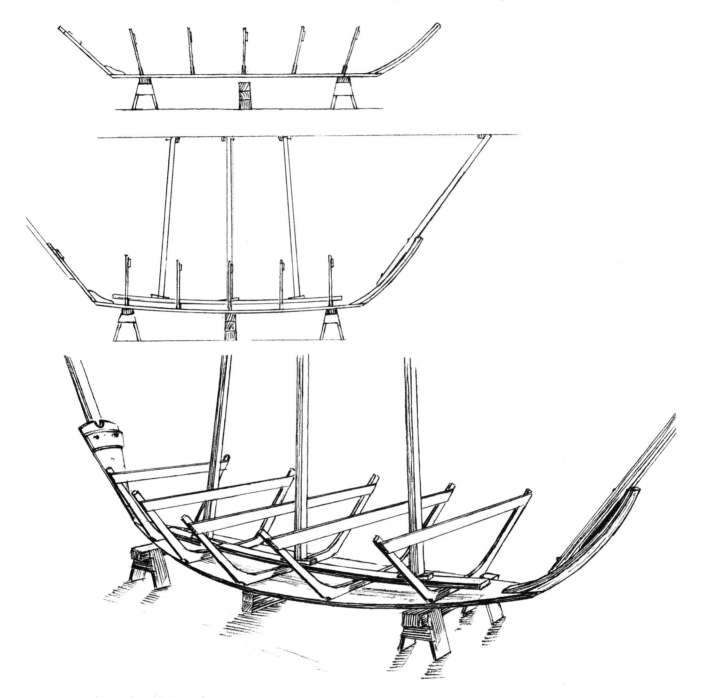

**19. Set-up for a flat-sided Bank dory, upright.** (Top) *Lay the prepared bottom across horses properly spaced and fastened down for the purpose.* (Middle) *Bend the bottom downward to the desired rocker by means of ballast piled inside, or by shores set against the ceiling. A sawn strongback may be incorporated if the loft plan is followed exactly* (Bottom) *Brace all frame members securely to the ceiling.*

*Alignment Check*

Finally after the set-up has been solidly braced and shored all around, it will do no harm to take a final fore-and-aft squint to see that the stem is still perfectly plumb and that it hits the centerline of the transom exactly. If a tight chalk line is stretched between nails driven into the centers of the stem head and the transom, it should pass directly over the vertical centerline mark on each frame assembly cross spall, and a plumb bob dropped from this line at any point should hit the centerline marked on the bottom. Likewise, if there is a centerline on the floor, the plumb bob hung from the stem head should hit it, as should the bob when it is hung from the middle of the outer face of the transom. Naturally, this check can be made only when the set-up is an upright one.

There are other checks that can be devised with plumb bob, spirit level, and chalkline. And it won't hurt to spend some extra time making doubly sure the set-up is true, for once the set-up is complete and everything is nailed rigidly in place, the final overall shape of the boat is established for better or for worse. If it is lopsided now, nothing can be done about it later.

*Sheer Ribbands*

Before leaving the set-up, we should mention a procedure highly recommended for Swamp-

scott dories. It is an excellent plan to spring a pair of stiff battens—one on each side—around the sheer running from stem to stern (see Figure 20). Put these on just above the sheer marks, nailing them temporarily to the timberheads. They will serve as ribbands. Should a frame be too narrow, it will show up here. To correct this the cross spall can be released to allow the frame to be pulled out until it is fair. Then the cross spall can be fastened back. Other times, a frame may be too wide, according to these sheer battens, so by the same method it can be pulled in until it is fair.

If the bottom and the sheer battens are fair, chances are that comparatively little fairing will be called for elsewhere. Besides assisting in establishing a true shape, these temporary sheer battens help greatly in holding the frames in place and the whole set-up rigid until the plank are on.

Temporary sheer battens are sometimes used in setting up Bank dories, but are hardly necessary. The straight side frames of the Bank dory may be sprung in or out slightly to achieve a fair boat as planking proceeds. The professional builder of Bank fishing dories depends on the natural bend of his plank to pull the frames true, regulated, of course, by his experienced boatbuilder's eye. Comparatively little attention to the beveling is required in fairing a boat of this sort.

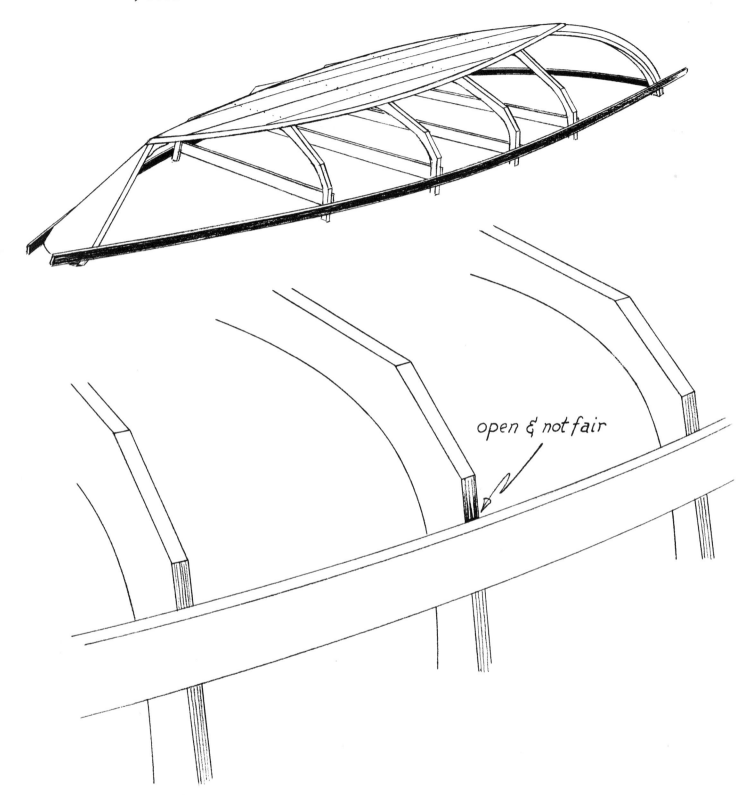

open & not fair

**20. A ribband or stiff batten applied to both sides of the boat just above the sheer mark insures alignment of all frame members during the construction process. It also indicates which frames need to be widened or narrowed by adjustment of the cross spall.**

*Horning*

The old method of setting a transom square with the centerline of the boat can be used to advantage. This is called "horning," because measurements are taken to the two outer corners of the "horns" of the transom (see Figure 21). A small nail is driven in the bottom on the centerline as far forward as possi-

ble. A tape, hooked over this nail, is drawn back tightly to either side of the inner face of the transom exactly on the sheer line. If the transom is square with the longitudinal centerline of the boat, port and starboard horning measurements will be identical, being the two equal sides of an isosceles triangle.

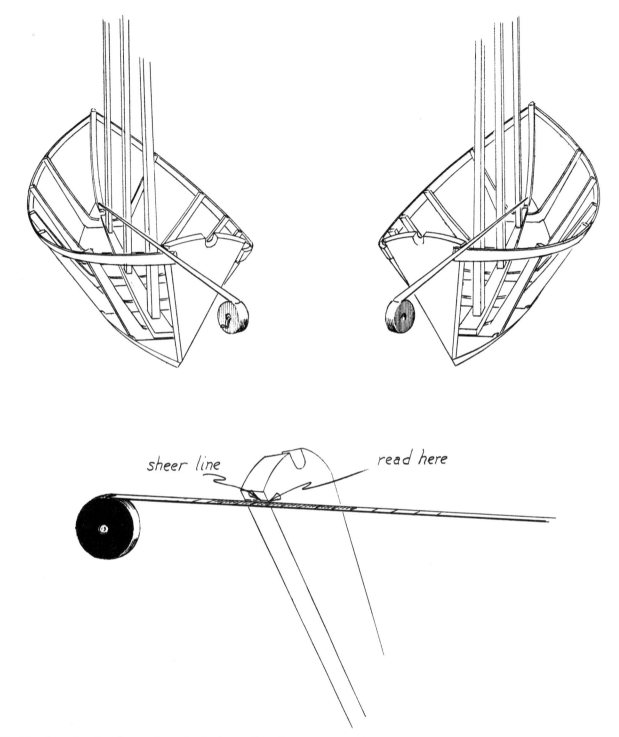

**21. Horning, the time-honored method of squaring the transom with the centerline by setting up an isosceles triangle.** *Anchor the tape as far forward as possible on the boat's centerline, then adjust the transom so that the same measurement is read at both interior corners or "horns" of the transom.*

*Fairing for Plank*

Fairing follows set-up. In this stage, the edges of the stem, transom, bottom, and frames are prepared to receive the plank. They must be smoothed, beveled, and equalized, so that wherever they come against the inner surface of the plank, they meet it with a touching fit. The natural bend of the plank is uniform and true, without kinks, flat spots, or abrupt changes in the flow of the curve. When the planking is wrapped around the inner members of the boat, it will not lie snugly and tightly and without deformity unless all irregularities on the outer faces of these members have been removed.

It is nearly impossible to make a laydown of lines that is exactly right in every detail. There is chance for error when the shapes are lifted from the floor, when the pieces are cut out, when the sub-assemblies are put together, and when the final assembly is made. It is a wonder, when all this is considered, that a boat gets set up as accurately as it does.

But no matter how accurately the preliminary operations have been done, there will likely be a few bunches to plane off and some beveling to be adjusted. Perhaps a frame or two will be slightly "heavy," requiring the removal of a few shavings.

In fairing a dory for plank, it is far more desirable to take off wood than to attempt to add it on. In the event that a frame turns out to be much lower than its neighbors, it can be beefed up by means of a thin strip of wood, or a shim, glued on the low edge (see Figure 22). However, the edges of the bottom, the stem, or the transom should never be built up with shims. A good builder is sparing with shims, and he resorts to them only as a last measure, and only when the discrepancy is comparatively great. Most of the time it is better to bring the fat frames down to correspond with the lean ones. A little wood removed this way does not matter. There will not be enough change in the final shape of the dory to be noticed or to affect its performance in any way that can be determined.

So, by and large, fairing boils down to a matter of planing off excess wood—a shaving here, a shaving there—until every bevel is just right and every curve blends with the rest.

Fairing is a deliberate job. Never hurry. Pause frequently and take the time to study the boat from all angles. A pipe smoker has the advantage here. He can clean his pipe and load it a few times and will be farther ahead in the end with a better job to his credit than the slap-dash fellow who tears into the job hell-bent-for-election.

Of course this would be a Swampscott dory that we are considering, like a gunning dory or a Beachcomber. They are fairly fussy boats. An ordinary Bank dory, with any decent luck, would have been faired and planked by this time.

The job goes better if the boat is faired as a whole and not in separate pieces. One side is worked against the other. The fairing process, let it be remembered, is largely an adjustment of parts to achieve an harmonious whole. What is done here will have its effect there. If you hang around one place too long, there is danger of taking off too much at that spot.

*Trying Batten*

Besides a sharp plane or two, the other kit required will be several battens, one of which will be a special thin, flat batten to simulate the lay and run of the planking. This is the *trying batten* (see Figure 22). About 2¼ to 2½ inches wide, and ⁵⁄₁₆ to ⅜ inch thick, made from clear, well-seasoned, northern white pine, and around half the length of the boat would be right. The aim is to have a flat, flexible strip that bends easily but uniformly. Cedar would do, or even a strip of thin plywood might answer.

The trying batten is moved about frequently to test for fairness. It is always applied with the run of the planking, that is, in the approximate fore-and-aft directions of the strakes. Sometimes the boatbuilder clamps it across several frames in order to stand back away from the boat to sight the bend. More often, in checking bevels and hunting for bunches or low spots on the frames, he holds the trying batten down with widespread arms and sights it either way from the middle.

Back and forth, all over the boat, the trying batten is applied and reapplied as excess wood is planed away, shaving by shaving. At last the batten will show true curves everywhere and will lie in exact contact with all parts it passes over. The boat is fair.

Sometimes the boatbuilder checks the bottom bevels with his folded two-foot rule extended down on the bottom edge of each frame in turn (see Figure 22).

*Lining Batten*

To make sure the run of the knuckle lines is not changed during the fairing process, a long lining or planking batten extending from the transom to the stem is tacked along the knuckles so that they can be relined and re-marked if necessary (see Figure 22). For dory work I like a lining batten that is approximately 1⅜ inches wide, ⅜-inch thick, and several feet longer than the boat. As always, seasoned, straight-grained, northern white pine makes the best battens, ones that can be nailed and re-nailed many times without splitting.

Fairing a dory can be pleasant if one takes his time, goes about it systematically, and refuses to get nervous. There is just enough uncertainty about the final outcome to keep the builder alert and in suspense. Fairing, at least in the case of the more difficult Swampscotts, is something of an art. The fairing process is to some extent creative, and it refuses to be reduced to a simple mechanical operation. No two builders will go about fairing a boat in exactly the same way, or achieve exactly the same result, although both may get fair hulls of nearly identical performance.

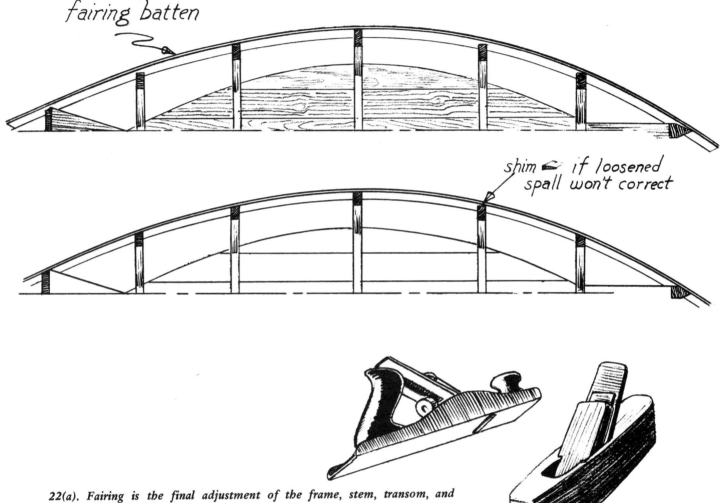

*fairing batten*

*shim — if loosened spall won't correct*

**22(a). Fairing is the final adjustment of the frame, stem, transom, and bottom bevels to receive plank with a watertight fit.** *Don't hurry with this step. A fairing batten is moved over all sectors of the boat in accordance with the lay of the plank. Frames are shaved or adjusted to width by their spalls. The final trimming is given to the bevels on the end members and the bottom. The batten must lie snugly and fairly on all timber surfaces. Roughing, smoothing, and block planes are some of the tools used in fairing the boat. Their blades must be kept sharp.*

*The example shown here is an extreme case; normally the frames will be much closer to fairness when the batten is first applied.*

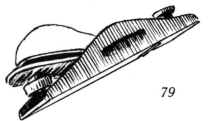

79

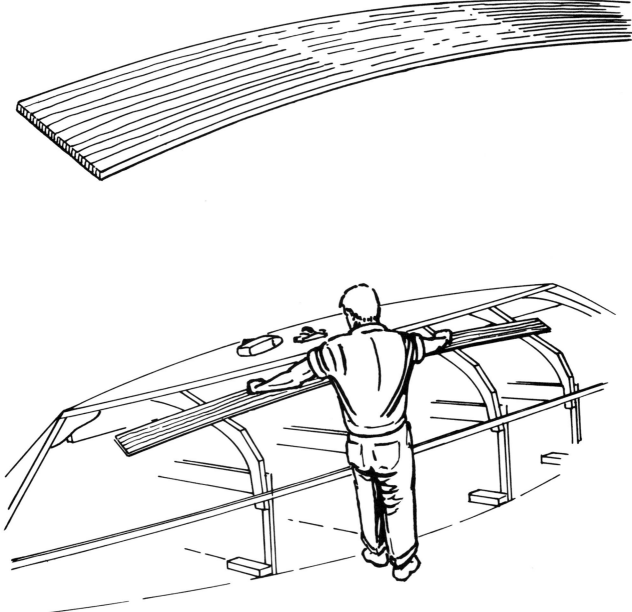

*22(b). Use of a wide "trying" batten on a Swampscott dory.*

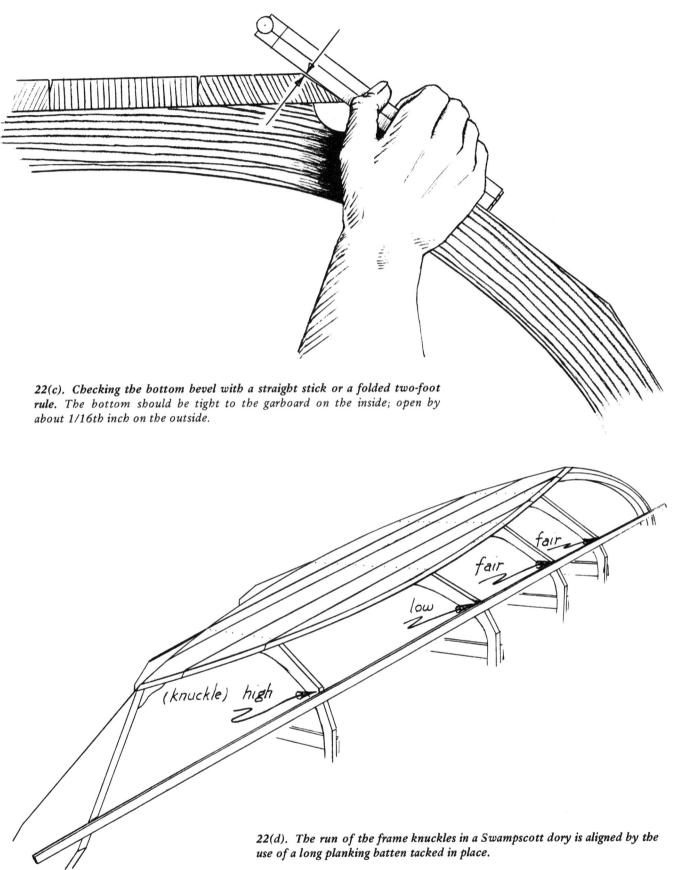

**22(c). *Checking the bottom bevel with a straight stick or a folded two-foot rule.** The bottom should be tight to the garboard on the inside; open by about 1/16th inch on the outside.*

**22(d). *The run of the frame knuckles in a Swampscott dory is aligned by the use of a long planking batten tacked in place.*

## STAGE 3: *Planking*

Dories are lapstrake, that is to say, clinker-planked boats. In general, the planking procedure is the same for all clinker boats. Planking is a trade within a trade. It is not that boatbuilders are secretive about planking, but probably because planking is so different from the common branches of woodworking that little has been written about it. Boatbuilders generally are not writers, and the writers are not plankers. Writers have skirted the subject, it appears, not only because they did not understand the planking process, but also because they failed to realize its key importance.

Boats on dory lines built from modern materials like plywood and plastic need not be planked in the traditional way. Glued batten seams characterize a substitute method of planking that is easy, strong, and best, perhaps, for plywood. This and other methods of planking will be covered in this book. (See Figure 23.) In time, plywood with seam-battens could largely replace the old lapstrake method, but for now, traditional clinker construction is still the first choice of most prospective dory builders.

The planking job is already partly done with the substructure framed and faired. Unless this preliminary work has been properly done, a first rate planking job is impossible.

Planking proceeds in stages, following a progressive series of steps. There are at least eight of these that fall into three slightly overlapping groups:

    1. Laying out, lining, and spiling.
    2. Getting out, splicing, and beveling.
    3. Hanging and fastening.

The first group of steps is mainly concerned with the *shape* of the planks. These steps include dividing up the hull surface for a predetermined number of planks; lining out and marking the "run" of the planks on the surface to be covered; taking or "spiling" from the curved surface of the hull the true shape of the planks in such a manner that this may be laid out in the *flat* on the planking stock.

The second group of steps involves cutting out the planks and otherwise preparing them to be fitted together on the boat. Most of this work is done at the bench, away from the boat, except that the lap bevels for Swampscott or round-sided dories must be taken from the hull for transference to the edges of the planks. Clinker plank are finished at the bench. No final planing is required after they are fastened in place on the boat. Dory plank may even be given a final sanding before they leave the bench.

The spiling operation overlaps into the second grouping somewhat, for spiling includes marking out the plank shape on the planking stock as well as taking it off the hull. Suitable boards are chosen for economical cutting and for the avoidance of defects, like checks, cross-grain, and loose knots. It is assumed that a sufficient amount of planking lumber of adequate lengths and widths is on hand to choose from. In this connection, a scale half-model can be of real service in helping the inexperienced builder estimate planking needs.

After a strake of plank is finished at the bench, it is bent on the boat and fastened. Bending and clamping the plank in position on the hull is called "hanging" by professionals. In fastening dory plank, a number of different kinds and sizes of metal fastenings are required, and tolerances are fairly critical. The importance of a thorough and careful fastening job should not be underestimated.

Now that the overall planking operation has been sketched in outline, let's turn to a more detailed description of the separate steps. It will not be possible to cover everything, but we will try to blaze a sufficient trail.

**23(a). Clinker or lapstrake construction.** *Permits the use of narrow or wide, thin plank stock. Seams are clenched or riveted with frame fastenings at the laps only. Extremely elastic construction. Appearance like clapboards.*

**23(b). Carvel construction.** *Seams are butted, caulked. Plank surface is flush. Relatively thick plank is required to hold the caulking successfully. Plank must be relatively narrow to inhibit excessive swelling or contraction.*

**23(c). Batten-seam construction.** *Modified carvel system permitting the use of wide, thin plank stock. The batten behind the seam permits the use of a sealant or caulking. However, splitting of plank will occur if contraction is excessive.*

*Laying Out*

For the dories in this book, most of the layout and lining for the planking has been done and is marked in the lines. This simplifies things a lot. All the builder need do is keep the planking spots obtained from the original laydown clearly marked (such marks are liable to get planed off in the fairing process) and line them through with a long batten. It will help, however, to have some idea of the shapes the various planks will take when laid out flat. Here it is that a scale half-model can be used to particular advantage. The novice, unsure of the planking operation, can see what is required much more clearly if he lays his planking out to scale in miniature before tackling the full-sized boat.

*The Effect of Flare*

First of all, it should be understood that a plank, when wrapped around the curved surface of a hull, will appear to have a different shape than when it is marked out on a flat board. Take a straight-edged board that is too wide to bend easily edgewise, and clamp it around the normally flaring sides of a Bank dory (see Figure 24). The ends of the board will shoot up high on the stem and transom, much higher than the middle of the board. There will appear to be a pronounced hollow curve in the upper edge of this plank, although we know that the top edge is perfectly straight when the board is laid out flat.

The more the side frames flare outward, as in the river batteau, the higher the ends of the straight-edged plank will shoot upward. Conversely, the more nearly upright the frames stand, the straighter the planking lines will show on the boat when straight-edged plank are used.

When this simple planking law is grasped, it becomes apparent why it is that most Swampscott dories require a sheer plank of so much curve (in the flat). In order to avoid cross grain and excessive waste of wide boards, it is standard practice to make this strake in two pieces, with a scarphed splice about one-third to one-fourth the length of the boat from the transom. The reason is that while the sheer line of the standard Swampscott model sweeps up at the ends like the garboard, the sheer knuckles of the frames stand nearly plumb. There is no outward flare at the top of the frames to pull the ends of the sheer plank upward (see Figure 24).

Because the side flare of the Bank dory runs straight to the sheer line without changing, sheer plank for such dories are nearly straight when laid flat. Consequently the sheer plank can be gotten out of fairly straight and comparatively narrow boards, and usually in one length, except when planking the extra-large models.

The accepted practice is to line dory plank so that they will be as straight as possible when laid out in the flat. Straight, or nearly straight plank are more economical of lumber and are stronger due to the avoidance of cross grain. Straight plank, furthermore, look better when bent in place on the boat.

*Right: 24(a). A scale half model or full model enables the builder to line off the side planking to best advantage. Note how a straight-edged batten applied to the side of this model has swept upward toward the ends of the boat. The amount of upsweep depends on how far outward the plank is canted in its bend around the hull.*

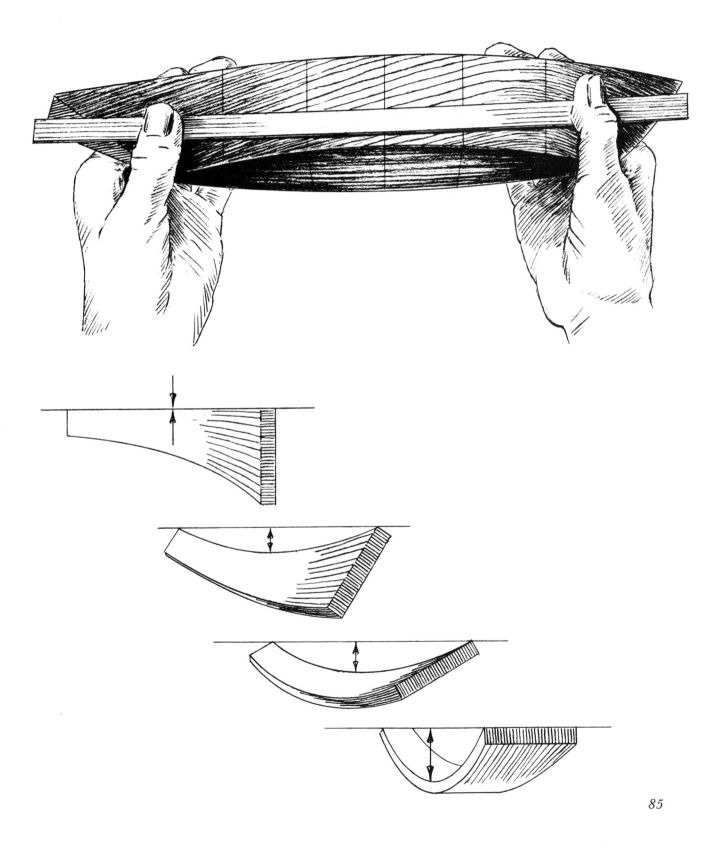

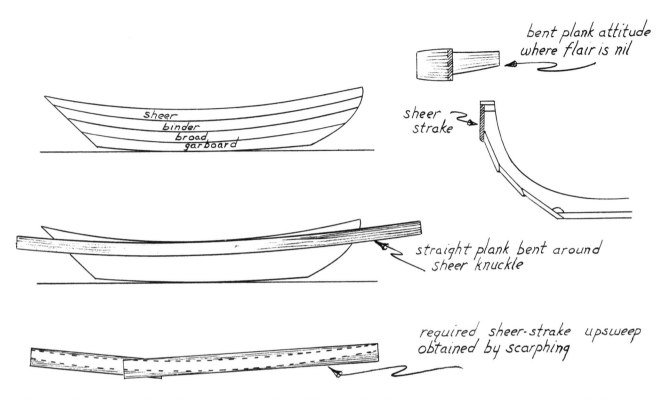

*bent plank attitude where flair is nil*

*sheer strake*

*straight plank bent around sheer knuckle*

*required sheer-strake upsweep obtained by scarphing*

**24(b).** *In a Swampscott dory, the garboard, broad, and binder strakes flare outward and sweep upward toward the ends of the boat. The sheer strake, however, has no flare and therefore does not sweep upward. Upward curve must be cut into the shape of this plank.*

*The Shape of Dory Garboards*

It is in the garboard, or side plank joining the dory's bottom, that the effect of flare on the shape of plank becomes most apparent. Applied to the flared sides of a Bank dory, a straight, parallel-edged board to be used for a garboard plank will shoot upward to its appointed location at the ends of the boat, while leaving considerable excess lumber overhanging the bottom panel at the middle of the garboard. If this excess wood were taken off flush with the bottom and the plank unbent for inspection, the plank would still exhibit a straight top edge, while the bottom edge would be seen to sweep inward in a concave curve along the length of the plank (see Figure 25). The flatter the "rocker" already established in the bottom panel of the dory, the deeper into the garboard plank this curve will cut. Conversely, the more "rocker" to the bottom panel, the shallower will be the curve cut into the garboard.

Thus, dories that are straight, or nearly straight fore and aft on the bottom will have garboards that are quite narrow amidship, although wide at the ends. Because the top edge of the garboard is laid out straight in the flat, or nearly straight, its ends will run up quite high on the stem and transom when it is bent on the boat. This accounts for its width at each end, and this must be taken into account in lining out the planks.

When wide boards of natural sawn lumber are used for garboards, the normal garboard shape just described produces relatively short, weak grain in the plank ends. This splits or "rents" easily and constitutes one of the weakest spots in the fabric of the standard dory. Plywood garboards avoid this weakness, but plywood does not stand prolonged soaking and drying as well as does natural lumber. However, this fault in plywood may be overcome to a large extent by sealing it with plastic. Another advantage of plywood is that it may be had in ample width for dory garboards, while sawn white pine lumber in boards 18 to 20 inches wide is almost unobtainable today.

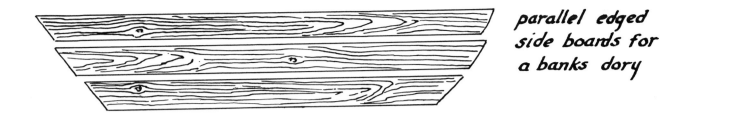

*parallel edged
side boards for
a banks dory*

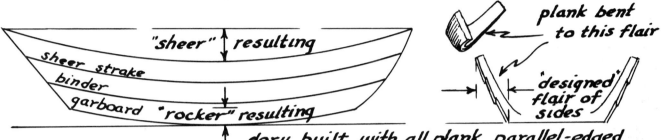

*"sheer"* $\uparrow$ *resulting*

*sheer strake*
*binder*
*garboard* *"rocker" resulting*

*plank bent
to this flair*

*"designed"
flair of
sides*

*dory built with all plank parallel-edged*

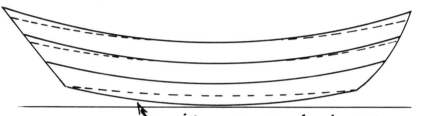

*if each strake is trimmed on one or both edges,
so as to lessen the upsweep of the hull,*

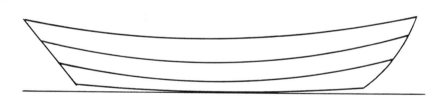

*these plank shapes will result.*

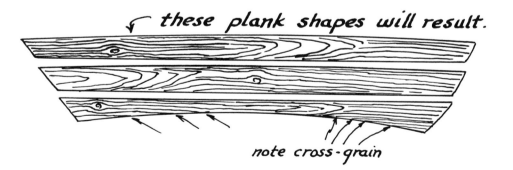

*note cross-grain*

25. *The natural upsweep of side planking in a boat is compensated for by controlling the shape of each plank applied.*
*This proves the need for lining off each plank edge on the model or on the boat (or both) to establish the appearance and coverage of each board.*

**Right: 26(a). Spiling with a sharp pencil compass.** *The idea is to regain the center of a circle that has been swung with a pencil compass. This is done by simply reversing the pointers. The pencil will mark through the center no matter where the point is set on the original circle.*

## Lining

About all the lining required in planking the Swampscott or other round-sided dories will be whatever is necessary to check, and more rarely to adjust, the alignment of the frame knuckles. As previously mentioned, this is done with the long fairing or planking batten. It does not matter if the knuckle lines are changed slightly during the fairing process. But they must run fair and both sides of the boat must correspond.

So far as the Bank dories and the straight-sided skiffs are concerned, it is permissible to change plank widths and, within moderation, the run of the plank as well, in order to make use of available planking stock to best advantage. The adjusted planking lines, which should follow the original lines as much as possible, will require testing for fairness and appearance with the planking batten tacked on the frames and carefully sighted.

## Spiling

Spiling is the method generally used by boatbuilders to take the precise shape of planks from the hull in order that they may be marked out on the planking stock. A plank carefully gotten out to accurate spiling will fit exactly when clamped in position on the boat. Various methods of spiling have been worked out. Some of the methods shown in books are more complicated than is necessary. Experienced plankers make spiling very simple.

In the spiling process, a thin batten substitutes for the plank. It will be narrower than the plank and thinner. Three-sixteenths to one-quarter of an inch in thickness is ample for dory spiling. The spiling batten is carefully bent around the frame in the approximate position that the plank being spiled will occupy, and it is temporarily tacked in place with 2d nails. "Spots" indicating the width and position of the plank on the frames, the stem, and the transom are marked on the batten in a manner to be detailed below.

After the batten has been marked, it is re-moved from the boat and laid out flat on the selected board. When its position has been adjusted to take best advantage of the planking stock, it is lightly tacked in place. Next the spiling marks are transferred to the planking stock (more detail later); the batten is removed; and the edges of the plank are lined out. This is done by tacking on a long, fair batten to conform to the line of spots just transferred from the spiling batten. It may be necessary to let the batten in or out slightly to bring the line to perfect fairness, but any large discrepancy will indicate error. When the batten sights true, a pencil drawn along its outer edge will line out the edge of the plank.

## Spiling with Pencil Dividers

There are several methods for marking the spiling batten. What is needed is a way to establish on the narrow spiling batten marks that will fix the positions of the edges of the wider plank relative to the batten while it is tacked fair to the frames, in such a way that these positions of the plank edges may then be reestablished on the planking stock when the batten is removed from the frames and tacked to the stock.

One may utilize pencil dividers set to a uniform radius throughout the operation (see Figure 26). The point is set in the planking line where it crosses each frame, and an arc for each frame is swung on the spiling batten. To reestablish this planking line on the stock, the dividers with the same setting are reversed, and two new arcs are swung on the stock with the point set on the original arc on the batten, first at one end of this arc and then at the other. The resulting two arcs will intersect precisely over the original point of setting on the frame. Thus, after the spiling batten has been removed from the boat and is laid out on flat planking stock, a line of spots for the plank edge at each frame can be established by swinging a series of intersecting arcs from the arcs previously marked on the spiling batten.

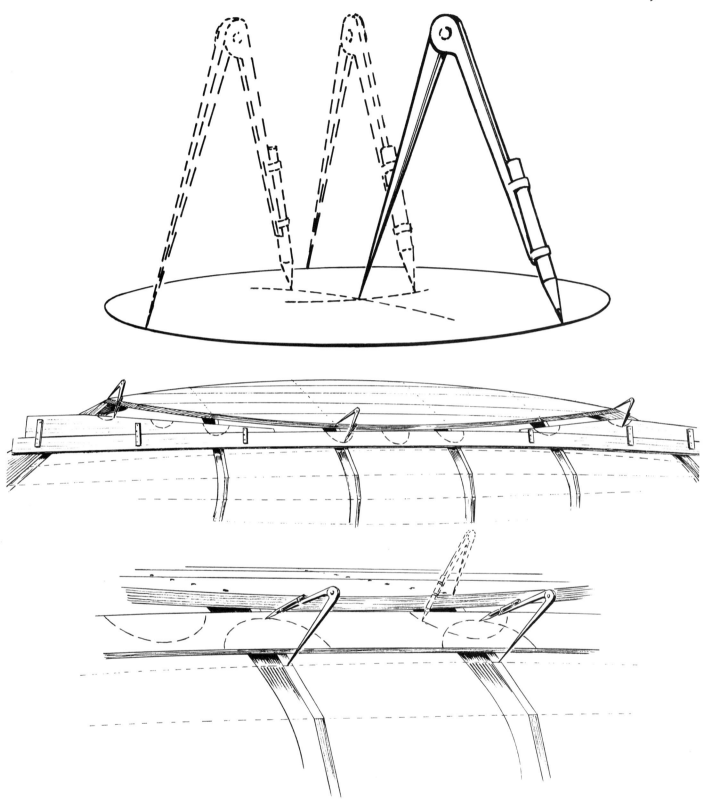

**26(b). When spiling plank-shapes with a pencil compass, the centers of many circles of equal radius are established with the compass point along the fine-line edge of the plank to be fitted to.** *Arcs of the circles are marked onto a batten clamped within reach of the set of the compass. The batten is removed from the boat, placed upon the plank stock, and the arcs are swung in reverse. Carefully done with a sharp instrument, each circle-center can be re-established to the accuracy of a pin prick. The whole locus of centers defines the edge of the matching plank, which, if cut fairly, should provide an airtight fit.*

*With a Spiling Block*

It is simpler to use a spiling block; that is, a small rectangle of wood or plastic, about 1½ inches wide and 2 or 3 inches long. The block is held so that its outer, long edge conforms exactly with the plank line on the frames, stem, and transom. Against the parallel inner edge of the block where it rests on the spiling batten a pencil line is drawn. This procedure is repeated at each station along the length of the boat. When the spiling batten is removed from the boat and laid out on the planking stock, the procedure is repeated in reverse. With the inner, long edge of the block set exactly on or over the lines on the batten, pencil lines conforming to its outer long edge are marked on the planking material (see Figure 27). A fair batten run through the spots so obtained gives the edge of the plank. One small caution: the spiling block should always be applied exactly parallel to the run of the plank. Some professionals don't bother to use a spiling block for dory work, but substitute their folded two-foot rule laid on the flat.

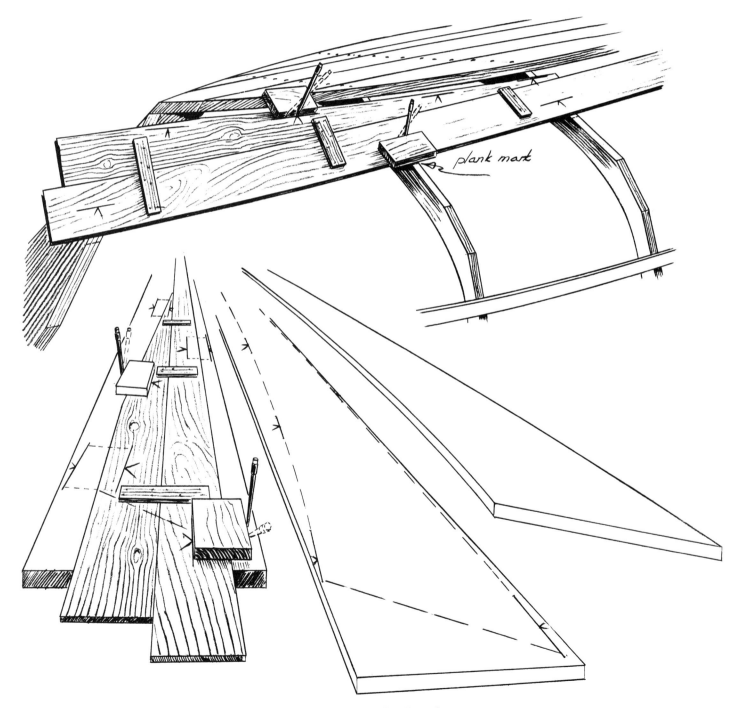

plank mark

27. *A spiling block used in lieu of a compass.*

*Adjustable Template*

One easily visualized method of spiling, similar to making a template, is simply to tack thin strips of wood across the spiling batten at each frame station and at the critical points of the stem and the transom. These cross strips or pointers are then trimmed off exactly where their ends extend across the plank line being fitted to. When the spiling batten is removed and laid flat on the planking stock, the ends of the pointers describe the exact perimeter of the upcoming plank. These points are marked on the planking stock, and a fair curve is run through them with a fairing batten. The plank is ready to be cut. Some boatshops employ a sophisticated spiling batten with sliding brass pointers to accomplish the same thing.

In order to receive the plank shape accurately, the spiling batten must lie snugly against all the frames as it is bent around the boat, but under no condition should it be forced into position by springing edgewise, even in the slightest, for that will cause distortion in the shape of the plank when it is marked out. A single, continuous length of batten running the full length of the boat is harder to put on without edge-set or distortion than two or three short lengths tacked on individually and then securely nailed or screwed together where the short pieces overlap. As a further precaution against edge-set, start nailing at the center of the batten when tacking it in place on the boat, and then nail outward in either direction toward the ends.

Sometimes both edges of the plank are spiled. But usually only the lower, that is to say, the overlapping, edge need be done for dory plank. It is quicker to line out the top edge from widths measured on the frames, as well as the stem and transom. Of course, the frame stations were marked on the spiling batten when it was tacked in place on the boat.

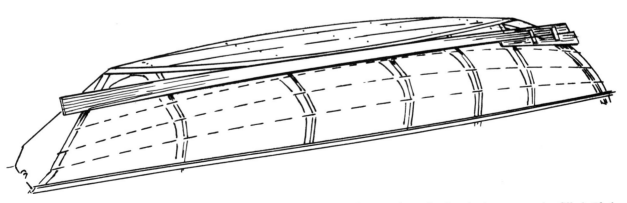

28(a). *To spile a dory garboard. Clamp or tack a suitable spiling batten through the plank space to be filled. If the adjusted compass won't reach the batten in some places, tack on some cardboard to increase the batten's width locally.*

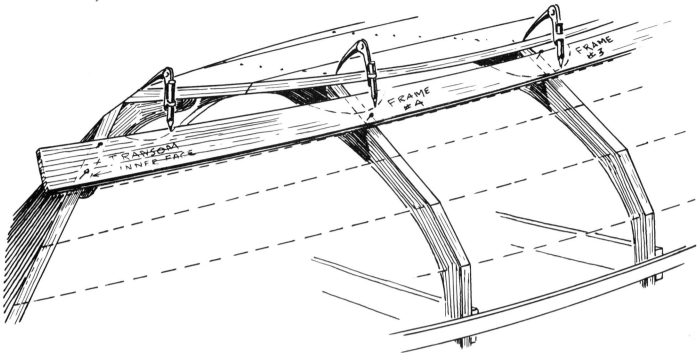

*28(b).  Swing compass arcs on the batten from enough locations along the perimeter of the plank space so as to describe the shape properly.* In this illustration the near side of the spiling batten is lying along the strake marks on the frames, eliminating the need to swing arcs on that side.

*Right: 28(c).  The spiling batten is transferred to a piece of plank stock.* The spots are marked by swinging the arcs in reverse.

*28(d).  The spots on the plank are connected with a pencil and fairing batten. The marked plank may now be cut to shape.*

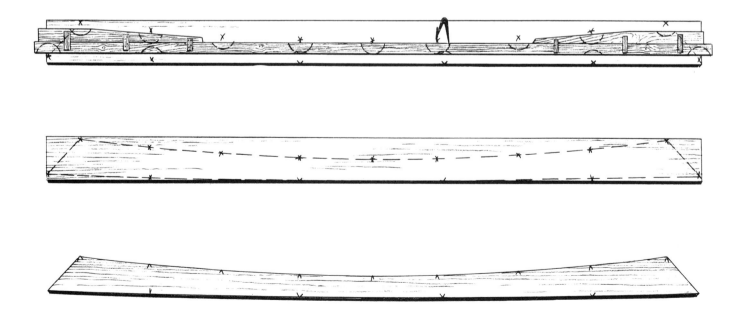

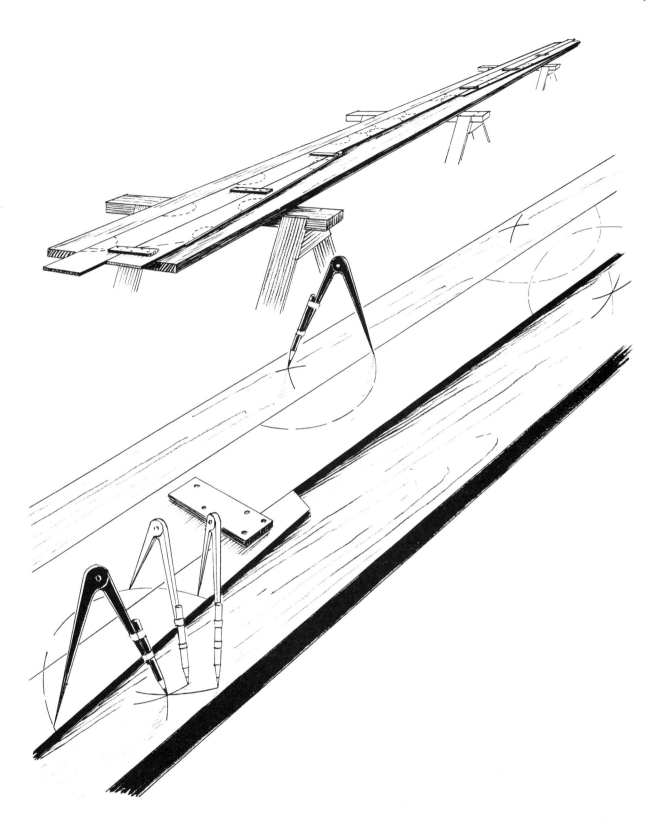

*Getting Out the Plank*

After the plank is marked, it is sawn out and then "jointed" to the line, that is to say the edges are planed to remove excess wood and to make them fair and square throughout. Ordinarily, a single plank will reach the length of the boat, forming one-half of a strake, for a complete strake goes around the boat. It is necessary for both sides to be planked together to insure uniformity, and to keep the structure from pulling out of shape. Thus each strake consists of two identical planks. Most of the time, when work is being done at all carefully and accurately, a spiling on one side only need be taken. A duplicate plank for the other side may be marked out, using the first as a pattern. In professional shops, after the first boat is built, dory plank are usually marked out from patterns, both sides of the strake being marked from the same pattern.

*Plank Splices*

If, for any reason, a side-length of plank has to be made in two pieces, it will be necessary to splice them. Butt blocks are awkward in clinker boats and unnecessary in dory construction, especially now that strong waterproof glues have been developed.

The customary splice in the sheer plank of Swampscott dories was generally located so the scarph came on the after frame. The scarph was cut square across the plank with 4 to 5 inches of overlapping taper. The inner face of the scarph was planed to a feather edge, which rested against the back of the frame. The covering side of the scarph ran by and over the inner part, hiding it against the frame so that the splice was not visible from the inside of the boat. On the outside of the boat the scarph end was not brought to a feather edge, but was left about ⅛-inch thick, which let into the after section of plank square and flush. At this end the scarph was fastened with small copper rivets (see Figure 29). At the top it was reinforced and partly covered by the gunwale. At the bottom it was held by the lap fastenings. Screws or boat nails into the frame completed the fastening of the splice and further strengthened the plank at this point. Only a thin line across the plank showed on the outside of the boat, and paint and putty hid it almost completely.

This is excellent construction, good for the hardest service and the lifetime of the boat, but this method of splicing is now outmoded by the modern glued splice, which is simpler, easier to make, and stronger (see Figure 29). A properly made glued splice is fully as strong as the natural run of the board, so that it is possible to make up wholly satisfactory long plank from a number of short lengths.

Both sides of the joining scarph are planed on a uniform straight taper to feather edges. After the glue has set and both sides of the joint have been sanded and painted, it will be difficult to find the splice.

Splicing up a strake in several sections involves extra labor, but this should not deter most amateurs who do not have to figure labor costs, and the savings in lumber could be considerable. Weak cross grain may be avoided in long, crooked plank by splicing up from several short, straight-grained pieces. Also, excessive wastage of wide boards may likewise be avoided.

Resorcinal resin glue makes an excellent splice, but requires considerable pressure, which means that splices will generally have to be glued up before the finished planks are hung on the boat. If plank sections are cut to exact width and shape before gluing, there is a chance of spoiling the plank through slippage in the clamping operation. Even a slight change of alignment of sections would ruin the fit of the plank. This danger may be avoided by first gluing up sections of board to the approximate shape, yet providing enough extra width so that the exact shape of the plank can be lined out from the spiling after the glue has set.

Or, sections of plank cut to finished shape may be temporarily nailed during the gluing process to the outline of the plank marked on a gluing table. A length of wide, heavy staging plank set on two saw horses might serve for this and would provide substantial clamping surface.

Epoxy adhesives do not require pressure. The joining surfaces need only be brought together and held in position until the glue has set. Thus, plank scarphs can be glued and fitted on the boat. A simple way to hold scarphed joints in place until the glue has set is to screw or nail them to temporary backing blocks shielded with paper against excess glue. When the glue is solid, the temporary blocks and fastenings are easily removed and the holes plugged.

Even though glued splices are very strong, it

is just as well to follow established practice by placing splices so that they are well scattered or "staggered," and in identical location on either side of the boat (see Figure 30). Also it should be taken into consideration that splices toward the ends of plank take less strain than those near the middle of the boat.

The length of the scarph joint should follow the general rule for scarphing plywood, that is twelve times the thickness of the material. A small, low-angle block plane, very sharp, set fine and worked diagonally with the grain, is the proper tool for cutting the scarph faces (see Figure 31). With epoxy adhesive the exact fit required for resorcinal resin glue is not necessary. Some of the epoxy adhesive should remain in the joint for the strongest bond.

*old-style sheer plank scarph - bedded in white lead*

*modern glue scarph*

*29. Two types of plank scarphs.*

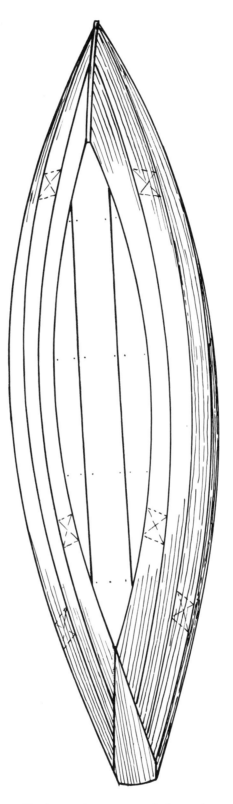

**30. Scarph locations on a Swampscott dory.** *Plank scarphs are properly located toward the ends of the boat, staggered on alternate strakes, and placed exactly athwartship of each other in the same strake of plank.*

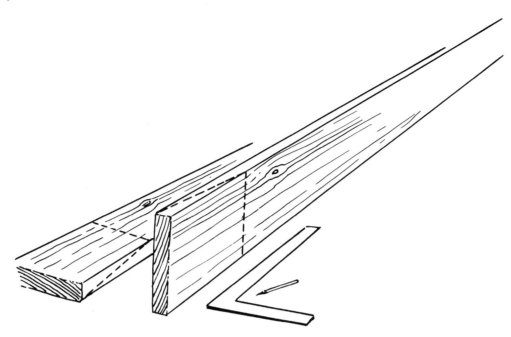

*31 (a). To cut a scarph, lay out the cut on both edges and the included side.*

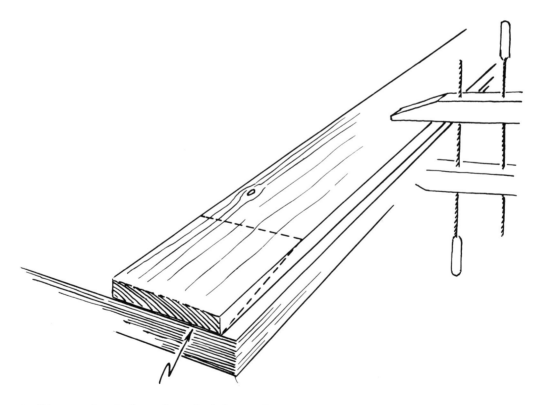

*31 (b). Lay the plank on the end of the bench so that the feather edge of the scarph will be supported during the final planing.*

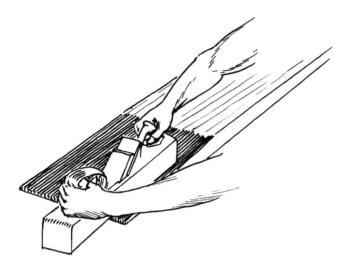

*31(c). Remove most of the wood with a draw-knife, scrub plane, or jack plane.*

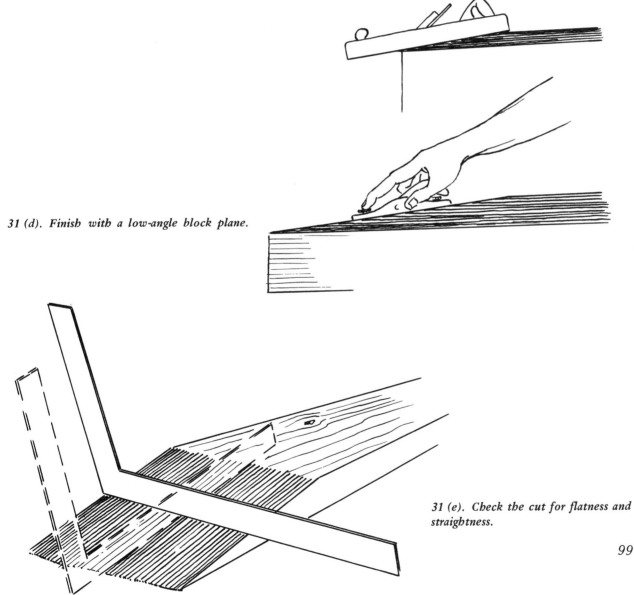

*31 (d). Finish with a low-angle block plane.*

*31 (e). Check the cut for flatness and straightness.*

*Lap Bevels*

Beveling the laps is not quite the bugaboo that some amateurs anticipate. For Bank dories and straight-sided skiffs, all lap bevels are uniform throughout, except for the "gains" at the end of the planks. Gains, it should be explained, are the diminishing tapers worked into the lap bevels toward the plank ends so that these will come together flush and lie flat on the transom and the stem.

For Swampscott and other knuckle-sided dories, inside lap bevels on the top edges of the planks will all be uniform throughout, the same as for a Bank dory. But the lap bevels on the overlapping, lower edges of the planks will change as the knuckle angle changes. Where there is no knuckle on the straight run of the deadrise at the top of the garboard, amidships, both lap surfaces (of garboard and broad strakes) will carry the same bevel, and the maximum amount on the boat, exactly as it would be on a Bank dory. But at the turn of the bilge on some Swampscott dories, where the knuckles are most pronounced, little or no bevel on the lap face of the outer plank is required.

*Lap Widths and Gains*

The first step is to gauge the width of the laps and mark them with pencil lines on diagonally opposite edges of the plank. The upper edge of the plank is marked on the outside, the lower on the inside face of the plank. Lap widths will vary slightly according to the size and type of dory, and the thickness of the plank (see Figure 32). Lap and beveling dimensions for each boat will be included in its separate specifications.

A Bank dory 19 feet long would normally show a lap width of about 1⅛ inch for a plank thickness of ⅝ inch. In beveling laps for a Bank dory, a uniform flat slope is planed on diagonally opposite edges of the plank, starting at the scribed lap line and running down to a remaining edge thickness of 5⁄16 inch (see Figure 33). About 3 feet from the ends of the plank, the "gains" start for this dory. The scribed width of the lap stays as is, but toward the end of the plank, wood is planed away so that the lap angle is gradually increased, diminishing the edge thickness from 5⁄16 inch to ⅛ inch on the extreme ends of the plank. This puts a slight twist into the lap surface for the length of the gains, but this is so gradual that the lap ends pull together tightly when the planks are fastened on the boat.

In a Swampscott dory of about the same length, with plank 9⁄16 inch thick, the lap bevel would be about 1 1⁄16 inch. The lap preparation on the upper edges of the plank would bevel uniformly to an edge thickness of ⅛ inch with gains starting 18 inches from the ends and edge thickness diminishing to slightly under 1⁄16 inch on the stem and transom (see Figure 33). The changing bevels of the lower, over-lapping edges of the plank must be taken off the boat at each frame station separately for each strake as the planking proceeds.

From the boat at each frame station, the correct angle of the lap bevel is taken with an adjustable carpenter's bevel, which is applied to the plank on the bench at the corresponding frame station as marked from the spiling batten. With a sharp chisel, a narrow section of the lap is pared away until the setting on the carpenter's bevel corresponds exactly (see Figure 33). The process is repeated at each frame station. Next, the stretches between the pre-beveled sections are carefully planed down so that they blend gradually and uniformly into the sections previously cut. As a rule, the amount of wood removed will increase toward the ends of the plank, where gains will increase the lap bevels still more.

In preparing lap surfaces with changing bevels, the greatest care must be taken to make the entire lap surface throughout its length flow in one continuous, gradual, even curve or twist. This ribbon of surface must also lie perfectly flat across throughout its length. If it is rounded, if there are holes, bunches, or abrupt changes in the twist, the lap will not come tight when the fastenings are put in.

The fitting of laps is not so critical as it was formerly, because now there are a number of good sealants or caulking compounds available for use. They will not only make a lap tight, but they will also reinforce it. Some of these flexible sealants are strong enough and adhesive enough to hold laps together without the help of metal fastenings.

For the most part, lap surfaces can be cut with a small plane, and for that purpose the same sort of low-angle block plane recommended for plank scarphs is excellent. Where there is much twist, however, as in the short gains of some of the smaller, lighter Swampscott dories and skiffs, a large spoke shave is the tool required.

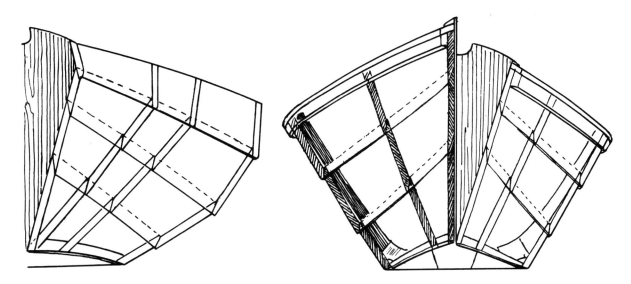

**32 (a).** *Cross-sections of the laps in a Swampscott and a Bank dory.* Through most of the boat, the laps are beveled just enough to insure a watertight match of the plank. Toward the ends, the planks are beveled into each other until they come flush at the stem and the transom.

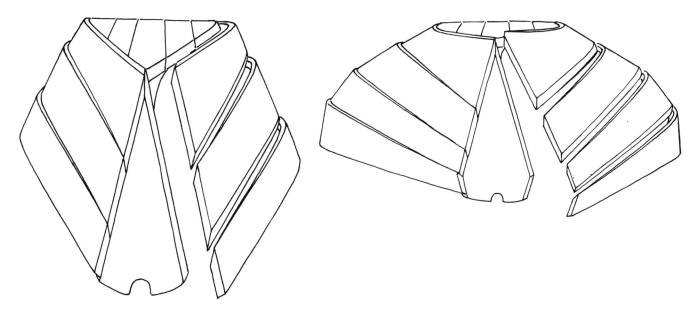

**32. (b).** *The appearance of the laps and the increased angle of the bevel, or gain, at the ends of a Swampscott and a Bank dory.* The scribed width of the bevel remains constant along the length of each plank, but the bevel depth increases.

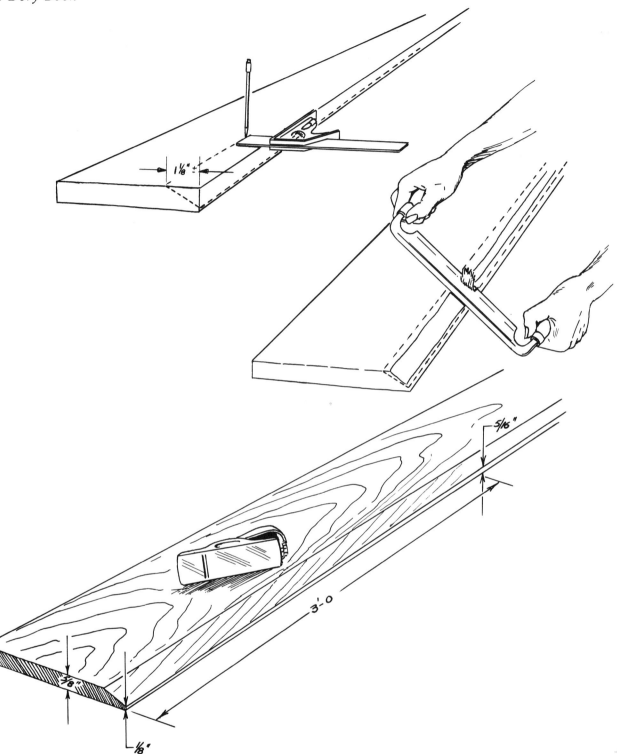

**33 (a). Plank bevels—the garboard.** *Scribe the width of the lap on the outboard side of the plank. Scribe the exposure and the gain along the inboard upper edge. The plank edge along the boat's bottom is to be left square until the plank is fastened; then it can be trimmed off. When cutting the bevel, strive for a smooth, flat bevel surface.*

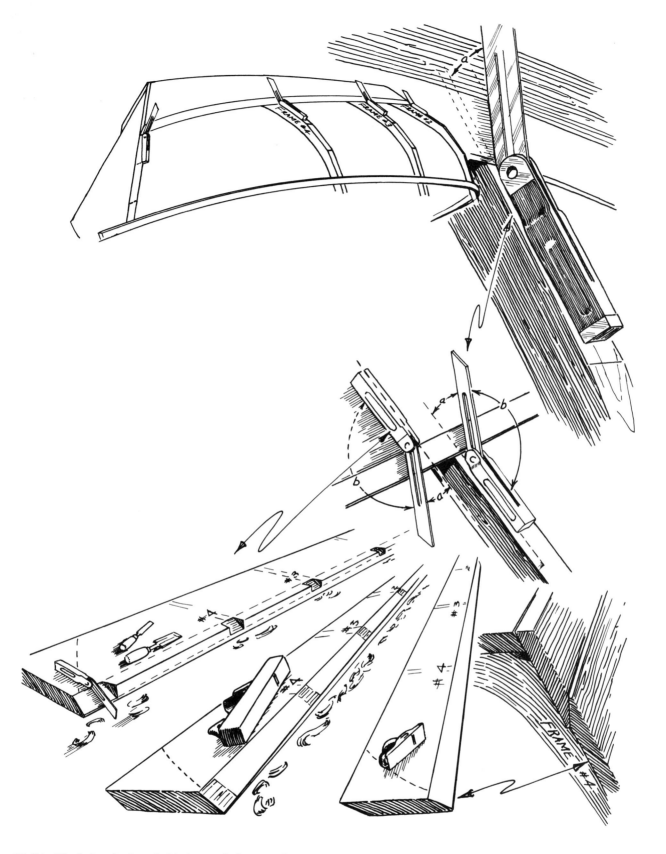

**33 (b). Plank bevels—broad, binder, and sheer strakes.** *Once the garboard is clamped or fastened to the boat, obtain the bevel to be matched at each frame station with a bevel square. Transfer these bevels to the spiled edge of the plank, and cut spots. Fair the spots together with a batten and trim the entire edge. Note that angles* **a** *and* **b** *are complementary, which allows the bevel square to be turned over when transferring the bevels. Remember that the bevels must also be established on the outboard upper edge of the broad and binder strakes before these planks are ready for fastening.*

*Hanging Plank*

"Hanging" is the boatbuilder's word for bending and clamping plank in place on the frames so that the plank can be fastened. In dory building, this is a relatively simple and easy operation, as a dory's shape is such that no hard bends or twists are required. No steaming is necessary for dory plank.

One elementary but urgent caution is necessary at the start. To attempt to draw or to pull plank into position with the fastenings is an invitation to disaster. All too frequently a split plank is the result. Joining members should touch wood-to-wood before fastenings are introduced. With clamps, wedges, and shores, plank are put exactly where they belong before any fastenings go in (see Figure 34).

The amateur dory builder can probably get along with half a dozen iron C-clamps. The 6-inch size is plenty large enough, and several 4-inch C-clamps will work in nicely. A few extra deep-throated clamps are handy. For drawing the laps together tightly in the "bays" between the frames, and especially where there is twist, a special clamping device is needed. This may be in the form of a large wooden "clothespin," slotted deep enough to slip down over the width of plank to grasp the lap on its lower side (see Figure 35). If the opposing fingers of this oversize "clothespin" are purposely made to fit loosely, so that a small wedge of softwood can be driven into the fork and against the outside of the lap, the pressure will squeeze the lap tightly. To reinforce the "clothespin" and to keep the force of the wedge from splitting it, the device is through-bolted or riveted just above the slot. Various other forms of this "clothespin" clamp are made, utilizing wedges for pressure, and sometimes special, deep-throated, wood handscrews are made up by professionals for clamping laps.

If dory plank are spiled correctly and gotten out accurately, hanging them is no job at all, for normally they will wrap around into place on the frames with a minimum of fuss and clamping. Not so with ill-shaped plank that must be sprung into place. Considerable edgewise bending is possible with plank that are either too straight or too crooked, but lots of effort and clamps are required to force these misfits into place and to hold them there until they can be fastened. One edge or the other will strain away from the frames, and the laps will gape open unless drawn together by plenty of "clothespin" clamps. Forced fitting of lapwork greatly increases the dangers of split planks, or open, leaking joints.

*Right: 34 (a). Hanging plank—the garboard, starboard side. Make sure that the plank is clamped firmly in place along its entire length before any fastenings are driven. The lower part of the drawing shows a workable clamping system to start the garboard onto the boat, beginning at the stem. A notched block enables the clamp to grip the inside corner of the stem. Put wood pads under the clamp faces to protect the finished surface of the plank. Place the clamps where they will not obstruct the drilling or fastening operations.*

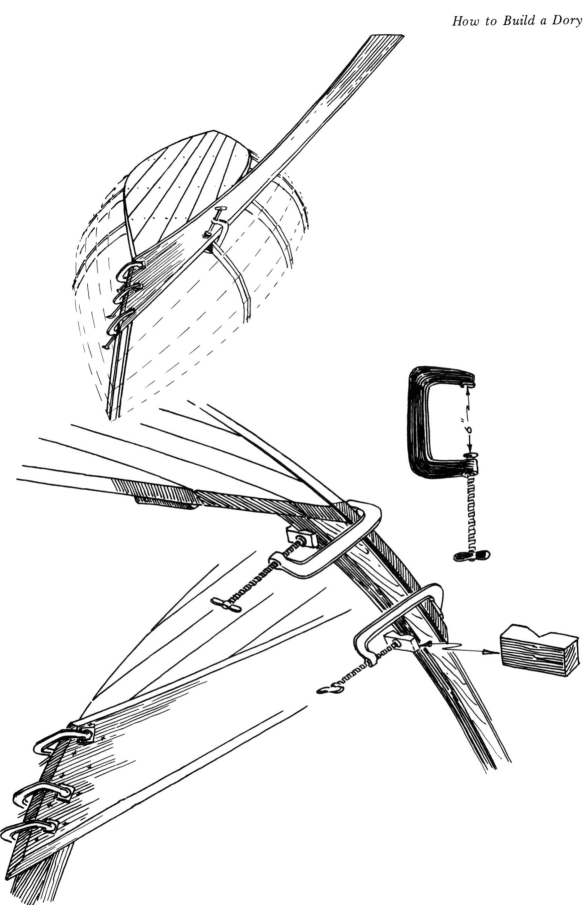

**34 (b). Hanging plank—the garboard, port side.** *Shores and wedges will be required to hold this plank at the stem and at the transom. The other garboard impedes the use of clamps. When using shores be sure that the opposite side of the boat is properly shored to prevent pushing the boat structure out of line.*

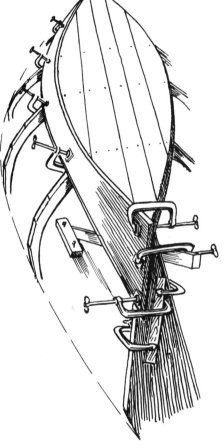

**34(c). Tips on hanging the garboard.** *It is quite possible for one man to bend the garboard and handle the clamps by himself. However, a helper to manipulate the outboard end of the plank is a good idea. Do the bending slowly and carefully, making sure that all clamping systems are secure as you move along the hull. A slipped clamp may result in a swiftly shattered garboard. Some builders apply luting of paint, red or white lead, or Cuprinol to all surfaces being joined; others prefer wood-to-wood joints.*

*The transom edges are too sharp in a dory for the seating of clamps. Temporary struts or blocking may be needed.*

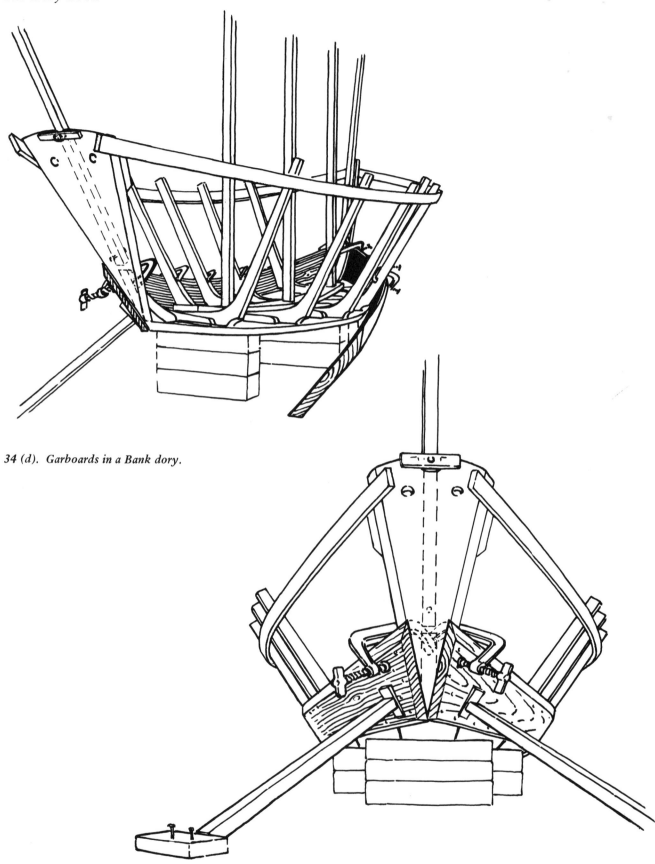

*34 (d). Garboards in a Bank dory.*

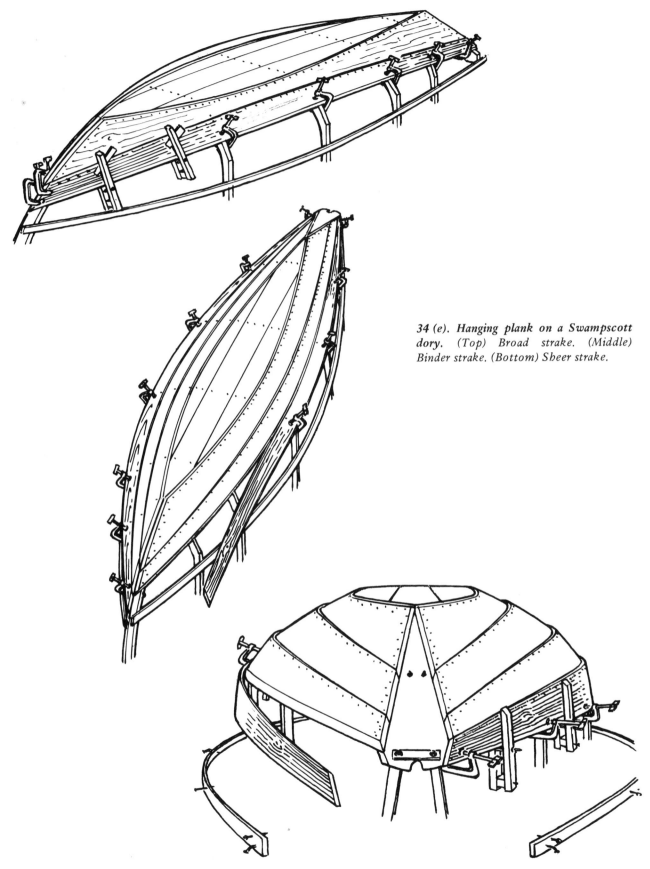

*34 (e). Hanging plank on a Swampscott dory. (Top) Broad strake. (Middle) Binder strake. (Bottom) Sheer strake.*

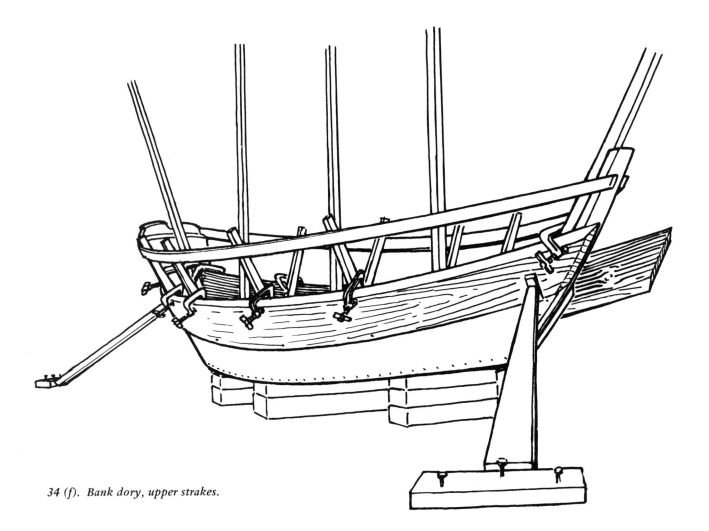

*34 (f). Bank dory, upper strakes.*

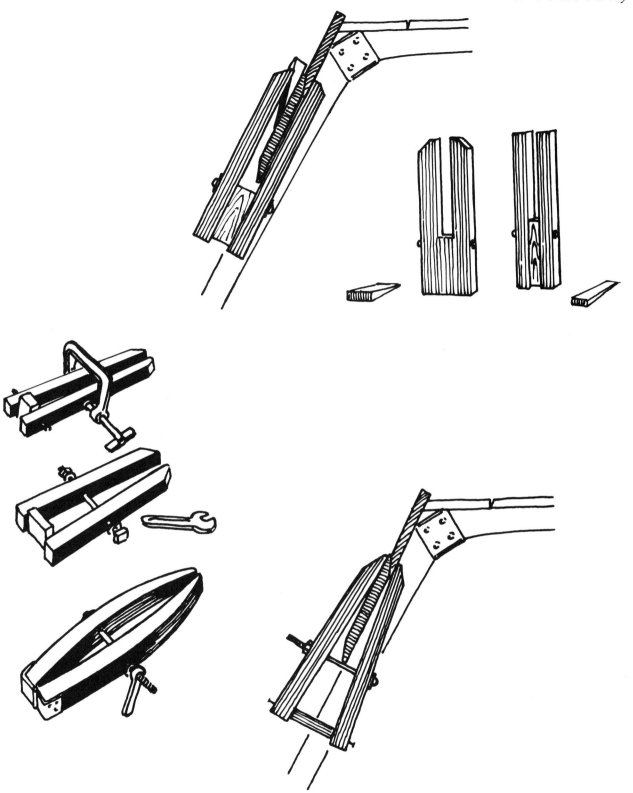

35. *Homemade lap clamps; some simple, some sophisticated.*

*Fastening Plank*

Fastening the plank is a critical job, and careful work up to now will be put in jeopardy should plank be nailed haphazardly. The final fastening operation tends to be underrated.

Years ago, dories were fastened throughout with galvanized iron (not steel) boat nails, because these were cheap, and easy and quick to put in. Old-fashioned galvanized iron (not steel) nails were good for at least twenty years in salt water, which is longer than most of the fishing dories lasted before they were smashed or worn out. Some of the better-cared-for old Swampscott racing dories did live long enough to undergo a complete refastening job after twenty-five or thirty years.

Today, genuine galvanized iron (not steel) boat nails, especially the chisel-point nails for dory laps, are no longer obtainable. Fortunately, there are alternative fastenings that are just as good or better for amateurs who are not going in for mass production.

*Copper Rivets*

Copper rivets make a better lap fastening than chisel-point nails and are probably easier for the inexperienced to work with. Suitable copper-wire nails are still abundant. An hour or two of practice riveting at the bench will suffice to get the knack. A few pointers: Rivets should be driven into pre-bored holes that are slightly smaller than the wire of the rivet. A heavy backing iron, firmly held, draws up the rivet and the lap. The unhandled head of a five- or six-pound top maul makes a good backing iron. After the burr or rove has been driven up tightly on the protruding end of the nail with the burr set, the excess point is clipped off. From $\frac{1}{16}$ to $\frac{1}{8}$ inch beyond the burr is left for the head, enough to swell out into a good head, but not enough to cripple under pounding. For swelling the head, a very light hammer is best—the lightest ball-peen hammer you can find. Many light, quick taps make the best head and draw the rivet up gradually to a tight, pulling fit. "Light blows kill the devil," as they used to say.

*Clench Nails*

If the laps are fastened with chisel-point nails, these must be bored for. There is a knack to driving them. As the nail goes through, the point is turned back into the wood again. This draws the lap together tightly as the nail is set up with the hammer against a hold-on in the other hand. It is not enough merely to bend these nails over on the inside of the lap; they must be turned back into the wood in a full "U" bend (see Figure 36). Here, again, practice at the bench is required before attempting to fasten the actual laps.

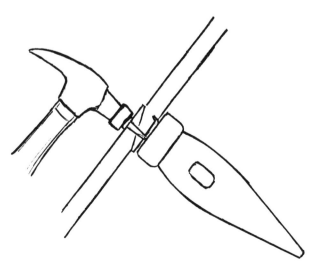

**36. Fastening the laps with chisel-point nails.** *The pilot hole should give a snug fit to the upper shank of the nail. Holes should be slightly staggered along the centerline of the lap, spaced about three inches apart.*

*Back the lap with a maul head or dopping iron held tightly against the wood but cocked away from the hole slightly to allow the point to come through. As the nail point comes through, roll the face of the dopping iron on it to turn the point back into the wood. The face of the dopping iron should be flat against the nail and the lap wood during the final blows of the driving hammer. Turn the nails across the grain into the thicker region of the lap.*

113

*Garboard-to-Bottom*

Fastening the garboard to the bottom is a tricky operation in standard dory construction, where this plank is nailed directly to the beveled edge of the bottom (see Figure 37). To begin with, it is essential for the bottom to be beveled so that the upper part of its edge (when the boat is right-side-up) is slightly strong. This edge must bear firmly against the inner surface of the garboard for its full length, and likewise must the ends of the garboard bear against the fayed edges of the stem and transom. But the lower part of the edge of the bottom should be slightly slack where the garboard comes against it, not open enough for caulking—and caulking should not be used here—but just enough for the paint to soak in nicely. In this way, a tight seal is formed all around the bottom. But should the bottom be beveled in reverse, so that the fit is closed on the outside but slightly open within, the dory will likely leak.

Ten-penny galvanized-wire nails are the standard fastening for the bottom edge of the garboard. Spaced 2 to 3 inches apart, these nails are driven exactly parallel to the flat of the bottom. Care must be taken that these long nails do not split out through either face of the bottom. Lead, or pilot, holes are best bored for these nails with a long, slim drill, substantially smaller than the wire of the nail so that its holding power is not lost. Because of the flare of the garboard, which is most extreme in Swampscott dories, the direction of the pilot drill requires accurate sighting. It may be lined parallel with a straightedge held athwartship against the flat of the bottom and projecting beyond it (see Figure 37).

The heads of the nails are sunk in enough below the outside of the garboard to be covered flush with putty. A small woodcarver's gouge, with its corners ground away, makes an excellent tool for countersinking for plank fastenings. After the lead hole is drilled, a twist with the gouge, and enough wood is removed to sink the nail head. In the past, the heads of the nails in the lower edge of the garboard were puttied over with white lead, which in time sets up like a rock. In cases of extreme side flare in some of the round-sided Swampscott dories, the middle section of the garboard is best fastened to the bottom with rivets.

If there should be any doubt as to whether a watertight fit has been achieved at this critical juncture between the garboard and the bottom, the seam may be covered with a reinforcing strip of fiberglass or polypropylene fabric set in epoxy resin. Two or three inches of overlap on both sides, stuck fast with epoxy, strengthens this joint greatly and makes it watertight. Of course, one of the several good elastic sealants that develop adhesive strength when cured can be applied before the joint is nailed. Such sealants are apt to be messy in application, but they insure a tight joint and reinforce the fastenings.

Anchorfast nails, either of bronze or Monel, might be substituted for the galvanized-wire nails. Anchorfast are more expensive. They resist corrosion better, but there is no conclusive evidence that they hold better than galvanized nails, or even as well. After a short time, galvanized nails develop a powerful adhesion to the wood.

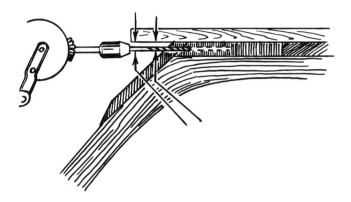

**37. Nailing the garboard.** *Accurate counterboring for the 10-penny nails along the bottom edge of the garboard is a critical operation. A good sighting gauge is a straight stick laid atop the bottom, extending over the drill as closely as possible. The drill bit is held parallel to the stick.*

*Clamps are neglected in the lower view to show the system of fastening required to hold a garboard in place. Nails along the bottom are spaced about three inches apart. Each is carefully counterbored, with the head countersunk.*

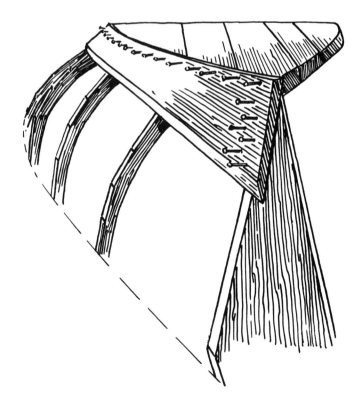

*Plank to Frames, Stem, and Transom*

For securing the plank to the frames, and the ends of the plank to the stem and the transom, either blunt-point galvanized boat nails or screws are used. Screws hold better but cost slightly more.

The only screws worth considering are bronze. Brass is too weak. The sharp threads of bronze screws pull so much better than the duller, hot-dipped galvanized screws (hot-dipped, however, is the only kind of galvanizing or plating that will stand up in salt water) that it is worth paying the extra for bronze.

Screws should not be too small. Even in the smaller dories, planking screws less than No. 10 should not be used. At the other extreme, the biggest dories will rarely require planking screws as large as No. 14. Lengths will range between two and three times plank thickness. Sizes and lengths, when critical, are specified for particular boats. Nail sizes are also given for those who prefer to fasten in the old way.

Holes must be bored for blunt-point nails. A little experimentation will determine the right size drill, for one that is too large will spoil the holding power of the nail. The large heads of such boat nails require countersinking. Here, also, the small, quick gouge ground round (and sharp) makes an excellent countersinking tool in soft lumber.

Plank fastenings into dory frames should not be too numerous. And if these fastenings are not properly located, they are apt to cause wide dory plank to split, as they swell and shrink. Dory plank "work" more than might be supposed, and, if rigidly fastened to the frames, they will pull themselves apart in time. Wide garboards must not be fastened to the frames anywhere except through the lap, or just below it. Fastenings into the frames near the bottom edge of the garboard are fatal. Splits and "rents" inevitably develop.

Sufficient fastenings for plank to frames may be had through the laps alone. But, if for any reason, one of these through-lap fastenings seems weak, an extra fastening may be added just below the lap.

*Plastic Reinforcement*

The foregoing considerations do not apply to plywood planking, which may be nailed anywhere without danger of splitting. A stiffer, more rigid hull, as well as a lighter and stronger one, can be built from plywood, especially if seam-batten construction is chosen instead of traditional lapstrake planking with sawn lumber.

If seam-battens are bound and sealed with strips of glass fabric or polypropylene cloth set in epoxy resin, structural strength is greatly increased, and perfect, permanent tightness is obtained. A modified construction utilizing plywood and laminations with the newer plastic adhesives offers much to the amateur builder. Such modified construction can be applied to all the different dories without requiring any change in basic hull lines. The new materials combined with the old sea-proven designs promise much for small craft development and restore wood to a favorable position in competition with molded plastic and light metals.

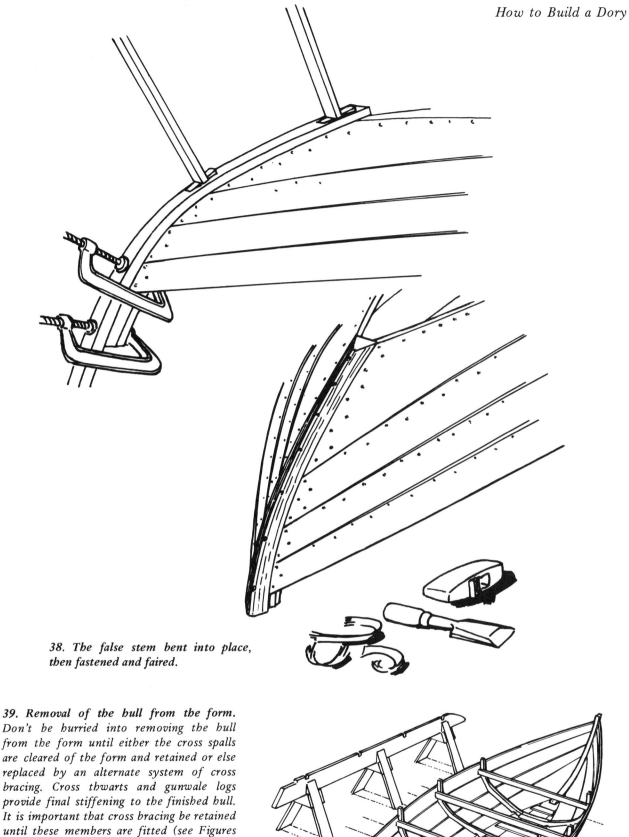

*38. The false stem bent into place, then fastened and faired.*

**39. Removal of the hull from the form.** *Don't be hurried into removing the hull from the form until either the cross spalls are cleared of the form and retained or else replaced by an alternate system of cross bracing. Cross thwarts and gunwale logs provide final stiffening to the finished hull. It is important that cross bracing be retained until these members are fitted (see Figures 40 and 41).*

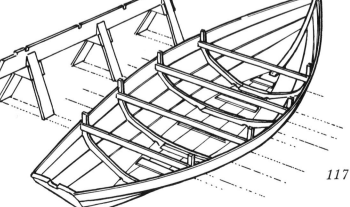

117

## STAGE 4: *Finishing the Interior, Painting, and Miscellaneous*

After the dory is planked, the rest is anticlimax and routine carpentry. There is little in finishing up the inside that requires special directions, or that cannot be determined without trouble from the drawings. Yet a few things should be mentioned in the way of special explanation. The different dories will show considerable variation in the dimensions of interior members, and the classic Bank interior is modified in various ways in Swampscott and Amesbury models for sailing and sport.

### Seat Risers

Seat risers, commonly pine, are quite thin, ½ to ⅝ inch generally, depending upon their width, just so they are strong enough to support the thwarts. Wider amidships, they taper toward their ends, mostly for appearance, but for lightness, too, as every bit of wood trimmed away helps. Risers, when laid out flat and before they are sprung into place against the frames, will show some curve. It is better to spile them from their frame locations and saw them to shape rather than to attempt to spring them edgewise into place. Also, before they go in, their top edges are generally beveled to conform to the under side of the thwarts.

### Thwarts

Removable thwarts, which made possible the "nesting" of Bank dories on the decks of fishing vessels, remain one of the dory's most distinctive features. Normally these are located so they brace against the frames. Lengths of stiff board, 8 to 10 inches wide, are notched at the ends for the frames, and are pushed down to rest in place on the riser. More rarely, thwarts are fastened in place permanently, and then mostly in Swampscott dories fitted for sailing. The thwart that holds the mast, in addition to being nailed or screwed to the riser, is usually braced against the sides with a pair of stout, sawn knees, well fastened through the plank and gunwales.

### End Decks

In some of the double-ended boats, like the Swampscott and Marblehead gunning and surf dories, there are seats in the ends supported by low bulkheads forming compartments, where foam flotation may now be stored. The tops or decks of these end seats should be snugly fitted and well screwed to the supporting cleats underneath, but at the same time be easily removable for painting and occasional checks for rot. The structure of these end seats must be contrived so as to prevent the holding or collection of rain water in any spot, for if this happens, sooner or later rot will surely start. It is better to provide limbers to drain off rain water from the ends than to depend upon perfect tightness in the decks. These low end decks are not only comfortable to sit on with good support for the back, but they form important bracing structures for the ends of the boat.

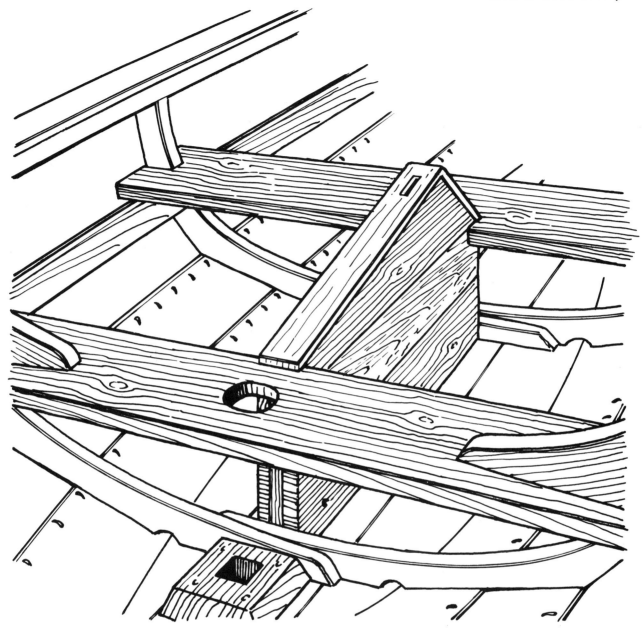

40. *The seat riser, thwarts, mast step, and centerboard case in a Swampscott dory.*

*Rot Spots*

At this point, a cautionary word is in order. While the dory is a simple, open structure, with fewer places to trap moisture than most boats have, nevertheless precautions against rot-producing dampness should be taken. Wherever wood comes together, it is possible, with poorly fitting joints or because of inadequate provision for drainage, for moisture to collect and eventually for rot to start. A potential trouble spot in the dory, besides the bow and the stern, could be under the gunwale cap; other spots are around the centerboard case and the mast step in sailing dories.

*Gunwales*

The solid gunwale standard on the Bank dory and the earlier Swampscotts was devised for thole pins. On more recent dories, the open gunwale has become common. The *open gunwale,* better suited for steam-bent ribs, is easier to put in and less likely to rot, but is not as stiff and bracing as the solid gunwale. In the Amesbury skiff, a famous adaptation of the smaller pulling dory, the gunwale is not an inwale but a substantial strip of oak bent around the outside of the sheer. This construction, which has much to commend it, I have adopted for the batten-seam gunning dory.

If thole pins are to be used, or if maximum stiffness and strength in the topsides are required, as when the boat is to be sailed hard, the solid gunwale is the better choice. The solid gunwale is built up of two parts, the inwale strip and the cap (see Figure 41). The former, running the length of the boat, is oak the same thickness as the frame stock, or slightly thinner. In the center of the boat, the inwale strip will be the same width as the frame heads, which it covers, tapering toward the ends of the boat. Bent around inside the sheer plank, this strip rests on top of the frame heads, which are mortised up into it an eighth of an inch or so, not enough to weaken the strip, but enough to give a solid grip on the timberheads. The inwale is nailed into the timberheads.

The cap, of thinner oak, generally ½ or ⅝

inch, is sawn to the half-breadth shape of the boat from a crooked board, preferably, to avoid cross grain. It covers both the inwale strip and the edge of the sheer plank, being nailed solidly to both, and it extends from the midsection of the boat both ways somewhat beyond the first and last frames. The thole pin holes are bored through this cap and the inwale strip underneath. From the ends of the cap, a narrower strip runs to the stem and the stern. This strip is beveled to shed water and for appearance. It covers the edge of the sheer plank as well as the joint between this plank and the inwale. It must be tight, well fastened, and sealed with paint to keep out the rain water.

On the outside of the sheer, the Bank dory requires no trim. Swampscott dories, however, usually carry a slight half round or half oval, planed to a taper at the ends, to dress them off. At the stem, the tapered ends of the inwales run to a small oak breasthook of the same thickness, which miters over them on a 45-degree cut. At the stern, the inwales run to the tombstone to land in notches let in to the tombstone cleat. No great strain comes on the ends at either bow or stern. Of course, the inwale is well nailed to the sheer plank throughout its length, which is especially necessary if the sheer plank is spliced, as it generally is in Swampscott dories. In the event of an open gunwale, as likely to be called for in Swampscott dories with intermediate bent frames, the gunwales or inwales are notched into the sawn frames and are fastened through these, and through the bent timbers, with copper rivets, which go through the sheer plank as well.

Some of the larger sailing and power dories are decked in, or partly decked, but here general boatbuilding practice applies. There is nothing distinctly dory about such work, and nothing further need be said about it here. It is the same for engine beds, shaft logs, rudders, and the like. All of this is either common boatbuilding procedure, or involves specialized detail amply covered in the various plans.

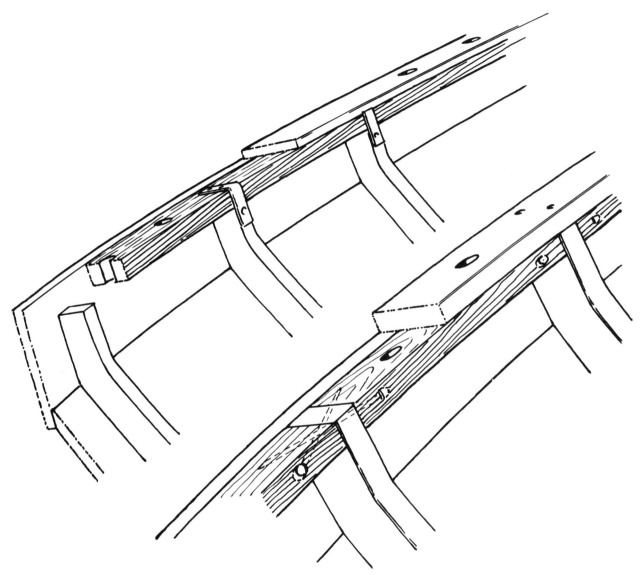

**41. Gunwale systems.** *(Top) A continuous gunwale log with a pieced cap and metal clips tying into the frameheads. (Bottom) A continuous cap of a heavier scantling with logs between the frameheads. This is very strong.*

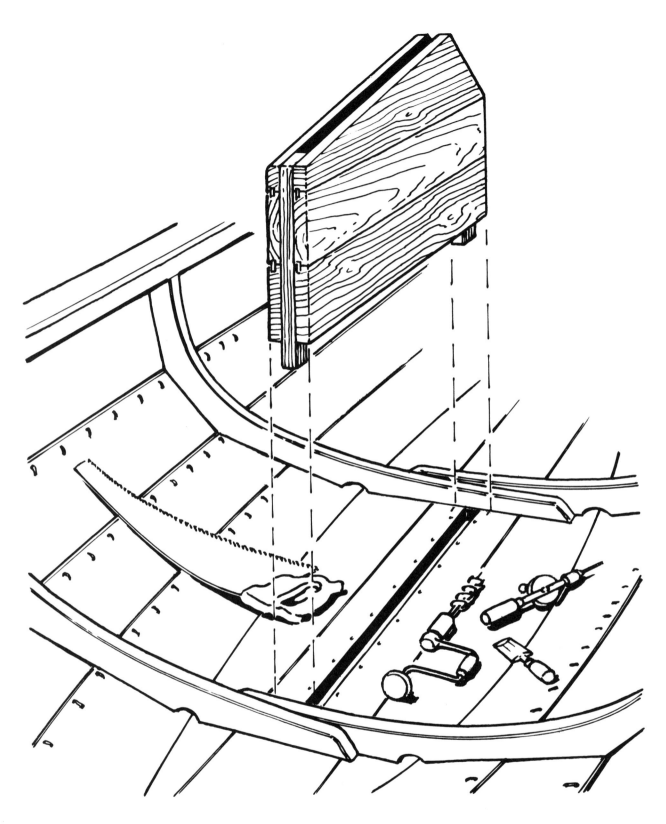

**42. Building the centerboard case.** *Join the side panels together. Glue and splines are sufficient.*

*Fasten the side panels to the oak posts, allowing sufficient length for the posts to pass through the dory's bottom. Fasten with screws or rivets.*

*Cut the centerboard slot through the boat's bottom, making sure it is parallel to the centerline. The slot width should permit a close slip-fit of the posts.*

*Insert the case and scribe it down to a tight match of the bottom along its length. Bed the case in a rubber seam compound.*

*Fasten upward through the bottom with long nails or screws. Through-bolted bed logs should be used in a big dory. The posts should be trimmed off slightly less than flush with the outside of the bottom.*

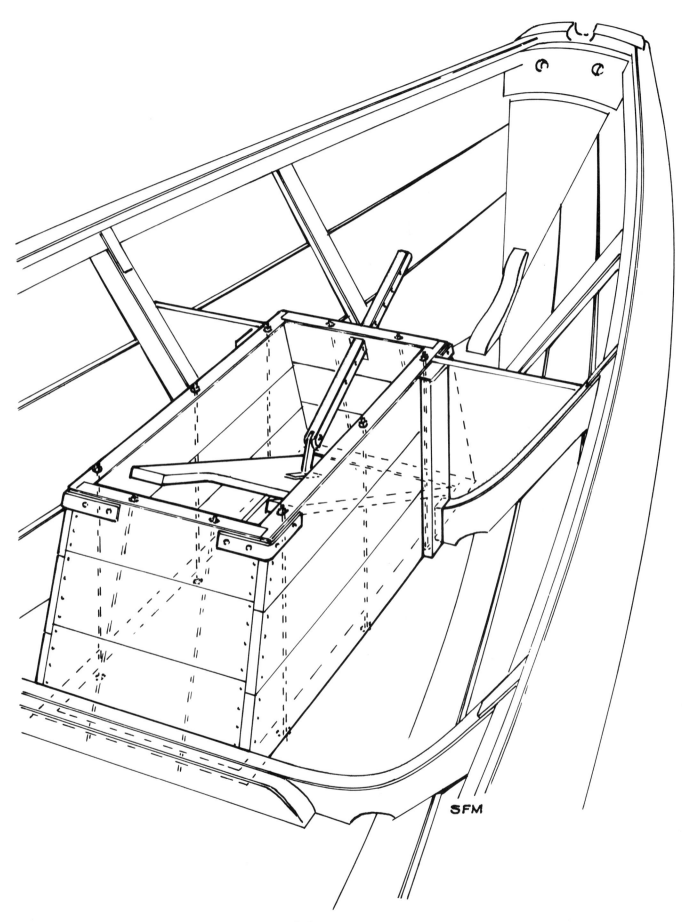

*43. A successful well for outboard power in a Bank dory.*

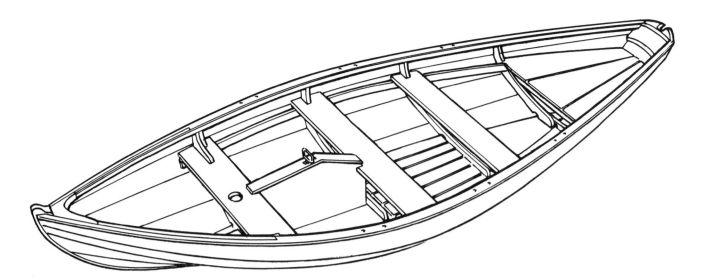

44. *The finished 17-foot Swampscott dory.*

45. *The nearly completed Bank dory.*

# 6 NEW MATERIALS

We have seen how materials to a large extent created the dory; how the dory took shape in direct conformance with the bending characteristics of wide pine boards; and how dory lines were in part determined by the manner in which materials at hand were best combined to get a good, low-cost, sea boat.

This was the way the dory evolved. But now what happens if we take away the wide, white-pine, clinker planks and the nail fastenings of galvanized iron? Is much of anything of the dory left? The question is not academic.

Various new building materials are now available, and these, when applied to dory design, make possible new and different methods of construction. Are craft of dory form, so produced, really dories? What difference does the material make to their being dories if they behave in the water as well or better than dories built in the old way, if they wear well, if they can take the abuse of rocky beaches, and, finally, if they are comparatively easy and inexpensive to build?

Sentiment must not stand in the way of utility and progress. Materials now familiar were once new and radical. There was a time when plentiful cheap boards of mill-sawn pine and machine-made nails were a novelty. These materials, producing the dories that we now know, displaced from common use the older types of workboat, including the Colonial wherry.

Once again new materials appear. Whether revolutionary changes in dory design will result from their use is not yet apparent. However, some of the new materials are already being used with satisfactory results that promise even more far-reaching innovations in the future. And the new materials are being forced upon home-workshop builders, because wide, pine lumber is scarce and expensive, and galvanized-iron boat nails are no longer obtainable. Fortunately, the new materials in most cases are not difficult to use. In some cases, they make the building operation easier than it was formerly.

## Metals, Molded Plastics

The fabrication of dories from aluminum or molded plastics is a factory proposition at the present time, feasible in mass production, but not for the backyard builder interested in producing a single boat. If the home-workshop builder is to make use of the new materials to best advantage, especially the expanding diversity of plastic products, including hull coatings, adhesives, elastic sealants, foams, and all the rest, he must be able to do so without the aid of elaborate molds, jigs, or other expensive equipment. Nor can he afford to buy in large quantity, or experiment widely in order to choose the product best suited for his special purpose.

The requirements of the home-workshop are

quite different from those of industry. The needs of the backyard builder demand packaging in small lots, pre-tested and reliable standards of quality, full information both as to advantages and disadvantages, and clear directions for use. The fact that purveyors of the new products frequently fail to meet these requirements, either in part or in full, partly explains why the application of the newer products in small craft design has lagged behind their potential, to the loss of all concerned.

## Plywood

Plywood is not exactly a new material. Yet, as far as dories are concerned, it is new, or comparatively so. Indeed, many conservative dory builders still despise plywood and refuse to have anything to do with it as planking. This is unfortunate, for plywood, properly used, is excellent for dories. In addition, it is one of the best values available today in boat materials. Plywood is obtainable everywhere, and it is easy to use.

Plywood is not likely to be improved. It is quite a wonderful material as it is, despite its disadvantages. By judicious use of the developing plastic coatings, adhesives, sealants, foams, and the like, most of plywood's weaknesses can be avoided or overcome, while its positive features are frequently enhanced.

The advantages of plywood (and Douglas Fir plywood in particular, for dory construction) include its great strength in combination with relatively light weight, its non-checking, non-splitting quality, the fact that it does not swell or shrink in width, and its high resistance to rot. Plywood is easy to work, is abundant and widely distributed, and is inexpensive compared to other boatbuilding materials. Unfortunately the quality of some of the plywood now produced leaves something to be desired. Care must be taken in its selection for boatwork.

Where boat curves are simple and one-directional, as in the sides of a Bank dory, plywood may be applied directly in panels. Where twisting curves are encountered, as in the sides of the round-sided dories, plywood, in strips, may be handled like ordinary plank. In terms of cost, availability, and versatility of fabrication, plywood remains tops on the list of new

materials available to dory builders in the home workshop.

Superior grades of exterior (waterproof) plywood are manufactured especially for boatbuilding purposes. Different manufacturers designate this special grade with various names, for instance "Armorbond," "Marine," and "Boathull." The latter is the designation used by member mills of the Douglas Fir Plywood Association to indicate a premium grade of exterior plywood suitable for the most exacting marine use. The inner plies of this grade, with respect to core gaps, solid veneer, and the like, are better than those of industrial, exterior-type plywood. However, there is no difference in glue, as all exterior grades have the same waterproof glueline.

Anyone who intends to use plywood for small boat construction will do well to inform himself thoroughly about plywood specifications, select his wood with care, and demand a product that conforms to standards. The requirements for small-boat construction are fairly critical, especially as dimensions must be kept down to save weight, but without sacrifice of strength.

There is an important reason why five-ply plywood is to be preferred over that of three plies for planking and other boat parts subject to immersion and soaking. That is because in the five-ply product, there is less wood in the thinner veneers to swell and shrink as the moisture content varies, hence less strain on the glueline. In the five-ply, a greater proportion of the wood is glue impregnated, reducing swelling and shrinking stresses still more.

Plywood is made with the grain of its composite veneers crossing at right angles to the recurrent stresses set up by expansion and contraction. Thus, the wood, as it gets wet and dries out, is always pulling at the glueline. Modern waterproof glues have tremendous holding power, but good boatbuilding practice calls for all possible measures to mitigate the strains to which the glueline of plywood will be subjected. One of these is to coat the surface of the wood with paint and special sealers to prevent it from soaking up water too fast or drying out too quickly. It is the powerful stress set up by abrupt change in moisture content that does the worst damage.

Because the edges of the plywood, by their exposure of endgrain wood, take up, or give off, moisture most rapidly, they are the most vulnerable part of the plywood and need special protection. On the edges, the veneers first separate or are split apart by accidental blows, abrasion, or other mechanical injury. Thus, the edges of plywood must always be sealed and hardened, or covered.

Plywood's comparatively thin surface veneer needs protection from abrasion. This last requirement is frequently met by fiberglassing the outside of the boat. A full covering of fiberglass has its drawbacks, however. Glass fabric is heavy, and the polyester resins still largely used with fiberglass in this country are brittle when fully cured and inferior in adhesion. A relatively recent fabric of Dynel modacrylic fiber is a good substitute for the glass cloth, when used as a surface covering for plywoods. It has nearly the same tensile strength but much greater resistance to abrasion than glass fabric, and it is easier to work with. The Dynel fabric for marine use is of loose weave and very elastic, so that it may be stretched tightly, without pulls or wrinkles, over any shape of hull and may be stapled in place before the liquid resin is brushed on and through the fabric in a single application. One advantage of Dynel/epoxy sheathing is the high resistance of Dynel to abrasion.

Special epoxy formulations are now obtainable which penetrate dry wood to some depth, hardening and sealing it against moisture. Such epoxy sealants give good result when applied alone to plywood without reinforcement with glass or synthetic fabrics. They must be painted, however, for protection against the degrading effects of sunlight, to which they are susceptible.

*As Panel or Plank*

The simplest and most obvious application of plywood is for side panels in the Bank dory and in other straight-sided dory types, where the entire side may be comprised of a single continuous panel bent in the fore-and-aft direction only. If standard sheets are not long enough, it is easy to splice them with plastic adhesives. A resorcinol resin glue, of which several well-known brands are sold for boat work, would be excellent. But some of the epoxy adhesives are even better, being just as strong or stronger than the resorcinol glues. With the epoxy adhesives, joint fit is not so critical, nor is pressure required in gluing.

Plywood can also be cut up into strips and handled exactly like ordinary clinker plank. Strong glue-splicing of plywood strakes is a simple operation. Long, crooked planks are easily and economically pieced together in this way from a number of short lengths. If one of the new flexible plastic caulking compounds or sealants is used between the laps, there is scarcely any need for metal lap fastenings, except to hold the laps together until the adhesive compound has set up. Not only do these compounds cement the lap surfaces together with a tough, flexible, completely waterproof bond, but also they permanently seal the otherwise exposed edges of the plywood strakes.

### Conventional Seam-batten Construction

In building the round-sided or Swampscott dory types, the apprentice builder frequently finds that beveling and fitting the laps is the operation that gives him the most trouble. Perfect bevels are not required if a plastic sealant is used to cement them. But the entire beveling and fitting operation can be bypassed if, instead of the usual clinker construction, the planks are butted on seam battens, glued with epoxy adhesive, and bound and reinforced on the outside of the seams with tapes of glass or polypropylene fabric set in epoxy resin, or in some instances the tapes may be omitted.

Such construction not only is light and exceptionally strong, but also is easy to build. This seam-batten method offers much to home-workshop builders. It brings within the range of ordinary capability a whole series of fine clinker craft that formerly might have been considered too difficult for the inexperienced amateur to attempt.

Actually, seam-batten construction for dories is not new. In about 1883, Higgins and Gifford, the Gloucester boatbuilding firm famous for their mackerel seine boats, patented an improved Bank dory planked on seam-battens. Fishing dories in those days took rough treatment on the Banks. Each season, many were smashed or quickly became too leaky for use. The seam-batten dory was devised to provide a stronger, tougher boat, but one that still could be put together cheaply enough to compete with the ordinary fishing dories mass-produced at Amesbury.

Seam-batten planking has had many successful applications. Chris-Craft has long used seam-batten planking to obtain lightness and flexibility in their large power hulls. More than twenty years ago, Walter J. McInnis, the well-known Boston naval architect and designer of power craft, got up a small, ultra-light double-ender as a cartop boat for sportsmen. Planked with ³⁄₁₆-inch plywood, with glued seam-battens as the sole internal framing, this round-bilged, multi-chine double-ender of modified dory lines was 14 feet long but weighed only 63 pounds, as originally put up by an Amesbury concern.

For its size, the McInnis boat weighed very little, yet if the designer had had at his disposal the plastic products now available, he might have made a still lighter boat; or, without subtracting from the weight, a stronger one, although all indications are that the original boat was quite strong enough for its purpose.

## Glued Seam-batten Construction

It is obvious that even with the lightest and strongest materials, appreciable increase in structural strength must almost certainly be paid for by some addition in weight. My 18-foot gunning dory, as described and detailed elsewhere, is designed for ¼-inch fir plywood plank, butted on epoxy-glued seam-battens. This is an example of a comparatively lightweight boat that could be built considerably lighter except that great structural ruggedness is required. Notwithstanding, this seam-batten boat, as built by Veli Holmstrom of Vinalhaven, Maine, for James S. Rockefeller, Jr., of Camden, Maine, weighed nearly one-third, or approximately 100 pounds, less than would a hull of the same lines built according to standard dory construction. This seam-batten dory is undoubtedly structurally stronger than a conventional dory, although controlled tests have not been made. However, I experimented with much the same sort of glued-batten reinforcement for plywood plank in building a light pram. The results have shown exceptional sturdiness combined with lightness for such construction and more than confirmed my first expectations.

The McInnis multi-chine double-ender depended upon its longitudinal seam-battens alone for internal framing. Apparently, the boats built at Amesbury were assembled and planked on a master form that held in place the chine strips, which served as seam battens until the ³⁄₁₆-inch plywood planking was hung and fastened, and until the hull shape was thus permanently established.

In the Rockefeller gunning dory, on the other hand, sectional frames of the usual sort, made of epoxy-glued, laminated spruce for lightness, served as building molds and were permanently retained in the boat. These frames were notched at the chine knuckles to receive the seam-battens, which were fastened in with screws. The result is an exceptionally stout frame grid that is easy to fair and to cover with plywood planks. This is the simpler, easier way of building a single boat, although the master form method is better for mass production. The sectional frames, serving as molds and normally retained in the structure for extra support, could be removed from the hull after the completion of planking to save weight, but rarely would the small saving so achieved warrant the considerable loss of structural strength.

Variations in handling seam-batten construction and in adapting it to the different dory types may sometimes be necessary or otherwise desirable. For example, some builders, in butting the plywood strakes on the seam-battens, will strive for such a precise fit that the epoxy adhesive used against the seam-batten will suffice for the edges of the plywood as well. Others may not trouble to make such a close fit, so that the butting edges of the plywood may not come together by as much as ⅛ inch or even ³⁄₁₆ inch. In that case, the gap may be filled with a plastic sealant. Filling with sealant will insure perfect watertightness, give flexibility and shock resistance to the hull, and add strength to the structure because of the sealant's adhesive power. In most cases, additional reinforcement and protection should be provided at the seam knuckles by binding them with a tape of glass fiber or polypropylene fabric anchored with epoxy resin.

This glued seam-batten method of planking with plywood is, of course, only one of many possible ways of utilizing the newer materials, especially the plastics. But the method deserves our special consideration here, for it is particularly suited to round-sided, knuckled dories as an easy substitute for traditional clinker planking. Generally, the batten-seam method will prove easier for the inexperienced builder, making it possible for him to undertake successfully dories like the Beachcomber and the gunning dory, which otherwise he might not dare tackle.

More than that, as will bear repeating, seam-batten construction produces a lighter and even stronger hull than does conventional construction, and one that in most cases will be cheaper rather than more expensive to build. Every round-sided dory of the Swampscott type shown in this book can be built to advantage by the glued seam-batten method, with no changes required in the lines and laydown, whether or not this is specifically indicated in the plans. In most such instances, it will be desirable to make the sectional frames lighter and to put in more of them closer together, following the example of the gunning dory.

## Plastics

Developments are coming so fast in the plastics field that some of these recommendations could be obsolete before they are printed. Enormous improvements in adhesives have been made in recent years, and greater gains are sure to come. But the perfect glue or glues for small craft needs have not yet been found. Some of the new epoxy formulations are far ahead of anything else to date in the marine field, especially in their ability to make strong joints by simple contact, without pressure from clamps. This is an advantage of tremendous importance in splicing plywood planking, to mention only one example.

In spite of advantages, unfortunately, the application of epoxy adhesives is restricted by their still narrowly limited temperature range, and the special problems attending their use in boatyards in winter.

### Fiberglass

All reinforced plastics in boatbuilding parlance are called "fiberglass." This is because the fabric reinforcement for thermosetting resins, and still by far the most widely used, was originally woven from glass fibers. The bonding resins originally used with glass fabrics, and still used for the greater part in "fiberglassing," are polyesters. But neither glass fabrics nor most of the polyesters are best suited for composite wood-plastic construction of small craft.

### Cloth

Today, glass reinforcement is far too heavy. It is not elastic enough, is too brittle, and, in combination with bonding resins, does not adhere as tenaciously to wood surfaces as some other materials. Besides, it has irritating "fly" — a term meaning that the tiny particles of glass broken off in sanding and like operations cause serious itching.

Likewise the polyester resins in common use are not elastic enough for best results with wood. Furthermore, they do not bond reliably to oak and some other woods, and are generally inferior to the epoxy resins in adherence to wood surfaces.

Fabrics woven from various synthetic fibers have been tried for thermoplastic reinforcement. These include nylon, Dacron, Dynel, and polypropylene. The first two of these we need not consider here.

For a time Dynel looked most promising, and probably is the best reinforcement for covering plywood decks because of its superior resistance to abrasion. But unfortunately, Dynel tends to be "notch sensitive." Cracks starting in the bonding resin are transmitted quickly through the fibers of the Dynel reinforcement, which offers little resistance to this type of failure. Thus, while a Dynel surface on plywood is superior, Dynel makes a very poor covering for planking that is going to "come and go" a lot, as the moisture of the wood varies, and Dynel's bad characteristic of "notch sensitivity" is greatly accentuated when it is used in combination with a brittle polyester resin. So far, the best fabric reinforcement available for composite wood-plastic construction is that woven from polypropylene multi-filament fibers. Polypropylene is an extremely versatile polymer or plastic synthesized from the hydrocarbon propylene, a cheap and abundant gaseous by-product of the gasoline cracking process.

### Polyester Resin

When fiberglass first flashed upon the boating scene, its silent partner was a thermoplastic polyester resin, rather rigid and brittle and not especially adhesive. This same sort of resin is still sold across the counter to the majority of uninformed boatowners today. Coverings of such resin in combination with glass, which is a relatively rigid and inelastic material itself, tend quickly and readily to work loose or crack if there is any movement of the wood beneath from the working of the structure in a seaway, or from swelling and shrinking following changes in the moisture content of the wood. Often cracks would be small but sufficient to admit and trap rain water, starting and forcing rot, which the fiberglass covering had been intended to prevent.

Why, with such grievous results manifest on every side, the practice of fiberglassing with rigid, brittle polyester resin has continued to grow is an unexplained mystery, especially as there is a wide range of polyester resins to choose from, including some that are quite tough and elastic and much more adhesive than the sort offered to the retail trade, even now. When the right materials are used, properly designed coverings of reinforced plastic can add greatly to the strength, durability, and even appearance, sometimes, of wooden construction. If a tough, adhesive, impact-resistant, polyester resin is not easily available to the builder of a small boat in retail quantity, it will pay him to use a suitable epoxy, although the latter may be priced somewhat higher, may be somewhat harder to apply, and may create a slight risk of skin irritation.

## Epoxy Resin

The most promising of the boatbuilding glues to date is epoxy resin. It gives an extremely strong and tenacious bond, yet one that can be made tough and flexible, if desired. When set, joints are colorless and completely waterproof. In fact the hardened resin is almost inert, being unaffected by oils or such acids and bases as are commonly found in boats. One great advantage is that pressure is not required in gluing, only firm opposition of joining surfaces. Precise fit or contact with the joint is not necessary. A film of resin between the joining surfaces makes the joint stronger, if anything. With epoxy, a wide range of splicing and laminating techniques that was not possible before has opened up for the small shop and the home-workshop builder.

Epoxy has drawbacks, however. It is a thermosetting resin, and most formulations will not set at temperatures lower than 60 degrees F. In some formulations, it sensitizes the skin of some people, especially if precautions are not taken. It is expensive in small quantities. It is marketed by many different concerns in a bewildering range of formulations, information about which is difficult to obtain outside of the industry.

By the end of World War II, epoxy resins were widely used in industry, more than ten years before boatbuilders heard about them. In fact the adhesive requirements of boatbuilders, in comparison with those of other users of epoxy resins, are so minor that there has not been much inducement for the plastics industry to consider boatbuilders' gluing needs. For example, the amount of epoxy resin now going into marine paint probably far exceeds any immediate potential demand for epoxy as an adhesive for building wooden boats.

## Conventional Adhesives

In the early 1940s resorcinol resin was introduced to American boatbuilders for waterproof gluing. Resorcinol resin is used for gluing marine plywood and large laminations, such as the laminated frames, stems, and keels specified at one time for non-magnetic minesweepers and other government craft. Heat and pressure are required for curing, and large pieces such as boat keels require special equipment and handling that only big industry can provide. Given optimum conditions of heat and pressure, special glue formulations for maximum strength and durability can be employed.

Less critical formulations of resorcinol resin are widely distributed for general boatbuilding use; these consist of two-part systems of liquid resin and powdered catalyst in separate cans to be mixed just prior to application. Excellent waterproof joints can be made with such glue, but some warmth and considerable clamping pressure are required, as well as a precise fit in the joining pieces of wood. A disadvantage of such glue in some cases is its brownish-purple stain. Although not equal to epoxy for some things, and not as versatile or as easy to use, resorcinol is still an excellent glue for many boatbuilding purposes.

Urea formaldehyde resin glue, on the other hand, which is sold in the form of a brownish powder to be mixed with water to the consistency of cream or thicker before using, is now obsolete as a boatbuilding glue. It is not waterproof, only water resistant, and is quite brittle besides, especially if the joint does not fit perfectly. It also stains somewhat. A limited use for interior joiner work might still be justified, possibly.

### Sealants

One of the newer adhesives is a caulking compound composed of epoxy resins and a synthetic rubber, more precisely, Thiokol's polysulfide polymer. This product is highly elastic, as well as tough, and is designed for joints where the natural expansion and contraction of the wood causes movement between adjoining members. Aside from filling seams, it would appear excellent for such purposes as bedding interior chine strips, the fayed surfaces of stem pieces, and the like. There are several places in dory construction where an elastic adhesive might be used to advantage.

As for Thiokol compounds for gluing wood, as a possible substitute for epoxy adhesives, I have not seen any yet that I should care to depend upon, that is, as a primary adhesive for wood. Highly penetrating formulations of epoxy resin have recently become available which sink in deeply when applied to dry wood, sealing it against moisture, hardening it, and stabilizing it dimensionally. Such sealants can be applied to plywood before it is put into the boat, for example to plywood strakes for a clinker dory hull, after they have been cut to shape and beveled.

### Plastics and the Oil Paints

The new plastic products and oil-based paints and preservatives may be combined on the same boat for maximum protection, but only if proper sequence is observed in applying them. Epoxy resins in paints, sealants, and adhesives are entirely unaffected by oil once they are fully cured, but these resins will not adhere to wood previously oiled, or to an oily surface of any sort. If a boat like the gunning dory is to have polypropylene tapes covering the planking seams, or is to be completely reinforced by an outside skin of Dynel fabric anchored in epoxy resin, these plastics should be fully cured before the inside of the boat is treated against rot and painted.

For the inside of the boat, it is recommended that the ¼-inch fir plywood first be soaked with a thin, liquid preservative of copper salts dissolved in a naptha vehicle. This is to be followed by a thorough soaking of dilute linseed oil, heated in a double-boiler, for maximum penetration. After the oil has thoroughly dried, the inside can be given a thin coat of pigmented paint.

### Foam Flotation

The inclusion of plastic foam for flotation is an indispensable safety measure for all pleasure dories. One way to install foam, and the way most commonly used so far, is to saw up pieces of slab foam to fit under seats, decks, coamings, and other out-of-the-way places. Surprisingly, little bulk of foam is required to provide adequate supplementary flotation for the ordinary dory. Another way is to pour in the liquid foam compounded on the job from a two- or three-part mixing system. The reacting foam swells to fill completely the spaces or compartments prepared to hold it. It becomes rigid and strong as it cures, and it develops tenacious adherence to the surfaces that enclose it. Some foams can also be sprayed on and will cling to overhead surfaces without sagging.

One danger to avoid in using foams that are flowed or frothed into place is the possible formation of moisture traps in inaccessible places where rot in the wooden part of the structure would be apt to start.

Plastics have already made a secure beginning. What the end will be is hard to guess. During and since Colonial times, American small craft, and dories in particular, have undergone a continual, diverse, and sometimes very rapid evolution. In that still-dynamic process, the advent of new materials and new processes based on these new materials are playing a large part. Considerations of economic need and utility have prevailed. It is normal and fitting that the new materials of our day, especially the new plastics, should find increasing application in small craft construction and design.

The amateur dory builder can make a valuable contribution with regard to new materials. He can try things that boat manufacturers wouldn't dare or couldn't afford to try. He has time to experiment, and if he has the inclination, he can do much to advance small-craft knowledge and design.

# PART THREE

# DORY PLANS

# 7 THE 32-FOOT MAINE RIVER-DRIVING BATTEAU

The Maine log-driving batteau, as perfected on the Penobscot River one hundred years ago, represents the ultimate refinement of the river-type dory. She is a boat for rapids and white water as well as for shallow, rocky, crooked streams. In basic form, the Maine river-driving batteau probably cannot be improved, although her construction can be appreciably lightened and strengthened by the use of modern materials.

Everything distinctive about the river-driving batteau was determined by the conditions of her use. She had to be light to be carried. In order to twist and turn among the boulders, the boat needed to be fast and maneuverable, hence the short bottom. The great bow rolled back the river in the boiling pitches; the long rake of the stem allowed the boat to slide over obstructions. The generous overall length of the boat contributed to stability. The extreme flare of the sides permitted the carrying of heavy loads in very little depth of water. Altogether, the Maine river-driving batteau is a daring watercraft, a combination of extremes that functioned brilliantly under the conditions for which the boat was developed.

So far as I know, no attempt has been made to power a river-driving batteau with an outboard motor in a well, but such an arrangement might be entirely feasible. If the well were properly designed and constructed so that the bottom could be closed tightly when the motor was removed, the batteau need not be spoiled for white-water use.

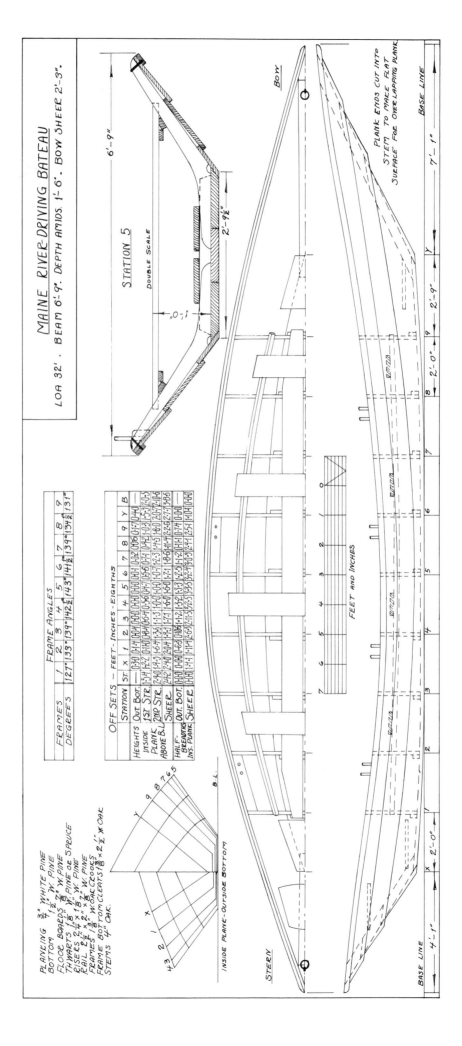

# MAINE RIVER-DRIVING BATEAU

## LOA 32'. BEAM 6'-9". DEPTH AMIDS. 1'-6". BOW SHEER 2'-3".

STATION 5

DOUBLE SCALE

6'-9"

2'-9½"

1'-0"

PLANKING ¾" WHITE PINE
BOTTOM 1½" W. PINE
FLOOR BOARDS ⅝" W. PINE
THWARTS 1⅛" W. PINE OR SPRUCE
RISERS 2¼" × 1⅛" W. PINE
RAIL 2½" × 2" W. PINE
FRAMES 1⅜" × 2" W. OAK
FRAME BOTTOM CLEATS 1⅜ × 2½" W. OAK
STEMS 4" OAK.

INSIDE PLANK - OUTSIDE BOTTOM

STERN

BOW

PLANK ENDS CUT INTO
STEM TO MAKE FLAT
SURFACE FOR OVER LAPPING PLANK

BASE LINE

7'-1"

2'-9"

2'-0"

BASE LINE

4'-1"

2'-0"

FEET AND INCHES

### FRAME ANGLES

| FRAMES | 1 | 2 | 3 | 4 | 5 | 6 | 7 | 8 | 9 |
|--------|---|---|---|---|---|---|---|---|---|
| DEGREES | 127° | 133° | 139° | 142½° | 143° | 144½° | 139° | 134½° | 131° |

### OFFSETS – FEET-INCHES-EIGHTHS

| | STATION ST. | X | 1 | 2 | 3 | 4 | 5 | 6 | 7 | 8 | 9 | Y | B |
|---|---|---|---|---|---|---|---|---|---|---|---|---|---|
| HEIGHTS ABOVE B.L. | OUT. BOT. | — | 0-3-0 | 0-1-4 | 0-0-4 | 0-3-0 | 0-3-0 | 0-3-0 | 0-4-1 | 0-3-2 | 0-0-6 | 0-1-7 | 0-4-0 |
| | INSIDE 1ST STR. | 1-5-4 | 1-2-2 | 0-1-0 | 0-8-4 | 0-6-4 | 0-5-6 | 0-4-7 | 0-5-6 | 0-7-1 | 0-4-2 | 1-0-3 | 1-5-3 | 2-0-5 |
| | PLANK 2ND STR. | 2-9-0 | 1-6-3 | 1-6-4 | 1-3-6 | 1-1-3 | 1-0-0 | 1-0-0 | 1-0-7 | 1-2-3 | 1-4-5 | 1-8-0 | 2-0-7 | 2-1-0-6 |
| | SHEER | 2-4-2 | 2-1-0 | 2-0-4 | 1-9-3 | 1-7-1 | 1-6-0 | 1-6-1 | 1-7-1 | 1-8-6 | 1-4-1 | 1-4-2-6 | 2-7-3 | 3-0-5 |
| HALF-BREADTHS | OUT. BOT. | 0-1-0 | 0-4-0 | 0-6-3 | 0-9-4 | 1-1-2 | 1-3-3 | 1-2-5 | 1-2-0 | 0-1-1 | 0-1-4 | 0-4-0 | | |
| | INS. PLANK SHEER | 0-8-0 | 1-4-1 | 1-1-4 | 2-6-3 | 2-1-5 | 3-2-5 | 3-3-5 | 3-2-4 | 3-0-3 | 2-4-1 | 2-5-1 | 1-4-0 | 0-4-0 |

# 8 THE 18-FOOT LIGHT BATTEAU

The Canadian batteau, which I have adapted from Adrian Neison's lines in his *Practical Boatbuilding for Amateurs*, which was published in 1901 and is out of print, is not intended particularly for white water, but more as a general hunting and fishing craft where a quick, easy-driving, shoal-draft boat is desired. This is a lightweight batteau, one which can be either paddled or rowed. She can take the place of a canoe for many purposes, and can do things that a canoe cannot do. She is more rugged than a canoe, and far easier and less expensive to build.

About the management of these light batteaux, Neison has this to say: "Small boats are usually propelled with a single-bladed paddle, and are exceedingly handy and manageable; larger boats are rowed and steered with a paddle, and under these conditions a Canadian boatman will run any rapid that it is possible for a canoe or boat to live through. As shooting boats they are exceedingly handy, as they are very steady, and draw little water, and in mud flats and marshes they may be wriggled over any ordinary banks with the help of a pole."

To compete with the canoe, this batteau is designed to be very light but amply strong. Finished weight should run between 90 and 100 pounds. Incidentally, I have not followed the considerably heavier construction shown in Neison's book, having taken advantage of modern materials that permit a much lighter craft than was formerly possible.

The sides and bottom of this boat are of ¼-inch fir plywood, ¼-inch being ample for the bottom the way it is reinforced and protected. The thwarts should be spruce for lightness combined with strength and stiffness. Everything else should be of oak for maximum strength. An alternative to oak, with a saving of weight, would be mahogany. For extreme lightness, you could use Sitka spruce, except for the three rubbing battens or "runners" on the bottom, which need to be extra tough and hard to stand abrasion. These fore-and-aft battens are also important structural members, being through-fastened into the bottom frames and thereby providing great additional strength and stiffness to the whole bottom.

Everywhere that wood lies against wood in the entire structure, there should be glue. I recommend a good grade of epoxy adhesive, of which there are many on the market. To seal the chine joint and to strengthen, stiffen, and reinforce the bottom, I have indicated a 4-inch band of epoxy and fiberglass to cover the chine knuckle. A much stouter job would be to fiberglass the entire bottom with epoxy resins and up two to three inches on the sides. This would add several pounds of weight, so if extreme lightness is desired, put on only the 4-inch band, as indicated. Under no circumstances leave off this band. Be sure the bonding resin is epoxy and not polyester, the more common and cheaper sort. I do not recommend polyester in this case.

Both ends of this boat are shown decked

over and sealed off with thin plywood bulkheads. The resulting compartments are packed with Styrofoam. This is very light stuff and adds little weight to the structure, but supplies great buoyancy high in the ends, where it will exercise a powerful self-righting action if ever the boat is capsized. This is the same principle that makes the self-righting surfboat come back right-side up. Besides, the end decks and bulkheads add greatly to the strength of the hull structure.

It is possible that light racks or floorboards will be desired. Such can easily be added. They are not shown in the interest of keeping down the total weight of the boat. Paddling in the ends may likely be done from the knees, in which case some sort of pad will be needed, possibly a cushion-type life preserver.

The 36-inch beam for this batteau is narrow for rowing, but no doubt the oars could be managed cross-handed as in the Adirondack guideboat. One reason why I favor an alternate 40-inch-wide model is its better width for rowing.

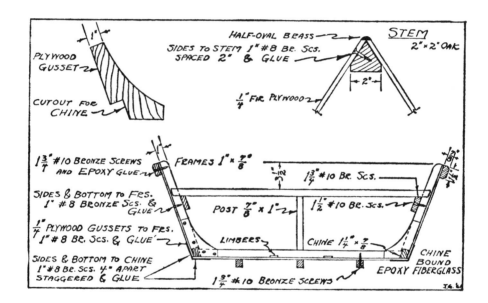

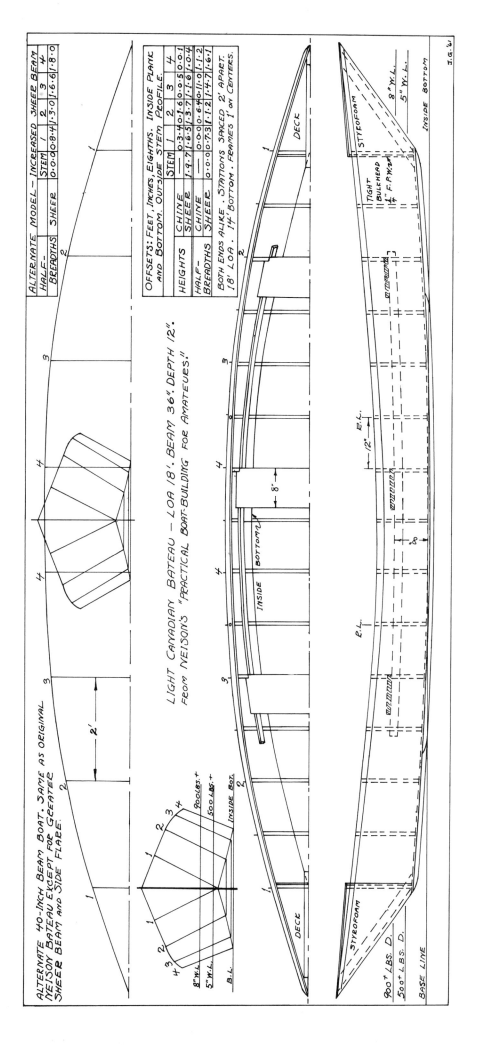

LIGHT CANADIAN BATEAU — LOA 18', BEAM 36", DEPTH 12".
FROM NEISON'S "PRACTICAL BOAT-BUILDING FOR AMATEURS."

ALTERNATE MODEL - INCREASED SHEER BEAM

| | | STEM | 1 | 2 | 3 | 4 |
|---|---|---|---|---|---|---|
| HALF-BREADTHS | SHEER | 0:0:0 | 0:8:4 | 1:3:0 | 1:6:6 | 1:8:0 |

OFFSETS: FEET, INCHES, EIGHTHS. INSIDE PLANK AND BOTTOM. OUTSIDE STEM PROFILE.

| | | STEM | 1 | 2 | 3 | 4 |
|---|---|---|---|---|---|---|
| HEIGHTS | CHINE | 0:3:4 | 0:1:6 | 0:0:5 | 0:0:1 | |
| | SHEER | 1:9:7 | 1:6:5 | 1:3:7 | 1:1:6 | 1:0:4 |
| HALF-BREADTHS | CHINE | | 0:0:0 | 0:6:4 | 0:11:0 | 1:1:2 |
| | SHEER | | 0:0:0 | 0:7:3 | 1:2:1 | 1:4:7 | 1:6:1 |

BOTH ENDS ALIKE. STATIONS SPACED 2' APART.
18' LOA. 14" BOTTOM. FRAMES 1" ON CENTERS.

ALTERNATE 40-INCH BEAM BOAT. SAME AS ORIGINAL NEISON BATEAU EXCEPT FOR GREATER SHEER BEAM AND SIDE FLARE.

2'

900 LBS.+
500 LBS.+
8" W.L.
5" W.L.
B.L.
INSIDE BOT.

DECK

INSIDE BOTTOM

8"
12"
8"

P.L.
P.L.

STYROFOAM
TIGHT BULKHEAD
1" F.P. N 2"
8" W.L.
5" W.L.
INSIDE BOTTOM

DECK
STYROFOAM
900+ LBS. D.
500+ LBS. D.
BASE LINE

J.G. '61

# 9 THE 19-FOOT HEAVY BATTEAU

This 19-footer is a larger, heavier, more able boat than the 18-foot Canadian batteau. She is suitable for larger lakes and rivers, and is not intended to be carried. She could easily be enlarged, if a bigger boat were needed, so long as the proportions were not too radically changed, though some increases in scantling would be required to take the additional strains. In case enlargement is contemplated, it is suggested that reference be made to the detailed drawing of the 32-foot Maine river-driving batteau.

This 19-foot batteau may be set up, framed, and planked lengthwise according to Bank dory procedure. Or the setup may be inverted and the boat framed for ⅜-inch plywood side planking, as shown here, and given ¾-inch pine cross planking on the bottom. Although not "dory" construction, the cross-planked method would eliminate the need for frames across the bottom and provide a surface stout enough to withstand the abrasion of down-river use. End decks are important for structural stiffness in this boat; they should not be omitted.

My draft of the 19-foot batteau shows an inner strip or keelson reinforcing the cross-planked bottom. In no case should this member be left out if the bottom is cross-planked, and also it should be securely nailed to each board. Cross-planking is an easy and economical method of building the bottom and is just as good as any other, especially if the bottom is to be covered with a reinforcement of epoxy-bonded fiberglass. The main disadvantage of cross-planking is that if the individual boards are put on too wide they tend to warp and "dish," making the finished bottom rough, uneven, and full of ridges. If too narrow, the cross planks are not stiff enough. Hence, they should not be over six inches wide, nor under four.

The method that I have shown as suitable for the 19-footer's lines follows rather closely the standard shape and scantlings found in the classic river-driving batteaux. All, that is, except the fiberglass reinforcement for the bottom, which is new.

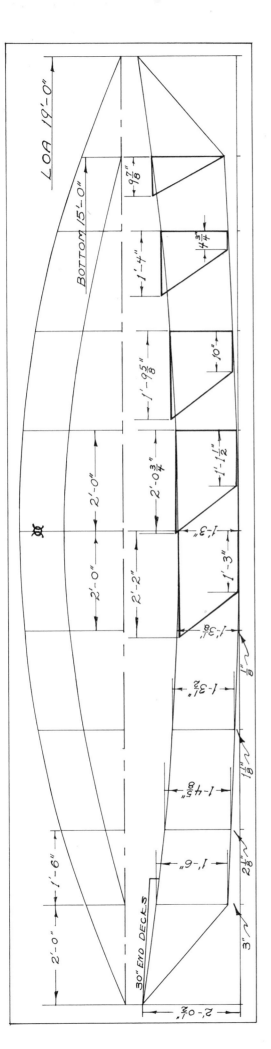

LOA 19'-0"

Bottom 15'-0"

9 7/8"

1'-4"

4 3/4"

1'-9 5/8"

10"

2'-0 3/4"

1'-1 1/2"

2'-2"

1'-3"

2'-0"

2'-0"

1'-3 1/8"

1'-3 1/8"

1'-3 1/2"

1/8"

1'-4 5/8"

2 1/8"

2'-0"

1'-6"

1'-6"

3"

2'-0 1/2"

30" END DECKS

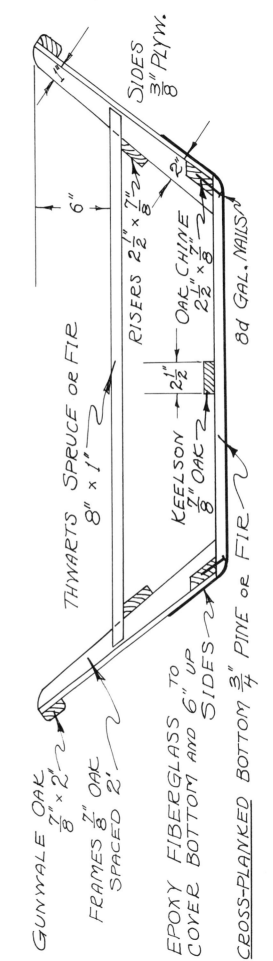

## MIDSECTION 19' LOA BATEAU

THWARTS SPRUCE or FIR
8" × 1"

SIDES
3/8" PLYW.

6"

RISERS 2 1/2" × 7/8"

OAK CHINE
2 1/2" × 7/8"

KEELSON
7/8" OAK

2 1/2"

8d GAL. NAILS

GUNWALE OAK
7/8" × 2"

FRAMES 7/8" OAK
SPACED 2'

EPOXY FIBERGLASS TO
COVER BOTTOM AND 6" UP
SIDES

CROSS-PLANKED BOTTOM 3/4" PINE or FIR

# 10  THE BANK DORIES

Bank dories were traditionally laid out according to the length of the bottom. The builder's principal mold—the halfbreadth shape of the bottom, gotten out of a single pine board and kept on a rack in the shop—governed everything.

The two dories detailed here are dories with 12- and 15-foot bottoms respectively. The 12-footer is about as small as is generally useful and safe, yet is not too large to be handled easily by a single oarsman. The 15-footer can be rowed by one man, but it takes two good oarsmen to handle her in rough water. There are dories that measure 16 feet on the bottom, and larger, but one with a 15-foot bottom is about as large as most people would want. It would be quite easy, however, to make this 15-footer (19 feet 5 inches long overall) a few feet longer. Both the 12- and the 15-foot models should be laid out according to the standard Bank dory procedure detailed in Part II of this book, and constructed right-side-up.

The lines and specifications for the 12-footer were worked out carefully by me from study and comparison of numerous dories for an article on the dory published in *Yachting* in March, 1954.

The plans for the 15-footer are those of a dory designed and built during World War II by Hiram Lowell & Sons, the famous Amesbury, Massachusetts, dory builders, for the U.S. Coast Guard. For all-around general use, it is probably the best Bank dory model ever worked out. It is less heavy and clumsy than some of the old fishing models, which were generally made very deep to carry enormous loads of fish. Such deep models in a light condition are cranky and hard to handle. In making this dory shallower, it was possible to give the sides greater flare, all in all resulting in a boat much better suited for general use.

It is instructive to compare the principal dimensions of this 19-foot 5-inch LOA Coast Guard dory with those of a 20-foot 0-inch LOA Gloucester fisherman's dory measured in 1917 by G.B. Douglas and described in *Rudder* that year.

Length on top: C. G., 19'5"; Douglas, 20'0". Length on bottom: C.G., 15'0"; Douglas, 16'5". Width, bottom: C. G., 2'10"; Douglas, 3'2". Extreme beam: C. G., 5'7"; Douglas, 5'7½". Depth amidships: C.G., 1'9½"; Douglas, 1'11". Height of bow above baseline: C.G., 3'0½"; Douglas, 3'0". Height of transom above baseline: C.G., 2'11"; Douglas, 3'1". Rocker of bottom at bow: C.G., 0'½"; Douglas, 0'2½", Rocker of bottom at stern: C.G., 0'2"; Douglas, 0'3½".

While the difference in overall length is only seven inches, the old fishing dory is 17 inches longer on the bottom. Thus, the entrance of the Coast Guard boat is more sloping and easier. The extreme beam of both boats is the same within one-half inch, yet the Coast Guard boat is four inches narrower on the bottom, giving more side flare. It is also 1½ inches shoaler. Altogether, the Coast Guard dory is a sharper, slimmer boat in the water. Yet it is rather surprising how closely similar these two sets of dimensions are, considering the interval between their development of approximately 30 years. This Coast Guard dory is no doubt basically the same boat as the dory built by Hiram Lowell & Sons for the USS *Mitscher*, and for which Commander (now Rear Admiral) Sheldon H. Kinney, U.S. Navy, is reported to have had such high praise in the *Maine Coast Fisherman* for May, 1957: "After giving it exacting tests," Commander Kinney reported, "the dory provides a rescue boat that can be lowered and recovered by a man-o-war in seas that make it impossible to lower the standard motor whaleboat." He also reported the dory was extremely popular with the *Mitscher*'s crew. "It is never idle when in port," he said "with the men waiting to use it for fishing, swimming, skin diving, or just plain rowing."

*A Bank dory used for inshore lobster fishing. (Photo by Edward D. Hipple)*

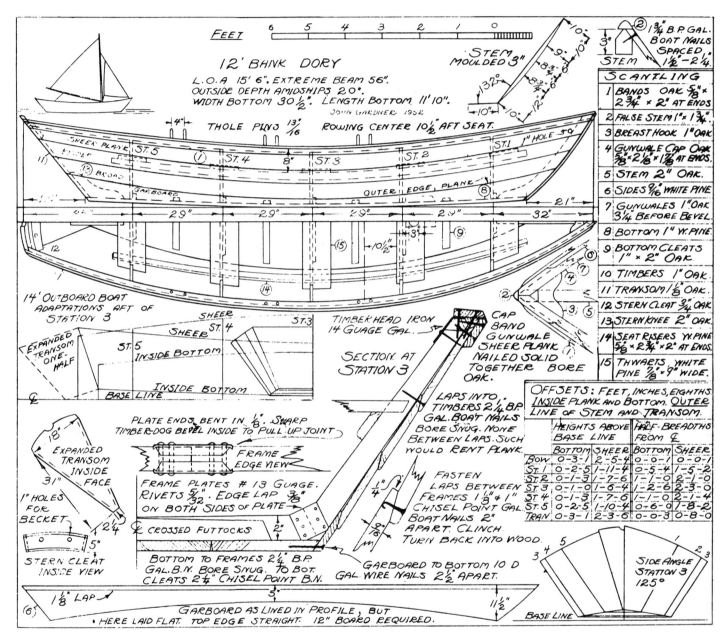

A 12-foot Bank dory.

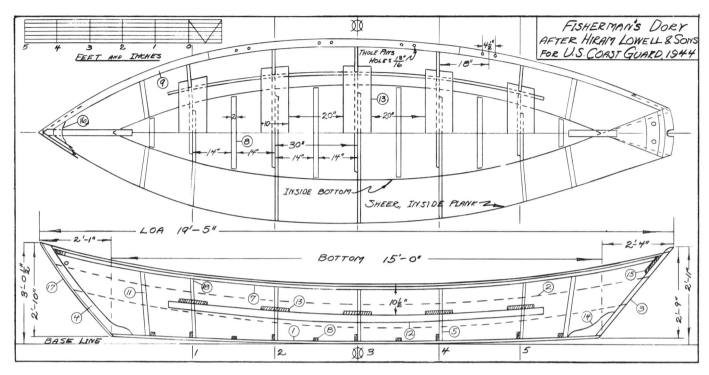

*The Lowell-Coast Guard 15-foot fisherman's dory. The lines and specifications for this boat are on the next page.*

*A Lowell-Coast Guard 15-foot fisherman's dory ready for delivery.*

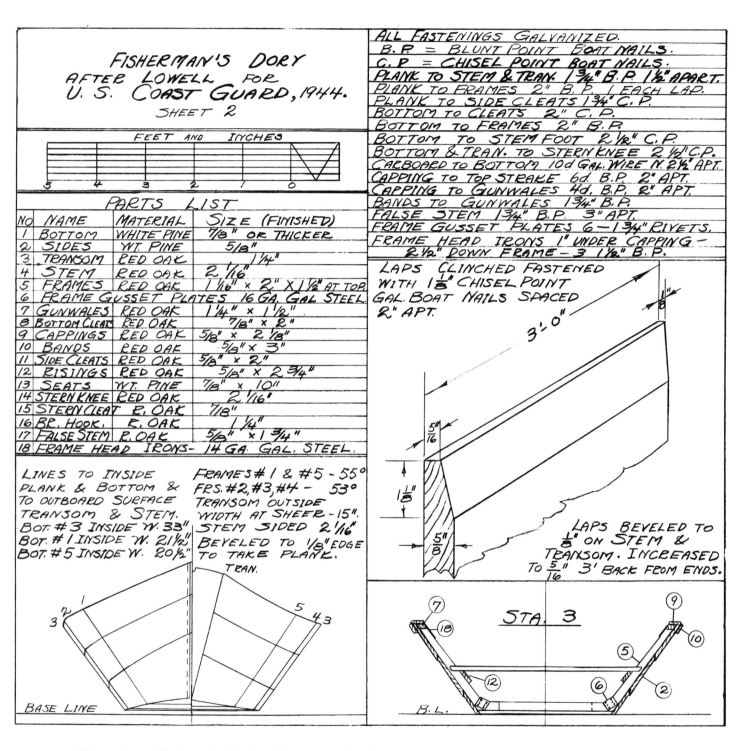

FISHERMAN'S DORY
AFTER LOWELL FOR
U. S. COAST GUARD, 1944.
SHEET 2

FEET AND INCHES

PARTS LIST

| NO | NAME | MATERIAL | SIZE (FINISHED) |
|----|------|----------|-----------------|
| 1 | BOTTOM | WHITE PINE | 7/8" OR THICKER |
| 2 | SIDES | WT. PINE | 5/8" |
| 3 | TRANSOM | RED OAK | 1 1/4" |
| 4 | STEM | RED OAK | 2 1/16" |
| 5 | FRAMES | RED OAK | 1 1/16" × 2" × 1 1/2" AT TOP |
| 6 | FRAME GUSSET PLATES | 16 GA. GAL. STEEL | |
| 7 | GUNWALES | RED OAK | 1 1/4" × 1 1/2" |
| 8 | BOTTOM CLEATS | RED OAK | 7/8" × 2" |
| 9 | CAPPINGS | RED OAK | 5/8" × 2 1/8" |
| 10 | BANDS | RED OAK | 5/8" × 3" |
| 11 | SIDE CLEATS | RED OAK | 5/8" × 2" |
| 12 | RISINGS | RED OAK | 5/8" × 2 3/4" |
| 13 | SEATS | WT. PINE | 7/8" × 10" |
| 14 | STERN KNEE | RED OAK | 2 1/16" |
| 15 | STERN CLEAT | R. OAK | 7/8" |
| 16 | BR. HOOK | R. OAK | 1 1/4" |
| 17 | FALSE STEM | R. OAK | 5/8" × 1 3/4" |
| 18 | FRAME HEAD IRONS | 14 GA. GAL. STEEL | |

ALL FASTENINGS GALVANIZED.
B. P. = BLUNT POINT BOAT NAILS.
C. P. = CHISEL POINT BOAT NAILS.
PLANK TO STEM & TRAN. 1 3/4" B.P. 1 1/2" APART.
PLANK TO FRAMES 2" B.P. 1 EACH LAP.
PLANK TO SIDE CLEATS 1 3/4" C.P.
BOTTOM TO CLEATS 2" C.P.
BOTTOM TO FRAMES 2" B.P.
BOTTOM TO STEM FOOT 2 1/2" C.P.
BOTTOM & TRAN. TO STERN KNEE 2 1/2" C.P.
CARBOARD TO BOTTOM 10d GAL. WIRE N. 2 1/2" APT.
CAPPING TO TOP STRAKE 6d B.P. 2" APT.
CAPPING TO GUNWALES 4d B.P. 2" APT.
BANDS TO GUNWALES 1 3/4" B.P.
FALSE STEM 1 3/4" B.P. 3" APT.
FRAME GUSSET PLATES 6 — 1 3/4" RIVETS.
FRAME HEAD IRONS 1" UNDER CAPPING —
   2 1/2" DOWN FRAME — 3 1/2" B.P.

LAPS CLINCHED FASTENED
WITH 1 1/8" CHISEL POINT
GAL. BOAT NAILS SPACED
2" APT.

3'-0"

5/16"

1 1/8"

1/8"

5/8"

LAPS BEVELED TO
1/8" ON STEM &
TRANSOM. INCREASED
TO 5/16" 3' BACK FROM ENDS.

LINES TO INSIDE
PLANK & BOTTOM &
TO OUTBOARD SURFACE
TRANSOM & STEM.
BOT. #3 INSIDE W. 33"
BOT. #1 INSIDE W. 21 1/2"
BOT. #5 INSIDE W. 20 1/2"

FRAMES #1 & #5 - 55°
FRS. #2, #3, #4 - 53°
TRANSOM OUTSIDE
WIDTH AT SHEER - 15".
STEM SIDED 2 1/16"
BEVELED TO 1/8" EDGE
TO TAKE PLANK.

BASE LINE

STA. 3

B. L.

*Lines and specifications for the Lowell-Coast Guard 15-foot fisherman's dory. The numbers in the parts list correspond to those in the drawing on page 145.*

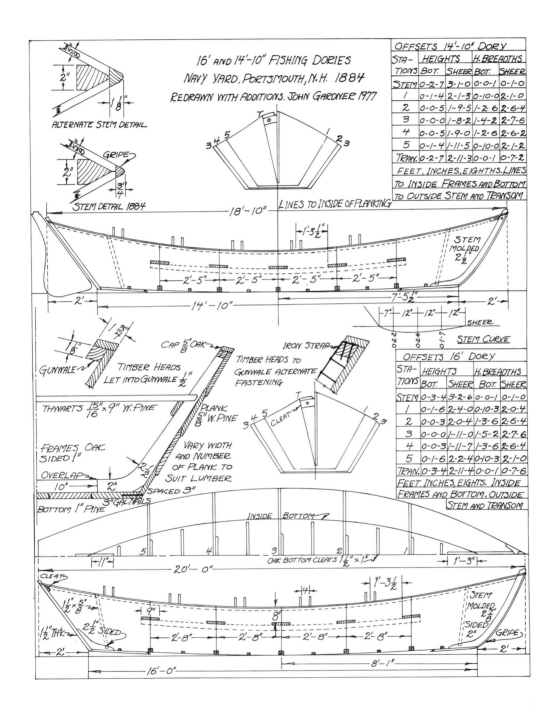

**16' AND 14'-10" FISHING DORIES**
**NAVY YARD, PORTSMOUTH, N.H. 1884**
**REDRAWN WITH ADDITIONS. JOHN GARDNER 1977**

ALTERNATE STEM DETAIL

GRIPE

STEM DETAIL 1884

LINES TO INSIDE OF PLANKING

18'-10"

14'-10"

STEM MOLDED 2¼"

7'-5½"

SHEER
STEM CURVE

GUNWALE

CAP ⅝" OAK
TIMBER HEADS LET INTO GUNWALE ½"

IRON STRAP
TIMBER HEADS TO GUNWALE ALTERNATE FASTENING

CLEAT

THWARTS 15/16" × 9" W. PINE

PLANK ⅝" W. PINE

FRAMES OAK SIDED 1"

VARY WIDTH AND NUMBER OF PLANK TO SUIT LUMBER

OVERLAP 10"   2"   SPACED 3"

3" GAL. NAILS

BOTTOM 1" PINE

INSIDE BOTTOM

OAK BOTTOM CLEATS 1½" × 1"

20'-0"

16'-0"

8'-1"

STEM MOLDED 2⅜" SIDED 2"   GRIPE

CLEAT 1½" × ⅝"
1½" THK   2½" SIDED

| OFFSETS 14'-10" DORY | | | | |
|---|---|---|---|---|
| STA-TIONS | HEIGHTS | | H. BREADTHS | |
| | BOT. | SHEER | BOT. | SHEER |
| STEM | 0-2-7 | 3-1-0 | 0-0-1 | 0-1-0 |
| 1 | 0-1-4 | 2-1-3 | 0-10-0 | 2-1-0 |
| 2 | 0-0-5 | 1-9-5 | 1-2-6 | 2-6-4 |
| 3 | 0-0-0 | 1-8-2 | 1-4-2 | 2-7-6 |
| 4 | 0-0-5 | 1-9-0 | 1-2-6 | 2-6-2 |
| 5 | 0-1-4 | 1-11-5 | 0-10-0 | 2-1-2 |
| TRAN. | 0-2-7 | 2-11-3 | 0-0-1 | 0-7-2 |

FEET, INCHES, EIGHTHS. LINES TO INSIDE FRAMES AND BOTTOM TO OUTSIDE STEM AND TRANSOM

| OFFSETS 16' DORY | | | | |
|---|---|---|---|---|
| STA-TIONS | HEIGHTS | | H. BREADTHS | |
| | BOT. | SHEER | BOT. | SHEER |
| STEM | 0-3-4 | 3-2-6 | 0-0-1 | 0-1-0 |
| 1 | 0-1-6 | 2-4-0 | 0-10-3 | 2-0-4 |
| 2 | 0-0-3 | 2-0-4 | 1-3-6 | 2-6-4 |
| 3 | 0-0-0 | 1-11-0 | 1-5-2 | 2-7-6 |
| 4 | 0-0-3 | 1-11-7 | 1-3-6 | 2-6-4 |
| 5 | 0-1-6 | 2-2-4 | 0-10-3 | 2-1-0 |
| TRAN. | 0-3-4 | 2-11-4 | 0-0-1 | 0-7-6 |

FEET, INCHES, EIGHTS. INSIDE FRAMES AND BOTTOM. OUTSIDE STEM AND TRANSOM

*Lines and offsets for a 14' 10" dory and a 16' dory, redrawn from the original draft done at the Portsmouth Navy Yard in 1884.*

147

# 11   THE ST. PIERRE WORKING DORY

Of the dories offered to amateur builders in the pages of the *National Fisherman*, the so-called French dory has been the most widely built. The French dory is a displacement-type workboat designed to carry heavy loads of fish and gear well offshore in all seasons and in most weather. Its hull is that of an overgrown Bank dory, with lofty bow and lofty stern resulting from accentuated sheer and rocker. The French dory, when converted to pleasure use, has been constructed for inboard power, outboard power (in a well), and sail. Sailing rigs for a French dory are not offered here.

In North America, the French dory has been employed in the sea fisheries surrounding the French colonies of St. Pierre and Miquelon, small islands in the treacherous Cabot Strait off the southern shore of Newfoundland. Locally she is known as "la grande doris de St. Pierre et Miquelon." These big dories are open boats, motor powered with low-speed, make-and-break engines. Their propeller shafts are retractable into the hull to permit the boats to be hauled ashore at night. Hundreds of these big dories have been employed in the St. Pierre fisheries since they were first introduced by the French government in the early 1930s. As a sea boat, in a region known for storm, ice, and shipwreck, the French dory has earned a remarkable record: there is no remembered instance of a "grande doris" being lost, or of any

fisherman being drowned from one. On several occasions these big dories have served as rescue boats, taking seamen from wrecks difficult to reach with ordinary lifeboats.

The standard St. Pierre dory is an open boat laid out for two fishermen, one working aft, the other forward. The sides are braced with thwarts, and the ends are partly decked. The exposed and rocky beaches force the fishermen to haul out their boats after each day's fishing. Each fisherman has his own greased plank ways and a simple winch or capstan turned by hand spikes to bring up his boat. In doing this, it is necessary that the propeller and shaft be pulled up out of the way and clear of the bottom. The rectractile feature of the propeller and shaft in combination with the flat dory bottom make this an ideal craft for shoal water and beaching.

One factor in the excellent roughwater performance of the grande doris is her large size. Mostly it is that huge, towering bow and the sharp fore sections that split the seas, which the flaring sides roll down, at the same time lifting the hull over and through. Perfect balance is achieved with an afterbody nearly identical in shape and displacement to the fore body. In a word, the boat is virtually a double-ender.

The high, narrow wedge of the tombstone transom is, of course, ideal in following seas.

*Fishing dories as used by the fisherman of St. Pierre et Miquelon. (Photos by Jean-Briand Ozon)*

The length of the boat is a factor for stability, permitting a beam of eight feet without making the hull stubby.

In short, the proportions of this hull combine to give an exceptional sea boat, as long years of successful fishing experience in all sorts of weather have demonstrated. This is a rough-water boat, not a speedboat.

## Comments on Design

The lines of la grande doris given here are those of the standard French fishing dory as taken from a blueprint prepared for the French fisheries by a government architect.

In the French islands the boats are roughly built with Canadian spruce for the bottom and side planking. Frequently, the strakes are of an uneven width, just as the boards come. Likewise the rub strips around the sheer, in place of gunwales, are sometimes nothing but saplings with the bark and occasional twigs left on. While these fishing boats are strong and solid enough, they are crude. We shall try for something more finished.

But before getting to the actual building, a few general observations remain for consideration. First, this dory is purely a *displacement* type. The hull will not plane, nor is it capable of speed. Thus, it is of no special importance for the hull to be lightly constructed, as it would be if it were a speedboat.

As most boats now are designed for speed, it has become second nature for designers and builders to lighten construction to the utmost, shaving scantlings to the minimum and cutting down safety margins as well. But some weight in the lower hull structure is advantageous in this dory, and its generous scantlings make the fits less critical and the fastening easier and more secure. Its comparatively heavy bottom gives a stouter, steadier boat, one that can stand beaching. Besides, this extra weight is easily handled by the powerful, slow-turning, make-and-break gas engine.

The deck and superstructure, if employed, should be kept as light as possible. The original working dory was an open boat and added top hamper must be offset by added weight or ballast below. To help in keeping top hamper to a minimum, spruce is specified for deck beams and thin plywood for decks and trunk.

For a proper job, the lines of this boat must be laid down full-size and faired carefully.

## Bottom Assembly

The bottom of the original St. Pierre dory is unusually heavy, being put together from plank of Canadian spruce about 1⅜ inches thick. In most cases, the great amount of rocker in the bottom would make it difficult for an amateur to spring a bottom of such thickness to the correct curve, especially if oak is used for the bottom plank instead of spruce. Extra thick bottom plank could be steamed and clamped over a form to allow the correct shape to set. If there are overhead beams stout enough, the bottom could be forced down to shape by heavy shores. In the Chesapeake, sometimes, rocker is put into a heavy bottom by suspending it on two stout horses, and throwing a ton or so of rocks on the unsupported middle part. An inventive mechanic could no doubt devise other ways, and possibly easier ones.

In the case of this dory, however, I especially recommend that the bottom be made out of two layers of ⅞-inch oak. If the inner bottom were a plump inch and the outer only ¾ inch, it might be even better. In the first place, the two layers will be fairly easy to bend separately. The outer bottom need not be put on until after the boat is planked. For a boat that is going to be grounded out on beaches, an easily replaceable outer bottom is highly desirable. The extra thickness, aggregating 1¾ inch, is also an advantage in this big dory.

As there are no separate bottom cleats to put on first to hold the bottom together, the bottom futtocks of the frames themselves will have to serve to cleat the bottom boards together. The side futtocks of the frames will not be riveted on until after the bottom assembly is sprung over the horses and secured in position.

In this boat the frames set plumb; so, because of the great camber of the bottom, it will be necessary to bevel the under surface of the bottom futtocks to allow the frames to set upright after the rocker is sprung.

Note should be taken that these bottom members of the frames are double the thickness of the side futtocks. The wide, heavy bottom of this big dory requires extra reinforcement, and the extra weight here does no harm. Besides, these thicker cross members provide better fastening. The entire structure of this boat depends on a solid bottom.

The lengthwise planks or boards that comprise the bottom taper to points as the

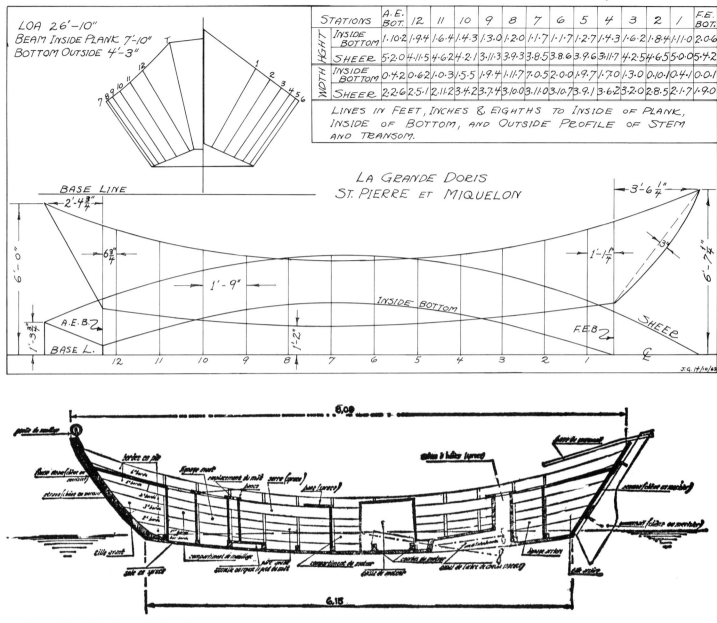

LOA 26'-10"
BEAM INSIDE PLANK 7'-10"
BOTTOM OUTSIDE 4'-3"

| STATIONS | A.E. BOT. | 12 | 11 | 10 | 9 | 8 | 7 | 6 | 5 | 4 | 3 | 2 | 1 | F.E. BOT. |
|---|---|---|---|---|---|---|---|---|---|---|---|---|---|---|
| HGHT — INSIDE BOTTOM | 1.10.2 | 1.9.4 | 1.6.4 | 1.4.3 | 1.3.0 | 1.2.0 | 1.1.7 | 1.1.7 | 1.2.7 | 1.4.3 | 1.6.2 | 1.8.4 | 1.11.0 | 2.0.6 |
| HGHT — SHEER | 5.2.0 | 4.11.5 | 4.6.2 | 4.2.1 | 3.11.3 | 3.9.3 | 3.8.5 | 3.8.6 | 3.9.6 | 3.11.7 | 4.2.5 | 4.6.5 | 5.0.0 | 5.4.2 |
| WDTH — INSIDE BOTTOM | 0.4.2 | 0.6.2 | 1.0.3 | 1.5.5 | 1.9.4 | 1.11.7 | 7.0.5 | 2.0.0 | 1.9.7 | 1.7.0 | 1.3.0 | 0.10.1 | 0.4.1 | 0.0.1 |
| WDTH — SHEER | 2.2.6 | 2.5.1 | 2.11.2 | 3.4.2 | 3.7.4 | 3.10.0 | 3.11.0 | 3.10.7 | 3.9.1 | 3.6.2 | 3.2.0 | 2.8.5 | 2.1.7 | 1.9.0 |

LINES IN FEET, INCHES & EIGHTHS TO INSIDE OF PLANK, INSIDE OF BOTTOM, AND OUTSIDE PROFILE OF STEM AND TRANSOM.

LA GRANDE DORIS
ST. PIERRE ET MIQUELON

The original St. Pierre fishing dory.

bottom narrows toward its ends. If the width of the bottom boards permits, it is a good plan to locate the ends so that their points fall on cross futtocks for support and fastening. The exceptional curve of the bottom puts quite a strain on these ends. However, in the complete boat, they will be supported by the backing cleats for the garboard if the frame futtocks don't catch them. In that case, a few temporary cleats may be needed until the permanent backing cleats are fitted and fastened.

## Bottom Outside the Garboards

Ordinarily in dory construction, the lower edge of the garboard covers the outer edge of the bottom and is nailed into it. In the St. Pierre dory, the garboards rest on top of the bottom.

The top, or inside must be beveled square with the rake of the sides to allow a square edge for the garboard—needed for a good caulking seam. In the original French dories, in the

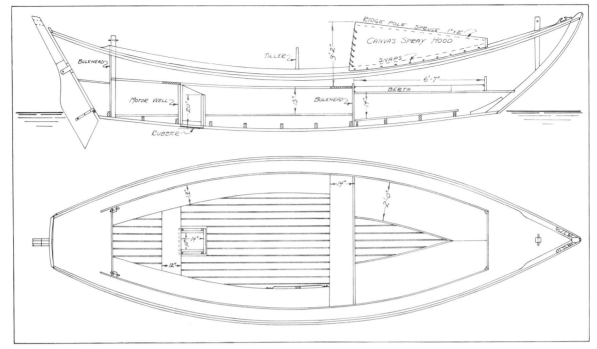

Above: The St. Pierre dory with an outboard motor well and spray hood.
Opposite page: The bottom construction of a St. Pierre dory using a box for a haul-up propeller arrangement.

spaces between the frames, nails were driven up through the bottom into the lower edge of the garboard to secure it. As the garboards are only ¾ inch thick, they are hard to nail accurately, and any accidental splits here could be critical.

A better way to support and to secure the bottom edge of the garboard is to fill in between the frames with backing cleats of ⅞-inch, or better, 1-inch oak, forming what amounts to a solid back rabbet, but with enough space at the ends of the separate cleats to provide free passage of water through the frame limbers. These cleats are easily fitted after the garboard is on. They are fastened securely into the bottom, and the garboards, in turn, are fastened into them. This makes a very solid job, and the extra weight is of no account.

### Stern and Knee

At the bow, the stem log, roughly pre-beveled, is fastened on to the bottom by bolting through a knee. The stem needs no partic-

ular comment. Because of the knee at the bottom end, not usually seen in dories, the stem can be cut out of a fairly narrow plank. If the ⅜-inch bolts through the knee seem on the small side, slightly larger ones are easily substituted. It is best, perhaps, not to try to cut the finished bevel at the bench, but to cut only an approximation, finishing the bevel after the stem is bolted on and the boat is set up and being faired for planking.

### Transom or Tombstone

The transom or tombstone, as it is often called, is pre-beveled as closely as possible from the full-size laydown of the lines, or from the scale half-model that I especially recommend all first-time amateurs make before they start the full-size job.

In this dory, and in the widened model especially, the transom is a substantial structure and must be planned for strength. I have suggested that the transom be made up of eight-inch-wide oak planks 1½ inches thick, running the long way of the transom. For the

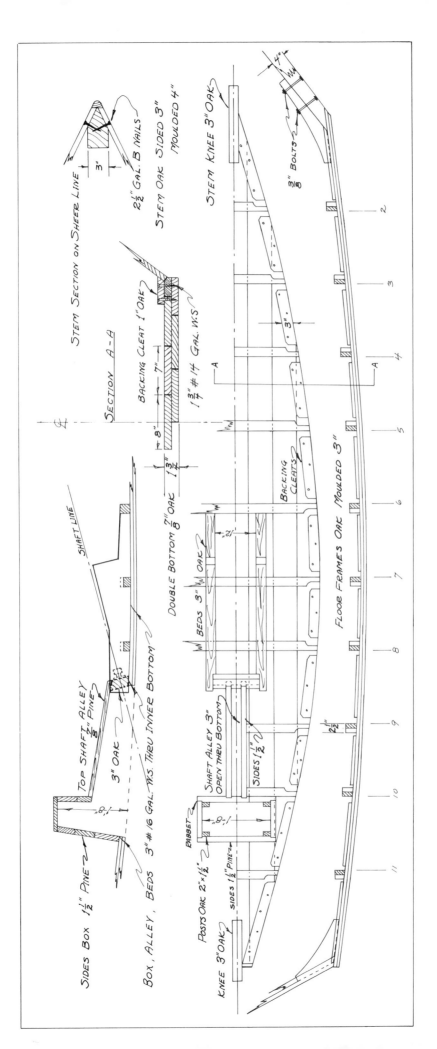

STEM SECTION ON SHEER LINE

2½" GAL. B NAILS

STEM OAK SIDED 3"
MOULDED 4"

STEM KNEE 3" OAK

3" BOLTS

SECTION A-A

BACKING CLEAT 1" OAK

1¾" #14 GAL. W.S.

DOUBLE BOTTOM ⅞" OAK

BACKING CLEATS

BEDS 3" OAK

FLOOR FRAMES OAK MOULDED 3"

SHAFT LINE

TOP SHAFT ALLEY ⅞" PINE

3" OAK

3" #16 GAL. W.S. THRU INNER BOTTOM

SIDES BOX 1½" PINE

BOX, ALLEY, BEDS

SHAFT ALLEY 3"
OPEN THRU BOTTOM

SIDES 1½"

RABBET

POSTS OAK 2"×1½"

SIDES 1½" PINE

KNEE 3" OAK

wide model, five planks will be required. This calls for solid framing to cleat them firmly together. Both cross cleats and lengthwise cleats of the same 1¼-inch oak stock are shown.

The two side cleats, running between the top and bottom cross cleats on either edge, project sufficiently to be beveled to support the side plank. The additional nailing surface and support that they provide is important. Also they are needed to support the shim ends of the outside planks.

The bottom cross-cleat gives extra support for nailing the bottom, and the stern knee is notched to fit over it. The top cross cleat also serves as a deck beam.

The transom may be fastened together with 2¼-inch No. 16 galvanized screws or with galvanized boat nails. In case the latter are used, they should be long enough to clinch over on the inside. Expansion of the transom, to obtain its true shape from the plans, will be explained further along.

### Frame Futtocks and Gussets

Now the side futtocks of the frames are put on with plates or clips of heavy galvanized iron that join with the bottom futtocks, being securely riveted through the ends of both. Enough of the outer corner of the knuckle is cut off to provide a good limber. The spread of the sides is checked for the correct flare, and temporary cross spalls are nailed on to hold the shape until the boat is planked.

The body sections in the lines indicate the frames, 12 in number. This is a greater number than is usual in most boats of the dory type. But this large boat, developed for the hardest kind of use, requires extra reinforcement. On the closely placed oak frames, sided 1¼ inches, is fastened ¾-inch lapped spruce planking in the original St. Pierre dory, making an extremely strong combination.

### Sheer Ribband

An oak ribband ⅞ inch thick and 2 inches wide is let into a notch, flush with the outside of the frames at the sheer, continuous from end to end of the boat. It may be pieced where necessary with butt blocks. This is an added member, not to be found in the original working dories, which are open boats. It is needed in our modified version, however, to provide reinforcement and fastening for the edges of the plywood deck and waterways. It also serves as a sort of binding strake to fair up the frames and to hold them in position for planking. The sheer ribband takes the place of a clamp and greatly stiffens and strengthens the boat.

### Selecting Plank

For the St. Pierre dory, six strakes of plank to the side are usual. This requires plank widths of seven and eight inches on the boat. In my opinion, this is rather wide, and seven strakes would be better.

In a 27-foot boat it will not be possible to have the planks run unbroken the full length, nor would it be desirable even if boards sufficiently long could be found. To make the strakes in unbroken lengths would mean much waste of lumber and weak cross grain where the planks are crooked. Better to make the strakes of two or three pieces, so long as the butts are well distributed and staggered, and not concentrated in the middle of the hull. In a lapstrake boat the lap fastenings take much of the strain off the butts.

The St. Pierre dory uses butt blocks of the usual sort. For a neat, light job, but a more than amply strong one, too, I recommend that the planks be spliced with glued scarphs. For glue, an epoxy adhesive is best as it does not require pressure to make a strong joint as is the case with most glues.

The St. Pierre hull is easy and economical to plank, as the strakes line out quite straight for the greater part. The side flare combines with the rocker and the sheer curve to give plank lines with very easy sweeps; some planks are practically straight.

### Garboards

In the St. Pierre dory, the fish-tailed shape of the garboard is less extreme than in some Bank dories. In lining the garboards for this dory, it is recommended that they be made quite narrow in the middle (between 4 inches

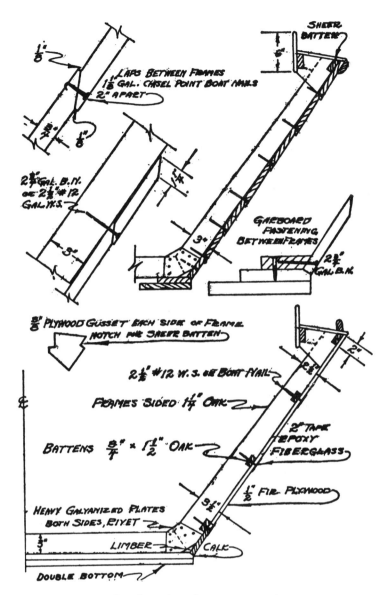

*St. Pierre dory frame construction.*

and 5 inches wide, including the lap) so that the ends will not be excessively wide. Thus, extra-wide boards will not be required, and there is less danger of splits or rents developing in the ends.

In this dory, because of its extreme sheer, the side width at the ends is slightly greater than the side width amidships. This means that one or more of the boards (planks next above the garboards) will also have to be fish-tailed to fill up the extra width, so that the top strakes may taper slightly narrower toward the ends for appearance.

## Lap Bevels

In a straight-sided dory like this one, the lap bevels are all uniform. About a foot or so from the ends, the bevels start to plane down gradually to a sharp, or feather, edge so that the ends of the laps will lie flush with each other on the fayed surfaces of the stem and transom. Planking bevels for the slightly rounded side of our modified model do not change enough to matter. In this boat, beveling the laps is easy and should not give the slightest trouble.

*Left: A St. Pierre dory built by Howard B. McClellan in Okinawa in 1964. She has sides built with two layers of plywood bonded together with resorcinal glue and reinforced with screws.*

*Below: A St. Pierre dory built by the Bluenose Boatyard in Chester, Nova Scotia.*

*Right: A St. Pierre built by John W. Friend in Dartmouth, Massachusetts.*

156

*A St. Pierre built in Seward, Alaska. (Photo by Dave Thompson)*

### Plank Stock

My first choice for planking lumber would be sap-free Northern white pine. Rift-sawn Douglas fir would be good, but heavier. Maine cedar with plenty of small, sound knots for toughness would also be good, but Western and Virginia cedar are too soft. Cedar can be disadvantageous because it soaks water.

Cypress and Philippine mahogany could also be used, but experience has taught me to distrust the lasting quality of the latter. Plywood may also be used as material for planking in the conventional clinker manner, and it will be economical to use in spliced-up fashion. Ten-foot panels would be good, giving three pieces and two splices to the strake. I recommend ⅝-inch exterior fir, although ½-inch could be used.

### Carvel Seam-Batten Construction

A more radical use of plywood, but one that has much to commend it, would be a carvel seam-batten construction utilizing ½-inch five-

ply exterior fir. Three battens are set into the side frames in addition to the sheer batten already specified. These seam battens of oak, ¾ inch by 1½ inches are jogged into the frames flush, and in consequence the molded depth of the frames would need to be increased slightly to make up for the notch.

The lowest of the three battens should be located quite close to the bottom to catch the upper edge of the narrow garboard of natural lumber. This garboard strip could be as narrow as 3 inches, and can be edge-set to make it come tightly against the bottom. It should be of ¾-inch lumber, planed after it is in place on the boat to make its top edge conform to the thickness of the ½-inch plywood above it.

Between this lowest batten and the sheer batten, the side space is divided approximately equally, and the two intermediate battens are lined in fair sweeps from stem to stern. The plywood strips that cover the side butt flush in the center of these battens. These strips, or narrow panels, are glued to the oak battens with epoxy adhesive and are well nailed with stout one-inch brads set just below the surface of the plywood. Because the panel strips are plywood, and because they rest tightly against the frames, as does carvel plank, they should be nailed securely into the frames with 1½-inch galvanized boat nails, with heads set just under flush for facing.

The procedure for scarphing and splicing the panel strips is the same as already detailed for narrower plank in Part II. However, in this batten construction, the outer end of the scarph should be located over a frame so that the scarph may be fastened through the outer lap into the frame with a row of 6d flat-head galvanized nails. This will pull the outside of the scarph in tightly, holding it securely until the glue is set and also adding substantial mechanical reinforcement.

Inside, the bend of the side curve of the boat will hold the inner lap of the scarph tightly until the glue has set, although a temporary backing block could be tacked in for extra security. The scarph joint on the outside may be covered with a piece of fiberglass tape set in epoxy resin.

The edges of the ½-inch panel strips, where they butt on the battens, need not be jointed tight, but may be put on just as they come from the saw. If they don't meet in all places by ⅛ inch or so, the voids can be filled by extended epoxy adhesive sanded smooth after hardening. It will be best to reinforce the joints with a 2-inch fiberglass tape set in epoxy resin, especially at the top of the garboard.

In this batten-seam construction, short pieces of plywood may be worked in, provided the scarphs are staggered, with no loss of structural strength, so there need be little or no waste. Even with plentiful splices, this construction is very strong and completely tight. It is probably easier for the amateur than conventional planking. Where good natural lumber is expensive and difficult to get, it is especially recommended. The batten-built carvel plywood side could be entirely covered with fiberglass, but this is not necessary. However, if this were done, the plywood need not be more than ⅜ inch thick.

## Finish Details

Planking of the St. Pierre dory proceeds according to the mode of planking a Bank dory as given earlier in the book. Seven strakes are required as shown in the sectional drawing presented here.

Decks, coamings, house—if desired—engine bedlogs, and/or outboard well are sketched out in the St. Pierre dory drafts and require no special discussion. How to build the rudder is covered in the text pertaining to the Beachcomber dory.

Power options, outboard wells, and spray hood for the basic St. Pierre dory are taken up on pages following. Some revised hull lines are presented also.

## Modified St. Pierre

Inasmuch as I intended to add a small house or cuddy for pleasure use that the original fishing boat never had, it seemed that a somewhat more powerful hull would be desirable. In the modified lines, I believe I have achieved a more powerful boat with only slight dimensional departures and no changes radical enough to upset the fine dynamic balance of the original time-tested design.

In the modified design, the profile shape, including rocker and sheer curve, remain unchanged. Mainly I have added a few extra inches of beam and bottom, and have rounded the sides slightly. This takes some of the slackness out of the bilge and adds to the displacement. Rounding the sides makes it possible to narrow the fore bottom somewhat without diminishing the flare, which should help when the boat is slamming into the sea.

Rounded sides of this sort are nothing new, of course. Flat-bottomed colonial batteaux used for transport in the French and Indian Wars were so built. Gaspé skiffs, New England wherries, and Swampscott dories all make use of rounded sides combined with a flat bottom. The power dories of the early decades of the present century, when these boats were our most numerous and popular small power craft, were mainly round-sided boats.

Actually straight-sided power dories are very much the exception; this feature was probably incorporated in the St. Pierre dory for ease in building. However, in this modified design there is not enough side curve to complicate construction. The side frames can still be cut out in single-piece futtocks from flitch-sawed oak plank without getting enough cross grain to weaken them materially. Naturally, it is desirable to have crooked planks for this, if possible. Generally, plank of appropriate curvature can be selected.

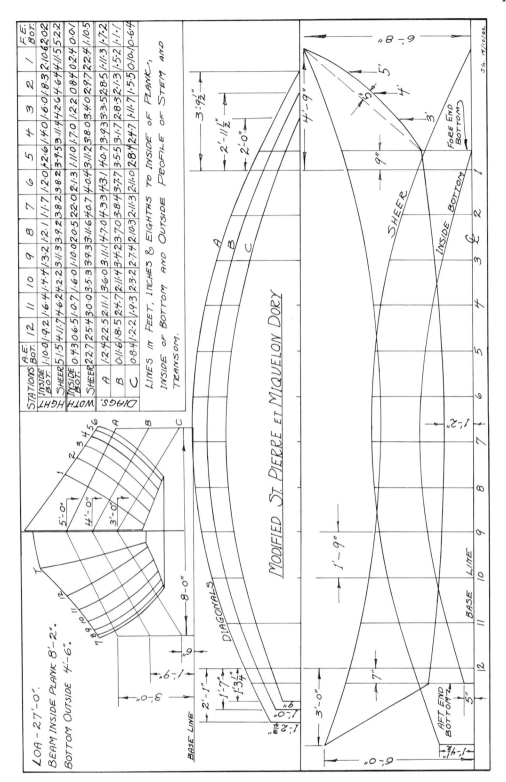

*Lines of the modified St. Pierre dory.*

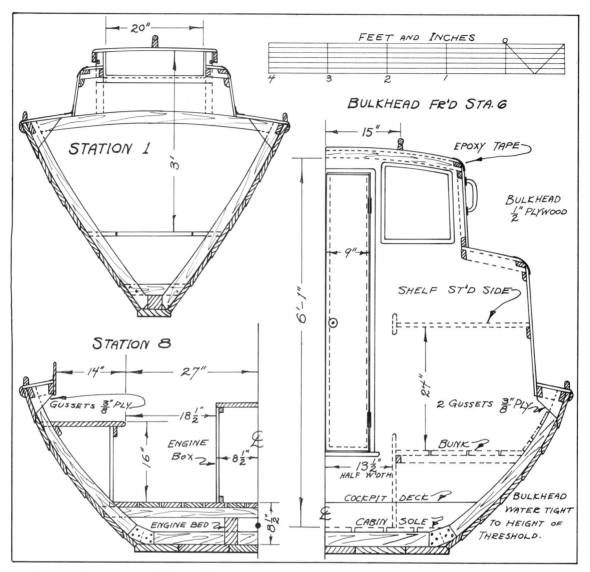

*Construction sections of the modified St. Pierre dory.*

As for planking, the side curve is not pronounced enough to change the lap bevels to any great extent or to make beveling the problem that some find in planking the much more rounded Swampscott.

**Widened St. Pierre**

I also want to offer for consideration the lines of a widened version of the St. Pierre dory, which I think might make a better boat for most readers than the slimmer model first presented.

The lines of the original type were scaled precisely from a blueprint for a standard fishing dory prepared under the direction of the fisheries division of the French government. This agency to a considerable extent subsidizes and supervises the fishing industry in this last French colonial outpost in North America.

In increasing the beam of this dory, I have not changed the profile in any way, which means that the sheer curve and bottom rocker remain unaltered. Length overall, length of bottom, and depth also remain the same; like-

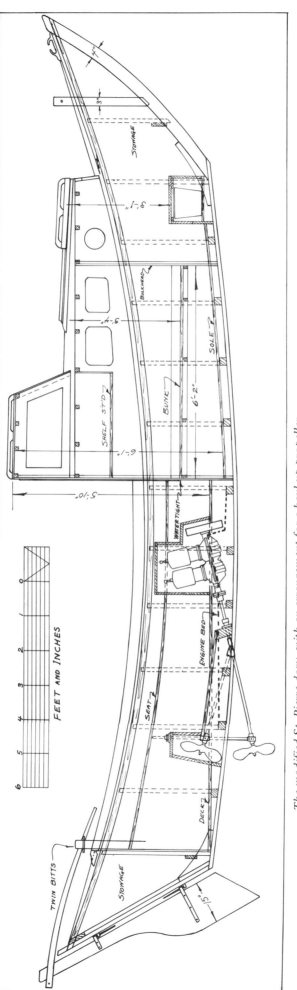

The modified St. Pierre dory, with an arrangement for a haul-up propeller.

| TABLE of OFFSETS | | STATIONS | AFT END B | 12 | 11 | 10 | 9 | 8 | 7 | 6 | 5 | 4 | 3 | 2 | 1 | FRD END B |
|---|---|---|---|---|---|---|---|---|---|---|---|---|---|---|---|---|
| | HEIGHTS | SHEER | 5-1-4 | 4-11-2 | 4-5-6 | 4-1-6 | 3-10-6 | 3-9-0 | 3-8-4 | 3-8-7 | 3-9-6 | 3-11-6 | 4-2-4 | 4-6-3 | 4-11-6 | 5-3-5 |
| | | BOTTOM | 1-9-7 | 1-9-0 | 1-6-3 | 1-4-1 | 1-2-6 | 1-1-6 | 1-1-3 | 1-1-7 | 1-2-5 | 1-4-2 | 1-6-0 | 1-8-2 | 1-10-7 | 2-0-5 |
| | HALF BREADTHS | SHEER | 2-5-6 | 2-8-4 | 3-3-7 | 3-10-1 | 4-2-5 | 4-5-4 | 4-6-2 | 4-5-4 | 4-3-2 | 3-11-7 | 3-6-7 | 3-0-1 | 2-4-3 | 1-10-4 |
| | | BOTTOM | 0-7-0 | 0-9-4 | 1-4-7 | 1-11-0 | 2-3-7 | 2-7-0 | 2-7-6 | 2-6-5 | 2-3-5 | 1-11-3 | 1-5-6 | 0-11-3 | 0-4-5 | 0-0-1 |

LINES TO INSIDE BOTTOM & PLANKING, TO OUTSIDE PROFILE OF STEM & TRANSOM. FEET-INCHES-EIGHTHS.

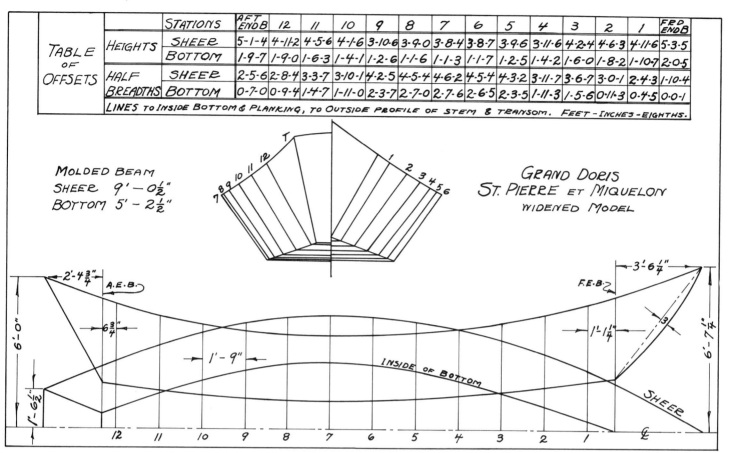

MOLDED BEAM
SHEER 9'-0½"
BOTTOM 5'-2½"

GRAND DORIS
ST. PIERRE ET MIQUELON
WIDENED MODEL

*Lines of the widened St. Pierre dory.*

wise the angle of side flare. But starting with nothing at the stem, I have increased the beam in a fair, easy sweep to an additional 7 inches half-breadth beam (14 inches total extra beam) amidships, diminishing to an extra 3 inches of half-breadth beam at the stern, a total of 6 inches extra transom width.

It should be noted that the added width has been distributed more toward the stern than the bow. This was done to keep the entrance as sharp as possible and to keep the bow sections narrow to obviate pounding into heavy seas. At the same time it was felt that the additional width and displacement would be more useful aft, especially in providing a roomier cockpit and lift for a larger, heavier engine.

This added width will not detract from the excellent sea qualities of the original dory, I feel sure. It will not require any changes in construction or add appreciably to building ex-

pense. No enlargement of scantlings will be required.

The widened boat will probably be slightly stiffer in the water, which is all to the good for general use. The added volume would normally make it float somewhat higher, but the additional weight of the house, decks, tanks, and equipment—and possibly a heavier engine—that the fishing hull did not have is likely to offset the added buoyancy, which is precisely why it is needed.

The additional cockpit room and the added width in the house will be great advantages in a pleasure craft. When I laid out the interior of the house as planned for the original narrower hull, I found myself a bit more cramped for room than I would have liked. The few added inches in the widened hull could make all the difference in providing comfortable accommodations. For this feature alone, the widened hull is worth considering.

### Expansion of the Transom

The transom of the widened dory is a more complicated structure than the usual dory tombstone. Before the transom can be cut out and fastened together, it is necessary to lay out its actual shape. Neither the sectional view nor the half-breadth view, as they appear in the lines, give the actual shape of the transom. Both show the transom shorter than it really is, although they do not distort its width.

The half-breadth view, which appears shortest of all, is what you would see looking down on the transom from above with your line of sight perpendicular to the baseline. The sectional view is what you would see viewing the boat from some distance astern with your line of sight parallel with the baseline, and focused approximately on the center of the transom.

To see the transom as it actually is, that is to see its true length, you would need to view it from the ground somewhat abaft the boat, with your line of sight exactly perpendicular with the rake or incline of the transom.

To draw this out in order to secure a pattern of the actual shape of the transom, an operation called *expanding the transom* is required. It is simple, but sounds hard, and sometimes scares people who are timid about geometry. It shouldn't. And if you will study the diagram a bit, it should soon become clear.

Several widths that have been laid out at convenient intervals on the *transom, as it appears in the half-breadth view of the lines,* are squared up to the raking line that represents the transom in the profile view. In profile, the transom appears in its true length. Where these several projections from the half-breadth view intersect the transom profile, lines are squared

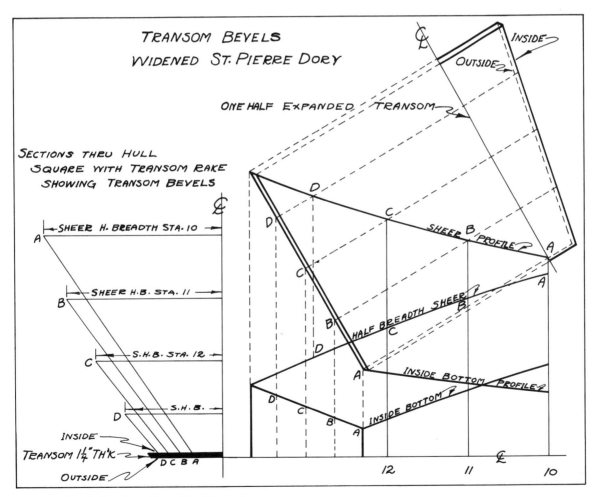

*Transom bevels for the widened St. Pierre dory.*

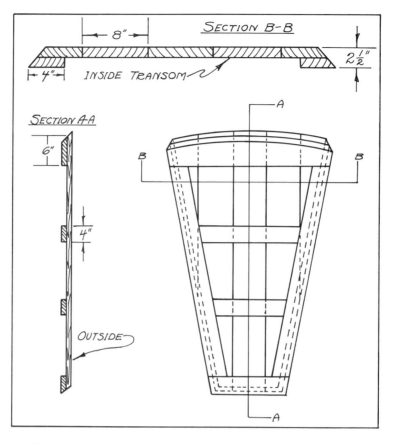

*Transom for the widened St. Pierre dory.*

out from the transom profile, which now becomes, in addition, the centerline for the expansion. On these lines just squared out, the widths from the half-breadth view, corresponding to them, are measured off, and through the points so established the line of the outer edge of the expanded transom is drawn.

I prefer to draw dories with lines shown to the *inside* of the plank and bottom, but to the *outside* of the stem and transom. So our expanded view, as it is now drawn, shows the *outside* face of the transom as it has been beveled to receive plank. Thus the inside face of the transom will be somewhat larger due to the bevel, and so the transom must be made up in the first place of sufficient size to permit beveling.

One can guess at the amount of extra wood or width needed, allowing plenty, and bevel after the transom has been fastened to the bottom with the frames and has been set up for planking. The transom bevels then are lined off the frames with a fairing batten.

But it is easier and neater to get the transom bevels off the laydown and to bevel the transom at the bench as it is being put together, before the boat is set up for planking.

### Transom Bevels

To get the required bevels from the laydown is also a simple operation that should become quite clear after a little study of our diagram. In beveling the edge of a plank or a flat assembly of planks such as our transom, the carpenter's bevel set to the proper angle is applied *square* with the working surface, that is to say, the stock of the bevel rests on the working surface, while the tongue of the bevel, set to the correct angle, lies in a plane at right angles to the working surface—in this case, the outside of the transom. Angles from the laydown, then, should be taken *square* with the rake of the transom. Several lines at convenient locations are drawn in the profile view perpendicular to the line of the raking transom. These perpendicular lines represent plane sections through the solid hull and are easily laid out in the flat in half-breadth view, from which the transom angle at each particular location may be directly taken.

These sections through the hull are trapezoidal in shape. The section line in the profile view that is squared from the raking line of the transom and carried to the sheer curve is the altitude of the trapezoid. The longer parallel side of the trapezoid, taken from the half-breadth view, is the width across the boat at the point where the section cuts the sheer. Likewise the shorter parallel side of the trapezoid is taken from the half-breadth view, being the distance across the transom at the point where the section starts and where that particular bevel is to be determined.

Laid out in the flat, this trapezoidal section, bounded as we have indicated, gives the right bevel directly. While we have explained this for the straight-sided dory, the same principle of expansion also works for both the knuckle-sided Swampscott dory and the round hull.

## Superstructure

In adapting this boat for pleasure use, regardless of which of the three hull variations is selected, the narrow waterways, low coamings, and short end decks should under no consideration be omitted. They are not difficult to put in and add greatly to the performance of the boat. From the structural standpoint, they stiffen and strengthen the hull to a surprising degree. The coaming makes a comfortable backrest for persons seated in the cockpit, and it also gives a convenient handhold in rough weather.

But most important of all, the marginal decking and coamings keep out a lot of loose water. The French fishermen, when the sea gets very rough, erect narrow bands of canvas supported by temporary pins stuck in holes in the gunwales. This expedient indicates that some addition to the sides is required in heavy going. The waterways and coamings as shown are superior in every way to temporary canvas bands, except for lightness. Here, again, a cautionary word is worth repeating. Top hamper must be kept to a minimum.

## Topside Weight Critical

Weight below the rail in this boat does not matter, and in the lower parts and the bottom I have indicated heavy construction, for one reason because it is much easier, since fits and fastening are not so fussy. This is not a speed-boat, as I said before. Overall weight, so long as it is kept down near the water, does not matter. There will be plenty of power to push it along as fast as it will be going.

But weight in the upper structure does matter! Deck beams should be spruce. Decks and waterways should not be heavier than $\frac{3}{8}$-inch plywood. Quarter-inch fir plywood covered with Dynel and epoxy would be better. The plywood gussets that we show tying the deck framing to the sides make an especially light, strong construction when the gussets are attached with screws and a good waterproof adhesive.

When properly used, epoxy resin is undoubtedly the best adhesive we have for a structure of this sort. For a strong joint with epoxy, a thin layer of the resin should remain in the joint. To prevent the resin from being squeezed out of the joint, one thickness of Dynel or fiberglass fabric thoroughly saturated with resin may be laid between the joining surfaces of the wood. This sandwich method insures that resin is retained within the joint, and the fabric also reinforces the wood, a feature of real benefit when the wood is cross-grained, as in the case of curved frames cut from straight lumber. This method of gluing gussets is recommended not only for the deck framing, but also for the frame splices at the bottom knuckle.

## Cabin

As mentioned before, the high bow will give depth enough for a two-stage trunk, sufficiently raised aft for headroom. This small cabin or cuddy will be separated from the open cockpit by a watertight bulkhead (that is, watertight below the knee-high entrance opening). In both the cockpit and the trunk, interior gratings on the bottom in usual dory style will serve for a standing surface.

A small section aft of the stem will also be decked and set off with a waterproof bulkhead

12 inches to 16 inches up from the bottom. Even should considerable water get into the open cockpit on occasion, it would be kept out of the ends of the boat.

Along the sides of the cockpit, narrow waterways and a low coaming will assist in holding back the loose water, as well as serve to brace the hull structure.

Within the cabin trunk or house are planned two berths, a simple cedar-bucket head, and a small Shipmate stove—all as compactly placed as practicable so as not to cut down on space for the cockpit. The forward part of the trunk will be kept quite low to cut windage and to keep weight down. But the after part of the trunk will be built up in a second stage sufficiently high for headroom. This will not require as much height as in most boats because the bottom of the dory serves as the cabin sole.

## Spray Hood, Alternative

For the essentially open boat, as shown with a spray hood in the accompanying drawing, either the original or the modified hull is recommended. This arrangement is roomy, simple, inexpensive, and not inconvenient. There is privacy behind the drawn curtains of the hood, and shelter in inclement weather. For two people this is not a bad rig for a wide cruising range, provided they are reconciled to roughing it just a little.

## Miscellaneous Equipment

Lights will be needed to satisfy Coast Guard requirements for craft over 26 feet. Minimum electric lights will do nicely, powered by a hot-shot battery or two. For interior lighting, small oil lamps in gimbals are the thing.

A lot of modern mechanical gadgets are hardly appropriate for this adaptation of a simple, not to say primitive, workboat type. The choice is up to the owner, however. Many of the fittings, cleats, chocks, and the like can be handmade. It is fun, and it keeps costs down. A cedar bucket makes an entirely adequate head, as such a yachting authority as L. Francis Herreshoff has explained on other occasions. No polish and varnish are required.

Good clean paint and a minimum of at-tention will keep this simple, unostentatious little craft sweet and shipshape.

## Power Options

In powering this boat there are a number of options to be investigated, both for inboard and outboard motors. In my consideration of the powering aspect, I proceeded from two underlying assumptions: (1) that this is not a speed boat, as has been thoroughly explained, and (2) that the dory's original feature as an easily beachable boat is to be retained. This second condition automatically rules out most, if not all modern American inboard engines of the size required for this boat. This is because nearly all modern engines turn up too fast for the haul-up device used on the fishing dory for pulling the propeller and jointed shaft up into the well inside the boat when it is beached. If a modern high-speed engine were used, a rigid log of conventional design would have to be added to the bottom of sufficient depth to permit the wheel to swing underneath. Such a projection below the bottom would prevent easy beaching. However, if one were willing to give up this feature, there are numerous small inboard engines that could be used. It would be easy to add the required shaft log and exterior fittings. In short, such an installation offers no difficult or unusual problems.

## Traditional Make-and-Break

Recommended power is the same as used by the St. Pierrais and the Newfoundland fishermen—for this boat a single cylinder, two-cycle, make-and-break gas engine.

Yes, engines of this sort are still made, and very fine ones, by Acadia Gas Engines Ltd. of Bridgewater, N. S., who have been manufacturing engines for Canadian fishermen since 1908, and by Lunenburg (N.S.) Foundry and Engineering Ltd., makers of Atlantic two-cycle engines. Long experience, the finest materials, and workmanship to match, now produce a much improved engine, especially as to compression and ignition, over earlier motors of this sort.

Those who have these engines say they are the easiest starting engines they have ever seen. And once started, they don't stop, unless you

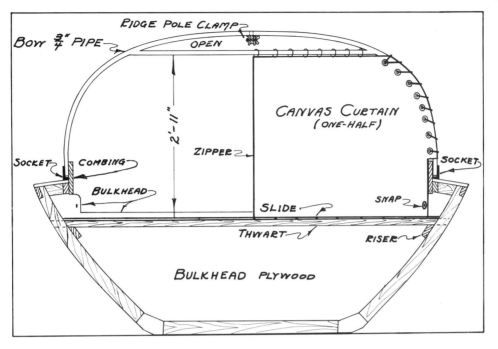

*Simple pipe frame for a canvas curtain.*

want them to, such make-and-break engines being practically weatherproof. In addition, such engines are economical in operation, easy to service, and good for a lifetime, with care.

For this boat a 5 hp make-and-break is sufficient. But these are real horses—king size, so to speak. The bore of the cylinder is 4½ inches; the stroke 5 inches. At approximately 550 rpm this engine turns a three-bladed propeller of 16-inch diameter and 16-inch pitch. Probably this will not push our heavily-rockered dory much more than 6 knots, but that is an honest 6 knots through anything and everything.

### Retractable Propeller Shaft

For such slow-turning engines, Acadia manufactures what they call a Power Dory Haul-Up, that is to say, a device for retracting the propeller up into a watertight box built into the bottom of the boat so that the dory may be hauled out on the beach. The shaft is hinged with a universal joint and passes through a collar, close behind the propeller, to which the lifting rod is attached. Thus the propeller may be lifted, or dropped back into the water at will.

This arrangement is standard on fishing dories in the French islands where the dories are hauled out at the end of each day's fishing. It is also used in Newfoundland. For boats that must ground out between tides, such an arrangement is most useful.

As for putting in the well for the retractile propeller and engine beds as well, I think I'd wait until the boat was planked. There'd be less chance of its changing shape.

### Engine Beds

The beds for a modern inboard engine must withstand powerful athwartship strain and pull. They must be braced accordingly. To be on the safe side in this respect, I show how two solid athwartship knees may be added for extra side bracing. If anyone wanted to add a couple more farther aft on the bed, it could be easily done. This might be considered if an extra-large engine is to be installed.

These knees are shown bolted through the bottom and cross-pinned through the bed logs. These bed logs, in turn, are also bolted through the bottom and notched over and into the cross timbers in a locking fit. I have indicated ⅜-inch galvanized carriage bolts, which I think

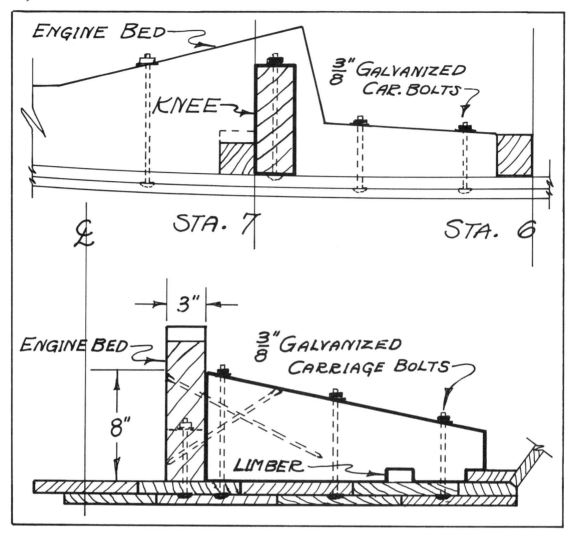

*Engine bed details .*

are heavy enough, but a larger diameter could be used.

Previously I showed a double bottom made up of two layers of ⅞-inch oak. Considering these bolts through the engine beds, it may be better if the inner bottom is at least one inch thick. One reason for the double bottom, as you recall, was to make it easier to bend the bottom to conform to the extreme fore and aft curve, or rocker, that this type of dory calls for. The other reason was so that the outer bottom layer could be replaced if it got banged up on the rocks in beaching, for which purpose this type of dory is especially designed. For this last reason the engine bed bolts should not go through the outer bottom, in case it has to be removed.

## Outboard Motors

By use of an outboard motor in a well, the beaching feature can be retained. Two problems present themselves, however: first, selection of a suitable motor; second, the design of the well.

It is not easy to find a satisfactory outboard equivalent for the powerful but economical, low horsepower, make-and-break work engine used by the French fishermen and recommended as first choice for these heavy dories. What is needed is a heavily made outboard that delivers powerful torque to a large, slow-turning wheel. There are precious few of these outboards manufactured today; the British Seagull and the Swedish Archimedes-Penta might fill the bill, though the former might not be big enough for this dory.

There remain, then, the standard multi-horse, high-speed pleasure outboards. In first cost such motors are fairly high, and they eat up tremendous amounts of gas in comparison with the Seagull and in relation to the torque delivered to the wheel, but they will do the job.

All in all, considering what outboards are available, I feel that outboard power is definitely the second choice for this boat. The first choice is still the heavy-duty, inboard, make-and-break Acadia or Atlantic engine.

## Outboard Wells

As for the correct type of well if an outboard is to be used, there is some latitude of choice, but I do recommend that in any case the motor be fixed in one position so it does not turn, and that steering be done with the rudder and tiller arrangement to be detailed later. This will give much more reliable steering for this boat, especially in rough water. Rudder steering can be guaranteed ahead of time, while motor steering is a gamble depending on such factors as the kind of motor, and the design and the position of the well.

A tilt-up arrangement for the motor is extremely convenient for shallow water and for beaching, especially when the motor is heavy. But it requires a fairly large well, including the opening through the bottom. Powerful high-speed motors develop tremendous suction under some conditions; this suction, for safety, must be provided for in the design of the well.

## Concentric Well

My first choice for a tilt-up well is the concentric well developed by Allan H. Vaitses, boatbuilder in Mattapoisett, Mass. This well was detailed and described in the *National Fisherman* for January, 1959. The concentric well, which closes the well opening when the motor is down, was developed from an earlier suggestion by L. Francis Herreshoff in *Rudder*.

Easier to build is the planing board well discussed by David R. Getchell in the *National Fisherman* for October, 1962. He tested it in his 22½-foot dory, finding it wholly satis-

factory and surprisingly efficient. A variation on this idea is a small box well covered across its bottom with a sheet of heavy rubber through which is a slot just large enough for the lower part of the motor to be forced through. The motor is fixed and steering is done with a rudder. At speeds in excess of 3 or 4 mph the well pumps itself dry. The only objection to this type of well is the necessity for lifting out the motor bodily instead of being able to swing it up easily by tilting. However, I have shown this type of well in the drawing of the St. Pierre with the spray hood. Such a well has the advantages of being easy to construct and of taking up but little room.

One further point comes up in connection with outboard power—the desirability of skegs to help the boat hold a steady course and to give a better grip on the water. Skegs are definitely needed on dories that have little bottom rocker. The St. Pierre has so much rocker, however, and such comparatively deep displacement amidships, that skegs are probably not needed. Besides the rudder helps steady the boat.

## Steering Rig

The St. Pierre dory is steered by a tiller affixed to a large outboard rudder. In our adaptation it is desirable to rig a wheel or stick conveniently close to the engine. The original long tiller should also be retained for emergency use.

One problem in converting the St. Pierre fishing dory is the steering. In the fisheries, these big dories are two-men boats. When one of the crew is standing aft at the tiller, the other is available amidships to tend the engine. But in adapting this boat for pleasure, it is highly desirable to work out an arrangement whereby a single individual can both conveniently steer and operate the engine. In a word, this means bringing the tiller forward to the center of the boat. This is easier said than done. Two difficulties peculiar to this particular craft must be overcome: (1) keeping the rudder easily dismountable so that the boat may be beached, and (2) creating a control system that will function despite the sharp angle at which the rudder is hung.

The easily demountable rudder is one feature we especially wish to retain, for this craft must be beachable. Its rugged flat bottom makes it a natural in this respect. For this reason, the rudder must come off quickly and easily even in rough water, and go back on again just as easily and quickly with nothing to get out of kilter.

The second difficulty confronting us when we set out to alter the original steering arrangement stems from the overhanging rake of the dory transom from which the rudder is hung. When a rudder stands straight up and down, that is plumb or nearly plumb with the waterline, it is easy to rig workable tiller lines, for these lead forward level and directly. But when the rudder post lays back steeply aft and the tiller arm points above the horizon, lines do not lead forward naturally in the desired horizontal direction. Also, the arc of the tiller arm as the rudder swings is downward as the arm moves to the side, further complicating things. Rigging workable tiller lines under these conditions requires planning.

What we have done is to hinge our tiller arm near its middle, so that its forward end, to which the tiller lines are attached, hangs down quite low in the boat, resting upon a flat deck of plywood. The tiller arm is a substantial bronze casting, so its weight holds it down. As it swings from side to side, it is supported by the surface of the deck. Any tendency for the end of the arm to drop lower as it swings out is taken up by movement at the hinge. Thus the outer end of the tiller arm, to which the tiller lines are attached, remains in the same horizontal plane at all times, corresponding to the surface of the plywood deck to which the tiller-rope blocks are bolted.

Although I have not shown it in the drawings, a strip of sheet metal could well be used to reinforce the deck surface upon which the tiller arm moves. It would prevent wear and minimize friction.

With the arrangement worked out here, all moving parts, in fact, the entire rig inside the boat, is enclosed and out of the way under the afterdeck and side seats. Nothing remains out in the open to get fouled or to be in the way. The lead of the tiller lines is pretty direct, with only one set of fairleads in addition to the minimum number of pulleys. The lines should pull freely and easily. The upright tiller stock moves against the edge of the seat on the starboard side abreast of the engine. Its lower end

is pivoted to a block bolted to the bottom of the boat.

The removal of the rudder in no way affects the steering rig inside the boat. The means devised for unshipping the rudder allows it to be lifted clear after the removal of a single toggle pin.

The rudder is held in its working position by being wedged into a rigid fork in the outboard end of the hinged tiller arm. This arm swings on a pin of ¾-inch bronze shaft held in bearing sockets permanently bolted through the transom. The forked tiller arm and its pivoted bearing assembly are not disturbed when the rudder is removed from the boat. The fork, purposely made heavy to insure adequate strength and rigidity, opens on a slight outward taper. In this way the rudder frees easily, but is gripped solidly when jammed up tightly into place with its toggle pin inserted. The side surfaces of the rudder stock, where it enters the tiller arm fork, are reinforced with plates of ¼-inch brass through-riveted with ¼-inch copper rod. These plates give a firm, exact bearing surface for the jaws of the fork and a tight fit that will not wear loose. It is absolutely essential that looseness or play does not develop here.

The toggle pin that holds the rudder in place is tapered at the end to facilitate entering and is secured with a lanyard to prevent its being lost overboard accidentally. If the matching holes through the rudder stock and the tiller arm fork are correctly located, the insertion of this toggle pin will draw these parts into a firm fit.

The two parts of the jointed tiller arm, including the forked outer section, are bronze castings. They need to be quite heavy for rigidity and strength. Fortunately, some extra weight is not a critical matter in this boat, as has been noted before. The two identical halves of the bearing socket are also cast and must be bored to receive the pivot pin of ¾-inch bronze rod.

The bottom end of the rudder is secured by the usual pintle-gudgeon arrangement, but with the pintle quite short for easy lifting out of the gudgeon socket when the rudder has been slacked in the tiller arm fork by pushing outward. The head of the rudder is mortised in the usual fashion to receive a standard, long, wooden tiller, and a spare tiller of this sort is

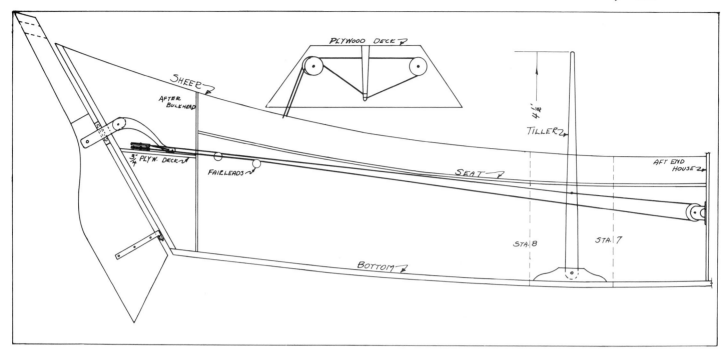

Steering rig.

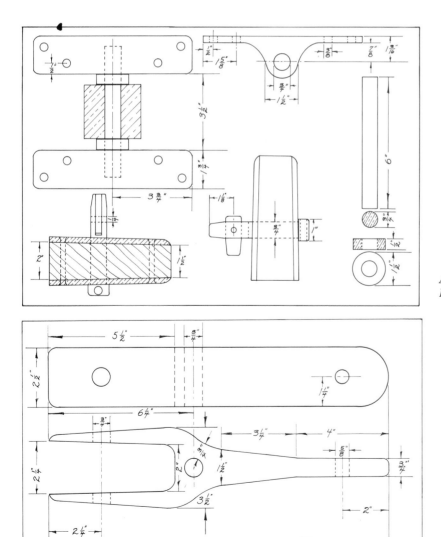

*Above: Details of the tiller bearing assembly.*
*Below: The outboard tiller fork.*

171

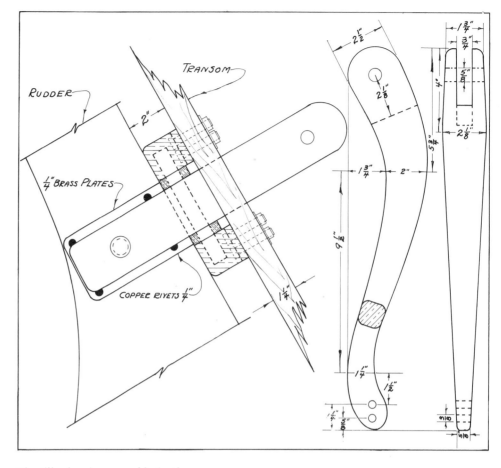

*The tiller bearing assembly in place.*

carried under the port seat in case of an emergency.

To remove the rudder is the work of an instant. The toggle pin is knocked out and another smart rap loosens the grip of the fork, permitting the rudder to be pushed outward and lifted free from the lower gudgeon. The rudder is just as quickly and easily re-attached. As mentioned before, the toggle pin should draw the rudder into the fork in a snug fit.

For tiller lines, 5/16-inch flexible wire tiller rope with standard blocks is adequate. The upright tiller is merely a strip of oak hinged to the block on the bottom of the boat with a carriage bolt. A keeper bent up from l-inch by ¼-inch flat brass may be screwed to the edge of the seat to form a slot for the tiller to move in. While we show the tiller as located on the starboard side, it could just as well be placed on the port side.

The hole in the transom through which the tiller arm passes is quite small and well above the waterline. However, a boot of flexible leather or a rubber seal may be easily installed to prevent water from squirting through this aperture in a following sea.

## Sail?

No doubt this dory would sail, given the proper rig, but I have not gone into that here, since I would prefer to see one sailing successfully before I recommend it widely. Perhaps the greatest danger lies in over-rigging. The standard hull is comparatively narrow and would undoubtedly prove tender under any great press of sail. Dories like these do not possess great initial stiffness and heel down easily to a certain point. They only go so far, of course, and recover quickly, especially with a load, and such quickness is an advantage in a seaway, allowing the boat to move with the water rather than to fight it. Such nice

*A sailing St. Pierre dory, said to be quite successful by her builder, Bill Gibbons of Petaluma, California.*

balance, however, as has been achieved with power, could easily be destroyed with a top-heavy rig. For anyone considering sail, probably my widened version of this dory would be best.

### Flotation

If ballast is added, its weight may be offset by the addition of extra flotation. It is strong-ly urged that the boat be made unsinkable by the inclusion of sufficient foam flotation to offset the weight of the engine, the ballast, and miscellaneous equipment. Ample bulk of flota-tion foam can be packed under the decks and waterways, and in slabs between frames. To make this boat absolutely unsinkable is com-paratively easy and inexpensive, and is one precaution I should certainly take myself, even though this dory is extraordinarily able as a sea boat.

# 12  THE HAMMOND 16-FOOT SWAMPSCOTT DORY

Here is a good boat for rowing. It pulls easily and can carry a load, yet it is not too large for one person to handle and is big enough and able enough to stand rough weather. The lines are pleasing, it is tough and sturdy and ideal for beaching, and, when fitted with a proper centerboard, it can sail.

More than seventy years ago, in the North Shore fishing towns of Massachusett's Essex County, before the gasoline engine took over, hundreds of fishermen in a thriving inshore fishing industry depended upon oars to get them to and from their traps and nets. Some fished both winter and summer. They required a lot from a boat, and the dory builders of the time supplied boats to meet the demand. Demand kept the boatshops busy, and competition was a spur to improvement.

The dory that developed is a handsome craft and in some ways a remarkable one. While the leading builders in the different towns styled differences that set them off from their rivals and provided a source of endless argument in the fishing shanties, still they all built what was essentially the same basic design. And this sweetly modeled craft was as different from the heavy, clumsy, straight-sided Bank dory as a blooded race horse is from a plodding farmer's nag.

In graceful lines, ease of rowing, and seaworthiness, these North Shore dories compare favorably with such famous round-bottom craft as the New Bedford whaleboat or the Glou-

cester seine boat. Yet its flat bottom makes it easier to beach, and its simple, sturdy construction will take abuse year after year. Just as important, it can be built for a fraction of the cost of round-bottom models, and this was particularly true more than seventy years ago when wide boards of good native white pine were plentiful and cheap.

I have called the boat shown here the Hammond dory after the man whose model it was, the late Jesse P. Hammond, who must have built hundreds of dories, all told, in his Danversport boatshop over a period of forty or fifty years. Jess, as his friends knew him, was a superb mechanic. He might have been rich and perhaps renowned had he pushed harder, been less friendly, and not been so exacting in his standards of workmanship. It was typical of the man that he was not content with building just a good boat—it must be the best boat that skill and patience could contrive, and to this end he often experimented with his models, making changes when he got an idea and testing the results in the water.

Around 1900, when the dory business was booming on the North Shore, Jess and his brother spent their winters building dories. The two could plank one in a day. At that time they built several sizes, including a heavy 19-footer for winter fishing. After local lobstermen gave up dory fishing, changing demand called for a smaller, lighter, more easily handled boat. Eventually Hammond sawed up

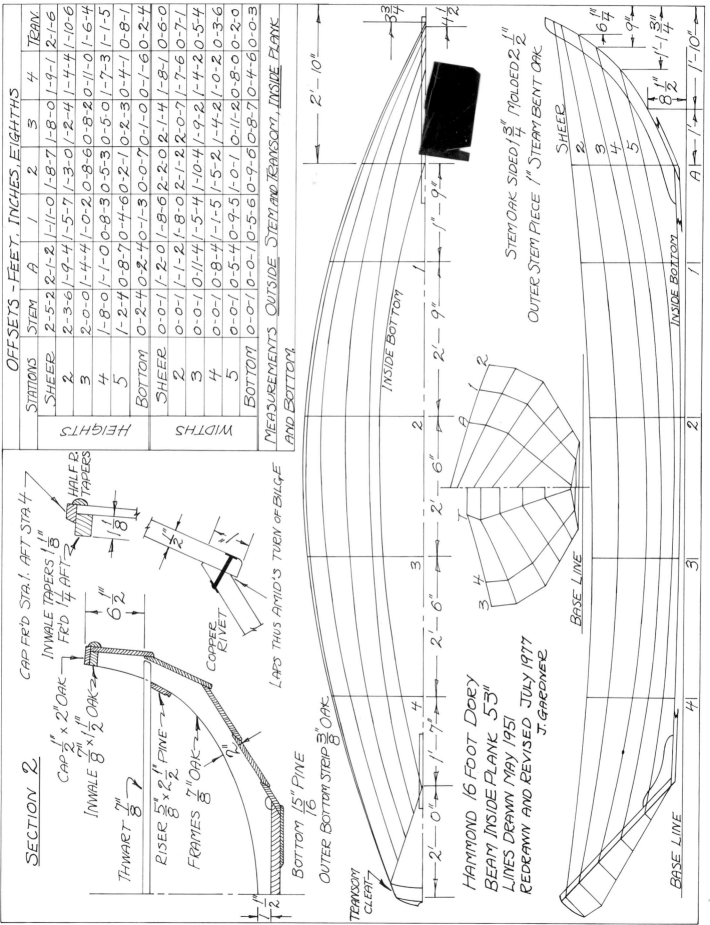

HAMMOND 16 FOOT DORY
BEAM INSIDE PLANK 53"
LINES DRAWN MAY 1951
REDRAWN AND REVISED JULY 1977
J. GARDNER

the patterns for his larger dories and built only the 16-footer, which he found to be his most popular model, about right for general purposes. He was proud of the towing qualities of this boat. He sold several finished bright for yacht tenders, and they proved highly satisfactory—following true and riding the deepest swells like a duck. To improve the model's sailing qualities, he added fullness to the lower knuckle of the after sections.

It is noteworthy that the Hammond dory shows more freeboard amidships than the model Chamberlain perfected in Marblehead, and Hammond's model does not favor the sharp stern of the Chamberlain double-ender. In fact this boat is closer to the so-called Swampscott dory, as developed and built in that town by Gerry Emmons, Small, and Chaisson.

Like other builders, Hammond sent his boats out with a bronze nameplate. In later years, long after he had given up dory building as an active business, he would still get inquiries about his dories, even from remote places up and down the coast.

The lines and measurements for the 16 foot Hammond dory were taken off in 1945 from molds made and many times used by Jesse Hammond. The essential dimensions are: length, 15 feet 11 inches; beam, inside planking, 53 inches; depth amidships 19½ inches. Four sets of sawn frames are set on the numbered stations, and five pairs of steam-bent timbers are spaced equally between the sawn frames and fore and aft of them, with five bottom cleats located in line with the bent frames. Laps are gauged one inch and are beveled to a scant one-eighth on the inside, with lap fastenings spaced approximately 3 inches apart. Copper rivets are the recommended replacement for the chisel-point, galvanized-iron nails, which are no longer obtainable. The garboard is fastened to the bottom with 10d (3-inch) galvanized wire nails, or bronze annular (ring) nails of the same size. The latter are recommended where copper rivets are used for the laps. The extra width between Stations 1 and 2 is left to provide for the installation of a centerboard, if one is desired. Removable gratings cover the bottom inside. Thwarts can be removable if merely notched to fit around the frames. The boat is lined for five strakes of planking in order to allow the use of moderate-width boards. If planked with four strakes, as originally done, exceptionally wide boards will be required for the garboards and the strake next above. Garboards may be spliced amidships with epoxy glue.

Scantling dimensions: Planking ½-inch Eastern white pine. Bottom, white pine, ⅞ inch to $1\frac{5}{16}$ inch thick. Thwarts, spruce, white pine, or Douglas fir, ⅞ inch thick, 10 inches wide. Transom, oak, 1 inch to 1⅛ inches thick. Transom cleat, ⅝ inch oak. Stern knee, oak, 1¾ inches sided. Stem, oak, 1¾ inches sided and 2½ inches molded. Sawn frames ⅞ inch oak, in two pieces spliced with metal clips or plywood gussets. Hammond's preference was one-piece crooks from apple limbs. Bent timbers, oak, ½ inch by 1 inch. Bottom cleats, oak, ⅞ inch by 1½ inches. Gunwales, oak, sided ⅞ inch, molded 1½ inches amidships, 1¼ inches aft, 1⅛ inches forward. Gunwale, cap, oak ½ inch by 2 inches, sawn to shape and running from Station 1 to Station 4, narrowing to a beveled capping strip, ½ inch by ½ inch by ¾ inch, which continues to the ends of the boat. Seat riser, pine, ⅝ inch by 2½ inches, tapering slightly at the ends. Half-round sheer trim, 1 inch amidships, tapering to ¾ inch at the ends. Bottom gratings, ½-inch pine strips on oak cleats.

# 13 FRED DION'S SWAMPSCOTT DORY

Around 1910 when everyone on the North Shore was sailing and rowing dories, Fred Dion of Salem decided to build himself one. He went over to Swampscott to the shop of E. Gerry Emmons, the noted dory builder, where he borrowed the molds and got the necessary measurements. Some of his friends, including Jack Moody, had worked for Emmons and others building dories, and they gave him pointers.

The dory Fred built followed the Swampscott model of the day in all particulars, except that he hauled the sides in a little, giving it a slightly narrower beam. This, Fred relates, was an improvement that was copied by others when they saw how well his new dory performed.

The Dion dory not only performed well, but also it was a life saver. Fred was living in South Salem on the harbor and his house was quite close to the water. He had not had the dory long when the great Salem fire destroyed that whole section of the city, and Fred's wife used the boat to get away in and to save a few belongings.

For the convenience of his wife, when she used the dory by herself, Fred fitted a long box inside one of the cellar windows on the water side where she could stow the mast and sails. The original mast was about 15 feet long and the boom around 10 feet, which brought it well inboard, permitting a backstay to be drawn through the rope becket in the stern of the dory. In spite of this very modest rig, the boat sailed smartly, and Fred claims that it did surprisingly well in comparison with the larger and more powerfully rigged Alphas, which were the class dories built at that time by Bill Chamberlain of Marblehead for the Salem Dory Club.

The light rig and the stability of the hull, for this is a very stiff dory, made it an excellent family boat. Mrs. Dion often went out in the harbor in it with her small children. Fred used it too, in all kinds of weather. He recalls one pull across to the Marblehead shore in a gale when the water was whipped up white. Most boats would have swamped, but with two men at the oars and another bailing they made it easily.

Since he built the Swampscott dory, Dion owned and sailed many yachts—vessels built by Lawley and Herreshoff and other well-known yards. But none, I gather, did he hold in higher esteem than this dory, which within the limits of her size and purpose was as much of a boat and as trim a craft as the best of them. Indeed, you would have to go far to find a better boat and a better example of the Swampscott dory.

It is worthwhile to call attention to some special features of this dory. First, she has a generous amount of sheer—more than most Swampscott dories. This is an advantage in heavy weather and the surf, though it makes her harder to plank. Also, the sheer plank is quite wide in its mid-portion. This calls for a

*A 17-foot Dion Swampscott built by Ed Coffin of Owls Head, Maine, in 1952.*

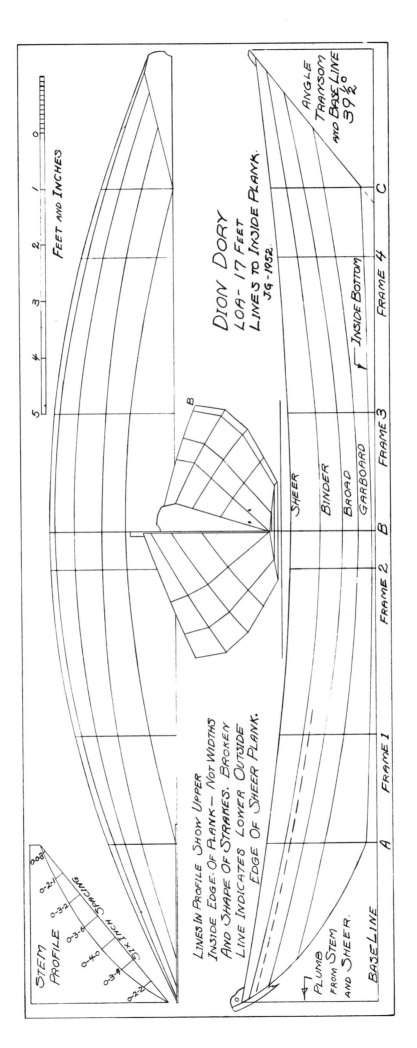

FEET AND INCHES

STEM PROFILE

0-0-0
0-2-1
0-3-2
0-3-6
0-4-0
0-3-4
0-2-2

THREE INCH SPACING

SIX INCH

DION DORY
LOA — 17 FEET
LINES TO INSIDE PLANK.
J.G.-1952.

LINES IN PROFILE SHOW UPPER
INSIDE EDGE OF PLANK — NOT WIDTHS
AND SHAPE OF STRAKES. BROKEN
LINE INDICATES LOWER OUTSIDE
EDGE OF SHEER PLANK.

ANGLE TRANSOM AND BASE LINE 39½°

INSIDE BOTTOM

SHEER
BINDER
BROAD
GARBOARD

A          B          C
FRAME 1   FRAME 2   FRAME 3   FRAME 4

PLUMB FROM STEM AND SHEER.

BASE LINE

## OFFSETS — DION DORY — 17' LOA

| FRAMES AND STATIONS | HEIGHTS above BASELINE | | | | | HALF-BREADTHS | | | | |
|---|---|---|---|---|---|---|---|---|---|---|
| | Bottom Inside Edge | Garboard Inside Top Edge | Broad Inside Top Edge | Binder Inside Top Edge | Sheer Inside Top Edge | Bottom Inside | Garboard Inside Top Edge | Broad Inside Top Edge | Binder Inside Top Edge | Sheer Inside Top Edge |
| STEM | 0-2-4 | 1-5-5 | 2-0-1 | 2-4-5 | 2-6-0 | 0-0-1 | 0-0-1 | 0-0-1 | 0-0-1 | 0-0-1 |
| STATION A | 0-2-4 | 0-11-5 | 1-4-1 | 1-8-3 | 2-0-2 | 0-0-1 | 0-7-6 | 0-11-1 | 1-1-4 | 1-2-7 |
| FRAME 1 | 0-1-5 | 0-7-3 | 0-11-4 | 1-4-1 | 1-9-3 | 0-5-6 | 1-0-5 | 1-5-2 | 1-8-3 | 1-9-6 |
| FRAME 2 | 0-0-7 | 0-4-0 | 0-7-3 | 1-0-2 | 1-6-7 | 0-10-3 | 1-3-6 | 1-9-5 | 2-1-6 | 2-2-7 |
| STATION B | 0-0-7 | 0-3-7 | 0-7-2 | 1-0-0 | 1-6-6 | 0-10-5 | 1-3-6 | 1-9-6 | 2-2-0 | 2-3-0 |
| FRAME 3 | 0-1-4 | 0-4-5 | 0-8-2 | 1-1-1 | 1-7-1 | 0-9-5 | 1-2-6 | 1-8-5 | 2-0-6 | 2-1-7 |
| FRAME 4 | 0-2-1 | 0-8-3 | 1-0-5 | 1-4-7 | 1-9-2 | 0-3-7 | 0-10-2 | 1-3-3 | 1-6-6 | 1-8-0 |
| STATION C | 0-2-5 | 0-10-7 | 1-3-3 | 1-7-1 | 1-10-6 | 0-0-0 | 0-6-6 | 0-11-3 | 1-2-5 | 1-3-4 |
| TRANSOM | 0-2-5 | 1-1-1 | 1-7-3 | 1-11-2 | 2-1-6 | 0-0-0 | 0-3-1 | 0-5-0 | 0-6-1 | 0-5-3 |

OFFSETS IN FEET, INCHES, EIGHTHS. TO OUTSIDE STEM AND TRANSOM. TO INSIDE PLANK AND BOTTOM.

PERPENDICULARS. LOCATED ON BASE LINE AFT OF PLUMB DROPPED FROM STEM AND FORE END OF SHEER.

| SHEER FORE END | BINDER FORE END | BROAD FORE END | GARBOARD FORE END | BOTTOM FORE END | STATION A | FRAME 1 | FRAME 2 | STATION B | FRAME 3 | FRAME 4 | STATION C | BOTTOM AFT END | GARBOARD AFT END | BROAD AFT END | BINDER AFT END | SHEER AFT END |
|---|---|---|---|---|---|---|---|---|---|---|---|---|---|---|---|---|
| 0-0-0 | 0-0-6 | 0-3-4 | 0-9-1 | 2-9-7 | 2-9-7 | 4-8-7 | 7-8-2 | 8-4-2 | 10-5-3 | 13-2-3 | 14-5-1 | 14-5-1 | 15-6-1 | 16-1-5 | 16-6-2 | 16-9-1 |

spliced sheer strake—too wide a board would be required to get it out in one continuous length. The splice is made on the third frame. Another thing to notice is the amount of bearing that this boat has amidships—a great deal more than some round-sided dories, so she is not tender and will stand up under sail.

Originally, the Dion dory had a false bottom of half-inch oak fastened with screws to the outside of the regular bottom. Instead of being beveled off on the edge to follow the flare of the sides, this false bottom was left square and a little "strong," projecting slightly beyond the lower edge of the garboard to which it gave protection. Such a false bottom is unusual. Fred says the boat sailed better for it. He noted a difference for the worse when he removed it. Also, the added weight, when it was in place, did not make the boat row harder, he observed.

Some details of the construction plan call for special mention. The forward thwart that holds the mast must be fastened in solid, braced to the sides with rugged knees and

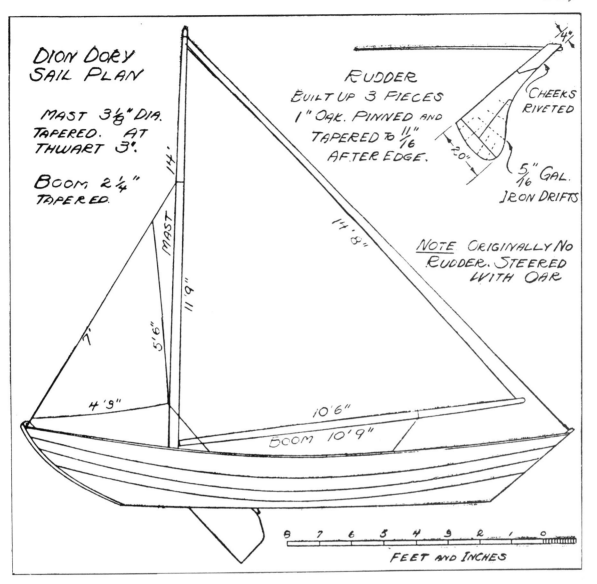

DION DORY
SAIL PLAN

MAST 3⅛" DIA.
TAPERED. AT
THWART 3".

BOOM 2¼"
TAPERED.

RUDDER
BUILT UP 3 PIECES
1" OAK. PINNED AND
TAPERED TO 11/16"
AFTER EDGE.

CHEEKS
RIVETED

5/16" GAL.
IRON DRIFTS

20°

¼"

NOTE ORIGINALLY NO
RUDDER. STEERED
WITH OAR

14'
MAST
11'9"
14'8"
5'6"
7'
4'9"
10'6"
BOOM 10'9"

8  7  6  5  4  3  2  1  0

FEET AND INCHES

secured to the centerboard box. A sturdy piece of oak board is fastened, with the grain running fore and aft, on the underside of the thwart to reinforce it where the mast goes through. Even so, care must be taken not to split or strain this thwart in taking down the mast in a blow. The mast and boom should be as light as possible—spruce is the proper timber.

Ample limbers should be provided so all parts of the bottom can drain through the one-inch drain hole just aft of the last frame. This hole is fitted with a pine plug. Removable gratings cover the entire bottom. The second and third thwarts are removable, and may be fitted with buttons on the frames to hold them in place. The second thwart helps brace the

centerboard box and is notched over the slant of the after side of the box. There is a handy stowage locker under the stern bench.

The stern bench itself lifts out freely and rests on a cleat on the slope of the transom and in front on a removable bulkhead or kip board that wedges against the after side of the fourth frame. The oak posts of the centerboard box mortise through the bottom, which is good construction generally. Corresponding with the hemp becket in the stern, there is at the bow a similar strap or grommet that is reeved through two seven-eighth-inch holes pierced just below the sheer planks close to each side of the stem so the pull is on that member.

The detail for the gusset plates or clips for

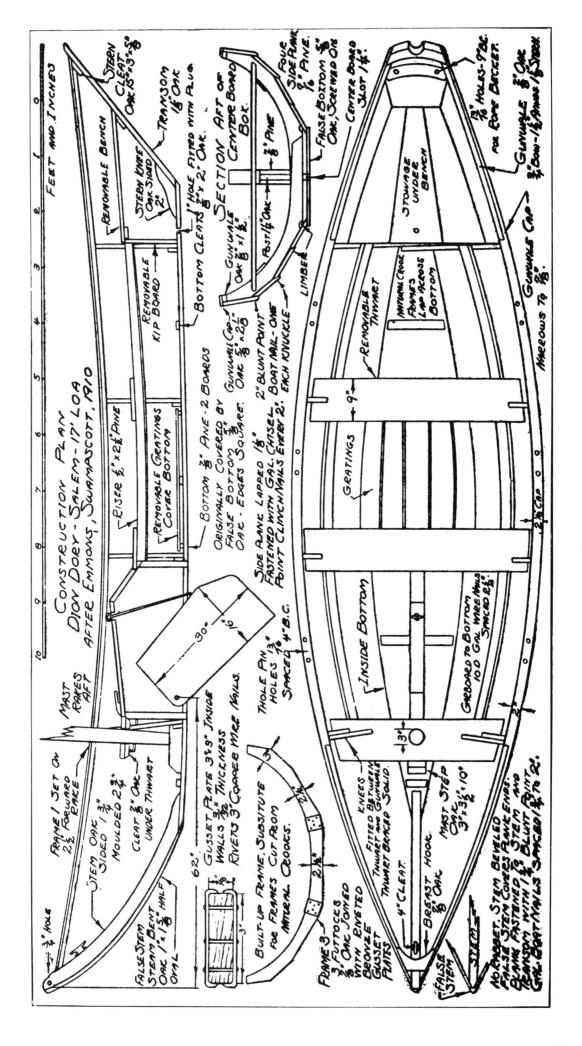

CONSTRUCTION PLAN
DION DORY - SALEM - 17' LOA
AFTER EMMONS, SWAMPSCOTT, 1910

built-up frames is to be noted in the construction plan. Suitable frame timber with the shape grown in is hard to get, so you may have to use built-up frames. These gussets or clips are plenty strong and have been used on commercial fishing dories for many years. It is important to design the clips so they extend around the edges of the timbers and clamp them. When a pair of these are put on a joint and drawn together with rivets, they form a socket around the ends that keeps the wood from splitting. Flat plates that don't grip the edges put all the strain on the fastenings, with the leverage transformed into splitting action. The clips shown leave enough space in the bottom knuckle for a good limber.

A great many dories were built with intermediate bent timbers between the sawn frames and fore and aft of them, making five on a side. The end ones were located at the extreme ends of the bottom and raked like cants to lie flat against the side without twisting. These intermediate frames were white oak bent on the flat- about- one-half by one inch, and fastened with chisel-point clench nails through the laps of the plank only, because nails through the center of the plank would eventually "rent" them. Such bent ribs are desirable when the dory is planked with thin stock—half inch or under. With heavy plank close to five-eighths of an inch thick, they can be dispensed with.

Don't spare the paint. A good carpentry job calls for a good paint job. In my experience, the best primer is red lead and linseed oil given plenty of time to dry. Grey is the usual final color. But if you intend to use the boat in the fall for duck hunting, a red-brown to blend with rock weed is what they use around Marblehead.

This boat was built originally for sail and oars, but it would go fine with a small air-cooled inboard engine. Also, it has possibilities for outboard use. It would drive easily at moderate speed, and would be safe anywhere.

When I drew up the sail plan for the Dion dory, there were no sails or mast to go by, as these had long since disappeared. Nevertheless, it was not hard to reconstruct the rig with fair accuracy. A three-inch hole in the forward thwart and the mast step beneath established the diameter and position of the mast. Upon questioning, Fred Dion recalled that when he stowed the mast diagonally across the thwarts, the after end of the mast used to project about a foot onto the stern sheets' bench. This would

make the mast about 14 feet long.

While the mast carried no side stays, Fred used to lead a backstay from the masthead through the stern becket of the dory to rake the mast aft, and as the boom had to swing inboard of this stay, this sets a reliable limit on the length of the boom. Further, Fred stated that his boom did not rise as high aft as was common in dory rigs of that time, for which reason I have drawn it quite low for a dory.

The jib is a typical dory jib as can be seen in many old pictures and plans. The jib stay was pulled taut through the hole in the stemhead; the distance between the stem and the mast determined, of course, the size of the sail. Fred said the jib as drawn looked all right to him, as did the rig in general. The sail is definitely smaller than the rigs represented in old pictures of fishing dory races, but perhaps these were racing sails rather than working sails, the latter being used when only one man would be handling the boat.

One thing not shown in the sail plan is an arrangement whereby the jib could be left to itself when sailing single-handed. A ring attached to the jib sheet passed along a rope traveller stretched athwartships forward of the mast. Sailing the boat alone, one sat on frame-three thwart, where it was easiest to manage the steering oar and hold the sheet.

Originally, the centerboard was hauled up by a length of iron rod with its upper end bent into a ring like an old-fashioned stove poker. When the board was down, this ring brought up on the top of the box prevented the board from dropping all the way out. Hauled out, the rod lay on the top of the box with its round end wedged under a special cleat, devised by Fred, which held the board from dropping.

This boat is drawn without a rudder, because that was how she was sailed. But a rudder could easily be fitted, and I have sketched one that might be used. Most dory rudders were turned with tillers, though Bill Chamberlain favored a yoke and lines for racing. The objection to a rudder for a boat like this, which will be rowed as much or more than it is sailed, is that the rudder must be removable, and that at best it will be cumbersome and will take up space in the boat. It is much simpler and easier to get along with an oar if you can. If the dory is hauled up on the beach when not in use, as many are, it would mean unshipping the rudder every time the boat came out of the water.

# 14  THE 17-FOOT NAHANT DORY

When the U.S. Navy first began to use dories, and to what extent they ever were used is not clear, but we do know for certain that sometime shortly prior to April, 1913, a lines plan and specifications for a 17-foot Nahant-type dory were drawn at the Naval Shipyard in Boston, Mass. Two years later this material, comprising several sheets, was published as Standard Plan No. 225 in the 1915 revised edition of *Standard Designs for Boats of the United States Navy*, a compendious work by Chief Constructor Philip Hichborn, U.S.N., the first edition of which was issued in Washington, D.C., in 1900 by the Government Printing Office. Both editions are now out of print and so rare as to be almost unobtainable, which is one reason for reissuing the details of the Nahant dory here.

Although no longer useful as a military vessel, this dory is adaptable to present-day recreational use and holds definite possibilities for amateur construction. The lines are excellent. What is needed, however, are some slight changes in the scantling dimensions to lighten the boat (especially in the topsides), a few additions to the parts list and a new schedule of fastenings. Some of the latter as originally specified are no longer obtainable, and others have since been improved upon.

The origin of this dory, as indicated by its name, may be of some interest. In all probability it was modeled on a type of local dory which had come into use at the Life Saving Station

formerly situated on the island of Little Nahant, and derived from the fishing dories of the immediate area, including those of the Lynn beaches and Swampscott. Nahant and Little Nahant are two scenic islands at the termination of a peninsula extending southward from Lynn, Mass., and connected to the mainland by a causeway built across a mile and a half of sand beach. Discovered in 1614 by Capt. John Smith and settled not many years later by farmers and fishermen, the Nahants were in time to become a celebrated watering place and summer resort. According to Lewis's *History of Lynn, 1829*, "Nahant is much visited by persons for the improvement of health, and by parties of pleasure ... two steamboats are constantly running from Boston during the pleasant season. . . . A spacious and elegant hotel has been erected of stone near the eastern extremity. . . ."

Racing in dories, both sailing and rowing, came into vogue here early, and in the 1890s, according to one contemporary account, Nahant, went "dory mad." The whole town was caught up in it, although summer visitors to a lesser extent. Rivalry was intense and the excitement tremendous. Fishermen's wives had to give up their regular duties, it is said, to sew sails.

In 1894 the Nahant Dory Club was formed. Probably the best known of the Nahant dories racing under club rules was the 23-foot Clipper dory built by R.H. Robertson, foremost Nahant dory builder. Lines for the Clipper dory pub-

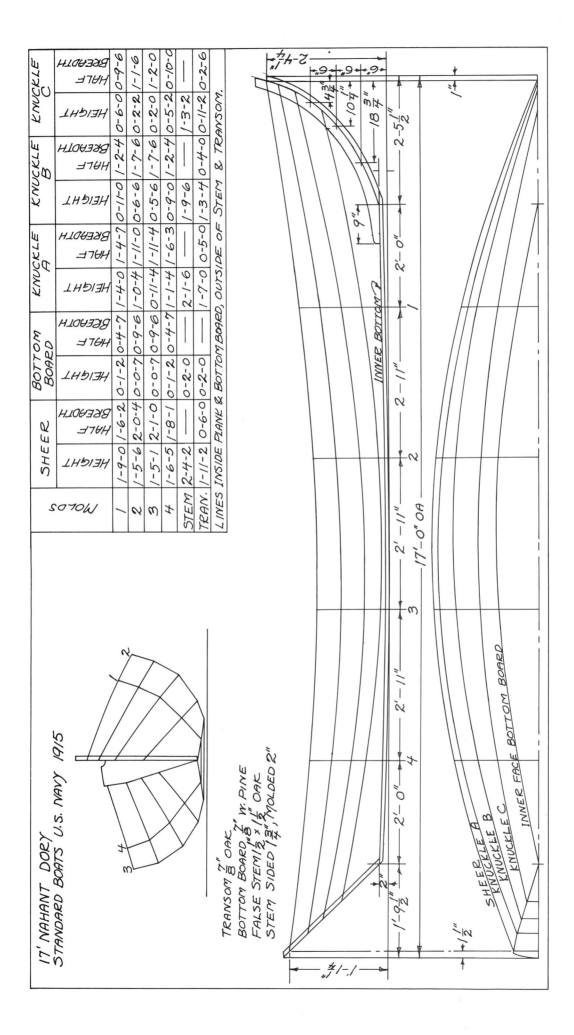

**17' NAHANT DORY**
**STANDARD BOATS U.S. NAVY 1915**

| MOLDS | SHEER HEIGHT | SHEER HALF BREADTH | BOTTOM BOARD HEIGHT | BOTTOM BOARD HALF BREADTH | KNUCKLE A HEIGHT | KNUCKLE A HALF BREADTH | KNUCKLE B HEIGHT | KNUCKLE B HALF BREADTH | KNUCKLE C HEIGHT | KNUCKLE C HALF BREADTH |
|---|---|---|---|---|---|---|---|---|---|---|
| 1 | 1-9-0 | 1-6-2 | 0-1-2 | 0-4-7 | 1-4-0 | 1-4-7 | 0-11-0 | 1-2-4 | 0-6-0 | 0-9-6 |
| 2 | 1-5-6 | 2-0-4 | 0-0-7 | 0-9-6 | 1-0-4 | 1-11-0 | 0-6-6 | 1-7-6 | 0-2-2 | 1-1-6 |
| 3 | 1-5-1 | 2-1-0 | 0-0-7 | 0-9-6 | 0-11-4 | 1-4-0 | 0-5-6 | 1-7-6 | 0-2-0 | 1-2-0 |
| 4 | 1-6-5 | 1-8-1 | 0-1-2 | 0-4-7 | 1-1-4 | 1-6-3 | 0-9-0 | 2-4-0 | 0-5-2 | 2-10-0 |
| STEM | 2-4-2 | — | 0-2-0 | — | 2-1-6 | — | 1-9-6 | — | 1-3-2 | — |
| TRAN. | 1-11-2 | 0-6-0 | 0-2-0 | 1-7-0 | 0-5-0 | 1-3-4 | 0-4-0 | 1-2-0 | 0-11-2 | 0-2-6 |

LINES INSIDE PLANK & BOTTOM BOARD, OUTSIDE OF STEM & TRANSOM.

TRANSOM 7/8" OAK.
BOTTOM BOARD 7/8" W. PINE
FALSE STEM 1/2" × 1/2" OAK
STEM SIDED 1 3/4", MOLDED 2"

INNER BOTTOM

SHEERLE A
KNUCKLEE B
KNUCKLE C
INNER FACE BOTTOM BOARD

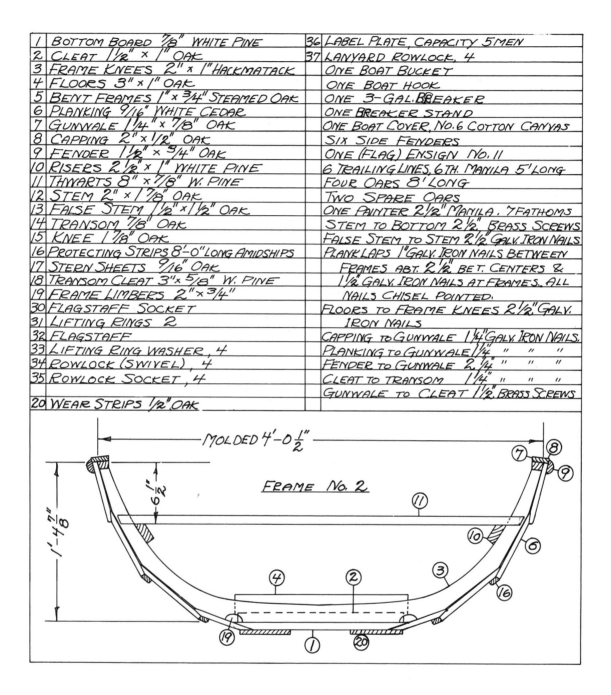

| 1 | BOTTOM BOARD 7/8" WHITE PINE | 36 | LABEL PLATE, CAPACITY 5 MEN |
|---|---|---|---|
| 2 | CLEAT 1 1/2" × 1" OAK | 37 | LANYARD ROWLOCK, 4 |
| 3 | FRAME KNEES 2" × 1" HACKMATACK | | ONE BOAT BUCKET |
| 4 | FLOORS 3" × 1" OAK | | ONE BOAT HOOK |
| 5 | BENT FRAMES 1" × 3/4" STEAMED OAK | | ONE 3-GAL. BREAKER |
| 6 | PLANKING 9/16" WHITE CEDAR | | ONE BREAKER STAND |
| 7 | GUNWALE 1 1/4" × 7/8" OAK | | ONE BOAT COVER, NO.6 COTTON CANVAS |
| 8 | CAPPING 2" × 1/2" OAK | | SIX SIDE FENDERS |
| 9 | FENDER 1 1/2" × 3/4" OAK | | ONE (FLAG) ENSIGN NO. 11 |
| 10 | RISERS 2 1/2" × 1" WHITE PINE | | 6 TRAILING LINES, 6 TH. MANILA 5' LONG |
| 11 | THWARTS 8" × 7/8" W. PINE | | FOUR OARS 8' LONG |
| 12 | STEM 2" × 1 7/8" OAK | | TWO SPARE OARS |
| 13 | FALSE STEM 1/2" × 1 1/2" OAK | | ONE PAINTER 2 1/2" MANILA. 7 FATHOMS |
| 14 | TRANSOM 7/8" OAK | | STEM TO BOTTOM 2 1/2" BRASS SCREWS |
| 15 | KNEE 1 7/8" OAK | | FALSE STEM TO STEM 2 1/2" GALV. IRON NAILS |
| 16 | PROTECTING STRIPS 8'-0" LONG AMIDSHIPS | | PLANK LAPS 1" GALV. IRON NAILS BETWEEN |
| 17 | STERN SHEETS 9/16" OAK | | FRAMES ABT. 2 1/2" BET. CENTERS & |
| 18 | TRANSOM CLEAT 3" × 5/8" W. PINE | | 1 1/2" GALV. IRON NAILS AT FRAMES. ALL |
| 19 | FRAME LIMBERS 2" × 3/4" | | NAILS CHISEL POINTED. |
| 30 | FLAGSTAFF SOCKET | | FLOORS TO FRAME KNEES 2 1/2" GALV. |
| 31 | LIFTING RINGS 2 | | IRON NAILS |
| 32 | FLAGSTAFF | | CAPPING TO GUNWALE 1 1/4" GALV. IRON NAILS, |
| 33 | LIFTING RING WASHER, 4 | | PLANKING TO GUNWALE 1 1/4" " " |
| 34 | ROWLOCK (SWIVEL), 4 | | FENDER TO GUNWALE 2 1/4" " " |
| 35 | ROWLOCK SOCKET, 4 | | CLEAT TO TRANSOM 1 1/4" " " |
| | | | GUNWALE TO CLEAT 1 1/2" BRASS SCREWS |
| 20 | WEAR STRIPS 1/2" OAK | | |

lished in *Rudder* in 1898 show an extreme racing type not at all like the Navy dory which we are considering.

By 1913 or thereabouts, New England dories both for fishing and pleasure were at their peak. Sailing dories at this time were by far the most popular and numerous racing class, and increasing numbers of power launches fitted with the then-new gasoline engines were being built on dory lines. No doubt this popularity was one

of the considerations which induced the Navy to add a dory at this time to its line of service small craft. That it should have selected one that previously had been developed and tested by the Life Saving Service would have been both logical and prudent.

Employed at the time at the Boston Naval Shipyard, where these plans were drawn, were several dory builders from Swampscott, of whom I have personal knowledge, as well as at

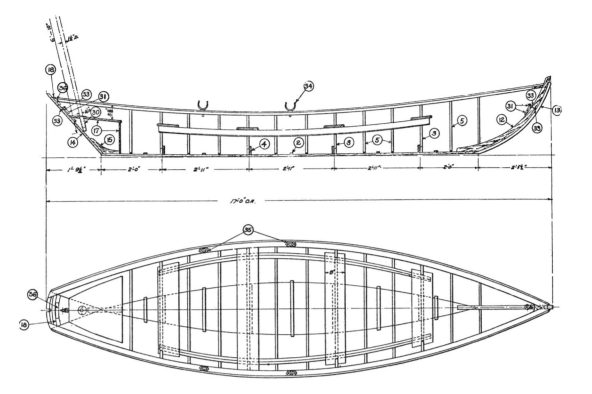

least one from Nahant. But whether they, or anyone else employed there at that time, built any of these Navy dories, I do not know.

In any event, some of the details shown in the Navy drawings differ from what was more or less standard for Nahant and Swampscott dories at that time and since. In view of this, my hunch is that these plans were done by a draftsman working from notes provided by dory builders, no doubt, but without dory building experience himself. The notes could have been incomplete, or he could have extrapolated details from other craft with which he was more familiar, or both. Whatever the reason, there are significant omissions from these Navy plans, and some of the things indicated are not according to the best building practice, or superior dory design. In what follows I shall cast a critical eye on each of the listed items in turn, commenting where required.

Omissions from the Navy plan include limbers in the bottom knuckles of the frame knees. However, I have shown limbers, No. 19, in redrawing the section view of Frame No. 2. In addition, the bottom cleats, No. 2, were shown extended with the ends beveled to fit tightly against the slant of the garboards. These I have

redrawn with the ends cut back so that water can easily drain around them. It is important to provide for the clear passage of water the length of the bottom. If an inch hole is bored through the bottom near the stern and fitted with a pine plug, it is easy to let the water run out by removing the plug, instead of having water trapped in every bay between frames the length of the boat.

Another serious omission was the lack of wear strips on the bottom to cover and protect the lower edges of the garboards. I have drawn them in, showing them as No. 20. If the boat is to be beached at all, protection is required here, otherwise the boat can easily be damaged to an extent that is difficult to repair. Sometimes it is advisable to cover the entire bottom with a thin, false bottom put on with easily removed short screws, so that it can be renewed when worn.

Narrow strips bent around the outside of the bottom, just wide enough to cover the bottom edge of the garboards, should never be used, as these cause drag and slow the passage of the boat through the water appreciably. The inside edges of wear strips fastened on the bottom should always be straight and parallel to the centerline of the boat.

Omitted also from the Navy plan were gratings of any kind to cover the inside of the bottom, to protect it from wear, and to give better footing. These are standard in knuckle-sided dories.

When the Navy plans were first drawn, no transom cleat, No. 18, was shown. This was added later as a dated correction as the published construction plan shows. This is an essential structural member, and its omission could indicate unfamiliarity on the part of the draftsman with dory construction.

The floors, No. 4, are unnecessarily heavy and high. Instead of being 3 inches by 1 inch oak, 2 inches by ⅞ inch would be more normal and plenty large enough. Three inches is entirely too high.

Frame knees, No. 3, need not be hackmatack. While hackmatack knees are still commonly used in Nova Scotia for the frames of Bank dories, the shape of the frames at stations 2 and 3 of this boat are not suited to the run of the grain in most hackmatack knees.

Planking, No. 6, could be white pine instead of white cedar; in fact, pine was standard for dories, and considering the added reinforcement of the intermediate bent frames, No. 5, ½-inch thick white pine would be heavy enough. Lacking other material, ⅜-inch marine plywood could be used, spliced from 8-foot panels with the edges well sealed.

The gunwale capping, No. 8, is shown to extend the whole length of the boat. This is unnecessary and adds appreciable extra weight to the topsides. Ordinarily, the gunwale capping stops slightly beyond the first and last frames, and from there to the ends is replaced by a narrow beveled strip just wide enough to cover the top edge of the sheer plank and its joint with the gunwale or inwale. Risers, No. 10, are unnecessarily heavy. Instead of 1 inch thick, ½ inch to ⅝ inch would be normal and ample.

Protecting strips, No. 16, put on to shield the edges of the laps in the center section of the boat are generally not added unless the boat is expected to receive extremely rough usage. If they are needed here, wear strips are most certainly needed on the bottom.

It is interesting to note all the equipment that this boat was supposed to carry, especially the 3-gallon water breaker. That would seem to indicate that this dory was not intended to serve merely as a harbor tender and for similar short trips but that it might be at sea for a considerable length of time on some occasions. It is further interesting to see that the capacity of this boat, in addition to the equipment specified, was set at five men. This is far greater than present Coast Guard regulations would permit.

When this dory was designed, chisel point, galvanized iron boat nails were standard dory fastenings. These are no longer manufactured, unfortunately. Copper rivets, even if they are slower to put in, are better and more lasting for the laps and the intermediate bent frames. For fastening into the frames, either bronze screws should be used or annular (ring) nails. Brass screws were the best available for boat work in 1913, but today's bronze screws are so much superior that brass should not be considered.

A serious omission from the Navy plan was any mention of fastenings for the lower edge of the garboard into the bottom. Generally 3-inch (10d) galvanized wire nails were used for this. Copper nails were not used, as they tend to become greasy as they corrode and do not hold well. Good quality hot-dipped galvanized wire nails will do quite well here, but not electroplated nails. Three-inch bronze annular nails are probably best.

Any unnecessary weight in the topsides of a boat of this sort is bound to have some adverse effect on performance, although some additional weight in the bottom may even be beneficial under certain conditions. The unnecessary extra weight in the capping strips has already been mentioned.

An even worse offender is the so called fender (No. 9), which is really huge for a dory. Instead of an oak half round 1½ inches by ¾ inch, one 1 inch by ½ inch and tapered toward the ends would be ample and a lot lighter.

This is not a particularly large dory. In fact its maximum molded beam of 4 feet 2 inches is rather slim for a 17-foot dory, and with her well-rounded bilges and easy lines, this boat will row and handle well, even with only one man at the oars. But, to say it again, construction as originally specified is unnecessarily heavy for present-day recreational use and scantlings should be reduced in size, as indicated.

# 15  THE 18-FOOT ONE-DESIGN SWAMPSCOTT SAILING DORY

We are indebted to Harvey P. Treat of New Haven, Connecticut for sending us the original blueprint for *Tweedledum* and *Tweedledee* of the Sea-Chanty one-design class. He acquired this print when he bought these two dories in 1922. They had been built to order in 1915 by George L. Chaisson of Swampscott for Floyd Clark, a retired attorney residing at Stony Creek, Connecticut. Treat immediately sold one of the dories, keeping the other, which he sailed with satisfaction for several years. As is often the case with old dory men, he now wishes he had it back again, or one like it.

When I asked Treat about his experience with this dory, he responded with the following information and comment:

> I put about 200 pounds of small, cobble ballast under the floorboards, which eased the quick action in heeling from a sudden puff, when going to windward, and seemed to make the boat more stable.
>
> As you know, these dories were almost all sides, with very little bottom. In walking forward of the mast, you had to get around the mast in one quick step, otherwise you found yourself in the water, and the dory dancing saucily alongside you.
>
> I went out sailing in any kind of weather, short of a hurricane (fortunately, there were no hurricanes in those days), with absolute safety and comfort. I belonged to the old New Haven Yacht Club at the time when they had a fleet of 18-foot Cape Cod knockabouts, which were raced regularly. I raced against these boats and won frequently.
>
> My dory was exceptionally well built, with the finest of workmanship, and should be alive and sailing today if it has had proper care.

In redrawing the original print, for publication, I have supplied a set of lines. These, I believe, are substantially correct for this model. The original print showed profile and deck views, as well as a construction section taken about amidships. This was supplemented by a list of principal dimensions. In addition, I had lines of other Chaisson sailing dories to go on, as well as the plans for C. D. Mower's early 21-foot racing dory for the Swampscott Club. Thus, I think that these lines as I have reconstructed them are not too far out of the way.

The original Chaisson print seems to indicate only five planks to the side. Three topside planks are clearly and unmistakably shown. To fill in the remaining space with only two planks would require boards of nearly impossible width. So I have laid out three strakes of plank here. Confirmation is furnished by old photographs of contemporary Swampscott boats showing six planks on a side, as is likewise the number on C. D. Mower's 21-foot sailing dory for the Swampscott Club.

While no offsets are given, the lines are accurate enough to be scaled for building. The original print specified bent frames spaced 8 inches on centers, with no mention whatever of sawn frames, usual in dory construction. However, several sets of sawn frames were probably used in lieu of molds, and remained permanently in the boat. Four sets would do nicely for this purpose, and if set on stations 4, 8, 12, and 16, as numbered in my lines, they would conform to the 8-inch spacing for the intervening bent ribs.

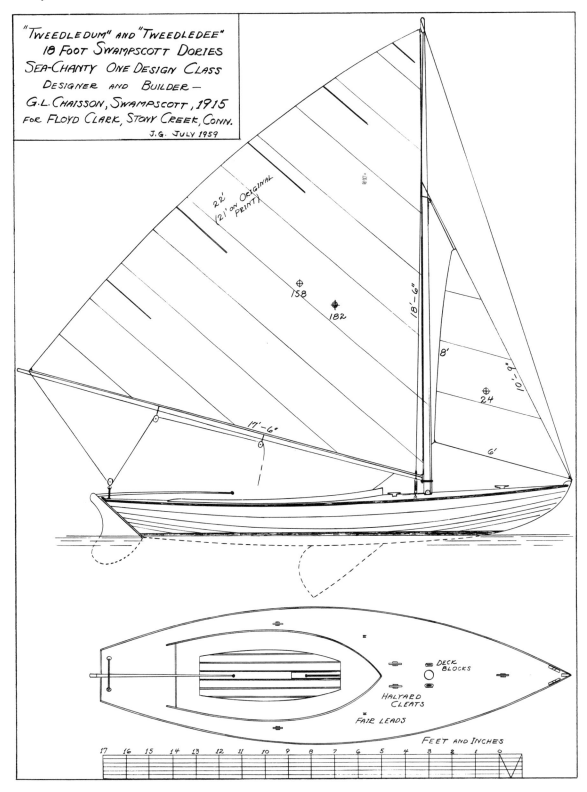

"TWEEDLEDUM" AND "TWEEDLEDEE"
18 FOOT SWAMPSCOTT DORIES
SEA-CHANTY ONE DESIGN CLASS
DESIGNER AND BUILDER—
G.L. CHAISSON, SWAMPSCOTT, 1915
FOR FLOYD CLARK, STONY CREEK, CONN.
J.G. JULY 1959

22'
(21' ON ORIGINAL PRINT)

158

182

18'-6"

8'

10'-9"

24

17'-6"

6'

DECK BLOCKS

HALYARD CLEATS

FAIR LEADS

FEET AND INCHES

17  16  15  14  13  12  11  10  9  8  7  6  5  4  3  2  1  0

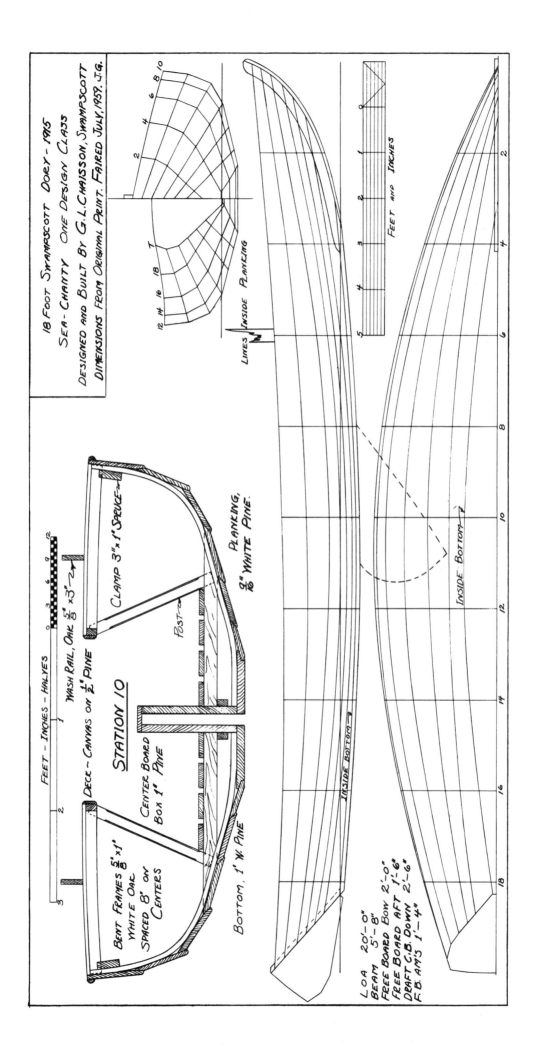

18 Foot Swampscott Dory - 1915
Sea - Chanty One Design Class
Designed and Built by G. L. Chaisson, Swampscott
Dimensions from Original Print. Faired July, 1959. J.G.

Lines Inside Planking

Feet and Inches

Feet - Inches - Halves

Wash Rail, Oak 5/8" x 3"
Deck - Canvas on 1/2" Pine

STATION 10

Clamp 3" x 1" Spruce

Post

Planking,
9/16" White Pine.

Bent Frames 5/8" x 1"
White Oak
Spaced 8" on
Centers

Center Board
Box 1" Pine

Bottom, 1" W. Pine

Inside Bottom

Inside Bottom

LOA 20'-0"
Beam 5'-8"
Free Board Bow 2'-0"
Free Board Aft 1'-6"
Draft C.B. Down 2'-6"
F.B. Am's 1'-4"

# 16 THE CHAMBERLAIN GUNNING DORY

The handsomest of all pulling dories is unquestionably the long, slim, but richly curving double-ender that originally came out of the Orne Street boatshop of William Henry Chamberlain of Marblehead. The Chamberlain gunning dory is a sporting boat modeled by a man who loved sports and excelled at them—sailing and gunning especially—just as he excelled as a craftsman.

Pictures fail, somehow, to catch completely the fine lines of the Chamberlain gunning dory. The camera lens flattens, foreshortens, and often distorts its complex curves. Nor can verbal description evoke the full perfection of the design. It is necessary to see, and, if possible, to row a gunning dory. But where's one to be found today? Chamberlain's shop has been closed for years. And there were never many of these gunning boats built to begin with.

It was in search of a gunning dory some years ago that I called to see Captain Gerald (Jerry) Smith, well-known North Shore yachting skipper, in the little shop at the rear of his Pond Street residence in Marblehead. I had heard that Captain Jerry was building a dory. It was not his first. I recalled a handsome, easy-rowing double-ender of the gunning dory type that he had built some 20 years previously.

In the Pond Street shop, a 17-foot double-ender was set up ready for planking. Jerry had framed it from a set of Chamberlain molds in his possession. Their years were evidenced by the deep, rich, brown color that age alone

brings to pine. As for the sheerline and the bottom rocker, Jerry had gone according to his own experience and judgment; in particular, he gave the bottom more fore-and-aft camber or rocker than Chamberlain, who made his dories closer to straight on the bottom. It is Jerry's opinion that a few inches of rocker make a better boat to row, and an easier one for getting off the beach with a load. As for the sheer, Jerry had lined out a nice, up-sweeping curve on his shop floor laydown that avoided the flatness that sometimes marred gunning boat lines.

Although originated by Chamberlain, double-ended gunning dories have since been constructed by several other builders, each of whom has added his own characteristic touches. The late Albert Cloutman built his own version, called the Sharpshooter. This was essentially the Chamberlain model, except the bottom was made a foot shorter.

Captain Jerry Smith, a gunning enthusiast and duck hunter from way back, was building his new boat for his own use. It was a labor of love, and consequently he took his time and used only the best of materials. Frames are of natural-crook elm, with twisting and interlocking grain that makes just about the toughest frames going. The bottom is a single width of native white pine, 19½ inches at its point of greatest breadth. Planking is of Northern white cedar. Pine is standard planking for dories, but gunning dories usually rate cedar as befitting their superior quality.

Gunning in Marblehead means duck shooting. The waters around the scattered rocky islands lying off the shores of Marblehead are natural habitats for numerous duck species that have long afforded sport in fall and early winter for town gunners. Ducks are found near the Dry Breakers, Ram Island, Tinkers, Coney Island, and the Inner and Outer Pigs, to mention some of the best gunning spots.

Years ago when the fishermen went gunning in the fall, they naturally went in their dories. But the standard lobster dory that had been soaking all summer was heavy and clumsy to drag over the rocks for the considerable distances often required, because of the movement of the tides. So gunning enthusiasts would plan to buy a new dory in the fall in order to have it as light as possible during the gunning season. In the early days, according to Captain Jerry, before Chamberlain, Graves, and others started building dories in town, Marbleheaders got their dories in Swampscott from Joshua Small and E. Gerry Emmons.

Early on a Sunday morning, generally, the two or three gunning partners who were to share the use of the new dory would set out on foot for Swampscott, some five or six miles distant. One would carry the leg-o-mutton sail rolled around its spar, another the oars. Arriving in Swampscott, and after paying their $18.00, then the price of a new fishing dory, they would start back by water. If the weather was fine and the breeze favored, they might take the long way home by way of Boston Harbor and Graves and Minots Lights, but that meant a late Sunday dinner.

Possibly Will Chamberlain built his first gunning boat even before 1900. He was an ardent gunner. He was born in 1864, and probably had hunted from boyhood. His big retriever, curled up under his workbench or sitting in the stern sheets of his sailing dory at the start of a race, is still remembered in Marblehead. Will Chamberlain's gunning partner, Arthur Bamford, was also his leading dory builder, so to speak.

Probably considerable experimentation was done before the light, double-ended Chamberlain gunning dory finally took classic shape. Gunning dories are remembered that were quite sharply pointed at the ends. Some, as already mentioned, had a rather flat sheer. As for rocker, Chamberlain is reported to have

once stated that he and Bamford had on one occasion tried putting in more rocker than their usual amount, but found it didn't seem to help.

The gunning dory from which I took the lines and details in 1942, and which I show here, was Chamberlain's own personal gunning dory, according to Charlie Briggs, who owned it in 1942 and who was using it for lobstering. I was a newcomer to Marblehead and unfamiliar with Chamberlain boats. But the superb lines of this double-ender hauled up on the beach at Barnegat caught my eye immediately. I spent a Saturday measuring the boat and am glad I did, for later the boat was broken up. Unfortunately, I had no camera at that time, so I failed to make a photographic record.

This boat had the lightest scantlings of any dory I have ever seen. Nevertheless, it was adequately strong, and stood up well under the abuse of lobstering, a use for which it was not originally intended. The bent ribs placed between the four sets of sawn dory frames are not usually found in dories. Undoubtedly they furnished needed support for the extra-thin cedar planking, only seven-sixteenths of an inch thick. This double-ender, unlike some, is higher at the bow than at the stern and is otherwise different at its ends. The extremely narrow ends of the sheer plank is a unique characteristic of Chamberlain designs, a strikingly handsome feature, adding grace and lightness to the lines. This dory is longer by nearly a foot than most gunning dories.

A hole through the forward thwart and a mast step underneath on the bottom showed that a sail was sometimes used, although mast and sail were missing when I took off the lines. No centerboard was built into these gunning dories, for lightness and simplicity, and also because they were primarily pulling boats. They had a light, unstayed mast, short enough to be stowed compactly inboard when down. The mast was round where it went through the thwart and in the step so that in a quick squall, when the single-part sheet was let go, the boom could swing around over the bow, and so prevent an overset.

The cut of the sail shown, as well as the dimensions, are typical, according to Captain Jerry Smith. When sailing, the dory steered with an oar; some fishermen placed oarlocks or

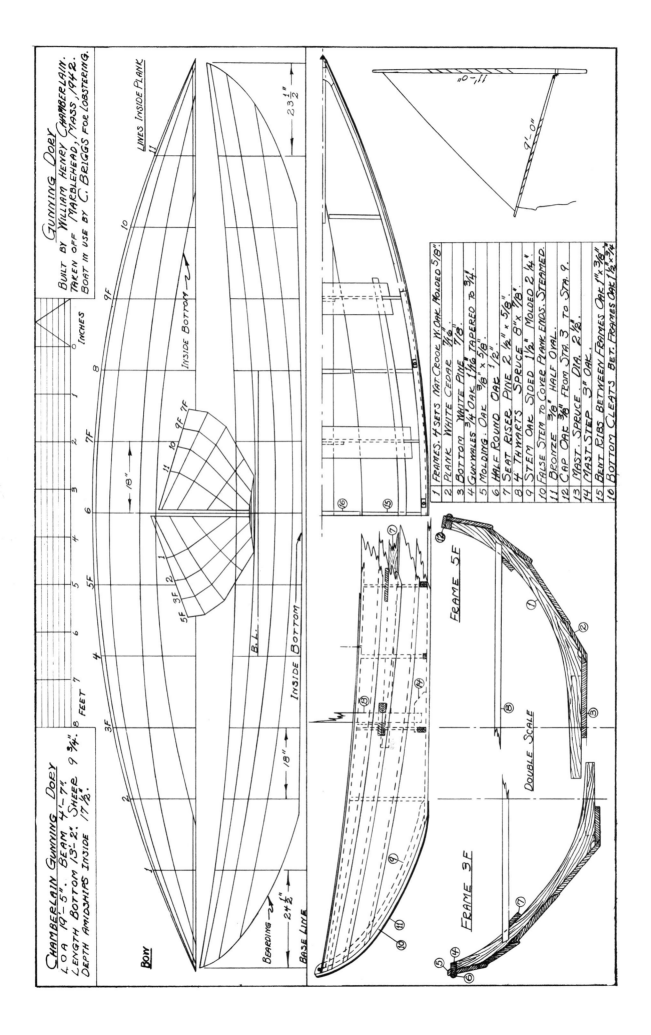

CHAMBERLAIN GUNNING DORY
L.O.A. 19'-5". BEAM 4'-7".
LENGTH BOTTOM 13'-2". SHEER 9¾".
DEPTH AMIDSHIPS INSIDE 17½".

GUNNING DORY
BUILT BY WILLIAM HENRY CHAMBERLAIN.
TAKEN OFF MARBLEHEAD, MASS. 1942.
BOAT IN USE BY G. BRIGGS FOR LOBSTERING.

LINES INSIDE PLANK

INSIDE BOTTOM

BODY

BEARDING

BASE LINE

INSIDE BOTTOM

B.L.

INCHES
FEET

FRAME 5F
FRAME 3F
DOUBLE SCALE

| 1 | FRAMES. 4 SETS NAT. CROOK W. OAK MOLDED 5/8" |
| 2 | PLANK WHITE CEDAR 7/16" |
| 3 | BOTTOM WHITE PINE 7/8" |
| 4 | GUNWALES 3/4 OAK 1½ TAPERED TO 3/4". |
| 5 | MOLDING. OAK 7/8" x 5/8" |
| 6 | HALF ROUND OAK 1/2" |
| 7 | SEAT RISER PINE 2½" x 5/8". |
| 8 | 4 THWARTS SPRUCE 8"x 7/8". |
| 9 | STEM OAK SIDED 1½ MOLDED 2¼". |
| 10 | FALSE STEM TO COVER PLANK ENDS. STEAMED. |
| 11 | BRONZE 3/8" HALF OVAL. |
| 12 | CAP OAK 3/8" FROM STA. 3 TO STA. 9. |
| 13 | MAST. SPRUCE. DIA. 2½". |
| 14 | MAST STEP 3" OAK. |
| 15 | BENT RIBS BETWEEN FRAMES OAK 1" x 3/8" |
| 16 | BOTTOM CLEATS BET. FRAMES OAK 1½ x 3/4. |

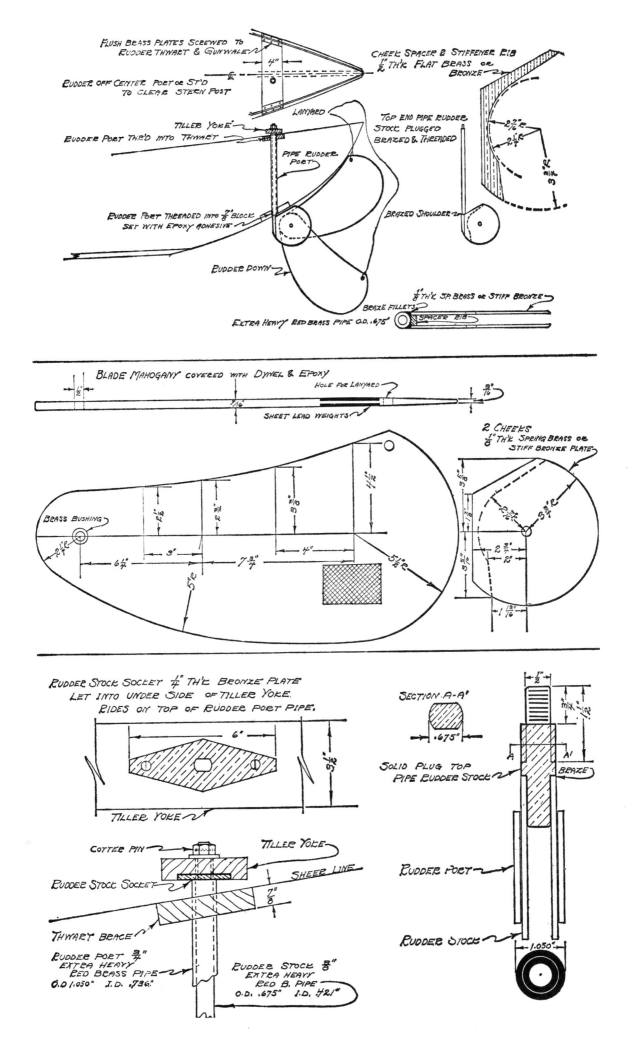

FLUSH BRASS PLATES SCREWED TO RUDDER THWART & GUNWALE

CHEEK SPACER & STIFFENER RIB ½" TH'K FLAT BRASS OR BRONZE

RUDDER OFF CENTER PORT OR ST'D TO CLEAR STERN POST

LANYARD

TILLER YOKE

RUDDER PORT THR'D INTO THWART

TOP END PIPE RUDDER STOCK PLUGGED BRAZED & THREADED

PIPE RUDDER PORT

RUDDER PORT THREADED INTO ⅞" BLOCK SET WITH EPOXY ADHESIVE

BRAZED SHOULDER

RUDDER DOWN

BRAZE FILLETS

⅛" TH'K SP. BRASS OR STIFF BRONZE

SPACER RIB

EXTRA HEAVY RED BRASS PIPE O.D. .675"

BLADE MAHOGANY COVERED WITH DYNEL & EPOXY

HOLE FOR LANYARD

SHEET LEAD WEIGHTS

2 CHEEKS ⅛" TH'K SPRING BRASS OR STIFF BRONZE PLATE

BRASS BUSHING

RUDDER STOCK SOCKET ¼" TH'K BRONZE PLATE LET INTO UNDER SIDE OF TILLER YOKE. RIDES ON TOP OF RUDDER PORT PIPE.

SECTION A-A'

.675"

SOLID PLUG TOP PIPE RUDDER STOCK

BRAZE

TILLER YOKE

COTTER PIN

TILLER YOKE

RUDDER STOCK SOCKET

SHEER LINE

THWART BRACE

RUDDER PORT ¾" EXTRA HEAVY RED BRASS PIPE O.D. 1.050" I.D. .736"

RUDDER STOCK ⅝" EXTRA HEAVY RED B. PIPE O.D. .675" I.D. .421"

RUDDER PORT

RUDDER STOCK

1.050"

The Chamberlain gunning dory re-designed by the author for James Rocke-feller. The construction photo shows the batten seam method used. The plans for this boat appear on pages 198-201.

*Rockefeller's gunning dory shows her form and carrying capacity.*

pins on the stern quarters to make it easier to keep the steering oar in place. As in all dories, the inside bottom is protected with the usual removable slatted gratings.

The fame of the Chamberlain gunning dory reached the ears of James Rockefeller, an enthusiastic duck hunter who finds gunning among the islands and ledges in lower Penobscot Bay around Vinalhaven, Maine, a fabulous and fascinating experience with a "certain mystique impossible to describe." He wanted to prolong the season into the first weeks of January, but that required a boat of unusual qualities, for as he observed, it can get quite nasty in a hurry on the offshore ledges in the winter time.

Rockefeller specified a boat large enough to hold two men with guns, decoys, and other gear, and to be managed safely and comfortably in a bad chop. At the same time he wanted something that might double as a

summer rowboat for his wife and two small children. It had to be light enough to drag up on the transom of his 36-foot lobsterboat with the aid of rollers.

In the beginning, Rockefeller had not considered the possibility of sailing a gunning dory, but when this was suggested he adopted the idea with alacrity.

The original length of the Chamberlain gunning dory of 19½ feet seemed excessive, particularly so, I suppose, in this decadent era of sawed-off, tubby, outboard boats, but I held out for an overall length of nothing less than 18 feet and won my point. The other changes in the lines were slight. I gave the modified version slightly more beam in proportion to length and widened the bottom a trifle aft. In lowering the deadrise angle just a bit, a somewhat harder knuckle at the junction of the second and third planks was attained, with the object of giving stiffer bearing for sailing. In

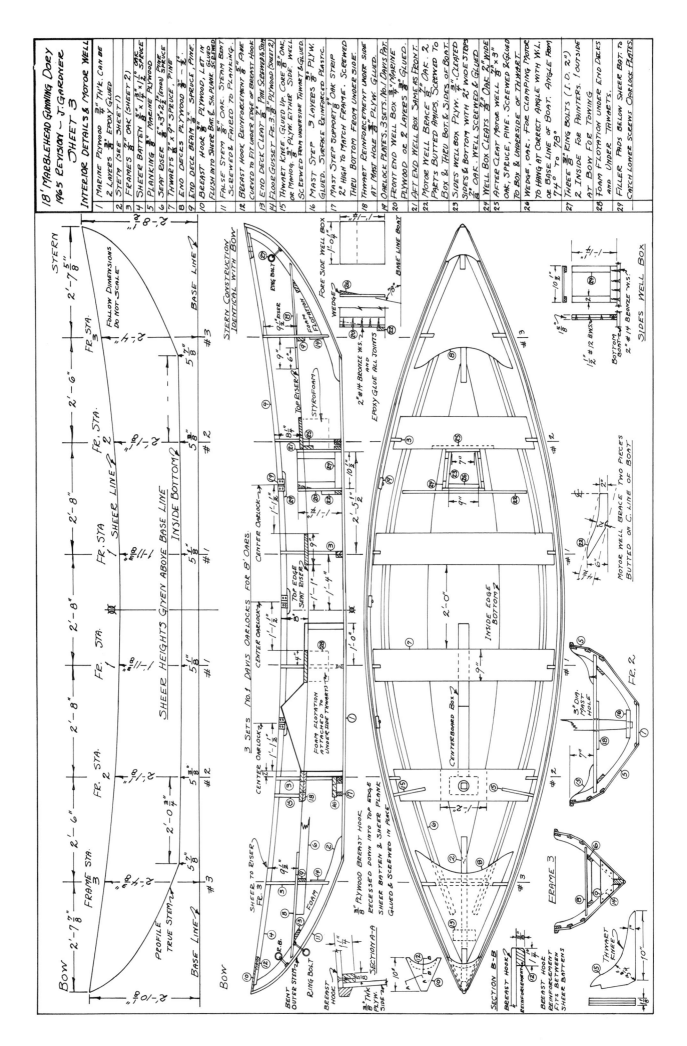

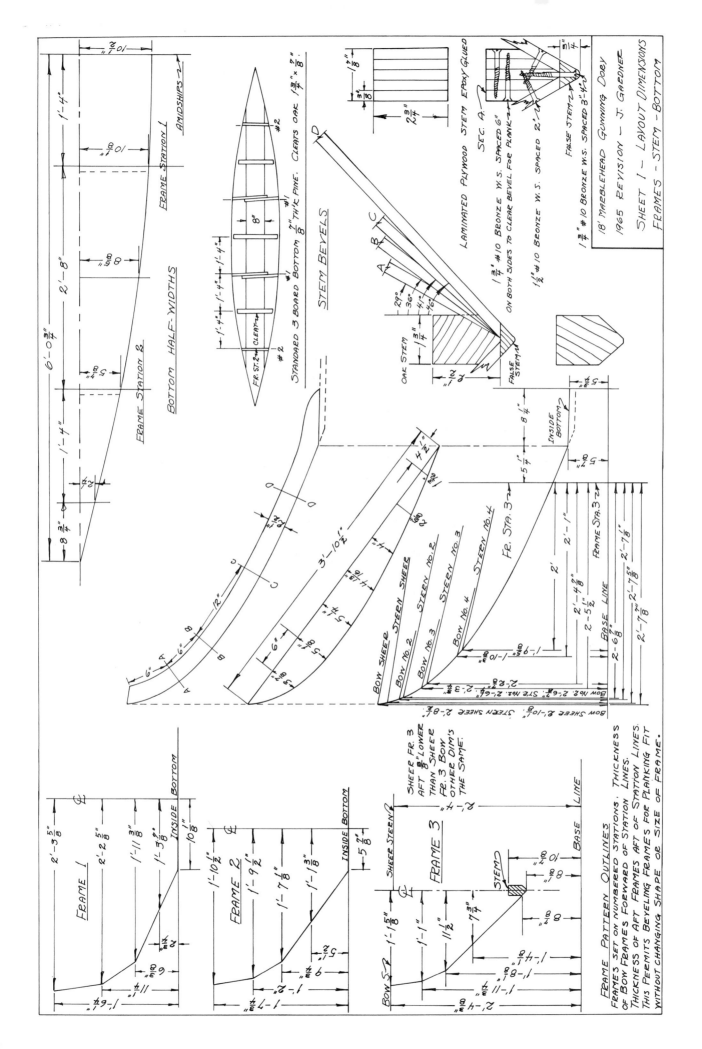

18' MARBLEHEAD GUNNING DORY
1965 REVISION — J. GARDNER
SHEET 1 — LAYOUT DIMENSIONS
FRAMES — STEM — BOTTOM

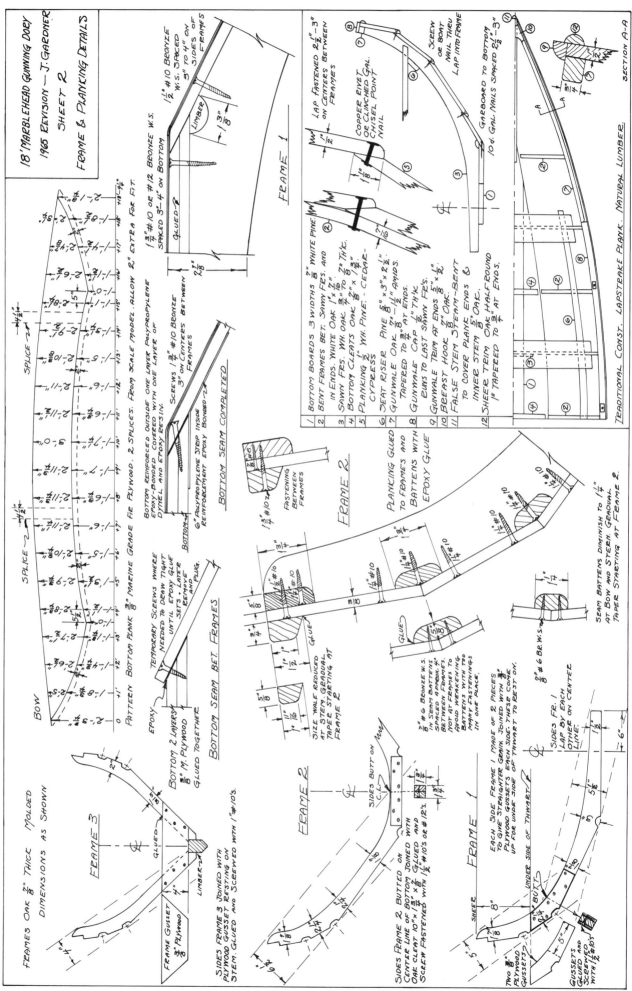

18' MARBLEHEAD GUNNING DORY
1965 REVISION — J. GARDNER
SHEET 2
FRAME & PLANKING DETAILS

FRAME 1

FRAME 2

FRAME 3

SECTION A-A

TRADITIONAL CONST. LAPSTRAKE PLANK. NATURAL LUMBER.

| | |
|---|---|
| 1 | BOTTOM BOARDS 3 WIDTHS $\frac{7}{8}$" WHITE PINE. |
| 2 | BENT FRAMES BET. SAWN FRS. AND IN ENDS. WHITE OAK 1" x $\frac{7}{16}$". |
| 3 | SAWN FRS. WH. OAK $\frac{3}{4}$"-$\frac{7}{8}$" THK. |
| 4 | BOTTOM CLEATS OAK $\frac{7}{8}$" x $\frac{7}{8}$". |
| 5 | PLANKING $\frac{5}{16}$" YH. PINE - CEDAR - CYPRESS |
| 6 | SEAT RISER PINE $\frac{5}{8}$" x 3" x 2$\frac{1}{2}$". |
| 7 | GUNWALE OAK $\frac{7}{8}$" - 2" AMIDS. TAPERED TO $\frac{3}{4}$" AT ENDS. |
| 8 | GUNWALE CAP OAK 1" THK. RUNS TO LAST SAWN FRS. |
| 9 | GUNWALE TRIM AT ENDS $\frac{5}{8}$" x 1" |
| 10 | BREAST HOOK $\frac{7}{8}$" OAK. |
| 11 | FALSE STEM STEAM-BENT TO COVER PLANK ENDS & INNER STEM $\frac{5}{8}$" OAK. |
| 12 | SHEER TRIM OAK HALF ROUND 1" TAPERED TO $\frac{3}{4}$" AT ENDS. |

FRAMES OAK $\frac{5}{8}$" THICK MOLDED DIMENSIONS AS SHOWN

PATTERN BOTTOM PLANK $\frac{3}{8}$" MARINE GRADE FIR PLYWOOD. 2 SPLICES. FROM SCALE MODEL. ALLOW 2" EXTRA FOR FIT.

BOTTOM REINFORCED OUTSIDE ONE LAYER POLYPROPYLENE EPOXY-BONDED COVERED WITH ONE LAYER OF DYNEL AND EPOXY RESIN.

BOTTOM SEAM COMPLETED

BOTTOM SEAM BET. FRAMES

FASTENING BETWEEN FRAMES

PLANKING GLUED TO FRAMES AND BATTENS WITH EPOXY GLUE

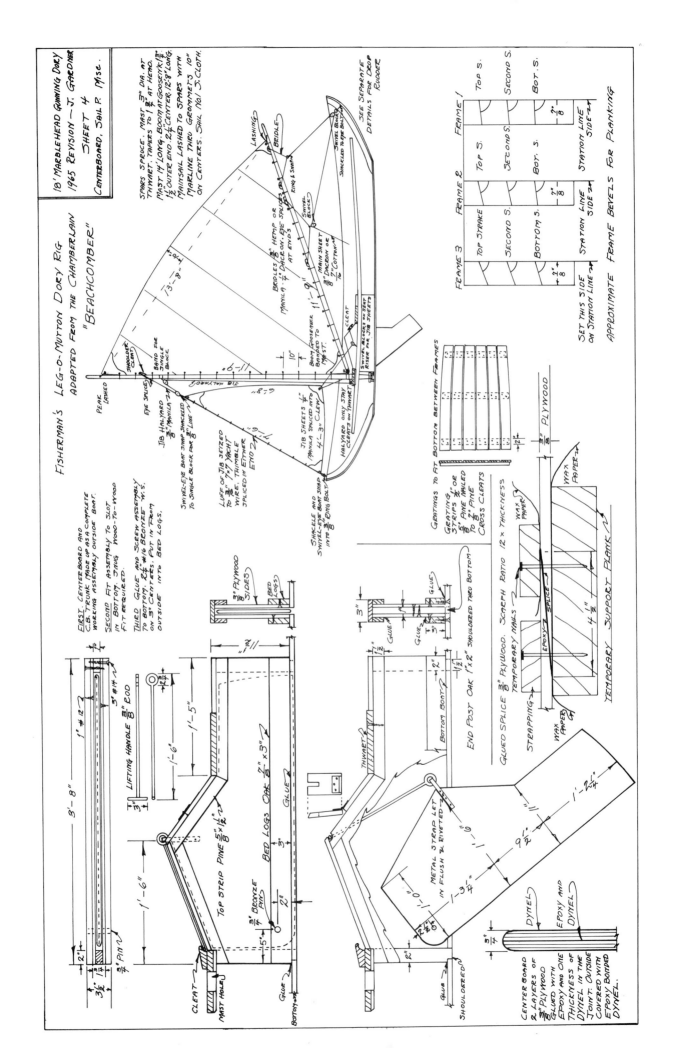

fact, all changes in the lines with the exception of shortening the length by about a foot under that of the original were made with the object of making the boat stiffer under sail, yet without impairing her easy rowing qualities to any noticeable degree.

As I mentioned previously, the gunning dories originally carried a light, unstayed mast and a small sail for running before the wind. Naturally, they required no centerboard. We had more ambitious plans for sailing and borrowed the details for the centerboard and centerboard case from Chamberlain's famous 21-foot Beachcomber sailing dory. Otherwise, we went about adapting this boat to sail cautiously and experimentally, starting out with a small sail area and an oar substituting for a rudder as originally used by the Swampscott and Marblehead lobstermen of 50 years ago when they sailed their working dories.

Even with meager canvas and the relatively clumsy steering oar, the new gunning dory sails surprisingly well. To some extent, this is certainly due to her exceptional lightness achieved without any sacrifice of strength by the use of seam-batten construction utilizing laminated spruce framing, epoxy adhesive, and ¼-inch plywood planking reinforced with Dynel fabric set in epoxy resin.

The boat sails well, but would obviously sail much better with a suitable rudder. For one thing, a rudder would permit the helmsman to place his weight where it would do the most good. For another, a well-adjusted rudder of suitable size would give much surer control. But fitting a rudder to this double-ended boat, considering the curve and rake of its stern post, or rather its "stern stem," if the term may be permitted, involves a few problems. For one thing, a rudder hung on an excessive rake tends to lift and lose its bite on the water when it is turned. Besides, the slant is awkward for the tiller or the tiller yoke. Certainly it was not possible to borrow the Beachcomber dory's rudder as we had its centerboard, because the Beachcomber's tombstone is straight and not raked excessively.

In addition to the problem of mounting the rudder on a curved and overhanging stern, there are other things to consider. It is desirable that the rudder be easily removed. The drop rudder shown comes off by loosening a single nut, but the hinged blade also swings up by itself to clear any obstructions, and lifts and secures above the bottom so that the boat may be drawn out on the beach without disengaging the rudder.

The installation—the way the rudder works as well as its fabrication—should be apparent from the drawings. It would be easy to substitute a larger blade, although the one shown is probably large enough considering its deep bite below the bottom of the boat.

There is enough clearance between the interior diameter of the ¾-inch, extra-heavy, red-brass pipe specified for the rudder port and the outside diameter of the ⅜-inch, extra-heavy, red-brass pipe used for the rudder stock to give a loose working fit, but not too loose. In locating the rudder port enough off center, either to port or starboard, sufficient to clear the stern post, no loss in rudder efficiency or any other undesirable effect may be expected.

Actually, this rudder is quite a simple contrivance, made entirely from standard, easily-obtained materials, and it is not difficult to construct.

The rudder stock and the rudder port are made out of standard brass pipe. The only lathe work is the solid plug closing the upper end of the rudder stock, which can be shouldered and threaded in 15 minutes. The two cheek pieces and the rib that joins and stiffens them can be cut out just as quickly from ordinary flat brass or bronze on a metal-cutting band saw. A few holes are bored on a drill press, and assembly is made by brazing. There is nothing beyond the skill of the capable amateur or the ordinary equipment of most boatshops.

Whether an ordinary stick tiller is used or a tiller yoke and tiller lines is a matter still to be settled. Yoke and lines are not seen much today, but Chamberlain favored them for dories and rigged his famous racing Beachcomber in this way. Besides some of the sailing dories, many of the old sailing canoes were steered with yoke and lines. Some of these now nearly forgotten craft carried light rigs to nearly ultimate refinement. With lines for steering, the helmsman could sit amidships and place his weight wherever he wished. It is necessary for a boat so equipped to carry a slight weather helm to keep a tight steering line.

The gunning dory, by the way, should not

be confused with another Chamberlain double-ender of about the same length built as a small surfboat and used in particular by the Metropolitan District Commission of Boston for life-saving and beach patrol work. Some will remember one of these surf dories that stood for many seasons on a cart on the sidewalk at the entrance to King's Beach, Lynn. While 19 feet long, or about the same length as the gunning dory, the surf dory had more sheer and a slightly different profile at the stemhead. Also, it was moderately deeper and fuller and had an additional strake or plank; that is, five strakes instead of the gunning dory's four. Further, the surf dory had no rocker, being dead straight on the bottom fore and aft.

# 17  THE 19-FOOT SURF DORY

Getting a boat on or off the beach in running surf requires a knack—also a special kind of boat. Several years ago, when the Texas Petroleum Company was in need of a small surfboat on the west coast of Nicaragua, they sent up to New England. The boat they picked was a double-ended, round-sided surf-dory of the sort developed in the North Shore fishing towns of Marblehead and Swampscott, Massachusetts. It was essentially a refinement of the fisherman's beach dory, with a trace of whaleboat, perhaps, and something from larger lifesaving craft as well as from the general heritage of scores of double-ended lapstrake workboat types once found on the North Atlantic coast.

The use for which the Texas Petroleum Company required a small surfboat was unusual. There was no dock at Puerto Masachapa, a small port south of Managua, Nicaragua, on the Pacific Coast, which the Texas Petroleum Company used as a terminal. When tankers arrived to discharge cargo, they were tended by two 24-foot power launches. These launches tied up just beyond the surf line. A small surfboat was required to carry men and equipment back and forth between the launches and the beach through the heavy surf. An exceptionally sturdy boat was required, as well as one of proper design, to withstand the powerful surf. The boat in use prior to the surf-dory was smashed.

The 19-foot surf-dory was designed to carry at least four men and several hundred pounds of equipment and lines. At Puerto Masachapa in heavy surf there is normally a helmsman with a steering oar and three men pulling single oars. Under less severe conditions, however, two men rowing in the ordinary manner with a pair of oars each, can handle the boat nicely and show a fair turn of speed. The boat is by no means so heavy or cumbersome that one capable oarsman cannot manage under most conditions, outside of surf.

The last builder to construct any number of surf-dories of this sort was the late George L. Chaisson of Swampscott, Massachusetts. Chaisson made them for local use and also shipped them to various parts of the country.

The surfboat built by Chaisson was certainly derived in large measure from the distinctive, round-sided work-dories developed by the fishermen on the flat, sandy beaches of Swampscott and Lynn. But William Chamberlain built these surfboats or lifeboats in his Marblehead boatshop before Chaisson. And it appears to have been Chamberlain who designed the model or derived it, rather, from the common round-sided work dory. Possibly Chamberlain was indebted also to the design of the larger (30-foot) lifeboats of the old Massachusetts Humane Society, which in Chamberlain's day maintained their Lifesaving Station No. 10 at Marblehead. The Humane Society's lifeboats, in turn, show a definite whaleboat influence.

The boat built for the Texas Petroleum

*The 19-foot surf dory designed and built by the author in 1955 for the Texas Petroleum Company. Note the stability of this boat.*

Company, the lines and offsets for which are reproduced here, follows closely the old Chamberlain 19-footer, except that the new boat was given slightly more depth and beam to increase its carrying capacity as a working boat. Both ends of the Texaco dory are identical to meet the breakers either way, and the inside arrangement is such that the boat can be rowed in either direction. The ends are sharp to cut the waves, yet full enough below to have lots of lift. They are also carried high enough to keep above the crests. This means that there is more than an ordinary amount of sheer when the ends are swept down to a moderate freeboard amidships to permit a good rowing angle for the oars and to keep down wind resistance. The bottom is straight and flat, which gives the boat a good seat on the beach and a very shoal draft, permitting the boat to go high up on the beach before grounding out. The bottom is also exceptionally solid to take pounding on a rough beach. The flotation is placed quite high in the ends to make the boat right easily in the water, should it ever capsize.

In building the boat for the Texas Petroleum Company, several departures were made from Chamberlain's construction. Intermediate to the standard sawn dory frames, steam-bent white oak ribs were placed in the manner adopted by Chaisson, a structural feature of great importance in adding strength and stiffness to the hull. The garboards were made of 5-ply, $\frac{3}{8}$-inch-thick Douglas fir marine plywood. A new method of locating the sawn frame splices up under the cross thwarts was employed to get a stronger frame and to avoid metal clips. An improved double-bottom was adopted from one seen on a dory built by Fred Dion of Salem. For flotation, Styrofoam was used instead of air tanks. Tanks can spring leaks, are difficult to make, and are expensive. Styrofoam is better in every way, and much cheaper. Instead of iron fastenings, bronze screws and copper rivets were used throughout. Modern waterproof glue as well as liquid rubber was employed. The inner bottom was made of mahogany, as mahogany gives a better hold for the garboard screws than pine, yet will not swell and shrink as much as an oak bottom would in the extreme conditions of the tropics.

For the 19-foot surf-dory, the plywood

selected was marine grade. This was used for the garboards, for gussets for splicing the frame futtocks as well as the two-piece stems, and for the bulkheads of the two end compartments enclosing the Styrofoam flotation. As the garboards of the surf dory are approximately 19 feet long, it was decided to splice them in the center, which is their narrowest part, and as the boat is identical at both ends, one pattern was all that was needed for marking out the four pieces needed for making up the two garboards. Thus it was possible, by taking care, to lay out the garboard pieces on a 4-foot by 12-foot sheet and to have enough left over to make the frame and stem gussets, as well as the end bulkheads. The procedure required laying out a garboard pattern before the frames were assembled and the boat was set up. Such a pattern may be obtained with sufficient accuracy from a scale half-model of the boat, most conveniently made 1½ inches to the foot.

Douglas fir plywood was chosen for the good and sufficient reason that it was the only kind of marine grade available. Apparently for such reasons as the abundance and the large size of Doublas fir timber, the good gluing qualities of that wood, and its high strength to weight ratio, Douglas fir dominates the plywood field. Some other wood or combination of woods might conceivably make a better marine plywood, but they were not available when the prototype boat was built.

In the surf dory, the lower edges of the garboards were not only coated with applications of sealer and paint, but also the ½-inch outer bottom of oak was extended to cover the garboard edges, with a liberal coating of bedding compound placed between. The upper edges of the garboards, beveled 1⅛-inches to lap under the broad strake, were coated with rubber sealer before the lap was riveted together. At both ends of the boat the garboards were sealed and bedded before being covered by the steam-bent false or outer stem. Thus all edges of the garboards were protected by sealing and covering with other members of solid wood. It may be positively stated that good building practice requires that plywood edges always be covered, and when plywood is adapted to traditional boat types, design and construction should be modified to permit such covering.

In the past the garboards of a standard 19-foot dory would have been of pine ⅝-

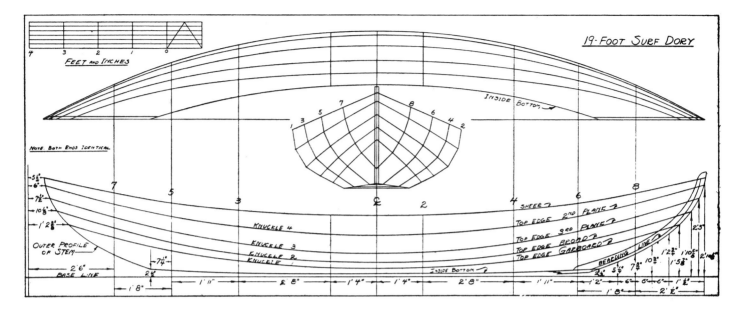

19-FOOT SURF DORY

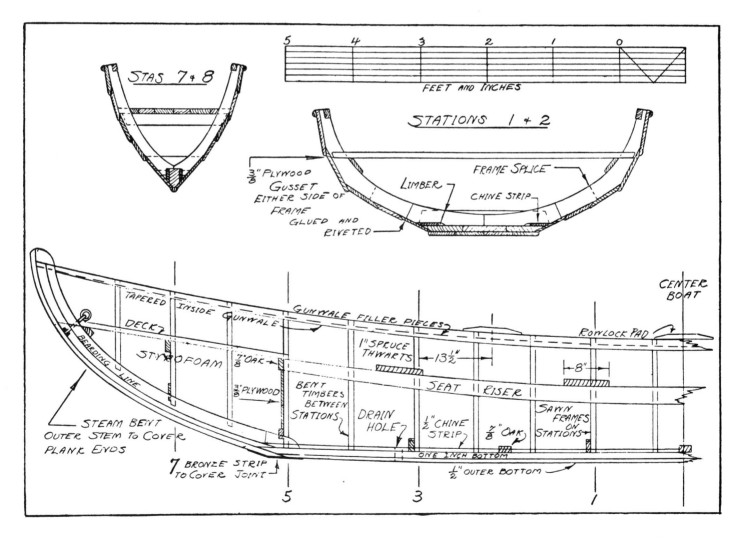

| | STATIONS | STEM | 7 + 8 | 5 + 6 | 3 + 4 | 1 + 2 |
|---|---|---|---|---|---|---|
| | | | | | | |

19-FOOT SURF DORY<br>OFFSETS — FEET, INCHES, AND EIGHTHS

| | STATIONS | STEM | 7 + 8 | 5 + 6 | 3 + 4 | 1 + 2 |
|---|---|---|---|---|---|---|
| **HEIGHTS** | SHEER | 2-10-1 | 2-4-6 | 2-1-2 | 1-10-7 | 1-9-2 |
| | KNUCKLE 4 | 2-7-2 | 2-1-1 | 1-8-6 | 1-5-1 | 1-2-6 |
| | " 3 | 2-3-0 | 1-8-4 | 1-3-5 | 0-11-4 | 0-8-4 |
| | " 2 | 1-10-5 | 1-4-6 | 0-11-6 | 0-8-0 | 0-5-2 |
| | " 1 | 1-5-7 | 1-1-8 | 0-8-6 | 0-5-3 | 0-3-2 |
| | IN. BOT. | 0-2-4 | STEM | 0-2-2 | 0-1-4 | 0-1-2 |
| **HALF-BREADTHS** | SHEER | 0-0-1 | 0-11-6 | 1-7-2 | 2-1-2 | 2-5-4 |
| | KNUCKLE 4 | " | 0-11-1 | 1-6-3 | 2-0-1 | 2-4-2 |
| | " 3 | " | 0-9-5 | 1-4-0 | 1-9-1 | 2-0-6 |
| | " 2 | " | 0-7-5 | 1-1-2 | 1-5-1 | 1-7-6 |
| | " 1 | " | 0-5-5 | 0-10-3 | 1-1-3 | 1-3-4 |
| | IN. BOT. | " | STEM | 0-2-2 | 0-7-6 | 0-11-3 |

OFFSETS MEASURED FROM BASELINE TO INSIDE PLANK,<br>TO INSIDE BOTTOM, TO STEM PROFILE.

inch thick; for light construction, 9⁄16-inch thick. Chamberlain, on the other hand, built his gunning dories with planking of ½-inch cedar. In substituting plywood for the garboards, that of ⅜-inch thickness is the best choice. Plywood ¼ inch thick, available only in 3-ply construction, is not solid enough for a boat of this size, nor is it stiff enough to bend fairly in the garboard width around frame-molds spaced 32 inches apart. On the other hand, ½-inch plywood would be unnecessarily heavy and stiff. Possibly a

5⁄16-inch 5-ply Mexican or African mahogany plywood would be the best choice of all for garboards for this 19-foot boat, if such plywood were available.

In the dry condition, ⅜-inch plywood garboards will be a little lighter in weight than garboards of ⅝-inch pine, in spite of the added weight of the glue in the former. But in a water-soaked condition, the thicker pine planking would certainly be considerably heavier, especially as a portion of the plywood is made impervious to water by its four layers of glue.

# 18  THE BEACHCOMBER-ALPHA

The Beachcomber-Alpha adventure comprises one episode in American boating history that deserves repeating. From about 1900 to 1910 these superb sailing dories were in their heyday. Designed and built by William Chamberlain in Marblehead for the Beachcomber Club of that town, whence this dory took its name, the same boat, with slight differences in rig, was adopted by the Alpha Dory Club of Salem, about 1906 or slightly before, where it was known as the Alpha dory.

The Beachcombers and the Alphas constitute the final chapter in the evolution of the sailing work dories of the North Shore, before sailing dories were transformed into purely racing craft, designed for speed rather than utility. The true Beachcomber is an open, undecked boat, fitted with rowlocks and oars, and as well suited to rowing as to sailing. It is still close to the working dories, a rugged utility craft that can be rowed, that can stand rough water, and that a lobsterman could tend his traps from. But although the Beachcomber is still a working dory, essentially, it has been fined out somewhat for fast sailing and easy handling. Like the Morgan horse, it has both stamina and speed.

Originally, the Beachcomber was built entirely of oak and pine lumber, with the exception of hackmatack for its four sets of natural-crook sawn frames, and sometimes for thwart knees and breast hook. It was fastened throughout with galvanized boat nails, and the fittings and hardware were all of galvanized iron. All in all, scantlings and fastenings were on the light side to give a hull that was as light as possible for fast sailing. It is a tribute to the inherent strength of dory construction, and the careful workmanship by which these dories were put together, that Beachcombers lasted as long and stood up as well as they did.

In some of the older boats, weakened by years of hard sailing or by collision, a brace in the form of a ⅜-inch iron rod with a turnbuckle in the middle ran from gunwale to gunwale just forward of the mast. This was not standard equipment, however, and I have not drawn it in the plans.

Today a lighter and stronger boat could undoubtedly be built by the judicious substitution of modern materials, including screws, plywood, glue, and resin-bonded fabric reinforcements. Safety flotation can be supplied by plastic foams. Undoubtedly, if Chamberlain were alive today and building dories, he would take advantage of the newer materials. As it was, I believe that screws had to some extent replaced nails in the last of the Beachcombers.

A list of "General Specifications" for the Beachcomber has been found among Chamberlain's papers. It is not complete, although nearly all items of importance are included. We shall use it as an outline, considering each of the headings in turn and adding such supplementary data as is needed.

The *bottom* is white pine, ⅞-inch in thick-

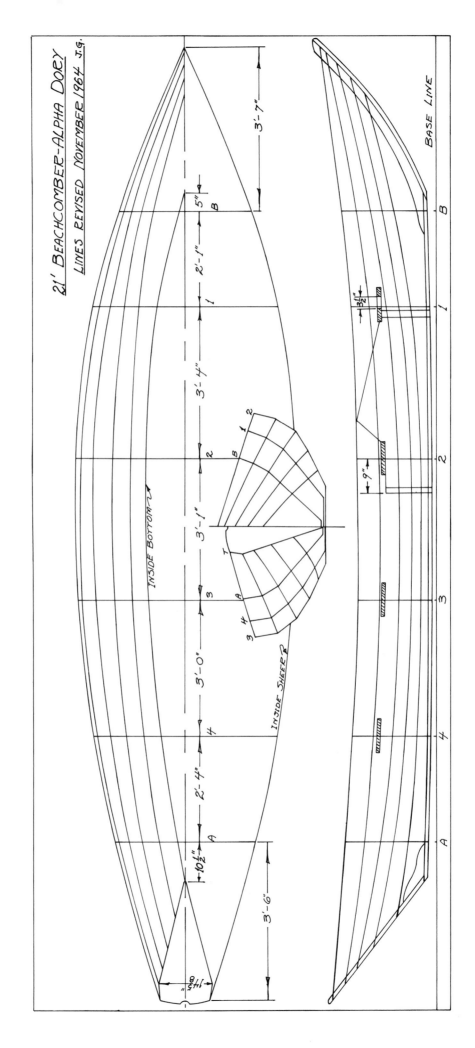

21' BEACHCOMBER-ALPHA DORY
LINES REVISED NOVEMBER 1964 J.G.

INSIDE BOTTOM

INSIDE SHEER

BASE LINE

| | STATIONS | T | A | 4 | 3 | 2 | 1 | B | S |
|---|---|---|---|---|---|---|---|---|---|
| HEIGHTHS ABOVE BASE-LINE | SHEER | 2-4-1 | 2-0-5 | 1-10-6 | 1-9-2 | 1-9-4 | 1-11-1 | 2-1-5 | 2-7-2 |
| | 1ST KNUCKLE | 2-0-5 | 1-7-4 | 1-5-0 | 1-3-2 | 1-3-3 | 1-6-1 | 1-9-7 | 2-5-7 |
| | 2ND KNUCKLE | 1-9-5 | 1-3-0 | 1-0-2 | 0-10-2 | 0-10-1 | 1-1-5 | 1-5-7 | 2-2-6 |
| | 3RD KNUCKLE | 1-5-1 | 0-11-4 | 0-8-4 | 0-6-6 | 0-6-7 | 0-10-2 | 1-2-5 | 1-11-2 |
| | 4TH KNUCKLE | 0-10-6 | 0-7-4 | 0-5-2 | 0-4-2 | 0-4-2 | 0-7-0 | 0-11-4 | 1-7-4 |
| | BOTTOM | 0-3-2 | 0-2-7 | 0-2-3 | 0-2-1 | 0-2-0 | 0-2-6 | 0-3-3 | 0-3-4 |
| HALF-BREADTHS TO INSIDE PLANKING | SHEER | 0-6-7 | 1-7-2 | 2-1-1 | 2-5-3 | 2-6-0 | 2-1-4 | 1-6-2 | 0-0-0+ |
| | 1ST KNUCKLE | 0-7-3 | 1-6-3 | 2-0-0 | 2-4-2 | 2-4-4 | 1-11-5 | 1-4-7 | 0-0-0+ |
| | 2ND KNUCKLE | 0-6-3 | 1-3-4 | 1-8-5 | 2-0-3 | 2-1-2 | 1-8-5 | 1-2-4 | 0-0-0+ |
| | 3RD KNUCKLE | 0-4-6 | 0-11-6 | 1-4-1 | 1-7-3 | 1-8-1 | 1-4-6 | 1-11-7 | 0-0-0+ |
| | 4TH KNUCKLE | 0-2-6 | 0-7-0 | 1-11-2 | 1-2-3 | 1-3-0 | 1-0-5 | 0-8-5 | 0-0-0+ |
| | | 0-0-2 | 0-1-7 | 0-6-3 | 0-10-0 | 0-10-6 | 0-7-6 | 0-1-3 | 0-0-0 |

BEACHCOMBER-ALPHA OFFSETS, FEET, INCHES, EIGHTHS. INSIDE PLANKING AND BOTTOM. OUTSIDE STEM AND TRANSOM.

T= TRANSOM. STATION A. 3'-6" FED. SHEER AT TRANSOM. STATION B. 3'-7" AFT SHEER AT OUTBOARD STEM. S= STEM. TOLERANCE, PLUS OR MINUS ⅛". REVISED NOVEMBER 1964. J. G.

ness, which is about a minimum bottom thickness for nailing on a garboard. Normally, either two or three boards will be required to make up a maximum bottom width of 21½ inches.

Standard nailing for garboards into the edge of the bottom is with 3-inch galvanized wire nails spaced about 2½ inches. A fine pilot hole for each nail is carefully sighted and drilled to prevent the nail from entering at the wrong angle, causing it to split through either one face or the other. As a substitute, bronze or monel Anchorfast nails will hold equally well or better, will last longer, but will cost considerably more.

If a plywood bottom is used, a thickness of ½-inch or even ⅝-inch would be required for fastening the edges of the garboards. For additional reinforcement and complete watertightness, the edges of a plywood bottom should be bound with glass fabric or Dynel set in epoxy resin.

*Bottom cleats.* The several boards making up the standard pine bottom are cleated athwartship between frame stations and at the ends with 2-inch strips of oak, ⅞ inch thick and laid flat. These are made short enough to let water run around the ends. They were originally fastened on from the outside with 2-inch galvanized chisel-point boat nails with the points turned back and clinched into the wood, but now it is generally easier to secure them with No. 12 or No. 14 screws 1½ or 1¾ inches long.

The *transom* is oak, ⅞ inch thick. If one board is used, a width of 16½ inches is required, which is probably wider than is commonly obtainable. Two boards will do, provided one is quite wide and the two are solidly joined with No. 12 or No. 14 1½-inch screws into the stern cleat.

The *stern knee* is 1⅞ inches thick, like the stem, fastened to the transom with No. 14 or No. 16 screws 1½ to 3 inches long. Originally this would have been fastened with galvanized blunt-point boat nails of approximately the same lengths.

The *stern cleat* is ⅞ inch thick. The molded width of 6 inches is sufficient to allow for through-bolting of the ⅜-inch eyebolt for the main sheet block.

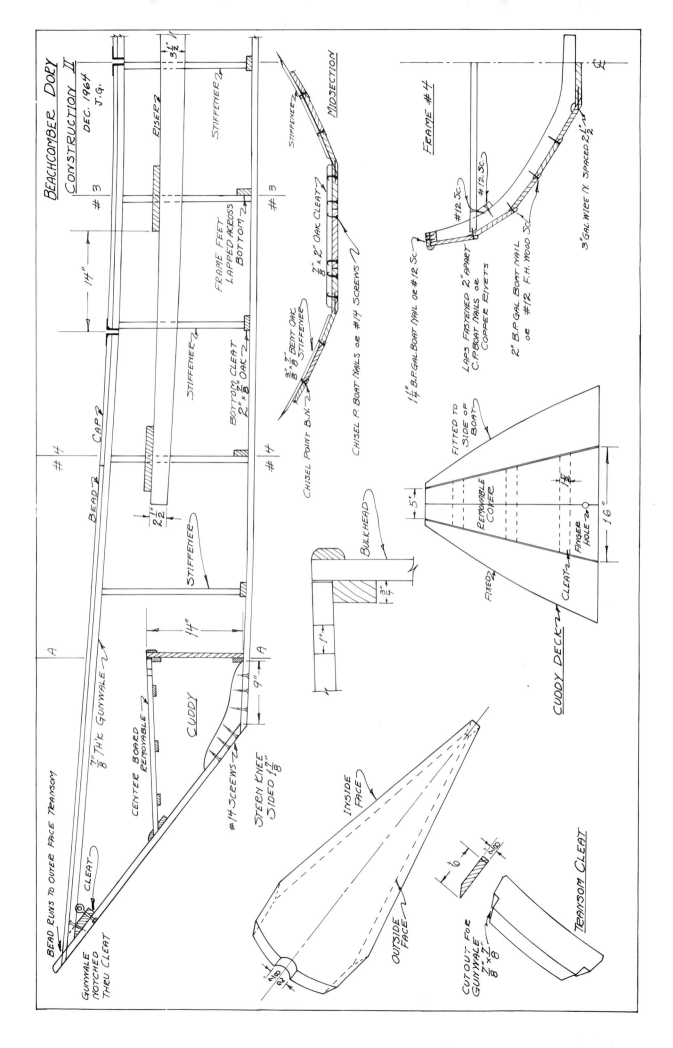

BEACHCOMBER DORY
CONSTRUCTION II

DEC. 1964
J.G.

#3

RISER

STIFFENER

14"

3½"

FRAME FEET
LAPPED ACROSS
BOTTOM

#4

BEAD

CAP

STIFFENER

2½"

STIFFENER

14"

CENTER BOARD
REMOVABLE

9"

#14 SCREWS

STERN KNEE
SIDED 1⅛"

A

BEAD RUNS TO OUTER FACE TRANSOM

GUNWALE
NOTCHED
THRU CLEAT

CLEAT

⅞" TH'K GUNWALE

CUDDY

BOTTOM CLEAT
2" x ⅞" OAK

STIFFENER

STIFFENER

MIDSECTION

⅞" x 2" OAK CLEAT

3" x ⅞" BENT OAK
STIFFENER

CHISEL POINT B.N.

CHISEL P. BOAT NAILS or #14 SCREWS

BULKHEAD

3"

1"

FRAME #4

#12 Sc.

#12 Sc.

LAPS FASTENED 2" APART
C.P. BOAT NAILS or
COPPER RIVETS

2" B.P. GAL. BOAT NAIL
or #12 F.H. WOOD Sc.

1¼" B.P. GAL. BOAT NAIL or #12 Sc.

3" GAL. WIRE N. SPACED 2½"

CUDDY DECK

FITTED TO
SIDE OF
BOAT

5"

REMOVABLE
COVER

FIXED

CLEAT

FINGER
HOLE 2"

1½"

16"

INSIDE
FACE

OUTSIDE
FACE

CUTOUT FOR
GUNWALE
⅞" x 1"

TRANSOM CLEAT

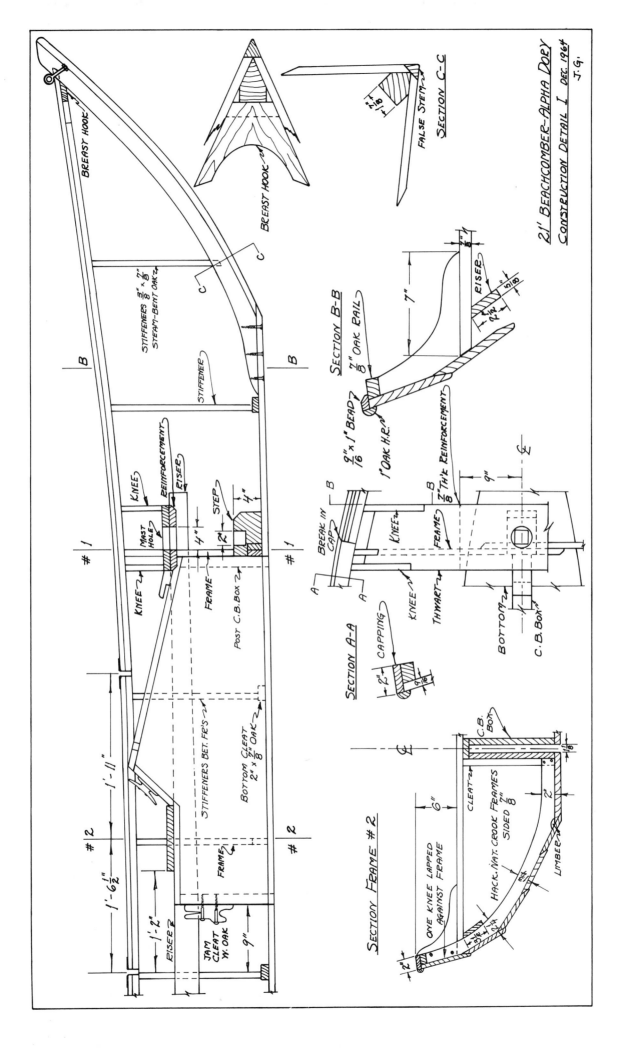

21' BEACHCOMBER-ALPHA DORY
CONSTRUCTION DETAIL I    DEC. 1964    J.G.

SECTION C-C
FALSE STEM
7/8"

SECTION B-B
7/8" OAK RAIL
9/16" × 1" BEAD
1" OAK H.R.
RISER
7/8"
7"
2½"
51/16"

SECTION A-A
2" CAPPING
9/16"
BREAK IN CAP
KNEE
THWART
BOTTOM
C.B. BOX
KNEE
FRAME
7/8" TH'K REINFORCEMENT
9"

BREAST HOOK
BREAST HOOK
STIFFENERS 3/8" × 7/8" STEAM-BENT OAK
STIFFENER
KNEE
REINFORCEMENT
RISER
MAST HOLE
STEP
4"
2"
4"
KNEE
FRAME
Post C.B.Box

1'-6½"
1'-11"
1'-2"
9"
RISER
FRAME
STIFFENERS BET. FR'S
BOTTOM CLEAT 2" × 7/8" OAK
JAM CLEAT YW. OAK

SECTION FRAME #2
ONE KNEE LAPPED AGAINST FRAME
6"
CLEAT
C.B. BOX
HACK. NAT. CROOK FRAMES SIDED 7/8"
LIMBER
2"
3½"
2"

*A Beachcomber-type dory built at Marblehead by Chamberlain.*

*A Swampscott X-dory, probably built by Emmons. This one is similar to those later built by Chaisson. Note the battened sails.*

*Model of a 21-foot Beachcomber dory built by the author and now at the Peabody Museum in Salem, Massachusetts.*

Hobo, *an Alpha dory that sailed out of South Salem, Massachusetts.*

*Dories racing in Marblehead in the late 1890s, before the advent of the Beachcomber dory class. Note the yokes and tiller lines. Marblehead dories were steered with a yoke and tiller lines, while Swampscott dories used a conventional stick tiller.*

*A Beachcomber dory built by Chamberlain. The scene is off Marblehead.*

The *stem* is oak, sided 1⅞ inches and molded 2¼ inches.

The *false stem* is oak, a strip about 2 inches wide by 1¼ inches thick, steam bent on the flat into place, nailed or screwed down tightly and finished to shape when cold.

*Frames.* Chamberlain lists: "Four sets hackmatack, sided ⅞ inch, molded 2 inches between knuckles, fastened to the bottom with 2-inch galvanized-iron boat nails." Such natural-crook hack frames crossed by each other across the bottom of the boat. More frequently, instead of such matched pairs of natural-crook frames, a three-part oak frame was substituted comprised of two side futtocks and a single piece across the bottom, the three joined together with riveted galvanized iron clips at the bottom knuckles. No matter how the frames were made up, No. 12 or No. 14 screws 1¾ inches to 2 inches long are fastened up through the bottom into the frames.

The *stiffeners* are of oak, ⅜-inch by ⅞-inch, of tough, select butt stock, steam-bent on the flat into place between the frame stations and in the ends to fit the shape of the boat, and fastened through the laps. Originally chisel-point boat nails were used, with the points turned back and clinched into the inside of the strip. Now that good chisel-point nails are difficult to obtain, copper wire nails riveted over burrs make an excellent substitute.

The *planking* is pine, ⁹⁄₁₆-inch thick. Boards as wide as 16 inches are required for the garboards. Now that planks can be spliced with waterproof glues, great savings are possible by using pieced-out strakes glued up from shorter lengths of lumber. For the wide-ended garboards, ⅜-inch plywood can be substituted; it can be scarphed and glue spliced from shorter pieces cut from 8-foot panels.

In fact, the boat can be planked entirely with plywood, and it is not necessary to lap the plywood in the conventional way. The strakes can be butted and glued to internal longitudinal seam battens. In that case, the joints can be bound with fabric tapes set in epoxy resin, or the whole outer surface can be covered with fabric set in epoxy.

In fastening conventional pine planking, No. 12, 1¾-inch or 2-inch screws go through the laps into the frames, but only through the laps, for screws through the planks into the frames between laps are liable to split the planks. As previously mentioned, the lower edges of the garboards are nailed with 3-inch nails to the bottom.

The laps were fastened originally with clinched chisel-point nails spaced 2 inches to 2½ inches apart. Now, riveted copper wire nails would probably have to be substituted, but are a better and more lasting fastening if properly put in. Incidentally, the ⁹⁄₁₆-inch planking is beveled a width of 1⅛ inches.

The *gunwales* are oak, ⅞·inch thick and 1⅜ inches wide between frames, but tapering at the ends to ⅞ inch at the stem and stern. These are bent into place and fastened down into timberheads and through the sheer plank from the outside. Nails or screws may be used in either case.

The *capping* is oak, ⁹⁄₁₆ inch thick and 2 inches wide, steamed, bent into place on the boat, and fastened down into the gunwales with nails or screws. The capping extends an inch or so past the frames at either end.

The *beading* is oak, ⁹⁄₁₆ inch thick by one inch wide, beveled on the inner edge, sprung to the shape of the boat at the ends, extending from where the capping stops to the stem and transom. The beading covers the top edge of the sheer plank and part of the gunwale. It is fastened with screws or nails.

The *breast hook* is a natural crook of hack, apple, or oak, ⅞ inch thick. It receives the ends of the gunwales, is fastened to the stem, and takes fastenings through the sheer plank from outside.

The *guard* is oak, half round, one inch wide. It is planed slightly tapering at the ends for appearance and is nailed or screwed.

The *thwarts* are pine, ⅞ inch thick by 9 inches wide. They are notched around the frames and screwed down to seat risers with No. 12, 2-inch screws.

The *thwart knees* are hackmatack, apple, or oak, ⅞ inch or ¾ inch thick. They are carefully fitted and screwed where possible to the frames, thwarts, gunwale, and sheer plank.

The *risers* are pine, ⅝ inch or ¾ inch thick, and 3½ inches wide in the center, tapering to 2½ inches at the ends. They are beveled on the top edge to receive the thwarts, and are screw fastened into the frames with 1½-inch, No. 12 screws.

The *centerboard trunk* sides are pine; the lower half is ⅞ inch thick, and the upper part can be ⁹⁄₁₆ inch thick for lightness. The end posts, mortised through the bottom, are of oak, 1¹⁄₁₆ inches thick by 1½ inches wide. The sides are copper riveted through the posts.

The *centerboard* is oak, finished ⅞ inch thick. It is pinned with drifts of ⁵⁄₁₆-inch rod and weighted with lead.

The *mast step* is an oak block, 4 inches by 4 inches by 6 inches, notched over the foot of the No. 1 frame.

The *mast hole reinforcement* is oak, ⅞ inch thick by 9 inches wide.

The *rudder* is oak, 1⅛ inches thick at the upper end of the stock, thinned to ¾ inch at the lower after edge. It is pinned with ⁵⁄₁₆- and ¼-inch rod.

The *rudder yoke* is oak, ¾ inch thick.

The *stern sheets cuddy* is pine, ¾ inch and ⁹⁄₁₆ inch thick, fastened with No. 12 screws.

The *gratings or racks* are pine, ⁹⁄₁₆ inch thick. The racks are removable.

The *spars* are Douglas fir or spruce.

## Lining Plank

It is important not to overlook that the lines are drawn to the inside of the planking. This is noted on the lines and offsets, but some readers, unfamiliar with dories and small-craft building practice, might overlook it. To work from the inside of the planking is easiest and most accurate, especially for clinker-planked boats with knuckled sides. It permits laying out directly the shape of the frames, which serve as building molds, without having to deduct plank thickness or to make allowance for lap widths.

However, the planking lines as drawn do not represent the outside appearance of the hull after it has been planked. The finished plank lines will be lower by the width of the lap. This shows up especially in the width of the garboard, which will be reduced by the width of the lap, and in the sheer, which will be increased by the same amount.

The hood end of the sheer plank as it appears on the profile view of the lines might seem excessively narrow where it lands on the stem, but it must be understood that this is the inside view, less the lap, and that actually the end of the sheer plank will be wider by 1⅛ inches, which is the width of the lap. Even so,

this makes the sheer plank quite narrow on the stem, but this is a characteristic of Chamberlain boats, and one of the refinements by which Chamberlain achieved a hull of outstanding grace and beauty. By keeping the hood ends of the upper planks quite narrow on the stem, and likewise on the transom, it is possible to peak up the ends of the garboard, and so straighten out its upper edge (when laid out flat) as well as straighten out the run of the plank above. This makes for less work in planking, more efficient use of lumber, and stronger planking because of the use of straighter grain.

A note on the table of offsets specifies a dimensional tolerance of plus or minus one-eighth inch. This is about as close as it is possible to scale offsets from a drawing laid out to a scale of one and one-half inches equals one foot. Even greater corrections or adjustments may be required in making a full-size building laydown of these lines. But this is to be expected, and as long as changes are kept as small as possible, and the general proportions of the lines sedulously adhered to while all is made fair and true, the result will be satisfactory.

## Rudder and Centerboard

No surviving rudder or centerboard for the Beachcomber-Alpha is now to be found for copying, yet I have been able to get together enough reliable data from one source or another to reconstruct these essential accessories with substantial accuracy. Both the rudder and centerboard are typical of sailing dories of the period. Their design and construction are quite simple, yet even so, pains must be taken in putting them together. There are several things that the amateur builder should be sure he understands before he sets to work.

Even if a single board wide enough to make the rudder in one piece were obtainable, it is better to make it of two boards, as I show, as a precaution against warping. With a two-board rudder, the lumber should not be slash sawn, but as nearly rift sawn as possible, that is, sawn with the grain of the annual rings running at right angles to the wide surface. Furthermore, when the two boards or parts are joined, they should be placed so that the grain in one runs opposite to the grain in the other. If warping

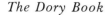

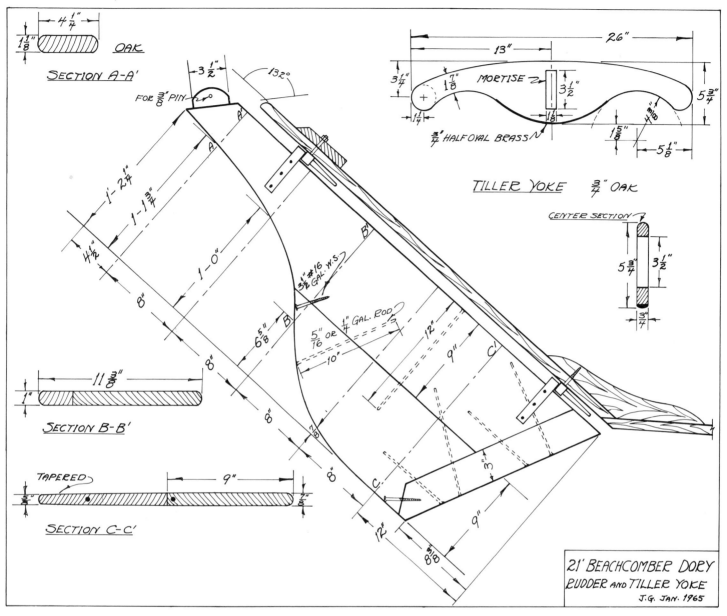

OAK

SECTION A-A'

FOR 3/8" PIN

132°

3 1/2"

1'-2 1/4"

1'-1 3/4"

1'-0"

4 1/2"

8"

6 5/8"

3/8" #16 GAL. W.S.

5/16" OR 1/4" GAL. ROD

10"

12"

9"

3"

8"

8"

8"

12"

9"

SECTION B-B'

11 3/8"

1"

TAPERED

9"

SECTION C-C'

26"

13"

3 1/4"

1 7/8"

MORTISE

3 1/2"

1/4"

1 5/8"

1/8"

5 3/4"

5 1/8"

3/4" HALF OVAL BRASS

TILLER YOKE    3/4" OAK

CENTER SECTION

5 3/4"    3 1/2"

3/4"

21' BEACHCOMBER DORY
RUDDER AND TILLER YOKE
J.G. JAN. 1965

takes place, the distortion in one part will tend to offset the distortion in the other, instead of adding to it, as happens when two or more boards are joined with their grain running in the same direction.

This precaution against warping is even more important in the construction of the centerboard, for there, if even a small amount of warping or "dishing" takes place, the board will stick in its slot. The cleats on the ends of the centerboard, like the cleat at the bottom of the rudder, are put there partly to stop warping or twisting, although they also help to hold these two assemblies together.

For both the rudder and centerboard, the lumber should be dry, well-seasoned oak. Green lumber, of oak especially, is bound to twist and warp. Oak is specified because it is standard for New England dories; it is what Chamberlain and other contemporary builders invariably used. A hard, solid grade of Philippine mahogany could be substituted. This wood keeps its shape and holds fastenings well, and is only a little more expensive, if at all, than a good grade of seasoned oak.

Plywood could also be substituted for oak for both the rudder and the centerboard, but if this is done, it would be best to cover the

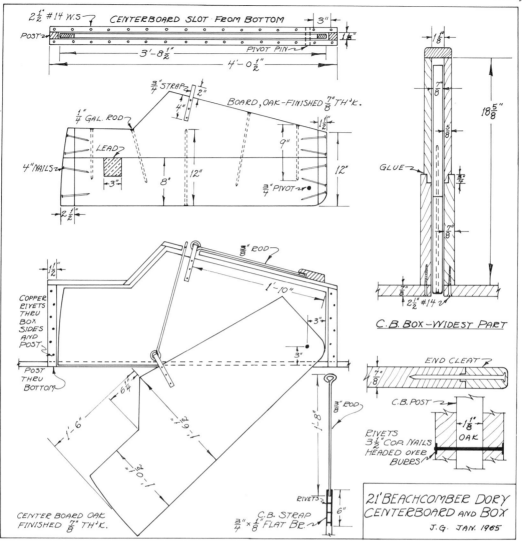

plywood with a skin of Dynel fabric bedded in epoxy resin. This covering serves both to waterproof and reinforce the plywood. By making up these parts from plywood, the need for pinning and cleating would be bypassed, for each could be made in a single piece. This would save a lot of labor and might more than offset the cost and trouble of adding the Dynel fabric and epoxy resin. Should the rudder be made of fir plywood, it would be necessary to reinforce the tenon that passes through the rudder yoke. With waterproof mahogany or birch plywood, such reinforcement would not be required.

### Pinning the Board

If oak is used, and pinned together as laid out in the drawings, the amateur should take care, for the operation is a fairly critical one that could easily be messed up for the want of the correct procedure. For instance, in boring for the pins, the uninstructed novice rarely gets his holes lined up accurately and too frequently puts his drill out through the side. Yet the operation is not essentially difficult.

For both rudder and centerboard, cut out the component pieces and fit them, temporarily assembling them on a flat surface, such as a level bench top. These pieces will all be of the same thickness of stock, for any tapering and thinning is left until the assembly is solidly pinned together. Clamp this preliminary assembly so it can't move, and exactly mark on the exposed upper surface the location of each pin with a firm, straight line the length of the pin. This line represents the center of the pin.

Separate the parts and square the pin lines, just marked, down across the edges of the pieces. Next, with a combination square or some other gauge that is set to half the thickness of the boards, mark through the lines already squared across the edges, gauging always from the upper, marked side of the boards.

Now the exact locations for boring the holes for the pins have been found and are marked on all edges by the intersection of the squared-down pin line with the gauge line. At these intersections, holes of the right size for the pins may be precisely centered and started with a sharp-spurred bit in a hand brace.

Where a pin is to pass entirely through a board, the hole is started on both edges and is bored halfway through from either side to halve possible error. If the two holes do not meet precisely, they usually come close enough so that the drill will lead through from side to side, so that, after reaming, a pin can be driven through. The important thing is that by this method the correct location of the holes on the edges of joining pieces is maintained. An attempt, starting at one edge, to bore a long hole edgewise through two or more thin boards will generally result in having the drill break out through one side or the other before the hole is complete.

A better way, when several thick pieces or boards are to be pinned together edgewise, is to bore each piece separately. If pre-assembled and properly marked to begin with, and provided the marks are followed, the holes will line up perfectly when the parts are reassembled again, and the pins can be driven without trouble.

A spurred bit is not suitable for boring long holes, for such bits have a tendency to run off. Either a barefoot ship's auger or a long twist drill is better. (A short twist drill may be lengthened by brazing on an extension of drill rod.)

It is assumed that an electric boring machine will be used. The builder will need assistance for sighting. The piece to be drilled is clamped flat on the bench. A straight, narrow strip of board is laid with one edge exactly on the marked line of the hole to be drilled, and it should extend somewhat beyond the piece toward the drill. By sighting along the edge of this stick, the man with the drill can line his hole one way. The hole is lined the other way, that is up or down, by an assistant standing off some distance at right angles. He calls out to the drill operator to move up or down to keep the shank of the drill exactly parallel to the run or line of the sighting stick.

By using this method, and exercising care, holes 8 or 10 inches or longer, of nearly perfect alignment, can be bored edgewise through thin, flat stock.

For the rudder, galvanized rod of $5/16$-inch diameter is recommended for pinning, although $1/4$-inch rod would do. Because the galvanizing adds slightly to the diameter, the drill should be the same size as the listed size of the rod. Even then, it may be hard to drive the rod without bending it, especially a $1/4$-inch rod. A heavy hammer is better for driving than a light one.

For the centerboard, because it is to finish $7/8$ inch thick or slightly less, $1/4$-inch rod should be used. If the holes as laid out are drilled according to the method described, that is, from both sides of each piece separately, no bored depth would be greater than $4\frac{1}{2}$ inches, so there should be little danger of running off.

### Pintles, Gudgeons, and Yoke

After the rudder is pinned, it is planed smooth and tapered. The position of the pintles and gudgeons are located. The top gudgeon is easily bolted through the transom cleat for extra strength. The pintles specified for the Beachcomber-Alpha open $7/8$ inch between the straps. The straps of the top pintle will be let in slightly, for the rudder at that point is $1\frac{1}{8}$ inches thick. The straps of the bottom pintle will slip on without cutting, since there the rudder is tapered to $7/8$ inch. The pintle straps are fastened on with copper rivets.

The tenon on the rudderhead must fit the mortise in the yoke snugly, so as not to wobble. A $3/8$-inch removable pin further secures it.

Only the weight of the rudder itself is required to keep the pintles from slipping out of the gudgeons under most conditions. If the rudder should come unshipped, the tiller lines will keep it from getting away.

The only feature of the yoke that needs mention is the reinforcement of ¾-inch half-oval brass that binds and reinforces the center part of the forward edge where there would be some danger, otherwise, of breaking because of the short grain. Normally this brass is secured by screws.

The centerboard box is rather light, but that is the way Chamberlain's specifications show it. I do not think that much weight is saved by reducing the thickness of the upper half of the box to ⅝ inch. In fact, I would prefer that the sides of the box be ¹⁵⁄₁₆ inch or even one inch throughout. The end posts should always extend through the bottom, as shown, both to stiffen the box and to permit caulking the ends from the outside. Copper rivets are the best fastening for the ends of the box, but these must be well headed over and set up tightly so they pull into the wood.

The box should be put together and bedded with waterproof adhesive, preferably epoxy, for additional strength as well as watertightness. The old builders like Chamberlain used white lead, which gave a tight seal, but did not make the construction any stronger.

The pivot pin is sometimes made of white oak or locust; if it is, it ought to be 1 inch in diameter. I have shown the pin as ¾-inch-diameter brass or bronze. It must fit tightly, yet be removable in case you wish to drop the board.

### Pivot and Rod

Sometimes a large screw eye or even an eye bolt was fastened to the top of the board for attaching the rod used for raising and lowering the board. I show a simple strap arrangement of ¾-inch by ⅛-inch flat bronze, attached with copper rivets. The handle is easily formed of ⅜-inch rod with an eye to hook into the strap on the board, and a T-shaped outer end. This tee or cross-bar rests on the top of the box when the board is down, preventing it from going farther. When the board is up, the T-end slips under a special cleat on the front end of

the box, locking the board in the up-position. This is a simple but effective device that was pretty generally used on centerboard dories of the Beachcomber period.

One thing that should be mentioned is that the lumber thicknesses given are quite critical in some cases and should not be reduced, even if retail lumberyards attempt to argue otherwise. For instance, ⅞-inch-thick pine for the bottom or the sides of the centerboard box should under no consideration be less than ⅞-inch thick. Most "one-inch" pine boards as sold today are actually only ¾-inch thick. So you may have to have your pine planed up specially, and, if you do, I would specify a "plump" ⅞-inch, which if it ran to ¹⁵⁄₁₆-inch, would be all the better.

### Sailing Rigs

The Beachcomber-Alpha is a good boat to learn to sail in. It is a safe boat for youngsters in their early teens, but no toy. In fact, sailed hard and up to its capacity, this craft can provide thrills and a vigorous workout for most adult sailors. It can be rowed as well as sailed, and handles easily under oars, like the working dories of the Massachusetts Bay shore fishermen of the late nineteenth century from which it was derived. With a full rig, 50 pounds of lead ballast on either side of the centerboard trunk, and a crew of three hiked out on the rail, this boat will draw smartly to windward and handle like a spirited colt.

This is also an economy boat. The standard rig, contrived to be lifted out of the boat and carried home at night in a compact roll on the skipper's shoulder, is just about as simple and inexpensive as it is possible for a workable rig to be.

It is not suggested that the rig about to be described in detail is the best one or the only one worth considering. But it is the rig most used around 1915, when the Beachcomber-Alpha class was at its peak of popularity. It will do to set a norm, but a norm that a present-day builder would probably want to depart from to some extent. It does constitute a tried and tested rig that is probably the least expensive and the least complicated of any that are workable and safe. But some of the newer things like Dacron yacht rope, stainless steel

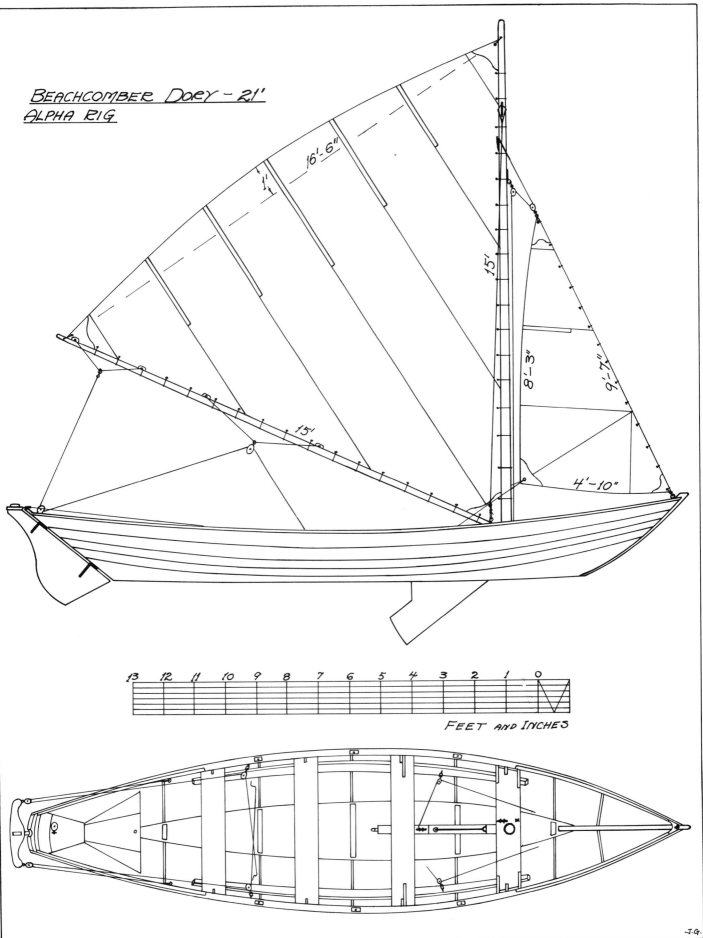

BEACHCOMBER DORY - 21'
ALPHA RIG

16'-6"

1'

15'

15'

8'-3"

9'-7"

4'-10"

13  12  11  10  9  8  7  6  5  4  3  2  1  0

FEET AND INCHES

-J.G.

wire, and some of the newer fittings are more than worth the extra cost.

In describing the rig, we shall start at the bow. The luff of the jib is laced or seized to a length of ³⁄₁₆ inch, 7 by 7 galvanized yacht wire with thimbles spliced in either end. The tack end is attached by a ³⁄₁₆-inch screw-pin shackle to a No. 1 galvanized swivel-eye boat snap, which hooks into a ³⁄₈-inch galvanized eye bolt through the stemhead. The upper eye of the jib luff wire takes another No. 1 swivel-eye boat snap, which is shackled to a single block for ³⁄₈-inch line. Another single block of the same size shackles to a 4- or 5-inch galvanized eye plate, which screws to the mast at the height designated on the rigging plan. Two ³⁄₁₆-inch screw pin shackles are needed for a fast-eye block; one shackle for a swivel-eye block.

The jib halyard of ³⁄₈-inch manila carries an eyesplice in the upper end just large enough to slip over the masthead, supported about 3 feet, 6 inches below on a wooden shoulder cleat. The lower end reeves through the block snapped into the thimble at the peak of the jib and back through the block fixed to the mast; it is hauled down taut, passing through a leader on the port top forward edge of the mast thwart, and securing to a 5-inch cleat on the after side of the thwart. This arrangement makes a separate headstay unnecessary.

The jib halyard arrangement is simplicity itself, but effective and generally substantial, although weak snaps have been known to break under the strain of pounding into a heavy chop. While ⁵⁄₁₆-inch manila might be sufficiently strong here, ⁵⁄₁₆-inch Dacron would be more than ample. Dacron, except for its higher cost, is to be preferred here, as in every other part of the rig, not only for its great strength and long-wearing qualities, but also because it handles easily and does not stretch.

The twin jib sheets of ¼-inch manila are permanently spliced into the clew of the jib, although some sailors preferred to have them on snaps. These sheets lead aft through swivel-eye single blocks shackled to ¼-inch galvanized eyebolts through the seat risers, either side, 15 inches forward of Station 2, and secure to a 4-inch cleat on the after slope of the centerboard box, above and forward of the second thwart.

The mast and boom are solid sticks of Douglas fir, according to Chamberlain's specifications, but Sitka spruce or eastern red spruce would be just as good or better. The mast is 3½ inches in diameter where it passes through the thwart and tapers to 2 inches at the head. It rises 16 feet above the thwart and extends 1 foot below, requiring a length of 17 feet in all. The gooseneck for the boom attaches about 5 inches above the thwart.

The gooseneck was generally of brass or bronze of a type that attached to the end of the boom with side straps fastened by through rivets. The boom, 15 feet, 6 inches long, is 2½ inches in diameter centrally, tapering to 2 inches at the inner end and 1¾ inches at the outer.

The mainsail is lashed permanently to the boom and mast with Italian hemp marline or suitable Dacron cord by a continuous series of half hitches passing through small grommets set close to the edges of the sail and spaced on 10-inch centers. Grommets of the same size and spacing are likewise pierced through the luff of the jib for its lashings.

Larger, heavier grommets in the corners of the sails permit lashings at the ends of the spars. The peak and the tack of the jib are held taut by lashings through respective eyes in the ends of the luff wire. The tack of the mainsail is lashed to the gooseneck. The peak, in absence of a main halyard, is pulled up by lashings passing through a ³⁄₈-inch hole bored through the top of the mast a couple of inches higher than the stretch of the sail. Likewise, a hole bored in the outer end of the boom allows a lashing from the clew that serves as an outhaul.

The two side stays or shrouds are ³⁄₁₆-inch, 7 x 7 galvanized yacht wire (stainless steel would be better) with eye splices served and varnished at the upper ends of a size to slip over the masthead and to lead neatly from ash shoulder cleats. Thimbles spliced into the lower ends allow lacing with light line to draw the stays taut. Turnbuckles are not used. Instead, ³⁄₈-inch galvanized iron eyebolts pass through the rail from 4 to 6 inches abaft the center of the mast. The eyes in the ends of the side stays hang about 6 inches above. A light line or lanyard threaded back and forth several times through these opposing eyes, and secured with a couple of half hitches around the standing parts, puts sufficient tension on the stay. In an emergency, two slashes with a knife will free the mast.

In the past, the main sheet was made of

cotton line because it was softer on the hands than hemp or manila. Dacron would be best today, and for Dacron only, ⅜-inch-diameter line would be required, while cotton for this purpose should not be less than ⁷⁄₁₆-inch.

The main sheet requires two bridles on the boom. Old photographs show considerable variation in the length and location of these bridles. It is suggested that the outer one at the end of the boom with the ring at its mid-point to take the snap in the end of the main sheet should be 1½ to 2 feet long with a drop of 6 inches, and the inner or center bridle that carries the main sheet block should be 3½ to 4 feet long with a 12-inch drop. And, further, there should be about 6 feet between the center points of the two.

These bridles have eye splices in their ends of a size to slip over the boom and are held in position by small ash stops fastened with two screws each. It is important that these bridles should not stretch, and no doubt hemp was originally used. Dacron resists stretching well, and the ⅜-inch Dacron recommended for the sheet would do nicely for these straps as well.

As previously mentioned, the outer end of the main sheet snaps into a ring tied in the outer bridle. Thence, it leads down through a single block, preferably swiveled, which is shackled to a ⅜-inch eyebolt passing through the center of the transom and vertically located slightly below the bottom of the sheer strake. From this block, the sheet leads forward and up through another swiveled single block secured at the mid-point of the inner and larger bridle. Thence, it leads downward and forward to be secured when desired on a jam cleat of ash or white oak bolted to the

after vertical post of the centerboard box. In the past, a few well-heeled skippers had brass snatch blocks attached to swivel deck plates, which bolted to the bottom of the boat about a foot aft of the centerboard box.

Since ⁵⁄₁₆-inch manila is ample for the two tiller lines, ¼-inch Dacron will do nicely. One end of the tiller line snaps into a ¼-inch ringbolt or an equivalent screweye set in the inner edge of the rail about 1 foot, 5 inches aft of Station 4. The tiller lines, one on either side, lead back to a single block, preferably a swivel-type, shackled to ¼-inch ringbolts or large screweyes in the outer ends of the yoke. From the yoke, the lines return inboard, reeving through another set of swiveled single blocks shackled to ¼-inch ringbolts or large screweyes fastened in the rail about 1 foot, 9 inches aft of Station 3. The resulting two-part purchase is sufficient to work the rudder easily from almost any location in the middle of the boat.

To secure the rudder, equivalent to lashing the tiller in other boats, the two lines are pulled tight athwartships and tied.

Rowlock sockets are set in the rail 12 inches aft of the after edges of the three forward thwarts so that the boat can be rowed from each of these thwarts if desired. When not in use, rowlocks are stored in the small after cuddy next to the transom. Here also could be stored the mooring line, which was used without mooring chocks, being tied through the mast hole and lashed to the eye in the stemhead to hold it centrally.

A pair of 8-foot oars tied under the front thwart on either side, with the blades extending to the stem, were always carried in the old Beachcomber-Alphas.

# 19   A 12-FOOT SEMI-DORY

The semi-dory, sometimes called a half-dory, gets its name from its resemblance to the forward half of a large Swampscott dory, as if the after half of the dory had been cut away and removed. Of course, this is not the case. Rather, standard Swampscott dory lines are widened aft to give a stern section wide enough and powerful enough to support an outboard motor without settling or "squatting." In the semi-dory, the after part of the bottom is also changed somewhat by widening it and by taking out the rocker to produce a nearly straight run aft. Fifteen or twenty years ago, semi-dories were a popular and much-used small craft type in New England, both for work and for sport.

This 12-foot semi-dory is a lightweight boat for oars or outboard and is well suited to carrying on the top of a car. It is easy to build, large enough for three adults to fish from comfortably, and able to stand considerable rough water. It is primarily designed for seam-batten construction with epoxy adhesives. The boat's weight, without racks or removable thwarts, is 80 to 90 pounds.

In this boat the stem and the frames, which serve as molds, are laminated from Sitka spruce ¼-inch thick. The several layers are spliced up from shorter pieces cut out and arranged to get as strong a grain combination as possible. Wherever pieced, a tapered, glued splice about three inches long for ¼-inch stock is used. If necessary, any of the strips or battens used in the boat may be spliced with a tapered wedge scarph. The ratio of the scarph length is 12:1, or twelve times the thickness of the stock being spliced. This ratio also applies to the scarphs in the plywood, when it is necessary to splice the planking.

For lightness and strength, Sitka spruce and Utile mahogany plywood have been chosen. Spruce for its weight is the strongest wood we have, and it glues well. And Sitka spruce, spar quality, while somewhat expensive, is completely clear and free of knots, and is widely obtainable. It is straight grained and saws up nicely into the narrow strips and battens required for this boat. The *Wood Handbook* gives Sitka spruce's weight dry as 28 pounds per cubic foot.

The Utile mahogany plywood recommended is 5 mm thickness for the side planking, and 6 mm thickness for the bottom, transom, and the reinforcements on the transom and the removable thwarts. Utile ply weighs only .615 pounds per square foot. Fir, ¼-inch, according to U. S. Plywood, and their thinnest marine plywood, weighs .77 pounds per square foot. Utile mahogany is a strong-lasting wood that bends well.

Only standard 4-foot by 8-foot panels of plywood are required. Thus, each plank will be spliced, as will the narrow, forward end of the bottom. Splices in the plank should be well staggered. However, if the splices are carefully made—scarph bevels planed accurately with a

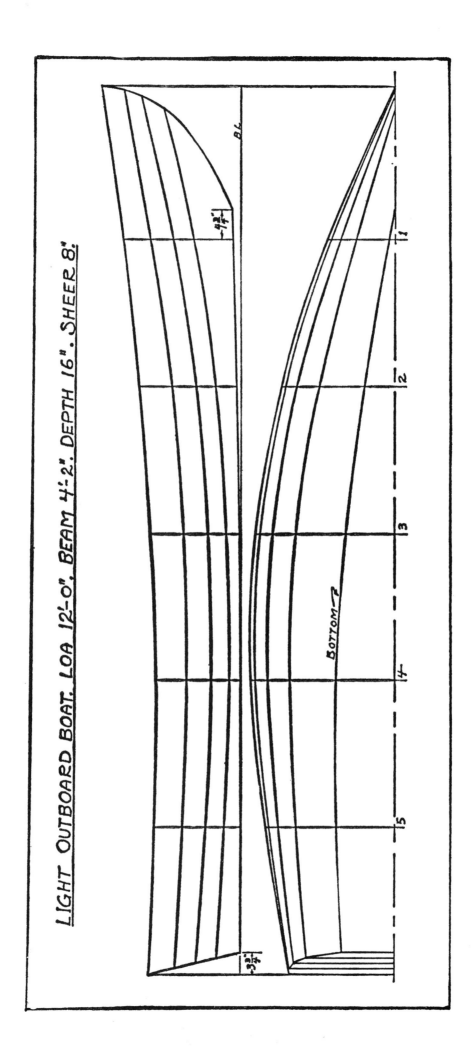

LIGHT OUTBOARD BOAT. LOA 12'-0". BEAM 4'-2". DEPTH 16". SHEER 8".

BL

BOTTOM

1  2  3  4  5

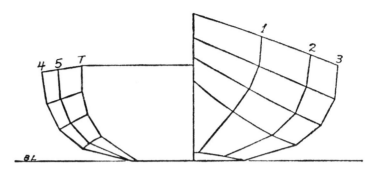

| OFFSETS in FEET, INCHES, & EIGHTHS to OUTSIDE of TRANSOM and STEM and INSIDE of PLANK and BOTTOM. | | | | | | | | |
|---|---|---|---|---|---|---|---|---|
| STATIONS | TRAN. | 5 | 4 | 3 | 2 | 1 | BOW | |
| **HEIGHTS** SHEER | 1-4-0 | 1-3-0 | 1-2-6 | 1-3-5 | 1-5-4 | 1-8-3 | 2-0-4 | |
| 1 | 0-11-4 | 0-10-2 | 0-9-4 | 0-10-1 | 1-0-1 | 1-3-5 | 1-8-5 | |
| 2 | 0-7-7 | 0-6-2 | 0-5-2 | 0-5-6 | 0-7-7 | 0-11-6 | 1-5-3 | |
| 3 | 0-4-1 | 0-2-7 | 0-1-7 | 0-2-4 | 0-4-2 | 0-8-1 | 1-1-2 | |
| BOTTOM | 0-0-0 | 0-0-0 | 0-0-0 | 0-0-0 | 0-0-4 | 0-1-1 | 0-1-2 | |
| **HALF-BREADTHS** SHEER | 1-6-2 | 1-10-2 | 2-0-6 | 2-0-0 | 1-7-3 | 0-11-3 | — | |
| 1 | 1-6-2 | 1-9-7 | 2-0-0 | 1-11-2 | 1-6-6 | 0-10-7 | — | |
| 2 | 1-5-3 | 1-8-2 | 1-10-0 | 1-9-1 | 1-4-5 | 0-9-2 | — | |
| 3 | 1-3-0 | 1-5-0 | 1-6-0 | 1-5-0 | 1-1-0 | 0-6-5 | — | |
| BOTTOM | 0-9-0 | 0-10-0 | 0-10-0 | 0-8-4 | 0-5-0 | 0-0-7 | — | |

block plane to a 12 to 1 slope, and pressed together evenly and firmly with epoxy adhesive—they should be just as strong as the rest of the wood

Bronze screws are recommended as fastenings for this boat, but they can be and should be smaller and less plentiful than is the general practice in boats of this type and size. In several instances, the screw sizes are indicated on the drawings. Each frame should be fastened to the bottom with one-inch No. 8s spaced about three inches apart. Of course, the frames are glued to the bottom with epoxy as well. In fact, it may be stated here, as general practice, that everywhere in this boat that wood joins wood, there should be a bond of epoxy. The metal fastenings are extra. And indeed, as where the frames are joined to the bottom, extra reinforcement is needed. Another place where screws are needed is through

the side plank into the several frames in the width of the plank between the seam battens. No. 6s, not over one-inch long, are sufficient, and should be spaced two to three inches. These provide reinforcement and serve to draw the plank tightly against the frames until the epoxy has set. For this, ⅝-inch No. 4s, the same as indicated to fasten the edges of the side plank to the seam battens, would be sufficient.

The screws into the seam battens need be spaced only so close as to hold the edges of the plank in firm contact with the battens until the glue has set. The meeting joint of the plywood strips should be filled with adhesive (which must be thick enough for this purpose) for strength as well as tightness. And the strip of epoxy fiberglass on the outside covering the seam will add greatly to the strength. The reason that the outside is not covered overall

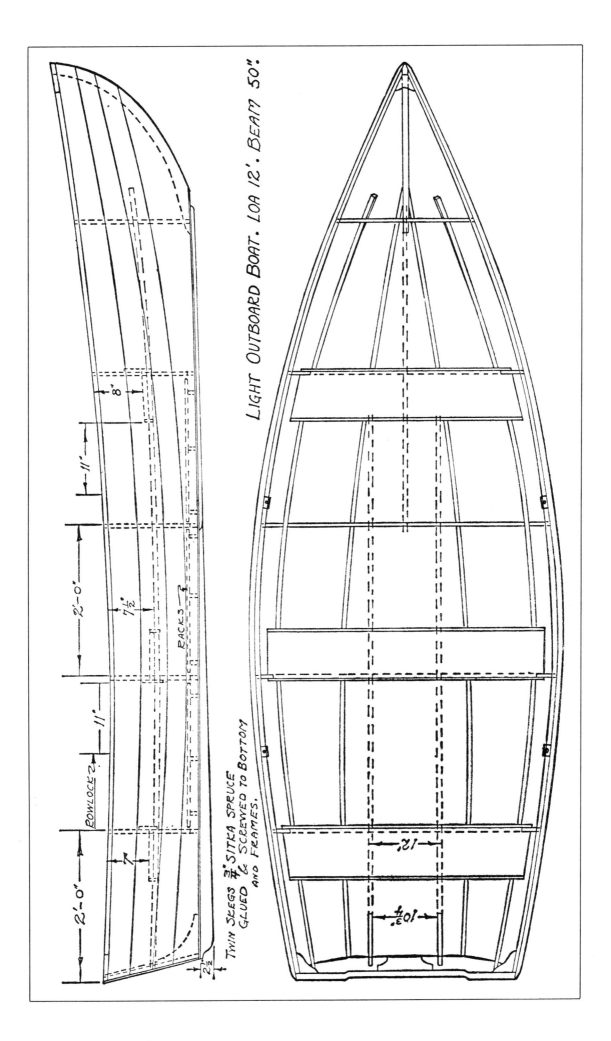

LIGHT OUTBOARD BOAT. LOA 12'. BEAM 50".

TWIN SKEGS ¾" SITKA SPRUCE
GLUED & SCREWED TO BOTTOM
AND FRAMES.

ROWLOCKS.

RACKS.

2'-0"   11"   2'-0"   11"   8"

7"   7½"

2½"

12'

10¾"

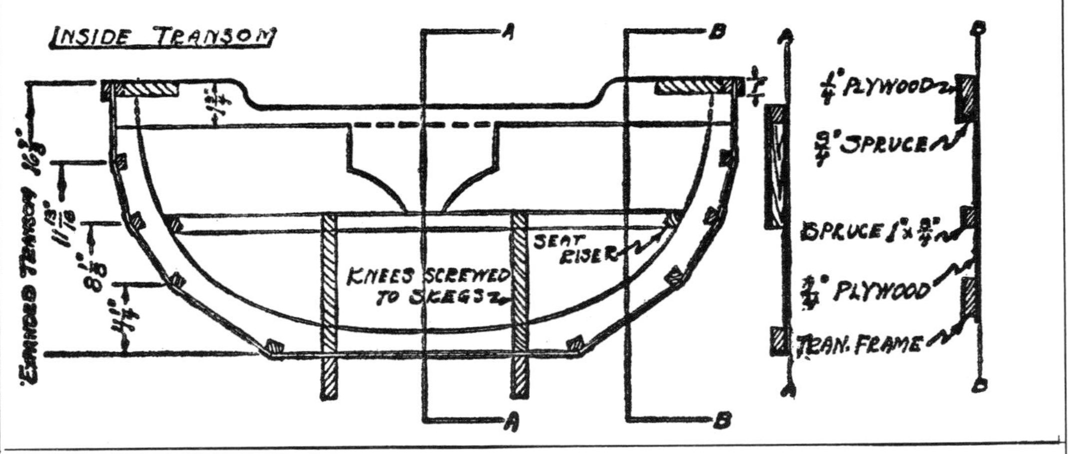
INSIDE TRANSOM
A
B
1/2"
1/4"
1/4" PLYWOOD
3/4" SPRUCE
SPRUCE 1" x 3/4"
3/4" PLYWOOD
TRAN. FRAME
SEAT RISER
KNEES SCREWED TO SKEGS
EXPANDED TRANSOM 16 3/8"
11 13/16"
8 1/2"
4 1/4"

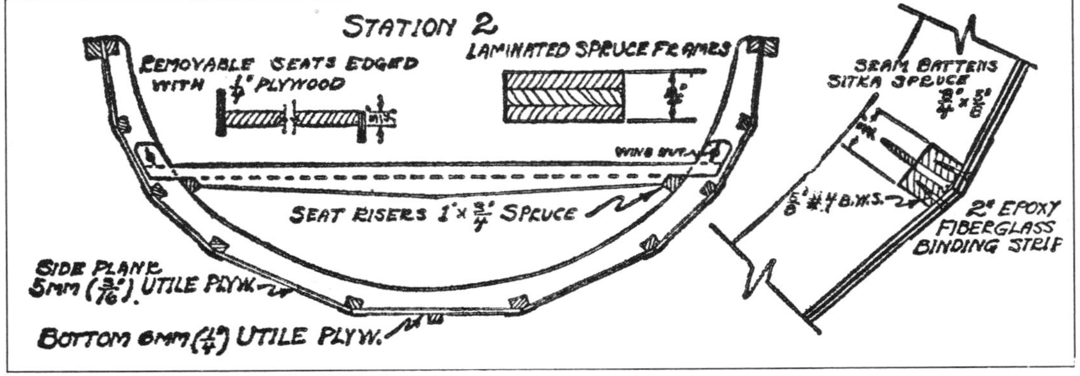
STATION 2
REMOVABLE SEATS EDGED WITH 1/4" PLYWOOD
LAMINATED SPRUCE FRAMES
WING NUT
SEAT RISERS 1" x 3/4" SPRUCE
SIDE PLANK 5MM (3/16") UTILE PLYW.
BOTTOM 6MM (1/4") UTILE PLYW.
SEAM BATTENS SITKA SPRUCE 3/4" x 5/8"
5/8" #4 B.W.S.
2" EPOXY FIBERGLASS BINDING STRIP

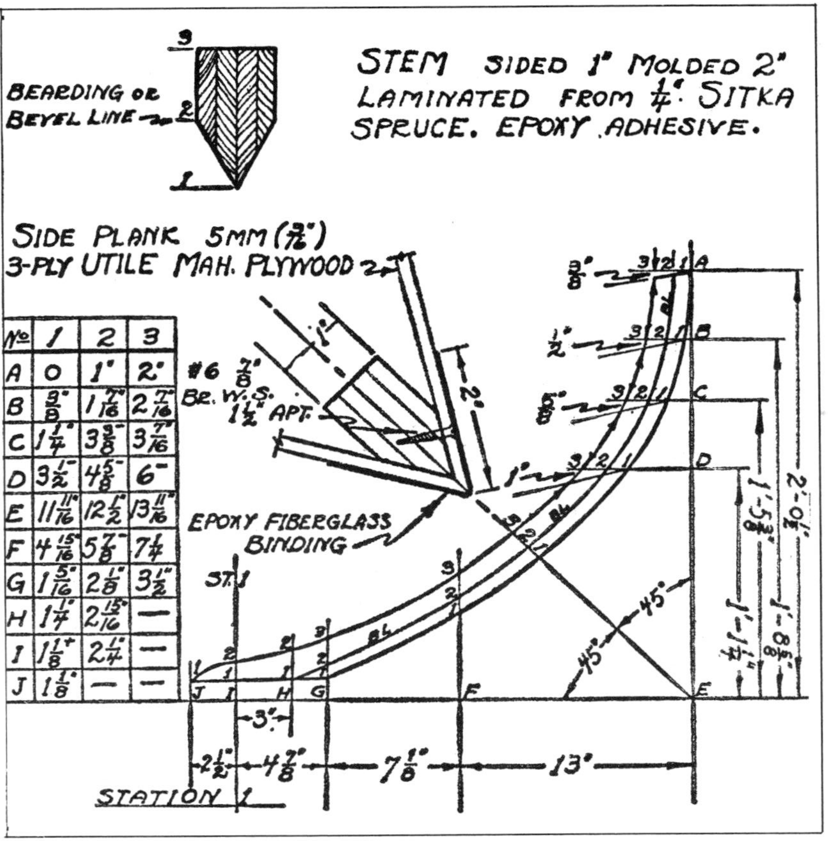
BEARDING OR BEVEL LINE
3
2
1
STEM SIDED 1" MOLDED 2" LAMINATED FROM 1/4" SITKA SPRUCE. EPOXY ADHESIVE.
SIDE PLANK 5MM (3/16")
3-PLY UTILE MAH. PLYWOOD
#6 7/8" BR. W.S. 1 1/2" APT.
2"
1"
EPOXY FIBERGLASS BINDING
3/8"
1/2"
5/8"
BL
45°
2'-0 1/2"
1'-8 5/8"
1'-5 3/8"
1'-1 1/4"
ST. 1
3"
2 1/2"
4 7/8"
7 1/8"
13"
STATION 1

| № | 1 | 2 | 3 |
|---|---|---|---|
| A | 0 | 1" | 2" |
| B | 3/8" | 1 7/16" | 2 7/16" |
| C | 1 1/4" | 3 3/8" | 3 7/16" |
| D | 3 1/2" | 4 5/8" | 6" |
| E | 11 11/16" | 12 1/2" | 13 11/16" |
| F | 4 15/16" | 5 7/8" | 7 1/4" |
| G | 1 5/16" | 2 1/8" | 3 1/2" |
| H | 1 1/4" | 2 15/16" | — |
| I | 1 1/8"+ | 2 1/4" | — |
| J | 1 1/8" | — | — |

with a continuous sheet of glass cloth is to save weight, as well as expense. One alternative that would make very little addition in weight would be to plank with 4 mm Utile (⅛-inch thick, .492 pounds per square foot) and cover the hull with a continuous sheet of glass cloth and epoxy resin.

The construction procedure for this type of dory, either with conventional plank or by the seam-batten method shown on the plan, is outlined in detail in Part II of this book.

An outboard of not over 7½ hp is recommended for this boat. The twin skegs with their bracing knees inside the boat against the stern stiffen the boat bottom and the stern, give the boat a better grip on the water, and provide protection when the boat is hauled out of the water. These skegs should be fastened up into the frames from the outside of the bottom with long screws, and, in addition to being glued on, should be fastened from the inside out through the bottom with screws that begin with a length of one inch aft and get shorter toward the bow.

Before sealing and painting or varnishing, the boat should be treated with a good rot preservative. Oil based preservatives may be used with impunity, as oil does not affect epoxy. The boat may be varnished, or one of the newer epoxy-base finishes may be used.

# 20  A 14-FOOT SEMI-DORY

For the home builder, this 14-foot semi-dory is a good one to start with. It is a tried and tested model, not too difficult to build, and a safe boat for children—one they can learn in and have a lot of fun with. But it is also a boat that will take Dad fishing, and that Mother can sail afternoons, if she has a mind to.

While this semi-dory has proved to be an excellent family boat, it was not offered as such in the first place. The lines for this particular boat were drawn for a series on tabloid lobster-boats printed in the *Maine Coast Fisherman* in the spring of 1954. Considered were a number of small fishing workboats suitable for outboard motors. Back then, Richard W. Hodgdon, who had never built a boat before, got busy and built this boat. Since then, this semi-dory has served him well and has taken hard usage in his home waters, yet remained in excellent condition. With motors of 6, 10, and 20 hp, its performance had been uniformly good, and, surprisingly, it did not row badly either.

After 15 years, Hodgdon had not forgotten a suggestion made in the original *Maine Coast Fisherman* article—that the boat could also be rigged to sail and would probably give a respectable account of herself with sails, as with motor or oars. The conversion made in 1969 proved even more successful than Hodgdon had counted on.

When asked for details, Hodgdon furnished a dimensioned sketch, which showed the location of the mast, centerboard, and rudder, as well as the dimensions of the latter two. It also gave the dimensions of the sails, with a combined sail area of 115 square feet. However, this boat had been used on an inland lake while under sail. For coastal use, a sail plan of somewhat less area seems advisable, so we offer a modified rig of 90 square feet with corresponding adjustment of the centerboard location. Hodgdon's drop rudder, convenient if the boat is beached frequently, has been retained. The details shown are one way of building it.

The result was not a racing machine certainly, but a good sailing knockabout, which was what Hodgdon was after. By lifting out the mast and unshipping the rudder, it is still possible for the boat to be used with an outboard as before. Incidentally, Hodgdon reports that this 14-footer performs well with motors ranging from 6 to 20 hp. The centerboard, when pulled up into its box, should not interfere with rowing.

Hodgdon built his boat standard dory fashion with sawn lumber, and he has since added Styrofoam to give greater buoyancy. When swamped, this semi-dory does not sink, but supports the occupants while they are bailing out.

A drawing showing how to set the boat up as well as how to proceed with the planking, the manner of fastening the laps, and so forth, appears in a subsequent chapter about building a

*The 14-foot semi-dory as originally built by Hodgdon.*

*Left: Hodgdon's 14-foot semi-dory rigged for sail.*

16-foot semi-dory, an enlargement of this 14-foot boat, which came first by some six years, so it applies equally well here.

It will be noted that the 16-footer is a four-plank boat, while the 14-footer is a five-plank dory. In both cases, the garboard and the next plank above are treated as a single plank, which is made of plywood. This could not be done with natural lumber, as the width required would be too great, but it is easily done with plywood, saving both labor and material. If one wanted to, however, this dory could be planked in the traditional manner with two bottom strakes of natural lumber replacing the one wide plywood strake as shown.

As can be seen, the various parts of the dory hull have been numbered. Under each number, in turn, we shall describe the part, its essential dimensions, material, manner of fastening, and

## 14-FOOT SEMI-DORY

| | HEIGHTS ABOVE BASE | | | | | | HALF-BREADTHS | | | | | |
|---|---|---|---|---|---|---|---|---|---|---|---|---|
| | BOT. | GAR. | 2 | 3 | 4 | SHEER | BOT. | GAR. | 2 | 3 | 4 | SHEER |
| STEM | — | 1-1-4 | 1-5-4 | 1-9-1 | 2-0-1 | 2-2-6 | 0-1-0 | 0-1-0 | 0-1-0 | 0-1-0 | 0-1-0 | 0-1-0 |
| STATION 1 | 0-1-6 | 0-9-1 | 1-0-2 | 1-4-2 | 1-8-0 | 1-11-7 | 0-1-0 | 0-5-3 | 0-8-5 | 0-11-0 | 1-0-2 | 1-0-5 |
| STA. 2 | 0-0-7 | 0-3-6 | 0-7-1 | 0-11-3 | 1-4-1 | 1-9-3 | 0-9-1 | 1-1-1 | 1-5-1 | 1-8-5 | 1-10-7 | 1-11-5 |
| STA. 3 | 0-0-1 | 0-2-1 | 0-5-3 | 0-9-5 | 1-2-4 | 1-8-2 | 1-1-5 | 1-4-3 | 1-8-6 | 2-0-5 | 2-3-3 | 2-4-4 |
| STA. 4 | 0-0-1 | 0-2-1 | 0-5-2 | 0-9-5 | 1-2-3 | 1-7-4 | 1-2-6 | 1-5-4 | 1-9-6 | 2-2-1 | 2-4-2 | 2-4-5 |
| STA. 5 | 0-0-2 | 0-3-1 | 0-6-2 | 0-10-1 | 1-2-5 | 1-7-5 | 1-1-5 | 1-5-2 | 1-9-5 | 2-1-2 | 2-3-1 | 2-2-5 |
| TRANSOM | 0-0-6 | 0-4-6 | 0-7-3 | 0-11-0 | 1-3-4 | 1-8-2 | 1-0-0 | 1-5-0 | 1-9-1 | 1-11-3 | 2-0-4 | 2-0-0 |

OFFSETS IN FEET, INCHES, & EIGHTHS TO INSIDE PLANK, BOTTOM AND OUTER STEM PROFILE. STATIONS SPACED 30". TRANSOM AT SHEER 26¾" AFT STA. 5. RAKED 5".

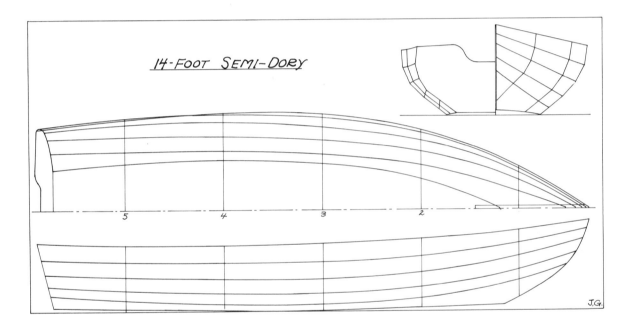

14-FOOT SEMI-DORY

J.G.

other related essential information. This, with the drawings, should provide sufficient information for building.

1. *Bottom.* Northern white pine, Philippine mahogany, cypress, cedar. Pine preferred. Thickness, ⅞-inch. Make out of three or four boards. Fasten to bottom cleats with No. 12 or No. 14 wood screws, 1½-inches long; likewise to frames, stem, transom, and stern knees.

2. *Bottom Cleats.* Oak, ⅞-inch thick, 2 inches wide. Midway between frames to stiffen bottom.

3. *Side Plank.* First two strakes from the bottom (garboard and broad) are made as a single plank of ⅜-inch marine plywood. Glued to bottom, stem, and transom with epoxy, polysulphide caulk, or equivalent. Nailed to bottom with 8d or 10d Monel Anchorfast nails, bronze Anchorfast, or galvanized wire nails, spaced approximately 2 inches apart. Fasten to stem with 1¼-inch, No. 10 or No. 12 screws; to transom with 1½-inch, No. 10 or No. 12 screws. Can also be made as two plank, as explained above, lapped and fastened like the upper plank. The upper plank to be made of northern white pine, Philippine mahogany, cypress, cedar ⁹⁄₁₆ inch thick, and lapped 1⅛ inches. Fasten through laps into frames with No. 10, 1½-inch or 1¼-inch screws, into transom with No. 10, 1¾-inch screws. On the

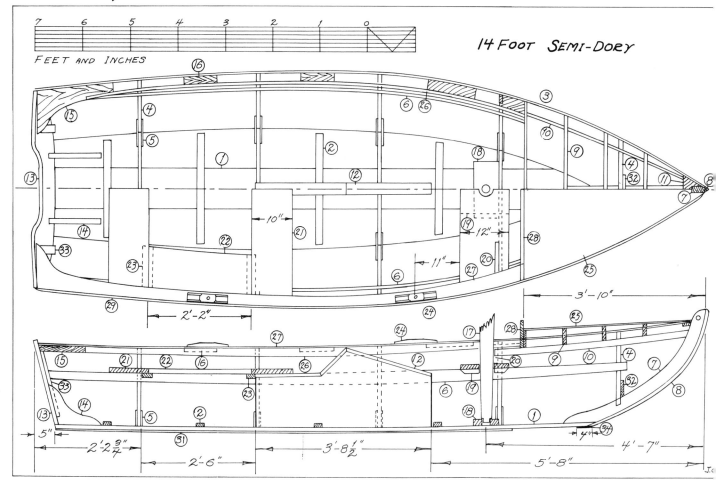

14 FOOT SEMI-DORY

FEET AND INCHES

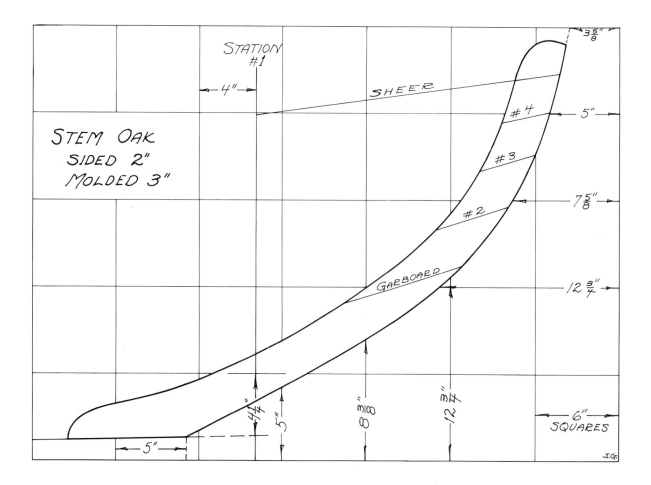

STEM OAK
SIDED 2"
MOLDED 3"

STATION #1

SHEER

#4

#3

#2

GARBOARD

6" SQUARES

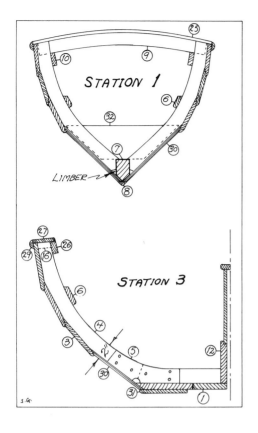

upper transom, use longer screws in the end grain. Fasten laps between frames with copper nails riveted over burrs spaced approximately 2½ inches.

4. *Frames*. Oak, ⅞ inch thick, molded approximately 2 inches. Side futtocks joined to bottom cross frame with plywood gussets either side.

5. *Frame Gussets*. ⅜-inch marine plywood fastened to oak frames with glue and 1-inch, No. 10 screws.

6. *Risers*. Same material as side plank, 3 inches wide amidship tapering at the ends to 2 inches. Fasten to frames with No. 10, 1½-inch screws.

7. *Stem*. Oak, 2 inches thick, molded 3 inches. Grain to follow the curvature of the stem as much as possible.

8. *Outer Stem*. Oak. Steam-bent strip applied after planking is complete. Fastened with No. 10, 1¾-inch screws, and faired to conform to the shape of the boat.

9. *Deck Beams*. Oak or mahogany ⅝ inch thick, molded 2 inches, and laid out to a curve rising 3 inches at the forward end of the deck.

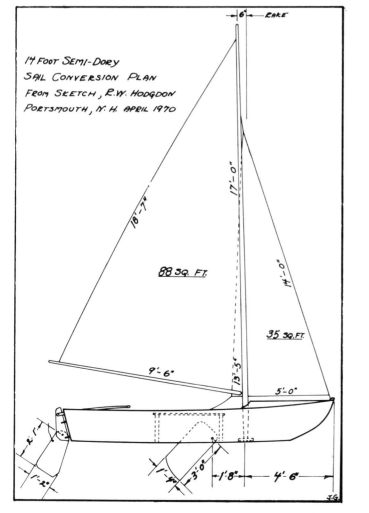

14 Foot Semi-Dory
Sail Conversion Plan
From Sketch, R.W. Hodgdon
Portsmouth, N.H. April 1970

88 SQ. FT.

35 SQ. FT.

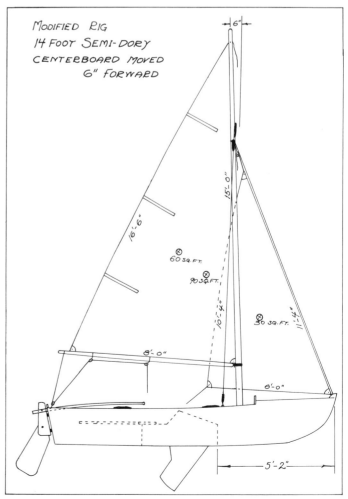

Modified Rig
14 Foot Semi-Dory
Centerboard Moved
6" Forward

60 SQ.FT.

90 SQ.FT.

30 SQ.FT.

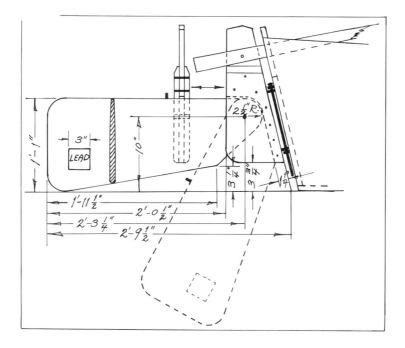

10. *Deck Beam Clamp.* Same material as the thwart risers. Fastened the same. Molded 2 inches. Fastened to the two forward frames and the stem to support the ends of the deck beams.

11. *Breast Hook.* Oak, ⅞ inch thick. Grain runs athwartships. Fastened to stem with long screw or drift. Takes fastenings from the sheer strakes and the fore end of the deck.

12. *Centerboard and Centerboard Box.* Fully detailed in accompanying drawing.

13. *Transom.* Philippine mahogany, 1 inch thick. Two or three pieces running athwartships glued and dowelled with ⅜-inch white oak dowels. Reinforced with stern knees and transom cleats.

14. *Stern Knees.* Oak, 1¼ inches thick, 10-inch length of either limb. Molded and located as shown. Fastened through the stern with No. 12 or No. 14, 2- or 2½-inch screws, bunged and plugged. Bottom fastenings may be longer than 1½ inches.

15. *Stern Quarter Knees.* Oak, 1¼ to 1½ inches thick. Ten-inch bearing on transom. Molded as shown. Fastening through transom same as stern knees. Sheer plank and inwale both screw into stern quarter knees with No. 10, 1½-inch screws.

16. *Filler Blocks.* ⅞-inch oak, mahogany, pine, located as shown. Fastenings from sheer plank, inwales, and capping.

17. *Mast.* Spruce. 19′6″ from step to head. 3½-inch diameter at deck, tapering to 2-inch diameter at head.

18. *Mast Step.* Oak, 1¼ to 1½ inches thick. To overlap at least two bottom planks.

19. *Mast Hole Cleat.* ⅞-inch-thick oak, 12 inches square. Underside of the center of the forward thwart, with grain running fore and aft, for reinforcement. Fastened with No. 12, 1½-inch screws, bunged and plugged.

20. *Thwart Knees.* Either side of the forward thwart to brace the mast. ⅞-inch thick. Preferably natural crooks of hackmatack, apple, oak, or other suitable hardwood. Can be glued laminations. Fasten to thwart, side planking, inwale, and capping.

21. *Thwarts.* Pine, Philippine mahogany, cypress, spruce. ⅞-inch thick. Notched around frames. Screwed to risers. No. 12, 1¾- to 2-inch screws, bunged and plugged.

22. *Side Benches.* Same material as thwarts. Between second and third thwarts either side. Fastened to thwarts by cleats on underside. Fastened with 1½-inch, No. 12 screws, bunged and plugged. Fastened to risers as well.

23. *Side Bench Cleats.* ⅞-inch oak, 3 inches wide.

24. *Rowlock Cleats.* Oak strips, 11″ by 2″ by ⅞″, beveled as shown, and screwed into capping and filler blocks.

25. *Fore Deck.* ⅜-inch plywood. Screwed to

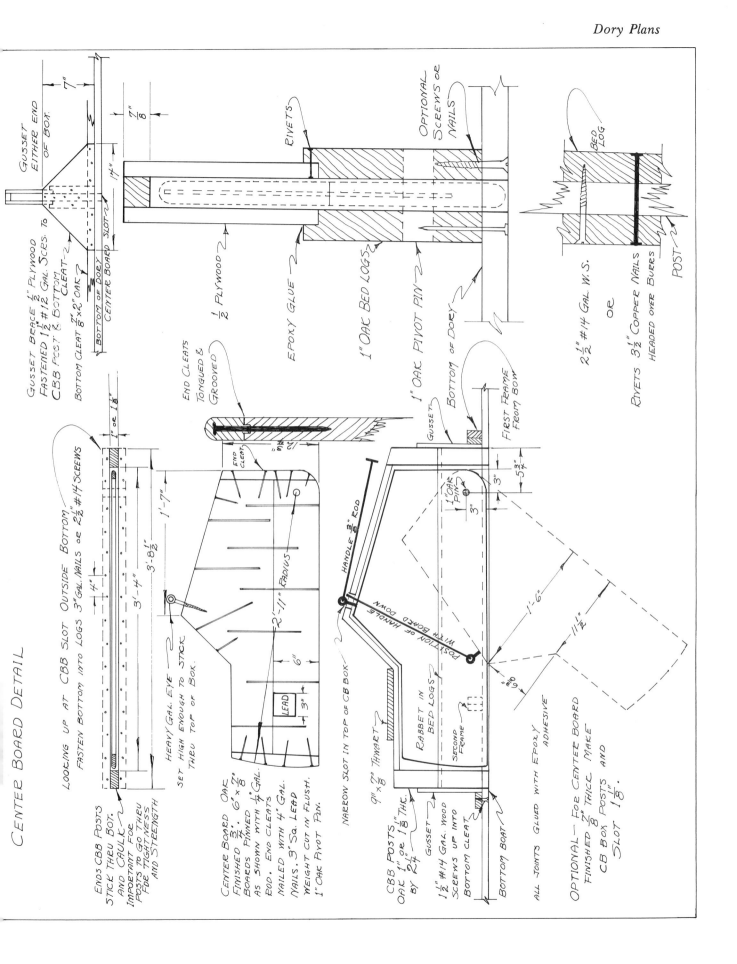

GUSSET EITHER END OF BOX.

GUSSET BRACE ½" PLYWOOD FASTENED 1½" #12 GAL. SCRS. TO CBB POST (& BOTTOM CLEAT. BOTTOM CLEAT ⅞"×2" OAK

RIVETS

½ PLYWOOD

EPOXY GLUE

1" OAK BED LOGS

1" OAK PIVOT PIN

BOTTOM OF DORY

OPTIONAL SCREWS OR NAILS

BED LOG

2½" #14 GAL. W.S.

OR

RIVETS. 3½" COPPER NAILS HEADED OVER BURRS

POST

BOTTOM OF DORY CENTER BOARD SLOT

CENTER BOARD DETAIL

LOOKING UP AT CBB SLOT OUTSIDE BOTTOM FASTEN BOTTOM INTO LOGS 3" GAL. NAILS or 2½" #14 SCREWS

ENDS CBB POSTS STICK THRU BOT. AND CAULK. IMPORTANT FOR POSTS TO GO THRU FOR TIGHTNESS AND STRENGTH

END CLEATS TONGUED & GROOVED

CENTER BOARD OAK FINISHED ⅞". 6"×⅞". BOARDS PINNED WITH ¼" GAL. AS SHOWN WITH ¼" GAL. ROD. END CLEATS NAILED WITH 4" GAL. NAILS. 3" SQ. LEAD WEIGHT CUT IN FLUSH. 1" OAK PIVOT PIN.

CBB POSTS OAK 1" or 1⅛" THK. BY 2¼"

HEAVY GAL. EYE SET HIGH ENOUGH TO STICK THRU TOP OF BOX.

2-11" RADIUS

LEAD

3"

6"

NARROW SLOT IN TOP OF CB BOX

9"×⅞" THWART

RABBET IN BED LOGS

SECOND FRAME

GUSSET

1½" #14 GAL. WOOD SCREWS UP INTO BOTTOM CLEAT

BOTTOM BOAT

FIRST FRAME FROM BOW

GUSSET

1" OAK PIN

3"

5¾"

3"

HANDLE ⅜" ROD

POSITION OF HANDLE WITH BOARD DOWN

1'-6"

1'-½"

6"

ALL JOINTS GLUED WITH EPOXY ADHESIVE

OPTIONAL — FOR CENTER BOARD FINISHED ⅞" THICK MAKE CB BOX POSTS AND SLOT 1⅛".

1" or 1⅛"

4"

3'-4"

3'-8½"

1'-7"

deck beams, sheer strake, and breast hook with 1¼-inch, No. 8 wood screws. Filler blocks along the outside between the deck beams and fastened to the sheer strakes can be installed for added fastening and reinforcement. Covered with thin canvas laid in paint, or with fiberglass or polypropylene, optional, or can be merely painted. Outside edges may be covered with fiberglass or polypropylene tape under half-oval trim.

26. *Inwale.* Oak or Philippine mahogany, ⅞-inch thick, 2 inches wide amidships, tapering to 1½ inches at ends. Fastened to stern quarter knees, frames, and filler blocks with No. 12, 1¾- to 1-inch screws.

27. *Side Capping.* Pine or Philippine mahogany, ½ inch thick. Forward end thinned slightly to fair into ⅜-inch-thick fore deck. Put on in two pieces. Butt splice under after oarlock cleat. Fastened to stern quarter knees, inwales, filler blocks, and sheer strakes with No. 10, 1¼- to 1½-inch screws. Heads slightly countersunk and puttied.

28. *Deck Coaming.* Philippine mahogany, ⅝-inch thick. Finishes after end of deck, covering the after deck beam and projecting 2 inches above the deck. Rounded ends cover the joints between the deck and side capping, and extend to the outside of the boat. Can be finished bright, in which case, inwales, side capping, and half-oval trim can be made of Philippine mahogany to correspond and be finished bright also. All fastenings through these members to be bunged and plugged.

29. *Half-Oval Trim.* Philippine mahogany or oak, 1 inch wide. Fore end approaching the stem tapered to ¾ inch. Fastened with No. 8, 1-inch screws, bunged ⅜ inch and plugged.

30. *Plywood Garboard.* (See No. 3)

31. *Bottom Strip.* Oak or Philippine mahogany, ½ inch thick. To protect the lower edge of the garboard and to take wear on the bottom. Inside edge of bottom strip must be straight and parallel with the centerline of the boat, otherwise it will create drag and slow the boat. Thus, these strips will be 8 inches wide at the center of the boat, ending at a point about 6 inches forward of the second frame, slightly forward of the mast location. Fastened with No. 10, 1-inch screws, bunged and plugged. Before the bottom strips are put on, and before any paint is put on the bottom, the lower edge of the garboard is to be covered and reinforced with fiberglass or polypropylene tape, 3 inches wide, equally lapped on the bottom and up the side. Tape is to be bonded with epoxy. A double thickness of tape to be applied at the base of the stem.

32. *Frame Cleat.* ⅜- or ½-inch plywood glued and screwed to the two sides of the forward, or No. 1, frame.

33. *Transom Cleats.* Oak strips, ⅞ inch thick by 2 inches wide, extending from the underside of the stern quarter knees to the bottom to reinforce the transom. Fastened with No. 12, 1½-inch screws, bunged and plugged.

34. *Bottom Plate.* Triangular piece of flat brass or bronze to cover lower end of false stem and fore end of bottom. Countersunk to fasten with No. 8, 1-inch screws.

# 21   A 16-FOOT SEMI-DORY

Here is a big, small boat. It is small enough for one man to build comfortably in his garage or backyard, and without too great a strain on the pocketbook. Also small enough to handle nicely on a trailer. Yet, it is big enough to stand some rough water, to fish three or four persons without crowding, and to take the family for a spin. This is no flashy speed boat, although it is capable of handling quite a lot of horsepower and of moving right along. Its straight bottom and powerful bearing aft insures this.

Primarily, this is a semi-dory for the fisherman who isn't in such a terrible hurry that he has to have the ultimate in speed. No doubt the boat would take a 25 hp motor, all right; but for many fishermen, 15 hp would be more useful and normal. Even with 10 hp, the boat should not do too badly.

This particular 16-footer is based in good part upon the 14-foot semi-dory described previously, which was designed for both outboard power and rowing. The 16-footer is really a much larger boat than its added two feet of overall would seem to indicate. It has proportionally greater sheer, more depth, beam, and bottom width aft. Its foredeck and side coamings will keep out a lot of loose water. Concealed Styrofoam flotation makes it unsinkable. The outboard motor well adds greatly to safety and convenience in handling the motor, and it improves the trim and performance of the boat.

While this semi-dory is not intended for regular rowing, as was the 14-footer, oarlocks are provided, and it can be rowed in an emergency. A pair of oars should always be along, secured out of the way under the side coamings.

Some pains have been taken in planning the construction of this boat to make it simple and inexpensive to build without any sacrifice of quality; also, to utilize modern materials where they can be used to advantage. The biggest innovation, or departure from standard dory practice is the plywood garboard, whose extra width eliminates one strake of planking, making only three strakes to the side, instead of the usual four or even five in a dory of this size.

The detailed drawings cover construction quite thoroughly, and, I hope, clearly. As you can see, each part is numbered, in most cases in two or more views. Also, each part is described in the following list. Dimensions, materials, fastenings, locations, and fabrications are given, and discussed when necessary. There should be no mystery about what goes into this boat and how it is put together.

1. *Frames*. Oak. Minimum siding (thickness), 7/8 inch; maximum, 1 inch finished. Molded width, 2 inches. There are eight sets of frames: one on each station, an extra set 22 inches aft of Station 6, and one cleated around the inside edge of the stern.

One of the first operations after the lines of the boat are laid down full size is to make up the frames, which serve as molds. Extra length of several inches should be left on the ends of the frames above the sheer to nail and shore to in setting up. After the boat is planked, and the sheer is faired, the excess is sawed off. The sheer line and the knuckle or plank lines must be clearly marked on the frames when assembled on the laydown.

2. *Frame Gussets.* ⅜-inch marine fir plywood. Extending 7 inches each side of the knuckle joint measured on the outside. Shaped to conform to the molding of the frames with extra wood on the inside of the knuckle to make an easy curve and to add strength to offset wood removed on the outside for the limber. Double gussets, that is, on both sides of the splice, each side fastened with six 1-inch, No. 10 bronze screws and waterproof glue. Alternate fastening: 8-penny copper nails, riveted over burrs.

3. *Bottom Cleats.* Oak. Same stock as the frames. Minimum thickness, ⅞ inch; maximum, 1 inch. Width, 2 inches. These lie on the bottom to cleat and to stiffen it midway between the frame stations. They are cut approximately one inch short of the bottom width to allow drainage around the ends. Fastened with bronze screws through the bottom from the outside. 1¾-inch, No. 12s or No. 14s. 1½-inch, No. 14s.

4. *Clamps.* Oak. Same stock as the frames. Width, 2 inches. Run from transom to bulkhead on Frame No. 2. Fastened to frames and filler block (No 21) with bronze screws, 1¾-inch No. 12s or 14s.

5. *Deck Beams.* Oak. Same stock as frames. Molded depth, 2 inches. Crown or camber, 4 inches in 5-foot span. One deck beam aft; four forward.

6. *Stringer.* Oak. Same stock as frames. Two inches wide. Supports second and third deck beams forward. Runs from Frame No. 1 to Frame No. 2. Fastened with 1¾-inch No. 12s or No. 14s, two to each frame. Deck beams notched in, one-half inch in stringer, one-half inch in beam. Beams countersunk to fasten with 2-inch bronze screws, or longer.

7. *Breast Hook.* Oak. Thickness, 1⅛ inches. Grain runs athwartships. Notched around stem with 3 inches of wood aft of stem face. Pinned to stem with ¼-inch rod or spike. Sheer plank fastened to breast hook with 1¼-inch, No. 2 bronze screws or larger.

8. *Stem.* Oak. Sided (thickness) 2 inches.

Molded shape from full-size laydown from lines plan. Requires plank approximately 10 inches wide by 5 feet long. Mark bevels obtained from laydown. Cut bevels part way to lines at bench. Leave enough wood for adjustment during final fairing of setup for planking.

9. *False Stem.* Oak. Can be same stock as frames. Best 1 inch thick. Approximately 2 inches wide. Steam bent. Put on hot after boat is planked and plank ends and stem face are faired to receive it. Fasten with bronze screws not smaller than 1¾-inch No. 12s.

10. *Bottom.* Northern white pine, mahogany, cypress, cedar, in that order of preference. Not less than ⅞ inch thick. Made up of boards approximately 7 inches wide (see plan of bottom assembly). Wide boards tend to curl and open too wide at the seams when dried out. Narrow boards are not as stiff and require more cleating. Fasten to bottom cleats, frames, transom motor well-box, and stem with bronze screws not less than 1¾-inch No. 12s, No. 14s better.

11. *Seat Risers.* Pine or same stock as bottom, 2½ inches wide. Runs from after frame to bulkhead at Station 2. Fastened to frames, two screws to a frame, heads flush. Screws, 1¾-inch No. 12s.

12. *Thwarts.* Pine, mahogany, cypress, or same stock as bottom, except white cedar. 10 inches wide. Not less than a full ⅞ inch thick. Notched around frames. Fastened to seat riser with bronze screws not less than 1¾-inch No. 12s.

13. *Fore Deck.* ⅜-inch exterior fir plywood in two pieces with seam on fore and aft centerline. Fasten into deck beams, blocking, breast hook, and top edge of sheer plank with bronze screws not less than 1 inch No. 8s. Larger screws better in soft wood of sheer plank. Space screws 4 to 6 inches apart. Glue with waterproof glue.

14. *Bulkhead.* ⅜-inch exterior fir plywood. Can be in two pieces with seam on vertical centerline. Fastened with screws (same size as fore deck) and glue on aft side of Frame 2 and first deck beam. Opening cut out and framed for door.

15. *Headledge or Splashboard.* ¾-inch mahogany. Covers end wood of plywood deck and runs out on side decking. Screw fastened through bulkhead into deck beam.

16. *After Deck Band.* ⅝-inch mahogany, molded 3 inches to curve of deck. Set flush

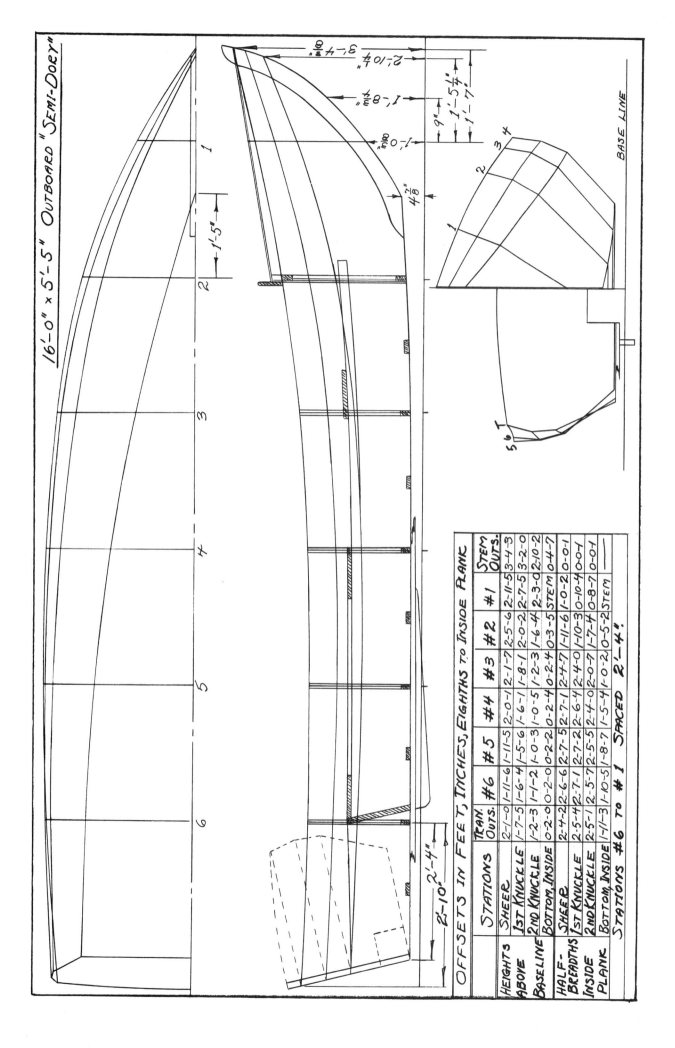

16'-0" × 5'-5" Outboard "Semi-Dory"

BASE LINE

OFFSETS IN FEET, INCHES, EIGHTHS TO INSIDE PLANK

| | STATIONS | TRAN. OUTS. | #6 | #5 | #4 | #3 | #2 | #1 | STEM OUTS. |
|---|---|---|---|---|---|---|---|---|---|
| HEIGHTS ABOVE BASE LINE | SHEER | 2-1-0 | 1-11-6 | 1-11-5 | 2-0-1 | 2-1-7 | 2-5-6 | 2-11-5 | 3-4-3 |
| | 1ST KNUCKLE | 1-7-5 | 1-6-4 | 1-5-6 | 1-6-1 | 1-8-1 | 2-0-2 | 2-7-5 | 3-2-0 |
| | 2ND KNUCKLE | 1-2-3 | 1-1-2 | 1-0-3 | 1-0-5 | 1-2-3 | 1-6-4 | 2-3-0 | 2-10-2 |
| | BOTTOM, INSIDE | 0-2-0 | 0-2-0 | 0-2-0 | 0-2-4 | 0-2-4 | 0-3-5 | STEM 0-4-7 | |
| HALF-BREADTHS INSIDE PLANK | SHEER | 2-4-2 | 2-4-6 | 2-7-5 | 2-7-1 | 2-4-7 | 1-6-1 | 1-0-2 | 0-0-1 |
| | 1ST KNUCKLE | 2-5-4 | 2-7-1 | 2-7-2 | 2-6-4 | 2-4-0 | 1-0-3 | 0-10-4 | 0-0-1 |
| | 2ND KNUCKLE | 2-5-1 | 2-5-7 | 2-5-5 | 2-4-0 | 2-0-7 | 1-7-4 | 0-8-7 | 0-0-1 |
| | BOTTOM, INSIDE | 1-11-3 | 1-10-5 | 1-8-7 | 1-5-4 | 1-0-2 | 0-5-2 Stem | | |

STATIONS #6 TO #1 SPACED 2'-4".

3'-4⅛"
2'-10¼"
1'-8¾"
9"
1'-5¼"
1'-7"
1'-0⅜"
4⅞"
1'-5"
2'-10"
2'-4"

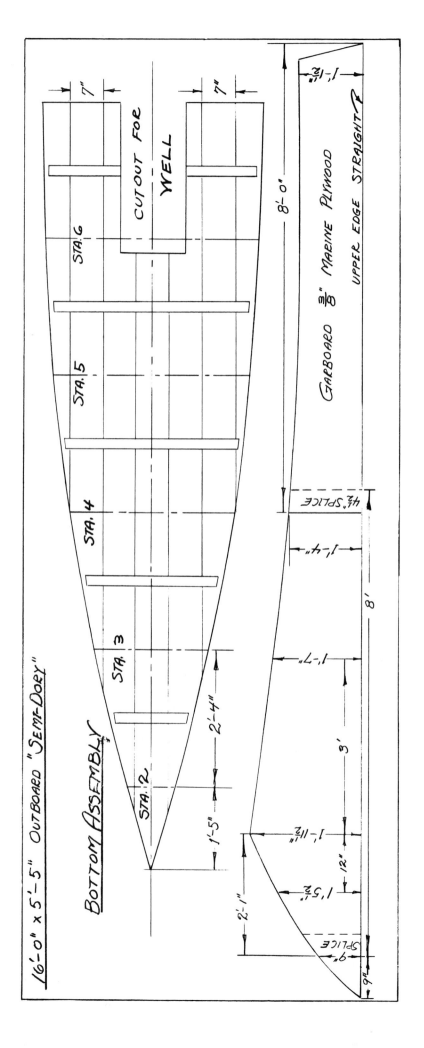

16'-0" x 5'-5" Outboard "Semi-Dory"

Bottom Assembly

STA. 2
STA. 3
STA. 4
STA. 5
STA. 6

CUTOUT FOR
WELL

7"
7"

2'-4"
1'-5"

Garboard ⅜" Marine Plywood

Upper Edge Straight

8'-0"

1'-1½"
4½" Splice
1'-4"
1'-7"
3'
8'

1'-11½"
12"
1'-5½"
2'-1"
Splice
9"
9"

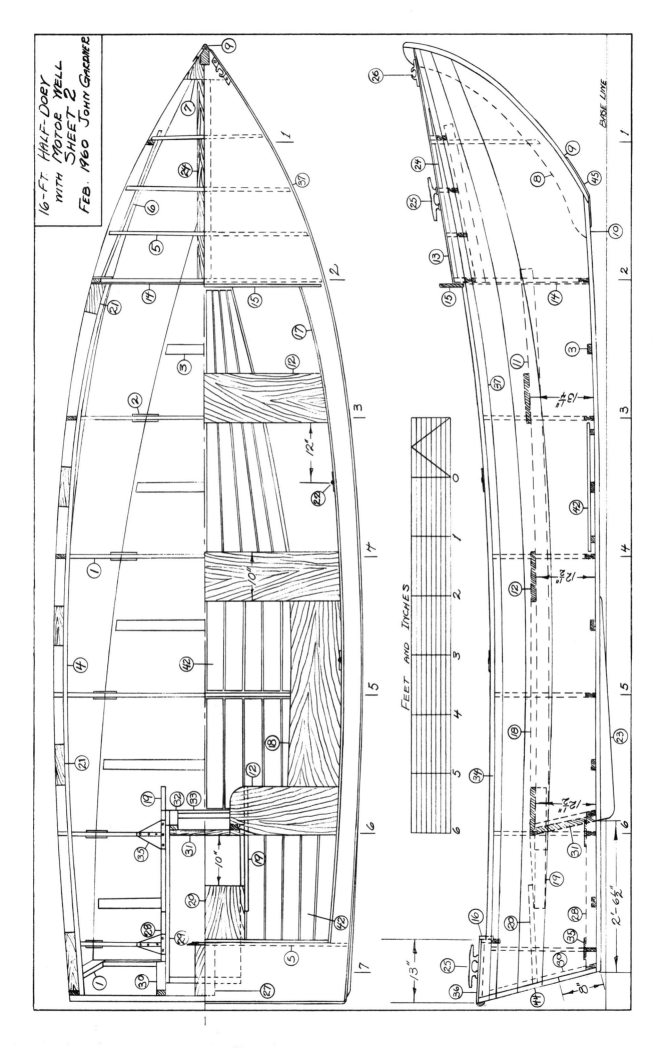

16-Ft. Half-Dory
with Motor Well
Sheet 2
Feb. 1960 John Gardner

Feet and Inches

Base Line

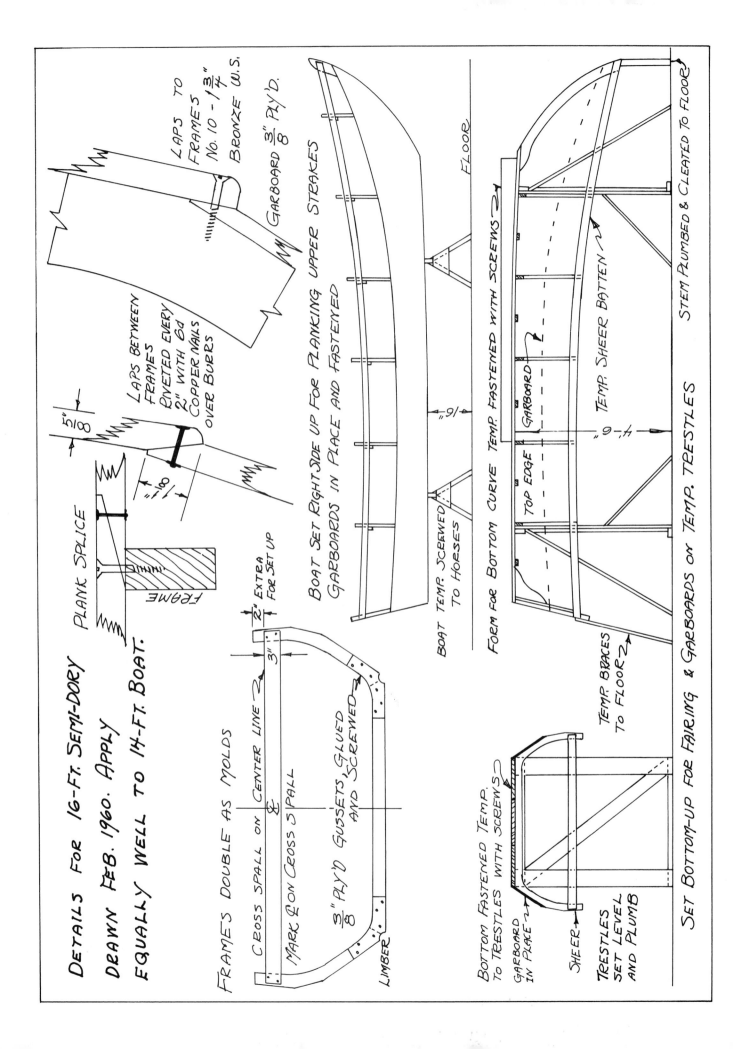

DETAILS FOR 16-FT. SEMI-DORY PLANK SPLICE

DRAWN FEB. 1960. APPLY

EQUALLY WELL TO 14-FT. BOAT.

LAPS TO FRAMES No. 10 - 14" BRONZE W.S.

GARBOARD ⅜" PLY'D.

LAPS BETWEEN FRAMES RIVETED EVERY 2" WITH 6d COPPER NAILS OVER BURS

BOAT SET RIGHT SIDE UP FOR PLANKING UPPER STREAKS GARBOARDS IN PLACE AND FASTENED

BOAT TEMP. SCREWED TO HORSES

FLOOR

FRAMES DOUBLE AS MOLDS

CROSS SPALL ON CENTER LINE

MARK ℓ ON CROSS SPALL

⅜" PLY'D GUSSETS GLUED AND SCREWED

2" EXTRA FOR SET UP

3"

LIMBER

FRAME

⅝"

FORM FOR BOTTOM CURVE TEMP. FASTENED WITH SCREWS

TOP EDGE GARBOARD

TEMP. SHEER BATTEN

TEMP. BRACES TO FLOOR

STEM PLUMBED & CLEATED TO FLOOR

16"

4-6"

BOTTOM FASTENED TEMP. TO TRESTLES WITH SCREWS

GARBOARD IN PLACE

SHEER

TRESTLES SET LEVEL AND PLUMB

SET BOTTOM-UP FOR FAIRING & GARBOARDS ON TEMP. TRESTLES

with top of deck to cover endwood of plywood. Ends cut to a snug wedge-fit against ends of side bands. Screw fastened, 1¼-inch No. 10s, ⅜-inch bungs.

17. *Side Bands.* ⅝-inch mahogany, molded to sweep of sheer, 3 inches wide. Runs from after deck beam to Frame No. 2 bulkhead. Fastened into clamp the same as No. 16. To cover edge of side decking.

18. *Bench.* Same material and thickness as thwarts. Two boards approximately 3 feet 2 inches long by 12 inches wide. Ends fitted against thwarts 2 and 3, supported by cleats screwed to underside of thwarts. Bench also screwed to cleats and to seat riser. Screws bronze; not less than 1¾-inch No. 12s except in cleats, 1½-inch No. 12s. Bunged ½ inch.

19. *Cleats for Third Thwarts.* Oak. Same stock as frame. 2 inches wide, 2 feet 2 inches long. Securely fastened to well box (from inside) with No. 14 screws. Thwarts fastened to cleats from above; No. 12, 1¾-inch screws, bunged.

20. *Well Cover.* Same stock as bottom and thwarts. Important that boards run athwartships to brace the well box against side pull. Fasten to sides of box with 1¾-inch No. 14s, bunged ½-inch; 2-inch No. 14s better, spaced 3 to 4 inches.

21. *Filler Blocks, Sides.* Can be oak, mahogany, or pine. Same stock as frames or bottom. Oak or mahogany give better fastening. 5 blocks to a side. Screwed to clamps and sheer plank. Forward block fastened to bulkhead at Station 2. Plywood covering of fore deck should lap back a few inches on forward filler block for added strength.

22. *Rowlock Sockets.*

23. *Skegs.* Oak. 1⅛ inches thick. Located 11 inches out on either side of the centerline. Fastened from inside bottom with No. 14 bronze screws. Bolted through bottom cleats and frame No. 5 with ¼-inch bronze carriage bolts.

24. *Deck Blocking.* Can be oak, mahogany, or white pine. Same stock as frames or bottom. Block under deck cleat (No. 25) fitted first and screw fastened at both ends through deck beams. Others screw fastened where possible through deck should be 1¾-inch No. 12s.

25. *Cleats.* 8 or 9 inches long. Bolted through deck beam and blocking. A second cleat on stern deck bolted through blocking.

26. *Chocks.* A 6-inch chock on either side, located as close to the stem as possible. Screw fastened through deck into breasthook.

27. *Block, Stern Deck.* Oak, mahogany, or white pine. Same stock as frames or bottom. Running from transom to stern deck beam under plywood deck. Notched and screw fastened into transom. Screw fastened through stern deck beam.

28. *Motor Well Bottom Cleats.* Oak 1⅛ inches thick by 2 inches wide. Screw fastened through bottom every 6 inches, 1¾-inch, No. 14 bronze screws. Screw fastened from inside of box 1¾-inch No. 14s. Set in white lead or equivalent bedding.

29. *Motor Well Sides.* Pine or mahogany. Same stock as bottom. Boards of sufficient width for two to a side if possible. Screws fastened with 1¾-inch, No. 14 bronze screws into transom cleats (No. 30); into well side stiffener (No. 31); into forward transom (No. 31); into forward well cleat (No. 32); into motor well cleat (No. 28). Fasten well. Screws 2½ to 3 inches apart through ends into Numbers 30 and 32. Also fastened along lower edge through bottom from outside, every 6 inches. Minimum 2-inch, No. 14 bronze screws. Set joints in white lead or equivalent bedding. After ends of well sides extend through opening in stern to come flush with outside. Fastened in transom aperture with 2-inch, No. 14 bronze screws or longer.

30. *Well Cleats, Stern.* Oak, 1⅛ inch by 2 inches. Serve as stiffeners for the stern transom, as well as the after cleats of the motor well. Extend vertically on the flat against the stern transom and outside the well box from the inside of the bottom to the underside of the deck. Notched over well bottom cleats. Fastened to stern transom (No. 44) with 2-inch, No. 14 bronze screws spaced every 3 or 4 inches, well staggered. Bottom bedded in white lead or equivalent.

31. *Motor Transom.* Oak or mahogany. 1¼ inches thick. Securely screw fastened to forward well cleats (No. 32) with 2-inch, No. 14 bronze screws. Also fastened to Numbers 19, 29, and 33. Bedded in white lead or equivalent.

32. *Forward Well Cleats.* Oak. 1⅛ inches thick, 2 inches wide. Fastened as previously specified.

33. *Forward Bottom Cleat.* Same as No. 28.

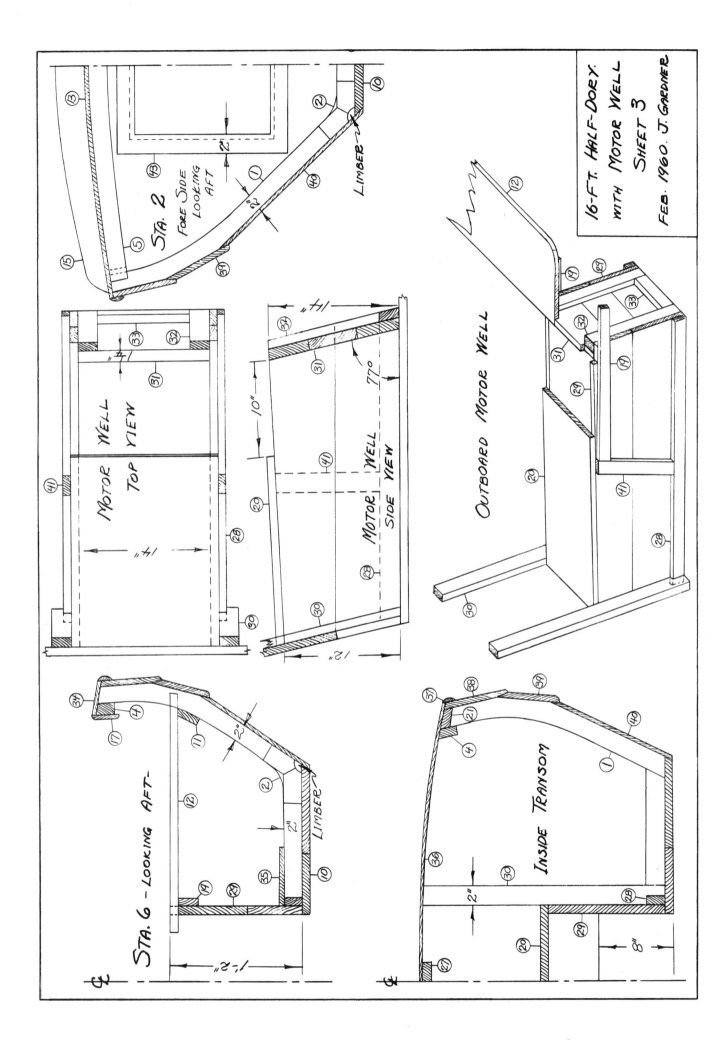

16-FT. HALF-DORY.
WITH MOTOR WELL
SHEET 3
FEB. 1960. J. GARDNER

STA. 2
FORE SIDE
LOOKING
AFT

LIMBER

MOTOR WELL
TOP VIEW

MOTOR WELL
SIDE VIEW

OUTBOARD MOTOR WELL

STA. 6 - LOOKING AFT-

LIMBER

INSIDE TRANSOM

34. *Side Decks.* ⅜-inch exterior fir plywood. To cover top of sheer and clamps. Can be in two lengths butted on filler block. After end to butt over stern filler block. Forward end to join forward deck at approximately midpoint of forward filler block. Fasten as No. 13, bronze screws not less than 1 inch No. 8s and waterproof glue. Longer screws better in top edge of sheer plank.

35. *Well Brace Gussets.* ½-inch exterior fir plywood. Three No. 14 screws into each frame end and three No. 14 screws into bearing on No. 28. Waterproof glue.

36. *After Deck.* ⅜-inch exterior fir plywood. Can be in two pieces joined over center block. Fastened the same as No. 13, fore deck.

37. *Trim.* Mahogany or oak half-oval, 1½ inches by ½ inch. Tapered slightly at the forward end. To cover edge of plywood decking.

38. *Sheer Strake.* White pine, mahogany, cypress, cedar. ⅝-inch thick. In two pieces, spliced on frame at Station 5. Fastened to stem, stern transom and frames with 1½-inch, No. 12 screws. 1⅛-inch laps riveted every 2 inches with 6-penny copper nails over burrs.

39. *Second Strake.* Material and fastening the same as sheer. Can be put on in one length or in two pieces spliced on frame at Station 3.

40. *Garboard.* ⅜-inch fir marine plywood laid out and spliced according to directions and diagram. Fastened to stern transom, frames, and stem with bronze screws, minimum 1¼-inch No. 10. Nailed to bottom with 8-penny Monel Anchorfast boat nails. Bottom and after edges sealed and bound with fiberglass tape set in epoxy resin.

41. *Well Box Side Stiffeners.* Oak. Stock same as frames, 2 inches wide. Fastened from inside well box with 1¾-inch, No. 14 screws.

42. *Gratings.* Of ½-inch pine on 1½-inch oak cleats, same stock as bottom cleats (No. 3). Fastened with galvanized nails. Removable.

43. *Frame, Bulkhead Openings.* Mahogany, pine. 2 inches wide. Glued and screwed to plywood bulkhead with 1-inch, No. 8 screws.

44. *Stern Transom.* Mahogany, white pine, 1⅛ inches thick. Made up of three 1-inch boards or four 7-inch boards. Cleated around inner outside edges and bottom with 2-inch-wide oak frame (No. 1). Cleated each side of well opening with stern well cleats (No. 30). Fastened to edge and bottom framing with 1¾-inch, No. 14 bronze screws approximately 3 inches apart.

45. *Brass Half Oval.* To bind bottom of false stem.

# 22 A 19-FOOT, 8-INCH SEMI-DORY

Following publication of the lines and commentary for the 16-foot semi-dory back in 1960, a number of readers requested lines for a larger boat of the same class. Sportfishing or lobstering in regions of extremely rough water were the reasons usually given.

The 19-foot enlargement (actually 19 feet 8 inches), shown in the accompanying drawing, is a lot more boat than the original 16-footer. Yet, the enlargement has been achieved without making any fundamental alterations to the original lines. The original construction details still apply, and can be followed for the larger boat with only a few simple and minor adjustments in the dimensions. The original scantlings were heavy, so it has not been necessary to enlarge these.

By adding and fairing in an extra frame—Frame A—between Frames 4 and 5, and by increasing frame spacing from 28 inches to 30 inches, the length is extended to 19 feet, 8 inches. Two inches added to the sheer height all the way is divided equally between the two top knuckles, so as to increase the width of the sheer plank below, each by one inch throughout. Four inches is added throughout to the width, giving a maximum beam to the outside of the planking of 5 feet 10 inches. The extreme width of bottom at the transom in the 19-foot boat is about 4 feet 5 inches to the outside of the planking, which should provide ample stability and support for any reasonably large motor.

If desired, more deck, wider waterways, and a higher coaming could be added. This would help in rough water. A small canvas spray hood, although not shown, could easily be installed. Higher sides for the motor are for a long-shaft motor, which I consider a must for a boat of this size.

Under no condition should the twin skegs, shown on the original boat as ending just forward of the motor well opening, be omitted. These strengthen and protect the bottom, serve as runners to drag the boat on, and greatly stabilize the hull when running.

Should plywood be substituted for the plank bottom as originally designed, it would be necessary to add extra longitudinal framing to stiffen it, unless plywood ½-inch thick or over were used.

Splices in the plywood garboards need not be joined with a glued, tapered scarph as shown in the construction details for the 16-foot boat. Plywood joints may be butted, backed by a double thickness of plywood in strips 5 or 6 inches wide for ⅜-inch plywood, the three thicknesses glued together and fastened with plenty of No. 8 or No. 10, 1-inch bronze screws. In case plywood is pieced or joined in this manner, it is highly recommended that an epoxy resin glue be used.

The amateur will do well to first make up as accurately as he can a solid half model of the hull to a scale of 1½ inches to 1 foot. From this he can make a cardboard template (to scale) of the plywood garboard showing where to splice and how to cut economically. He can also get the shape of his upper planks from his half model. These upper planks can be made of ⅝-inch plywood if desired, and it is advisable to splice them up from several short lengths. A tapered, glued scarph, at least 12 times as long as the thickness of the planking stock, should be used.

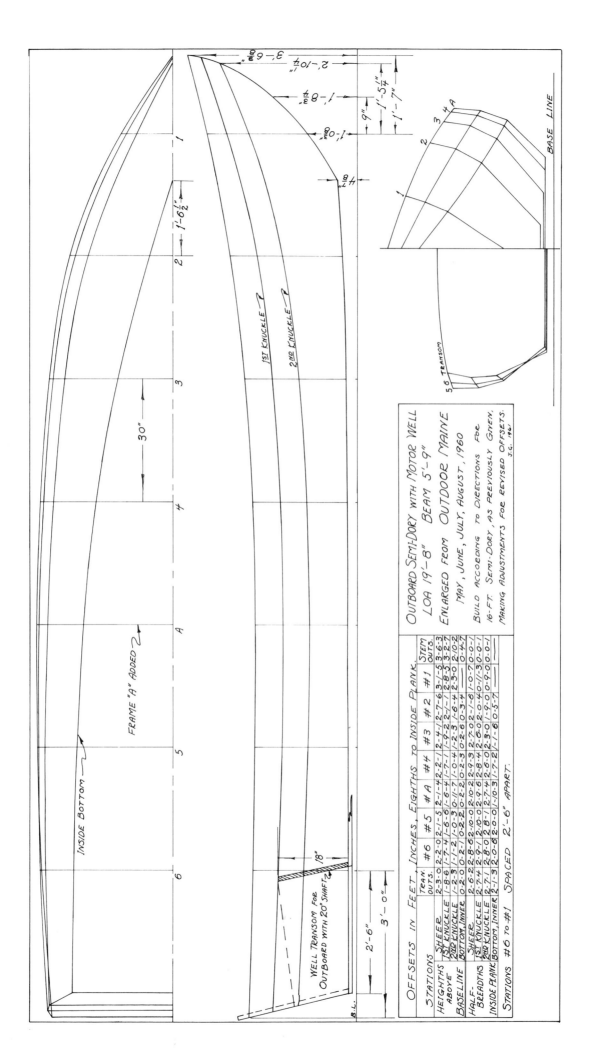

BASE LINE

1ST KNUCKLE

2ND KNUCKLE

INSIDE BOTTOM

FRAME "A" ADDED

WELL TRANSOM FOR
OUTBOARD WITH 20" SHAFT

30"

18"

2'-6"

3'-0"

5 6 TRANSOM

OUTBOARD SEMI-DORY WITH MOTOR WELL
LOA 19'-8"   BEAM 5'-9"
ENLARGED FROM OUTDOOR MAINE
MAY, JUNE, JULY, AUGUST, 1960
BUILD ACCORDING TO DIRECTIONS FOR
16-FT. SEMI-DORY, AS PREVIOUSLY GIVEN,
MAKING ADJUSTMENTS FOR REVISED OFFSETS.
J.G. 1961

OFFSETS IN FEET, INCHES, EIGHTHS TO INSIDE PLANK.

| STATIONS | | TRAN. OUTS. | #6 | #5 | #A | #4 | #3 | #2 | #1 | STEM OUTS. |
|---|---|---|---|---|---|---|---|---|---|---|
| HEIGHTS ABOVE BASELINE | SHEER | 2-3-0 | 2-2-0 | 2-1-5 | 2-1-4 | 2-2-1 | 2-4 | 2-7-6 | 3-1-5 | 3-6-3 |
| | 1ST KNUCKLE | 1-8-6 | 1-7-4 | 1-6-6 | 1-6-4 | 1-7-1 | 1-9-2 | 2-2-1 | 2-8-5 | 3-2-7 |
| | 2ND KNUCKLE | 1-2-3 | 1-1-2 | 1-0-3 | 0-11-7 | 1-0-4 | 1-2-3 | 1-6-4 | 2-3-0 | 2-10-2 |
| | BOTTOM, INNER | 0-2-0 | 0-0-2 | 0-1-2 | 0-0-2 | 0-2-2 | 0-2-3 | 0-2-6 | 0-3-4 | 0-4-7 |
| HALF-BREADTHS | SHEER | 2-6-2 | 2-8-5 | 2-10-0 | 2-10-2 | 2-9-3 | 2-7-0 | 2-1-6 | 1-0-7 | 0-0- |
| | 1ST KNUCKLE | 2-7-4 | 2-9-1 | 2-10-6 | 2-9-6 | 2-8-4 | 2-6-0 | 2-0-2 | 1-0-3 | 0-0- |
| | 2ND KNUCKLE | 2-7-1 | 2-8-0 | 2-8-1 | 2-7-4 | 2-6-0 | 2-3-0 | 1-9-0 | 0-9-0 | 0-0- |
| | BOTTOM, INNER INSIDE PLANK | 2-1-3 | 2-0-6 | 2-0-0 | 1-10-3 | 1-7-2 | 1-1-6 | 0-5-7 | | |

STATIONS #6 TO #1 SPACED 2'-6" APART.

# 23 THE CHAISSON 10-FOOT DORY TENDER

The lines and details which follow are for a superior yacht tender built sometime before World War II by George L. Chaisson of Swampscott, Mass., who produced these boats in three lengths, this 10-footer being the smallest. Chaisson was building these dory tenders at least as early as 1916. These dory tenders were a specialty of the Chaisson boatshop, and were widely known and distributed. Over the years I have come across more than a few of them in use, and always their owners set store by them and praised them highly.

There were two grades, although the difference was primarily one of finish, for the construction of both kinds was uniformly excellent and to the best of my knowledge, both performed and lasted equally well. One was finished bright, copper fastened and brass fitted. The other was painted and galvanized fastened. It was from one of the latter that the measurements and details set forth here were taken. This particular boat is the prized possession of George Stadel, the well-known Stamford, Conn., naval architect who is a connoisseur of classic small craft, and whose opinion based on a lifetime of experience can be depended on.

George rates these tenders tops, as I do. They tow beautifully, row and handle well, have exceptional carrying capacity, and are fine sea boats. In addition they are strong and rugged due to their dory construction. In spite of their narrow, flat bottoms, which incidentally are great for landing on the beach, they are essentially round-hull boats and behave as such, being in their performance on a par with classic yacht tenders by Lawley and Herreshoff, although they are only half as difficult to build.

This boat will require molds for each of its four 2-foot stations, and, unlike standard dory construction in which the pre-cut frames serve as molds, the molds for this boat will be removed after the boat is planked. Construction starts with the bottom assembly, which consists of the bottom with the inner stem and the transom attached. The bottom, which is 19½ inches at its widest part, is normally made out of two Eastern white pine boards ⅞ inch thick and cleated together. For this boat, cleats 1⅛ inches wide and ⅞ inch thick are spaced on 12-inch centers. They should be securely fastened from the outside through the pine into the oak with 1½-inch #12 wood screws.

It is important that the bottom be no less than ⅞ inch thick. If Eastern white pine is used, a few sound knots not too large will make the bottom even tougher. Good quality, rift sawn, seasoned Douglas fir or mahogany would serve as acceptable substitutes. Cedar or cypress would be too soft.

Although dories are frequently built upside down over a plank-on-edge strongback, I recommend planking this dory right-side up. One way to do this would be to set the bottom assembly on two stout horses about 28 inches high, and to spring the bottom to its required fore-and-aft camber by shoring from overhead. If the ceiling

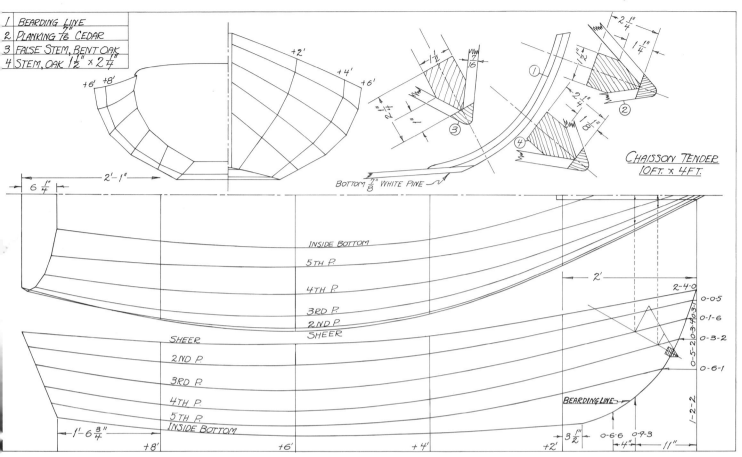

| 1 | BEARDING LINE |
| 2 | PLANKING 7/16 CEDAR |
| 3 | FALSE STEM, BENT OAK |
| 4 | STEM, OAK 1½" x 2¼" |

CHAISSON TENDER
10 FT. x 4 FT.

BOTTOM 7/8" WHITE PINE

INSIDE BOTTOM
5TH P.
4TH P.
3RD P.
2ND P.
SHEER

SHEER
2ND P.
3RD P.
4TH P.
5TH P.
INSIDE BOTTOM

BEARDING LINE

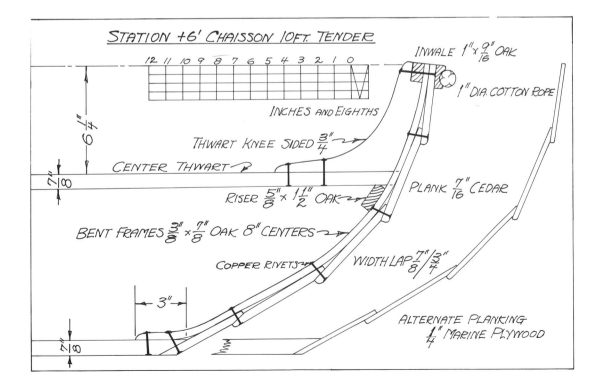

STATION +6' CHAISSON 10 FT. TENDER

12 11 10 9 8 7 6 5 4 3 2 1 0

INCHES AND EIGHTHS

INWALE 1" x 9/16" OAK

1" DIA. COTTON ROPE

THWART KNEE SIDED 3/4"

CENTER THWART

RISER 5/8" x 1½" OAK

PLANK 7/16" CEDAR

BENT FRAMES 3/8" x 7/8" OAK 8" CENTERS

COPPER RIVETS

WIDTH LAP 7/8"/3/4"

ALTERNATE PLANKING
¼" MARINE PLYWOOD

is too high or there are no rafters to brace from, other methods can be devised for bending the bottom to its required curvature and securing it in place.

While it is a little harder to fit the plank bevels when a boat is planked upright, it does become possible for one man to rivet the laps by himself, which is more than sufficient compensation when one is working alone.

The transom should be ⅞ inch thick, or even an inch if made of Eastern white pine or Douglas fir, but it can be ¾ inch thick, finished, if a good grade of mahogany is used, which would be de-

sirable if the boat is to be varnished. Even if the boat is to be painted, mahogany would be an excellent choice for the transom, as it does not swell, shrink, or twist excessively, like oak for example, yet affords good fastening for the plank ends.

The boat under consideration had its transom cut down sometime during its career for an outboard motor. I have not shown this. If one desired the transom, it could easily be done, although some additional reinforcement should be added for the motor.

| CHAISSON TENDER — 10 FT. x 4 FT. | | STEM | +2' | +4' | +6' | +8' | TRAN. |
|---|---|---|---|---|---|---|---|
| HEIGHTS | SHEER | 2-4-0 | 1-11-6 | 1-8-0 | 1-6-4 | 1-6-7 | 1-8-4 |
| | 2ND P. | 2-2-1 | 1-9-2 | 1-4-7 | 1-2-7 | 1-3-3 | 1-6-1 |
| | 3RD P. | 1-11-0 | 1-5-5 | 1-0-7 | 0-10-3 | 0-11-5 | 1-3-0 |
| | 4TH. P. | 1-7-4 | 1-1-7 | 0-9-0 | 0-6-7 | 0-8-1 | 0-11-2 |
| | 5TH P. | 1-2-2 | 0-10-0 | 0-5-6 | 0-4-3 | 0-5-3 | 0-8-3 |
| | BOTTOM | 0-4-5 | 0-4-4 | 0-3-1 | 0-2-5 | 0-3-5 | 0-5-6 |
| HALF-BREADTHS | SHEER | 0-0-6 | 1-0-2 | 1-8-6 | 1-11-6 | 1-9-6 | 1-4-2 |
| | 2ND P. | 0-0-6 | 0-11-7 | 1-8-4 | 1-11-2 | 1-9-4 | 1-4-6 |
| | 3RD. P. | 0-0-6 | 0-10-5 | 1-6-3 | 1-9-1 | 1-8-0 | 1-4-1 |
| | 4TH P. | 0-0-6 | 0-8-6 | 1-3-2 | 1-5-3 | 1-4-4 | 1-2-2 |
| | 5TH. P. | 0-0-6 | 0-5-7 | 0-11-1 | 1-0-4 | 1-0-1 | 0-10-5 |
| | BOTTOM | 0-0-6 | 0-1-7 | 0-7-6 | 0-9-2 | 0-8-1 | 0-6-0 |

OFFSETS – FEET, INCHES, EIGHTHS, MEASURED TO INSIDE PLANKING, INSIDE BOTTOM, OUTSIDE TRANSOM AND TO BEARDING LINE.

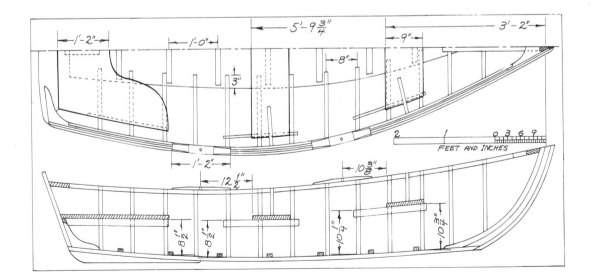

FEET AND INCHES

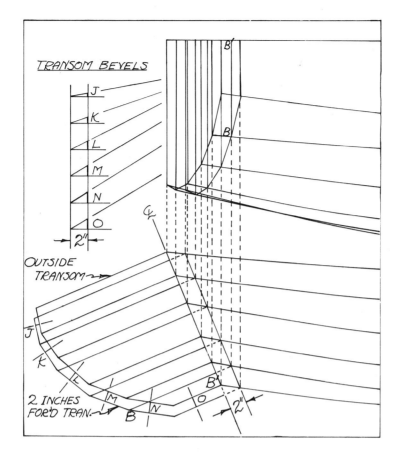

TRANSOM BEVELS

J
K
L
M
N
O

2"

OUTSIDE
TRANSOM →

J
K
L
M
N
B
2 INCHES
FOR'D TRAN.

2"

# 24 A 12-FOOT, 6-INCH SWAMPSCOTT DORY TENDER

Every now and then somebody gets a notion to build a small dory. Usually I try to discourage this, because, as a rule, small dories aren't much good, especially Bank dories. In such craft overall length is critical. A dory reduced in length to 14 feet, let us say, would not be safe, in my estimation, unless built with extra width of beam and with high freeboard as well, in which case, a tubby, clumsy craft would result that could hardly be called a dory.

Swampscott dories are different. These knuckle-sided craft, because of their rounded shape, behave in the water much like ordinary round-hull boats, and so can be safely built in shorter lengths, if correctly proportioned. Such a boat of proven ability and performance is the 12-foot 6-inch LOA Swampscott dory which we have under consideration here. This boat is modeled on one which I ran across at the Lynn Yacht Club in Lynn, Mass., more than 20 years ago. It was the smallest Swampscott dory (not skiff) that I had seen, and because of this and its striking appearance, I went out of my way to make inquiries about its performance.

From several of the club members I learned that this little dory, which had been around the club for some years, had proved to be a fine tender of exceptional carrying capacity, besides being an excellent sea boat. Further, I found that it had been built by George Chaisson in his Swampscott shop not far distant, which in itself was strong commendation, for Chaisson was never known to build a mean dory, and in fact Chaisson dories were about the best you could get.

I did not have the necessary equipment with me at the time for a complete lines-taking job, but I did have a camera and a rule, and was able to get photos and the principal dimensions, which I set down in my notebook. However, it was not until many years later that I got around to making use of these dimensions to lay the boat out on paper. The shape as I have reconstructed it is close to the original, I am quite sure, if not identical with it for all useful and practical purposes. One change that I have made is to draw the boat for five strakes of plank instead of four.

When Chaisson built this dory some 35 to 40 years ago, wide white pine boards were still to be had at reasonable cost. Today such lumber is priced out of reach, if any at all is to be found. Actually, five strakes of plank instead of four will make a better boat, although more work will be required in building it.

The diagram of the planking shapes is provided to enable the builder to estimate what he will need for planking stock as well as the approximate lengths and widths required for the selection of his lumber. The planks are shown continuous for their full length, but in all probability the builder will find it advantageous to splice them up out of shorter pieces. The planking shapes were taken from a half model made to a scale of 2 inches equal one foot. While the model was accurately made and the shapes

# Dory Plans

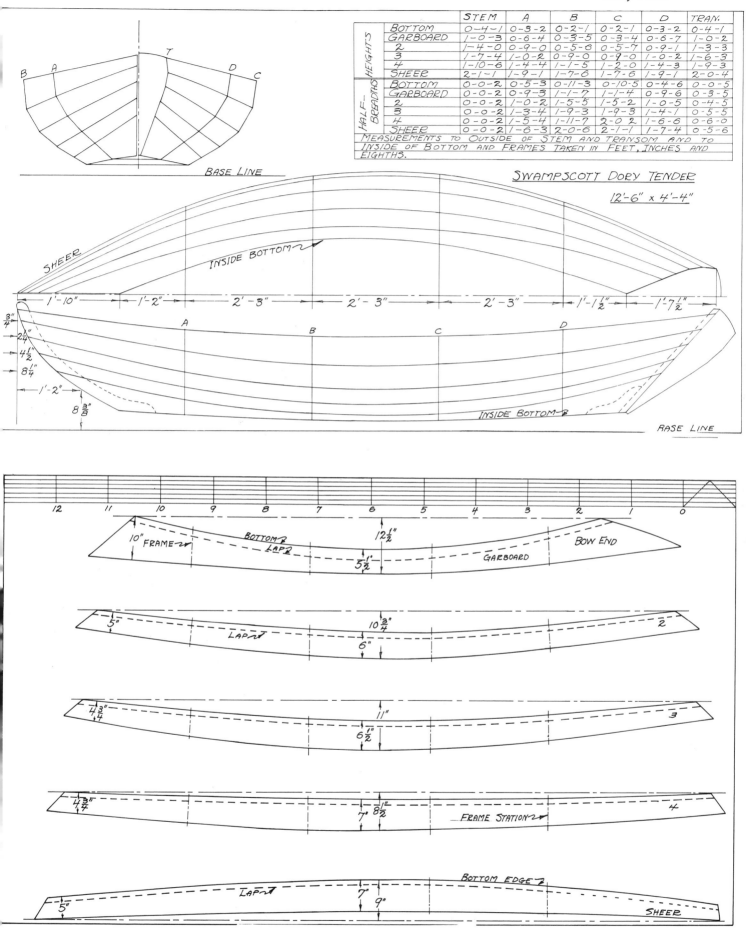

|  |  | STEM | A | B | C | D | TRAN. |
|---|---|---|---|---|---|---|---|
| **HEIGHTS** | BOTTOM | 0-4-1 | 0-3-2 | 0-2-1 | 0-2-1 | 0-3-2 | 0-4-1 |
|  | GARBOARD | 1-0-3 | 0-6-4 | 0-3-5 | 0-3-4 | 0-6-7 | 1-0-2 |
|  | 2 | 1-4-0 | 0-9-0 | 0-5-0 | 0-5-7 | 0-9-1 | 1-3-3 |
|  | 3 | 1-7-4 | 1-0-2 | 0-9-0 | 0-9-0 | 1-0-2 | 1-6-3 |
|  | 4 | 1-10-6 | 1-4-4 | 1-1-5 | 1-2-0 | 1-4-3 | 1-9-3 |
|  | SHEER | 2-1-1 | 1-9-1 | 1-7-6 | 1-7-6 | 1-9-1 | 2-0-4 |
| **HALF-BREADTHS** | BOTTOM | 0-0-2 | 0-5-3 | 0-11-3 | 0-10-5 | 0-4-6 | 0-0-5 |
|  | GARBOARD | 0-0-2 | 0-9-3 | 1-1-7 | 1-1-4 | 0-9-6 | 0-3-5 |
|  | 2 | 0-0-2 | 1-0-2 | 1-5-5 | 1-5-2 | 1-0-5 | 0-4-5 |
|  | 3 | 0-0-2 | 1-3-4 | 1-9-3 | 1-4-1 | 0-6-0 |  |
|  | 4 | 0-0-2 | 1-5-4 | 1-11-7 | 2-0-2 | 1-6-6 | 0-6-0 |
|  | SHEER | 0-0-2 | 1-6-3 | 2-0-6 | 2-1-1 | 1-7-4 | 0-5-6 |

MEASUREMENTS TO OUTSIDE OF STEM AND TRANSOM AND TO INSIDE OF BOTTOM AND FRAMES TAKEN IN FEET, INCHES AND EIGHTHS.

BASE LINE

SWAMPSCOTT DORY TENDER

12'-6" x 4'-4"

SHEER

INSIDE BOTTOM

1'-10"  1'-2"  2'-3"  2'-3"  2'-3"  1'-1½"  1'-7½"

A  B  C  D

3/4"  2¼"  4½"  8¼"

1'-2"

8 3/8"

INSIDE BOTTOM-B

BASE LINE

12  11  10  9  8  7  6  5  4  3  2  1  0

10" FRAME  BOTTOM  LAP  12½"  5½"  GARBOARD  BOW END

5"  LAP  10¾"  6"  2

4¾"  11"  6½"  3

4¾"  7' 8½"  FRAME STATION  4

BOTTOM EDGE

LAP  7"  9"

5"  SHEER

carefully taken, it is not likely that enlargements made from them would provide an exact fit for a full-size boat. For that reason it is desirable for the builder to spile his own shapes after he has got his boat set up and faired for planking.

The original boat had more than the usual number of bent ribs, but apparently there were only three standard sawn dory frames. Chaisson made more use of bent ribs than other dory builders, and some of his tenders of modified dory construction were framed entirely with bent ribs. In working out the details for my reconstruction of this dory I have gone back to the more conventional framing layout, making provision for four sets of standard sawn dory frames located at stations A, B, C, and D as shown in the lines plan. Midway between each pair there should be a bent rib, and, at either end of the boat, two sets of bent ribs spaced to give maximum reinforcement.

Scantlings for this small dory should be the same as that for the larger versions, except for the width and location of the thwarts. These should be 10 inches wide instead of 8 inches, and they should be screw-fastened to the risers. The frames at Station B should be notched into the after edge of the thwart at that station so that its after edge lies flush with the after face of the frames. And at Station C the forward edge of the thwart should notch around frame C in like manner to bring the forward edge of the thwart flush with the forward face of the frame. This will place the two thwarts far enough apart to permit two oarsmen to row at the same time without interference. A single oarsman would usually row from Station B.

# 25 THE 13-FOOT CHAMBERLAIN DORY SKIFF

The smallest, but most numerous member of the dory family is the skiff. The many fine qualities of dory design make it a favorite. In and around Marblehead, for instance, there are more small boats of the dory-skiff type than any other kind. They range all the way from the humble flat-iron with sides as square as a box, to rounded models like the skiffs by Chamberlain and Lawton.

On the smaller ponds and sheltered harbors, a wide, flat bottom is all right. Drawing little water and skimming along easily, if the water is smooth, the flat bottom is stiff and steady. Add high sides and you have a boat that small children can't tip over or fall out of easily. But don't take such a boat out where the big ones are rolling. Out there you will be much better off in something like the Chamberlain skiff.

Look over the lines of this Chamberlain model. Note the narrow, well-rockered bottom that sits deeply in the water when the boat is loaded, giving it a firm grip down underneath where it counts. The turn of the bilge rounds out big and full with plenty of lift. Properly trimmed and handled right, this little boat will accomodate itself to the motion of rough water with ease. The bow is high enough and full enough to keep her head up, but freeboard has been held down to cut windage. The stern has been tucked sufficiently high to prevent drag. Also narrowed and raking, the stern can dodge the smash and smother of a following sea and ride away from it. For a rowing sea boat, you can't do much better within the 13-foot limit. Of course, a longer boat, other factors being equal, will take more weather.

When the outboard motor came along, it was hung over the transoms of boats like this Chamberlain skiff, which is about perfect for rowing but unsuited to outboarding. Their relatively slender sterns were never intended to support all this added weight concentrated so far aft. To take the weight, their bottoms were widened and straightened, and sterns spread out big and square. Such boats did pretty well with motors that had the brute force to push a clumsy hull, but naturally they did not row easily. Their awkward sterns dragged water and slammed about in a following sea.

Some years ago, Tom Plant, who was a rowing enthusiast, approached me for the design of a small rowing boat that he might build for himself, as well as have a few built for sale by his crew in the shop in the wintertime when outside work happened to be slack. He liked the idea of planking with plywood on seam battens to be covered with a layer of reinforced thermoplastic.

I can't for the life of me recall at this writing whether Plant used fiberglass, Dynel, or Vectra polypropylene for his reinforcing fabric, but I believe it was before polypropylene was brought forward for boat work. Today I would definitely recommend polypropylene, as it is only one-third the weight of equivalent fiberglass, and it is tougher and more elastic.

*Above: A 13-foot Chamberlain dory skiff built by Thomas G. Plant, Jr., of San Francisco. This rowing model is fitted with a sliding seat and spoon-blade oars.*
*Below: The same model dory skiff built by Plant and rigged for sail.*

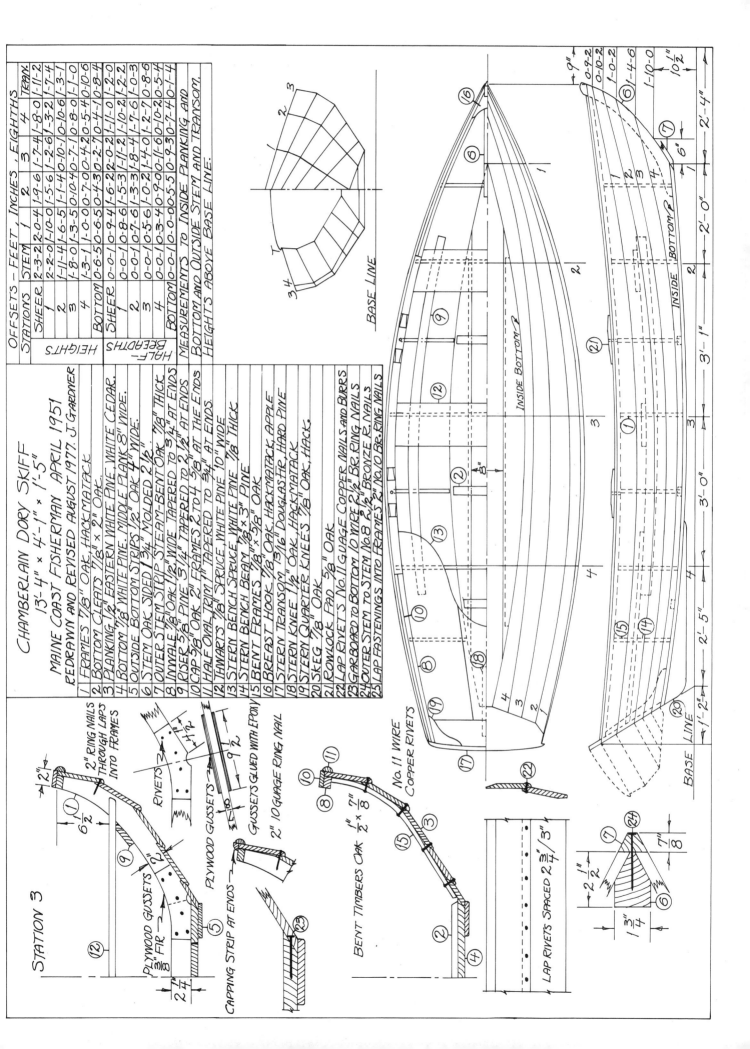

## CHAMBERLAIN DORY SKIFF
### 13'-4" × 4'-1" × 1'-5"
### MAINE COAST FISHERMAN APRIL 1951
### REDRAWN AND REVISED AUGUST 1977. J. GARDNER.

1 FRAMES 7/8" OAK, HACKMATACK.
2 BOTTOM CLEATS 7/8" × 2" OAK.
3 PLANKING 1/2" EASTERN WHITE PINE, WHITE CEDAR.
4 BOTTOM 7/8" WHITE PINE. MIDDLE PLANK 8" WIDE.
5 OUTSIDE BOTTOM STRIPS 1/2" OAK 4" WIDE.
6 STEM OAK SIDED 1 3/4" MOLDED 2 1/2".
7 OUTER STEM STRIP STEAM-BENT OAK 7/8" THICK.
8 INWALE 7/8" OAK 1 1/2" WIDE TAPERED TO 3 3/4" AT ENDS
9 RISER 5/8" PINE 3 1/4" TAPERED TO 2 1/2" AT ENDS
10 CAP 3/8" OAK 2" FRAMES 2 TO 4 5/8" AT THE ENDS
11 HALF OVAL TRIM 1" TAPERED TO 3/4" AT ENDS.
12 THWARTS 7/8" SPRUCE, WHITE PINE 10" WIDE
13 STERN BENCH SPRUCE, WHITE PINE 7/8" THICK
14 STERN BENCH BEAM 7/8" × 3" PINE
15 BENT FRAMES 1/2" × 5/8" OAK
16 BREAST HOOK 7/8" OAK, HACKMATACK, APPLE
17 STERN TRANSOM 13/16" DOUGLAS-FIR, HARD PINE
18 STERN KNEE 1 1/2" OAK, HACKMATACK
19 STERN QUARTER KNEES 7/8" OAK, HACK.
20 SKEG 7/8" OAK
21 ROWLOCK PAD 5/8" OAK
22 LAP RIVETS No.11 GUAGE COPPER NAILS AND BURRS
23 GARBOARD TO BOTTOM 10 WIRE 2 1/2" BR. RING NAILS
24 OUTER STEM TO STEM No.8 2 1/2" BRONZE R. NAILS
25 LAP FASTENINGS INTO FRAMES 2" No.10 BR. RING NAILS

### OFFSETS — FEET, INCHES, EIGHTHS

| | STATIONS | STEM | 1 | 2 | 3 | 4 | TRAN. |
|---|---|---|---|---|---|---|---|
| **HEIGHTS** | SHEER | 2-3-2 | 2-0-4 | 1-9-6 | 1-7-4 | 1-8-0 | 1-11-2 |
| | 1 | 2-2-0 | 1-10-0 | 1-5-6 | 1-2-6 | 1-3-2 | 1-7-4 |
| | 2 | 1-11-4 | 1-6-5 | 1-1-4 | 0-10-6 | 0-10-6 | 1-3-1 |
| | 3 | 1-8-0 | 1-3-5 | 0-10-4 | 0-7-1 | 0-8-0 | 1-0 |
| | 4 | 1-3-1 | 1-0-0 | 0-7-0 | 0-4-2 | 0-5-4 | 0-10-6 |
| | BOTTOM | 0-0-0 | 0-6-5 | 0-6-5 | 0-4-3 | 0-2-7 | 0-0-4 |
| **HALF-BREADTHS** | SHEER | 0-0-0 | 0-9-4 | 1-6-2 | 2-2-1 | 1-1-0 | 1-2-0 |
| | 2 | 0-0-0 | 0-8-6 | 1-5-3 | 1-1-2 | 1-10-2 | 2-2-2 |
| | 3 | 0-0-0 | 0-7-6 | 1-3-3 | 1-8-4 | 1-7-6 | 1-0-3 |
| | 4 | 0-0-0 | 0-5-6 | 1-0-2 | 1-4-0 | 2-7-0 | 8-6 |
| | BOTTOM | 0-0-0 | 0-3-4 | 0-9-0 | 0-1-6 | 0-20-5 | 1-1 |
| | BOTTOM | 0-0-0 | 0-0-0 | 0-0-5 | 0-9-3 | 0-7-4 | 0-1-4 |

MEASUREMENTS TO INSIDE PLANKING AND
BOTTOM AND OUTSIDE STEM AND TRANSOM.
HEIGHTS ABOVE BASE LINE.

STATION 3

2" RING NAILS
THROUGH LAPS
INTO FRAMES

RIVETS

PLYWOOD GUSSETS

GUSSETS GLUED WITH EPONY

2" 10 GUAGE RING NAIL

PLYWOOD GUSSETS
3/8" FIR

CAPPING STRIP AT ENDS

BENT TIMBERS OAK 1/2" × 7/8"

No.11 WIRE
COPPER RIVETS

LAP RIVETS SPACED 2 3/4/3"

BASE LINE

INSIDE BOTTOM

BASE LINE

# 26  THE 13-FOOT LAWTON DORY SKIFF

This 13-foot dory skiff, was redrawn from a sketch made by the late Charles A. Lawton when he was at the point of retiring as a boat-builder from the James E. Graves Beacon Street boatshop in Marblehead, Massachusetts, at the age of 90. Charlie, as everyone knew him, came from St. John, N. B., in the 1880s to work for H. V. Partelow & Co. of Boston at its factory at Auburndale on the Charles River. There he built St. Lawrence River skiffs, and his favorite, the varnished Adirondack, both with a transom-stern and double-ended. The turn of the century found him working in Swampscott, Massachusetts, building dories for Elbridge Gerry Emmons, who at that time had the leading dory business in the country. Dories were then the most popular small-craft type both for sail and power.

To those interested in a better dual-purpose boat for general rowing and outboard use, this model by Charles Lawton is offered for consideration. The conflicting requirements for rowing and outboard use raise some knotty problems. It is no simple job to work out a good dual-purpose design. That is what Charles Lawton was driving at with this 13-foot outboard skiff, and the lines speak for themselves. Lawton drew it up and built one in 1950 when he was past the age of 90, and after more than 70 active years of boatbuilding. Charlie lived for many years in Marblehead, in which town he became famous for his varnished yacht tenders unsurpassed for quality and finish. He was one of the last of the old-time dory builders. It was Charles Lawton, I believe, who many years ago first adapted the bent timber and open gun-wale construction to dory skiffs.

Construction for this outboard dory skiff proceeds in the usual manner for a Swamp-scott-type dory. Assuming that the lines have been laid down full-size, faired, and the necessary patterns made, the first step is to cut the bottom to shape from a couple of ⅞-inch pine boards and permanently cleat them together. The stem is fastened to the bow end and the tran-som to the stern. This assembly is then placed upside-down on the sawn frames that serve as molds and which have been set bottom-up in position on their respective stations and at a convenient height. When all has been made true, fair, and secure, the planking proceeds from half-inch pine or cedar, starting with the garboard.

After the planking is in place, the hull is lifted from the forms and turned right-side up. The bent timbers are put in, the fastening of the laps is completed, and the interior work is finished.

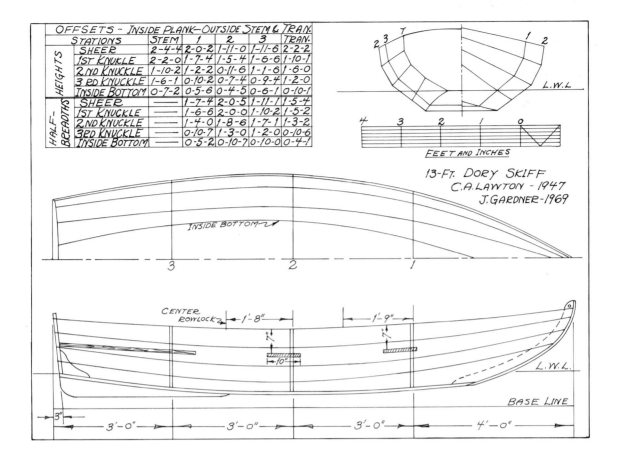

| OFFSETS - INSIDE PLANK—OUTSIDE STEM & TRAN. |        |        |         |        |        |        |
|---------|---------------|--------|--------|---------|--------|--------|
|         | STATIONS      | STEM   | 1      | 2       | 3      | TRAN.  |
| HEIGHTS | SHEER         | 2-4-4  | 2-0-2  | 1-11-0  | 1-11-6 | 2-2-2  |
|         | 1ST KNUCKLE   | 2-2-0  | 1-7-4  | 1-5-4   | 1-6-6  | 1-10-1 |
|         | 2ND KNUCKLE   | 1-10-2 | 1-2-2  | 0-11-6  | 1-1-6  | 1-6-0  |
|         | 3RD KNUCKLE   | 1-6-1  | 0-10-2 | 0-7-4   | 0-9-4  | 1-2-0  |
|         | INSIDE BOTTOM | 0-7-2  | 0-5-6  | 0-4-5   | 0-6-1  | 0-10-1 |
| HALF-BREADTHS | SHEER   | ———    | 1-7-4  | 2-0-5   | 1-11-1 | 1-5-4  |
|         | 1ST KNUCKLE   | ———    | 1-6-6  | 2-0-0   | 1-10-2 | 1-5-2  |
|         | 2ND KNUCKLE   | ———    | 1-4-0  | 1-8-6   | 1-7-1  | 1-3-2  |
|         | 3RD KNUCKLE   | ———    | 0-10-7 | 1-3-0   | 1-2-0  | 0-10-6 |
|         | INSIDE BOTTOM | ———    | 0-5-2  | 0-10-7  | 0-10-0 | 0-4-1  |

FEET AND INCHES

13-FT. DORY SKIFF
C.A. LAWTON - 1947
J. GARDNER - 1969

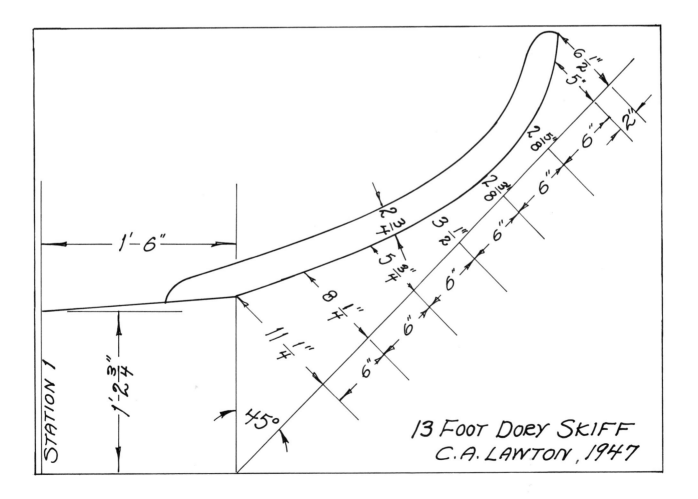

STATION 1

13 FOOT DORY SKIFF
C.A. LAWTON, 1947

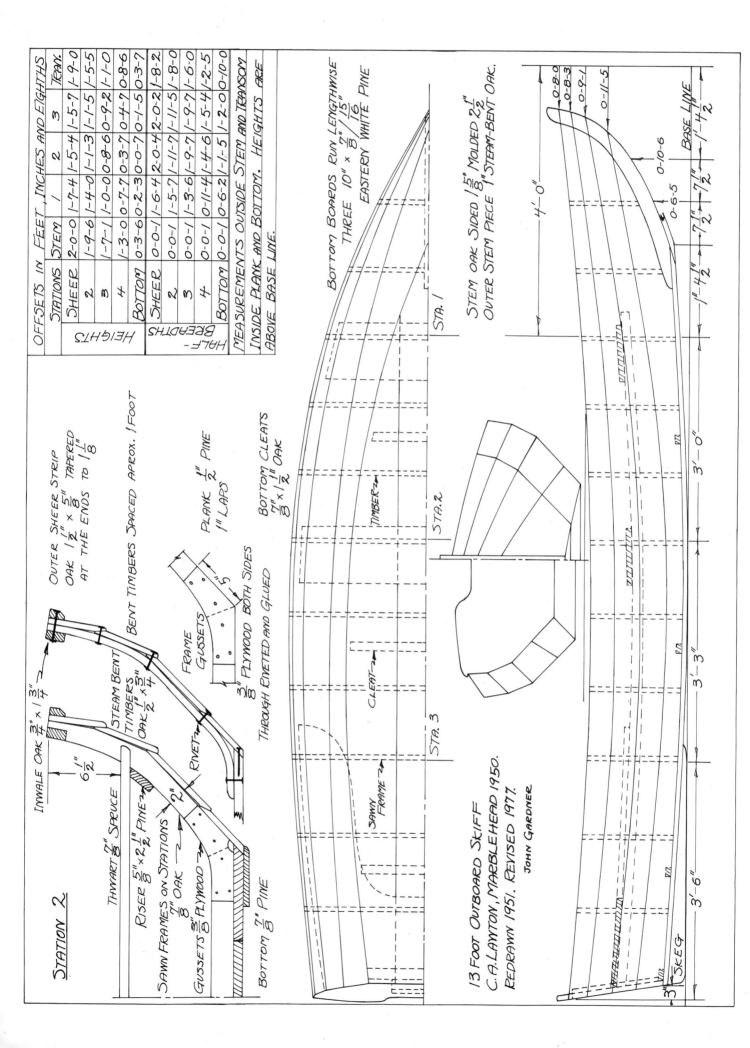

13 Foot Outboard Skiff
C.A. Lawton, Marblehead 1950.
Redrawn 1951. Revised 1977.
John Gardner

# 27 A 14-FOOT DORY SKIFF

This 14-foot skiff is offered as one possibility to be considered in the selection of a general-purpose rowboat, one which will row easily and be a good sea boat, as well, within the limits of its size. It is a proven model, being a slightly altered and enlarged version of the 13-foot 6-inch dory skiff designed and formerly built in the early decades of this century by William Chamberlain of Marblehead.

From the load line as drawn in the lines plan, the draft, including the thickness of the bottom, is shown to be 6¾ inches, and the displacement at this depth figures to be approximately 9 cubic feet, or something like 560 pounds. Allowing 150 pounds for the weight of the ⅜-inch marine fir plywood hull, the displacement remaining would be about equivalent to the combined weight of three medium-size persons. With this loading, the bottom of the transom would barely touch the water, so there would be no stern drag. The entrance is fairly sharp—the additional 6 inches at the bow helped this, and, with its somewhat narrow bottom and relatively steep deadrise, this hull is bound to row easily.

Because of the characteristics just noted, initial stability will prove somewhat tender, so that a landlubber stepping into her carelessly when she is light might get a start. Yet this is a stable hull where stability counts, and because of her ample side flare, beam, and length, a fairsize boy could sit on her rail without putting it under.

This design has been worked over and altered so it can be built easily and inexpensively. Planking of ⅜-inch marine plywood has been laid out to be cut economically from standard 4-foot by 8-foot panels, the pieces to be glue spliced. The planking could just as well be butted on seam battens, but some amateurs have had trouble with this method in building other round-sided dories, for which reason an easier substitute technique for securing the edges of the planking has been devised.

In spite of its flat bottom, which of course is relatively quite narrow, this dory skiff has virtually a round hull, and, for all practical purposes, behaves as one. Indeed, this skiff closely resembles the old-time New England wherry, which was a fine sea boat.

It is worth mentioning that this skiff fitted with a centerboard and a proper rig would sail smartly, but she is unsuited for an outboard.

*A 14-foot dory skiff under construction by Mark M. McChessney in 1969.*

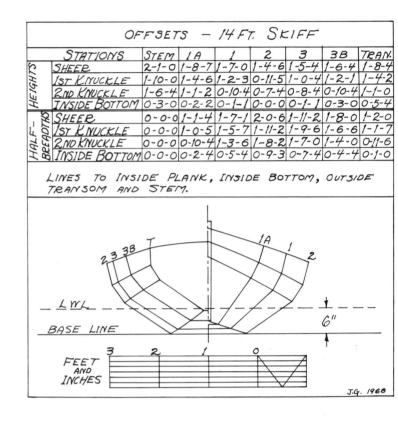

| | STATIONS | STEM | 1A | 1 | 2 | 3 | 3B | TRAN. |
|---|---|---|---|---|---|---|---|---|
| **HEIGHTS** | SHEER | 2-1-0 | 1-8-7 | 1-7-0 | 1-4-6 | 1-5-4 | 1-6-4 | 1-8-4 |
| | 1ST KNUCKLE | 1-10-0 | 1-4-6 | 1-2-3 | 0-11-5 | 1-0-4 | 1-2-1 | 1-4-2 |
| | 2ND KNUCKLE | 1-6-4 | 1-1-2 | 0-10-4 | 0-7-4 | 0-8-4 | 0-10-4 | 1-1-0 |
| | INSIDE BOTTOM | 0-3-0 | 0-2-2 | 0-1-1 | 0-0-0 | 0-1-1 | 0-3-0 | 0-5-4 |
| **HALF-BREADTHS** | SHEER | 0-0-0 | 1-1-4 | 1-7-1 | 2-0-6 | 1-11-2 | 1-8-0 | 1-2-0 |
| | 1ST KNUCKLE | 0-0-0 | 1-0-5 | 1-5-7 | 1-11-2 | 1-9-6 | 1-6-6 | 1-1-7 |
| | 2ND KNUCKLE | 0-0-0 | 0-10-4 | 1-3-6 | 1-8-2 | 1-7-0 | 1-4-0 | 0-11-6 |
| | INSIDE BOTTOM | 0-0-0 | 0-2-4 | 0-5-4 | 0-9-3 | 0-7-4 | 0-4-4 | 0-1-0 |

LINES TO INSIDE PLANK, INSIDE BOTTOM, OUTSIDE TRANSOM AND STEM.

J.G. 1968

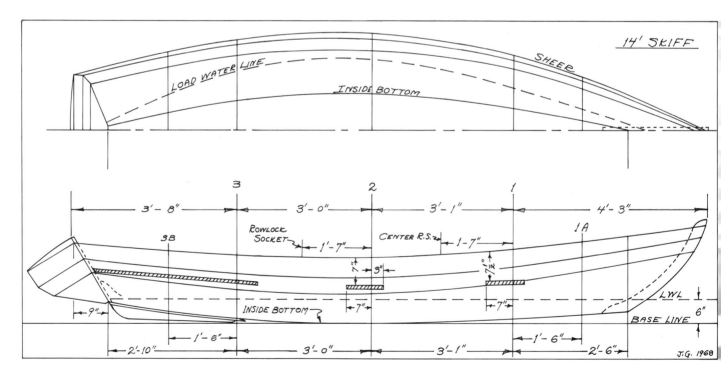

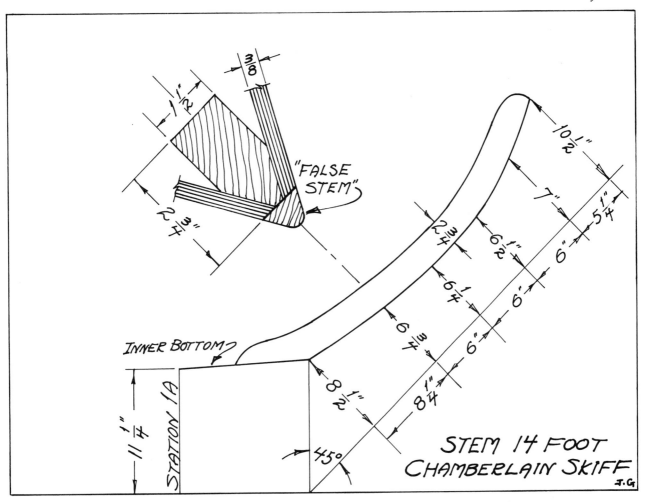

"FALSE STEM"

$\frac{3}{8}$

$1\frac{1}{2}$"

$2\frac{3}{4}$"

$10\frac{1}{2}$"

7"

$5\frac{1}{4}$"

$2\frac{3}{4}$"

$6\frac{1}{2}$"

$6\frac{1}{4}$"

6"

$6\frac{3}{4}$"

6"

6"

6"

$8\frac{1}{2}$"

$8\frac{1}{4}$"

INNER BOTTOM

$11\frac{1}{4}$"

STATION 1A

45°

STEM 14 FOOT
CHAMBERLAIN SKIFF

J.G.

# 28 A 14-FOOT, 4½-INCH OUTBOARD FLATIRON

An old friend, Paul Hanson of Chicago, wrote to see if we had plans for a skiff. Paul builds his own boats, and after building two ordinary plywood skiffs, he took a notion to build another skiff. "Good flat-bottom skiff plans are hard to find," he wrote. "Have you something with the flare of a Bank dory, something about 14 feet overall, 4½- to 5-foot beam, that could be rowed in a pinch, but would ordinarily be driven by a 5- to 10-hp outboard mounted on the transom?"

In reply, I mailed Paul the plans and building directions for the 14½-foot flatiron skiff shown here. His response was enthusiastic: "You hit the nail on the head. I see no reason why the flatiron shouldn't be a good boat for hauling on a trailer and for fishing for perch in Lake Michigan, when you are hardly ever more than a mile or so offshore."

Paul did not wait long to start building, and it didn't take him long, once he had started—within a period of 2½ weeks, he spent 40 hours, he estimates, which is close to the minimum for the simplest sort of boat. Considering that he built it in his backyard without benefit of power tools, we may be sure he hustled and made no false moves. In fact, when it comes to reporting the performance of this skiff, it seems best to let Paul describe it in his own words:

Today I took the skiff out with a 12 hp Sea King. I did not have any way of getting the correct speed, but I think it was between 15 and 18 mph. I also made full-speed turns in about 75-foot circles, and she just went around like she was on a straight course. We had waves only 2½ to 3 feet high, and when running into them, there was no pounding, and no spray entered the boat. And that I think is something for a flat-bottom boat. This boat does not squat either. It seems that only the bottom between frames 3 and 4 was in the water... This boat also rows well and seemed to move right along with a pair of 7½-foot oars.

A month later, Paul had more to say.

I have only had a chance to go out a couple of times in that flatiron. Last time, I had it out in a southerly chop with the wind about 20 mph. My motor had a miss in it, so I don't think I got all I should have out of this boat. But I can say one thing: I did not experience pounding or any slapping, so common to flat-bottom skiffs. Maybe it didn't plane too well, because I didn't have my son in it to hold the bow down. I weigh 225 pounds, and that is a lot of weight at the stern. But I still could see over the bow at all times, while another skiff that I was in recently under similar conditions squatted so much it seemed as if the bow was six feet in the air...

I don't think you should go out in a storm with this boat, but I am pretty sure it will give a very good account of itself, if caught out. In fact, I think it is just as good as any 14-footer you can find, if you handle it right. And another thing, it has plenty of flare to lift. Also, it is easy to launch off and on a trailer. It would serve anyone real well as a fishing or hunting boat because it draws only about 4 or 5 inches. I don't think you can find a better skiff of its size anywhere.

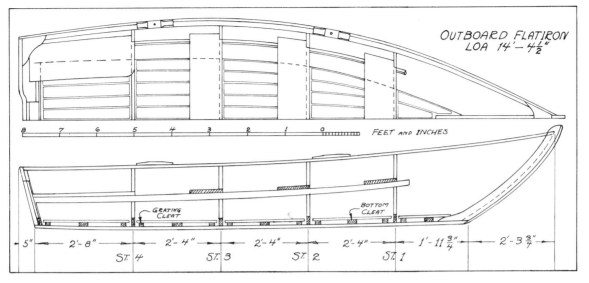

OUTBOARD FLATIRON
LOA 14'-4½"

8  7  6  5  4  3  2  1  0    FEET AND INCHES

GRATING
CLEAT

BOTTOM
CLEAT

5"    2'-8"    2'-4"    2'-4"    2'-4"    1'-11¾"    2'-3¾"

ST. 4    ST. 3    ST. 2    ST. 1

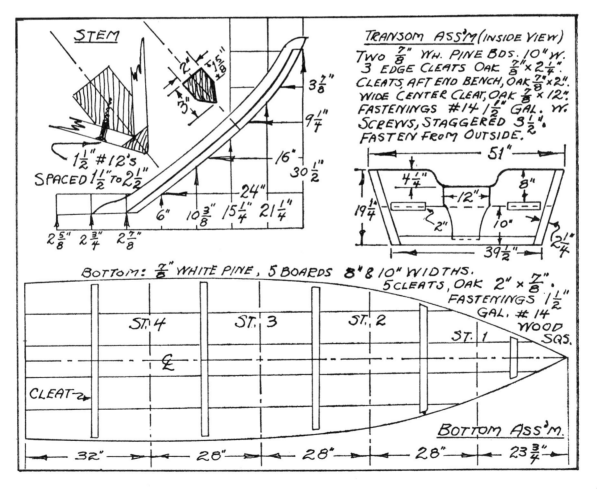

STEM

2"    1 5/16"

3"

1½" #12's
SPACED 1½" TO 2½"

2 5/8"   2 3/4"   2 7/8"

6"   10 3/8"  15 1/4"  21 1/4"

24"

3 7/8"

9 1/4"

16"

30 1/2"

TRANSOM ASS'M (INSIDE VIEW)

TWO ⅞" WH. PINE BDS. 10" W.
3 EDGE CLEATS OAK ⅞" × 2¼".
CLEATS, AFT END BENCH, OAK ⅞" × 2".
WIDE CENTER CLEAT, OAK ⅞" × 12".
FASTENINGS #14 1½" GAL. W.
SCREWS, STAGGERED 3½".
FASTEN FROM OUTSIDE.

51"

4 1/4"    8"

19 1/4"    12"

2"    10"

2 1/4"

39 1/2"

BOTTOM: ⅞" WHITE PINE, 5 BOARDS 8" & 10" WIDTHS.
5 CLEATS, OAK 2" × ⅞".
FASTENINGS 1½"
GAL. #14
WOOD
SQS.

ST. 4    ST. 3    ST. 2    ST. 1

Ç

CLEAT

BOTTOM ASS'M.

32"    28"    28"    28"    23¾"

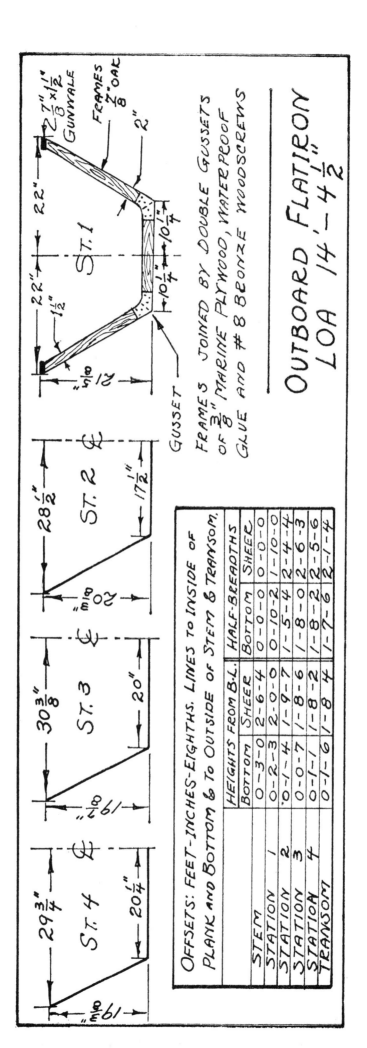

# OUTBOARD FLATIRON
## LOA 14'-4½"

GUNWALE — 2 $\frac{7}{8}$" x $\frac{1}{2}$"

FRAMES $\frac{7}{8}$" OAK

FRAMES JOINED BY DOUBLE GUSSETS OF $\frac{3}{8}$" MARINE PLYWOOD, WATERPROOF GLUE AND #8 BRONZE WOODSCREWS

GUSSET

ST. 1 — 22" — 22" — 1½" — 10¼" — 10¼" — 2" — 2½"

ST. 2 ₵ — 28½" — 17½" — 20"

ST. 3 ₵ — 30⅜" — 20" — 19½"

ST. 4 ₵ — 29¾" — 20¼" — 19"

OFFSETS: FEET-INCHES-EIGHTHS. LINES TO INSIDE OF PLANK AND BOTTOM & TO OUTSIDE OF STEM & TRANSOM.

| | HEIGHTS FROM B.L. | | HALF-BREADTHS | |
|---|---|---|---|---|
| | BOTTOM | SHEER | BOTTOM | SHEER |
| STEM | 0-3-0 | 2-6-4 | 0-0-0 | 0-0-0 |
| STATION 1 | 0-2-3 | 2-0-0 | 0-10-2 | 1-10-0 |
| STATION 2 | 0-1-4 | 1-9-7 | 1-5-4 | 2-4-4 |
| STATION 3 | 0-0-7 | 1-8-6 | 1-8-0 | 2-6-3 |
| STATION 4 | 0-1-1 | 1-8-2 | 1-8-2 | 2-5-6 |
| TRANSOM | 0-1-6 | 1-8-4 | 1-7-6 | 2-1-4 |

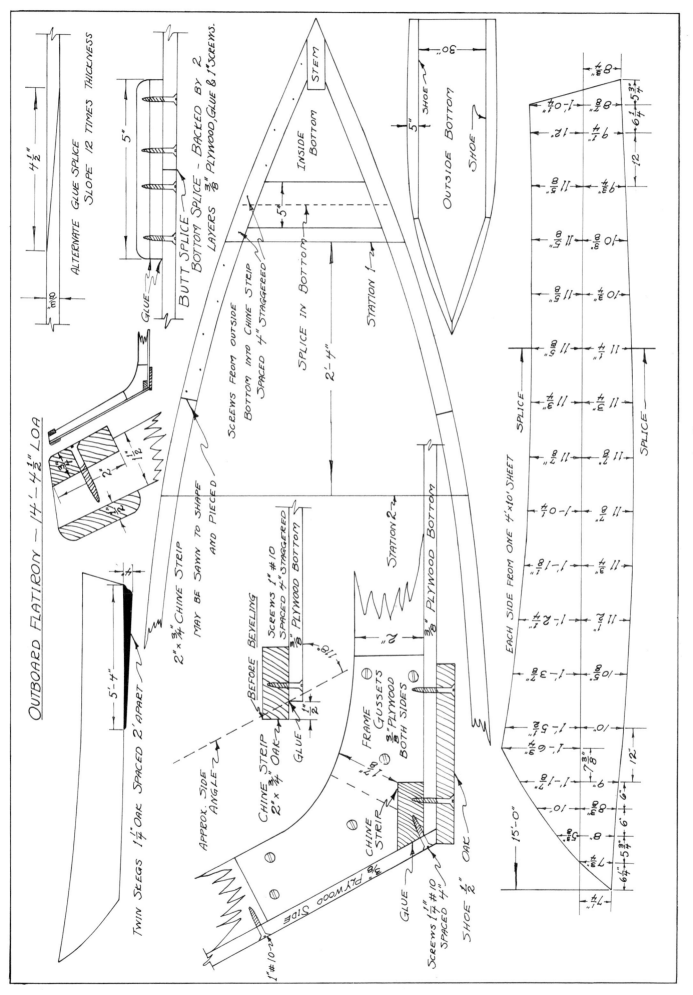

*The plywood version of the 14' 4½" outboard flatiron.*

# 29  THE 14-FOOT, 9-INCH LOWELL DORY SKIFF

Here we have a tried and tested dory skiff of large size. This substantial rowboat will give good service for fishing and general recreational use on all but the most exposed waters. This is a sturdy craft, built for rough treatment, and stout enough for a workboat. Its flat bottom and shallow draft make it easy to beach. Considering its weight and size, this skiff rows easily and handles well. But it should be well understood at the beginning that the skiff is not a model for the violent, open sea, and that in this respect, it is not in a class with such rough-water types as the larger Bank and Swampscott dories, the peapod, or the Rangeley Lakes boat.

The flat, comparatively wide bottom of this skiff affords great initial stability, making it a steady, comfortable boat to fish from, and that dogs and children cannot tip easily. Likewise, this flat bottom draws little water even under a load, giving a craft well suited to extremely shallow water. While the boat would row easier with a narrower bottom, it would lose in steadiness.

A small outboard motor can be used to push this dory skiff along at moderate speeds, but considerable alteration of its lines would be required to make this boat suitable for large motors and high speeds. Features that make this skiff row easily and handle well under oars would need changing. The rocker would have to be taken out of the bottom, aft, to make a straight, flat run from amidships to the transom. The transom, itself, would need widening and should be set more upright—by at least 15 degrees—to give a better angle for the motor.

These are not difficult changes to make and might well be considered if one were interested primarily in an outboard boat capable of a smart turn of speed. The resulting craft would be what is now frequently called a semi-dory. Boats of this type are now popular and widely used with large outboard motors. If one is mainly interested in rowing, however, the skiff is best left as she is.

The lines and the construction details in the accompanying drawing were taken from a boat owned by Mr. H. C. Riggs in Essex, Mass. This boat was built for Mr. Riggs by Hiram Lowell & Sons, Amesbury, Mass. The model was the old New York Club tender, so called, lengthened by two feet. Originally, this tender was designed and built by Toppan of Medford, Mass., at one time a famous dory-building concern, whose advertisements, incidentally, may be seen in the back files of *Rudder* magazine of many years ago.

This need not be an expensive boat to build, nor should it be a difficult model for the amateur builder. There are no hard bends and no steaming. Even fitting the laps is not hard, if the beginner will take time to study the operation.

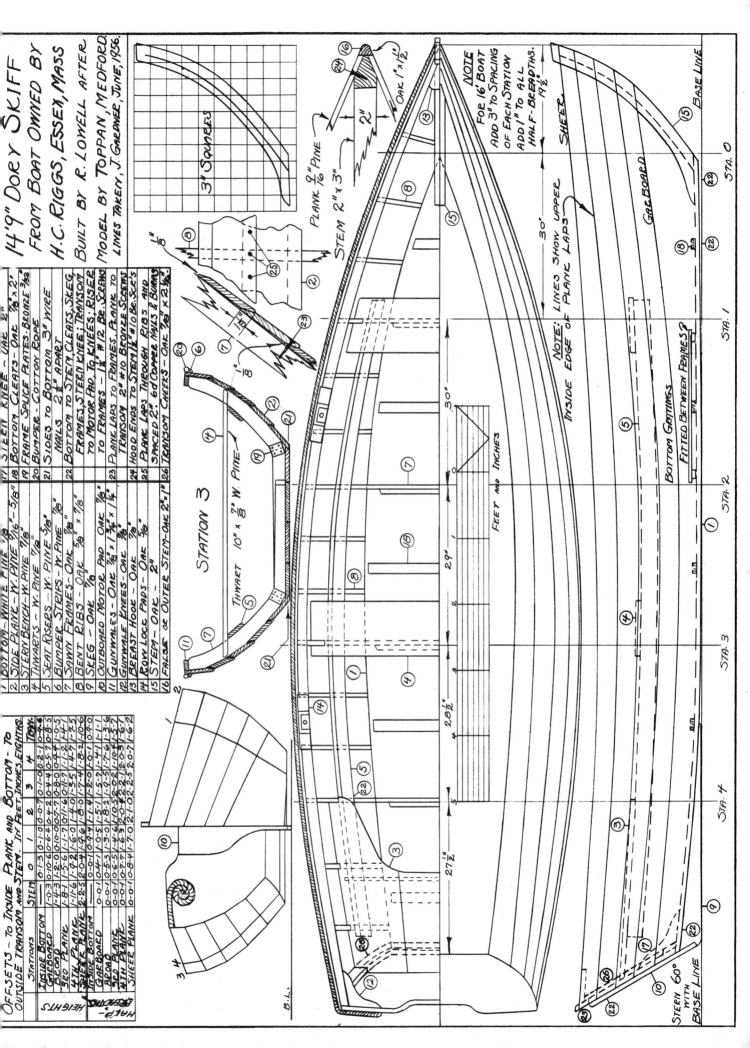

# INDEX

Pages of illustrations are given in italics